CASTE SYSTEM UNTOUCHABILITY AND THE DEPRESSED

Japanese Studies on South Asia No. 1

Caste System, Untouchability and the Depressed

Edited by

H. KOTANI

MANOHAR

2020

First published 1997
Reprinted 1999
POD reprint 2020

ISBN 978-81-7304-204-1

Published by
Ajay Kumar Jain *for*
Manohar Publishers & Distributors
4753/23 Ansari Road, Daryaganj
New Delhi 110 002

Printed at
Replika Press Pvt. Ltd.

Contents

Preface

This volume reflects the outcome of the many academic and field activities undertaken by a select group of Japanese researchers which was organised in 1989 to conduct intensive, multi-faceted research on the caste system and untouchability (in Japanese, Fukashokuminsei Kenkyukai). Nearly 50 members individually specializing in history, anthorcpology, religion, literature, politics, economics, geography and other fields participated in this study group.

As a result of five years of strenuous efforts made by the group, a series of five lengthy volumes under the general title of *Caste System and the Depressed* was published in Japanese from 1994 to 1995 by Akashi Shoten Publishers. From among more than 60 articles contained in this series of books, 10 articles focusing specifically on untouchability accompanied by two short introductory notes were selected for the English translation to constitute this first volume of *Japanese Studies on South Asia.* These volumes are to be a series of books on South Asia written in English by Japanese scholars under the general editorship and auspices of the Japanese Association for South Asian Studies.

The problem of untouchability has continued to attract considerable attention of Japanese people due to the fact that there still exist in Japan discriminatory social practices against a segment of people having a striking similarity to untouchability though not without some fundamental differences. Historical studies of untouchability are thus expected to serve in promoting a better understanding of the origin and development of the continued social discrimination against this segment of the Japanese population.

I am grateful to the Japanese Ministry of Education, Science, Sports and Culture for the Grant-in-Aid for Publication of Scientific

Research Results accorded this publication. I am also appreciative of the Mitsubishi Foundation for its financial aid received for the years 1989 and 1990 to support the activities of the Fukashokuminsei Kenkyukai. My gratitude is also due to Akashi Shoten Publishers (Tokyo, Japan) for undertaking the enormously labourious task of publishing five extensive volumes on Indian society in Japan. Finally, I am pleased to thank Ms Keiko Yamada, Research Fellow of the Japan Society for the Promotion of Science, for her considerable service to me in helping prepare the camera-ready copy for this volume.

14 February 1997 HIROYUKI KOTANI

Contributors

HIROYUKI KOTANI: Professor, Tokyo Metropolitan University. *Marx and Asia* (in Japanese), Tokyo, 1979. 'The Vatan–System in the sixteenth–eighteenth century Deccan' in D.N. Jha, ed., *Society and Ideology in India: Essays in Honour of Professor R.S. Sharma*, New Delhi, 1996.

GEN'ICHI YAMAZAKI: Professor, Kokugakuin University. *The Legend of Aśoka: A Critical Study* (in Japanese), Tokyo, 1979. *Society in Ancient India: The Social Structure and Middle/Low Classes* (in Japanese), Tokyo, 1986.

NOBORU KARASHIMA: Professor, Taisho University. *South Indian History and Society: Studies from Inscriptions A.D.850–1800*, Delhi, 1984. *Towards a New Formation: South Indian Society under Vijayanagar Rule*, Delhi, 1992.

MASANORI SATO: Professor, Asia University. *State and Society in Mughal India* (in Japanese), Tokyo, 1982. *Economy and Polity of Rajasthan: A Study of Kota and Marmar* (with B.H. Bhadani), Jaipur, 1997.

TSUKASA MIZUSHIMA: Professor, Institute for the Study of Languages and Cultures of Asia and Africa, Tokyo University of Foreign Studies. *Socio-cultural Changes in Villages in Tiruchirapalli District, Tamilnadu, India*, Tokyo, 1983.

MASAO NAITO: Professor, Institute for the Study of Languages and Cultures of Asia and Africa, Tokyo University of Foreign Studies. *Social Groups and Social Mobilization in Modern and Contemporary South Asia* (in Japanese), Tokyo, 1991 (ed.).

TOSHIE AWAYA: Research Associate, Tokyo University. Dept. of Oriental History. 'Situating the Malabar Tenancy Act, 1930', in *Local Agrarian Societies in Colonial India: Japanese*

Perspectives, Peter Robb et al., eds., London, 1996.

MASAYUKI USUDA: Professor, Tokai University. 'Historical evolution of a Talukdari village in southern Bangladesh', *The Bulletin of the Faculty of Letters, Tokai University,* nos. 51, 52, 55 (1989–91).

MASAHIKO TOGAWA: Research Fellow of the Japan Society for the Promotion of Science. 'From court ritual to popular ritual: Ethnohistorical analysis of the spread of Durga Puja in Bengal' (in Japanese), *Japanese Journal of Ethnology* 57, no. 2 (1992).

I

Untouchability in History

1

Introduction

Social Discrimination in Ancient India and its Transition to the Medieval Period[1]

GEN'ICHI YAMAZAKI

The varṇa system that was established in ancient India functioned as the larger framework within which the caste society was formed. According to the *Ṛg Veda*, the oldest of the four Vedas, the distinction of the four varṇas dates back to the origins of the human race. That is to say, at the time of Creation, the brāhmaṇa were born from the mouth of Puruṣa (the Primeval Man), the kṣatriya from His arms, the vaiśya from His thighs, and the śūdra from His feet. However, the four varṇas were actually established during the middle of the Later Vedic Era (1000–600 B.C.), which marked the formation of Aryan agrarian society. It was during this time that the above myth was created and inserted into the *Ṛg Veda*, the most important scripture of Brahmanism, in order to legitimize the four-varṇa system.

The brāhmaṇas, who made up the highest ranked varṇa, monopolized the positions of priest and teacher of the Vedas; the kṣatriyas took charge of politics and the military; the vaiśyas formed the commoner ranks of cultivators, herders and merchants; and the śūdras were relegated to the position of servants. The top three varṇas were the regular members of Aryan society. They were called the dvijāti, or 'twice born', and were allowed to participate in the religious worship presided over by the brāhmaṇas. Their 'second' birth was the initiation ceremony into the Vedic studies (upanayana) which they performed while they were young. In contrast, the śūdras were segregated from the dvijāti as ekajāti, who were born only once from their mothers' wombs. Below the śūdras a class of inferior people existed, in which the caṇḍālas, or 'untouchables', were placed. In other words, social discrimination appeared in a stratified form. The sections that follow are designed to introduce to the reader the pertinent items contained in the available documentation concerning this dual system of social discrimination.

THE CASE OF ŚŪDRA

The Dharmasūtras

When the four-varṇa system was first established, most of the people who were given the status of śūdra were indigenous Indians who had been conquered by the Aryans. While it is true that a portion of the Aryans were also designated as śūdras, their numbers were very small in proportion to the whole. As to the origin of the term 'śūdra', some think that it is a derivative of *śuc*, to be sorrowful; others think that it derives from *kṣudra*, or trifling. In either case, these explanations are merely attempts made after the fact at word coincidence. No one is certain about the meaning of the term, but as to its origin, it is probably a name given to an indigenous tribe that was conquered by the Aryans and then became a common term used to call subjected people in general.

The four-varṇa system was over time ideologically refined by orthodox brāhmaṇas. The *Dharmasūtras*, which were compiled between 600 and 300 B.C., represent the crystallization of these efforts by the orthodox brāhmaṇas whose homeland was the upper-Ganga basin. However, from the very beginning, the four-varṇa system was filled with contradictions. Therefore, the brāhmaṇas had to revise the basic principles to conform to the realities of daily life, resulting unavoidably in quite loose interpretations and relaxation of the rules. In the *Dharmasūtras*, we can see such difficulties incurred by the brāhmaṇas in defining the status of śūdra. First, let us look at the basic principles.

According to the rules contained in the *Dharmasūtras*, because śūdras were born from the feet of the Universal Soul Brahman, they were destined to serve the three upper varṇas born from his mouth, arms and thighs.[2] They were to support themselves and their families with the small compensation received for the services they rendered. The *Dharmasūtras* determined this compensation as 'cast-off shoes, umbrellas, garments, mats, and left-over food' of the twice-born varṇas.[3] A śūdra whose master had fallen into poverty was required to assist him with the wealth he had accumulated during his servitude. On the other hand, the *Dharmasūtras* also require masters to care for and support their śūdras.[4] Śūdras were also allowed to become artisans;

however, those who did become artisans were required to provide one day of service per month to the king.[5] Generally speaking, we can say the śūdras who became artisans received more social and economic independence than their servant counterparts.

The śūdra was strictly forbidden from participating in the Veda religious ceremonies of the Aryans. Accordingly,

> If a śūdra intentionally overhears the Veda chants, he shall have his ears filled with molten tin and dark-red pigment. If a śūdra dares to recite the chants himself, he will have his tongue cut out; and if he learns the chants by heart, his body shall be split in twain.[6]

Such punishments were probably not actually carried out, but they do tell us how strictly śūdras were excluded from Aryan customs and behaviour. However, the *Dharmasūtras* did permit śūdras to perform their own religious rituals and chant the holy word 'namaḥ'.[7]

Because ritual purity was sought by the twice-born varṇas, it was forbidden in principle to eat anything cooked by a śūdra or drink water from a śūdra's hand.[8] These restrictions on food and drink were especially strict among the brāhmaṇas, who were obliged to preserve the highest level of purity.

In principle, marriage was permitted only within one's own varṇa. This rule was often broken, but any twice-born male who took a śūdra to be his wife would become the object of particular scorn. If a twice-born male had only one wife and she was of śūdra status, he would be considered to be in a state of ritual impurity and would be forbidden to attend family ceremonies like śrāddha ancestor worship.[9] On the other hand, any śūdra male who approached a twice-born female, behaved like a twice-born varṇa in everyday life, or did any harm to a twice-born person would be subject to serious punishment, sometimes even death.[10]

Despite all of these regulations intended to segregate śūdras from Aryan society, in their everyday life the twice-born varṇas were unable to adhere to them thoroughly. After outlining these rules and restrictions, the *Dharmasūtras* then discussed how to compromise in practice, by offering some loopholes for getting around them. There were in general two kinds of loopholes: prāyaścitta (penance or purification) and exceptions to the rules.

In the case of eating and drinking, if one had received food or drink from a śūdra, he was ordered to do prāyaścitta by 'suppressing his breath seven times a day for seven days',[11] or there could be an exception like 'it is permissible to take food cooked by a śūdra under the supervision of a twice-born person'.[12] Intra-varṇa rules of marriage were so often broken that the *Dharmasūtras* were finally forced to recognize the practice of anuloma, or marriage to women of a lower varṇa. Whether or not śūdra women were to be included in this practice was often debated among the orthodox brāhmaṇas, but the affirmative opinion always predominated.[13] A small inheritance was even given to the sons of twice-born males borne by śūdra wives.[14] In contrast, the practice of pratiloma, marriage to a women of a higher class, continued to be discouraged and scorned.[15] Any śūdra male who had had sexual relations with a twice-born women would be heavily punished by 'having his penis severed and his wealth confiscated, and if the women has a husband or patron of some kind, these above two punishments will be followed by death'.[16]

The most important loopholes of the exception type were the āpaddharma, or rules for times of distress. These rules allowed the prohibitions on contact with śūdras to be ignored in time of distress or emergency. For example, receiving food from a śūdra to ward off starvation, or working in a śūdra occupation or working for a śūdra in time of extreme poverty was not considered sinful.[17] Of course, as soon as the distress had passed, such practices were to be ceased immediately.

Buddhist Scriptures and the Arthaśāstra

The Buddhist scriptures and the *Arthaśāstra*, which were sources written a little later than the *Dharmasūtras*, came into existence in the process of the formation of new urban societies in the mid-Ganga basin. The former were compiled by the Buddhist clergy, the representatives of the unorthodox sects of those days, while the latter was the work of political thinkers. And they both describe a society different from the one contained in the *Dharmasūtras* compiled by orthodox brāhmaṇas with their roots in the agrarian regions of the upper-Ganga basin. A summary follows of how these two sources regard the status of śūdras.

Buddhist scripture describes the four varṇas as a pre-existing truth. When describing a country or region, society is inevitably divided up into kṣatriyas, brāhmaṇas, vaiśyas, and śūdras, adding at times statuses inferior to śūdras like caṇḍālas and pukkusas.[18] However, in Buddhist Jātaka tales, hardly any distinction is made between the varṇas of vaiśya and śūdra in descriptions of everyday life. That is to say, while brāhmaṇas and kṣatriyas stress their respective varṇas in everyday life, the members of the two lower varṇas do not refer to themselves as being vaiśyas or śūdras, and are not called so by the members of other varṇas. Rather, in their everyday lives, kinship relationships, wealth, and occupation were more important reference points. The social segregation of śūdra as determined by the *Dharmasūtras* cannot be observed as such in the urban life of the mid-Ganga basin.

The Buddhist scriptures called kṣatriyas, brāhmaṇas, and gṛhapatis (wealthy upper-class vaiśyas) as ucca-kula (noble families) and inferior statuses, like caṇḍālas, nesadas, veṇas, rathakāras and pukkusas, as nīca-kula (mean families).[19] Between the noble and mean families are placed the common people consisting of the middle and lower classes of the vaiśya and the śūdra. The society described here is different from that idealized by the orthodox brāhmaṇas, being that there is ample allowance for social mobility. One Buddhist scripture states:

> Even kṣatriyas, brāhmaṇas and vaiśyas will rise earlier and go to bed later than a śūdra who has amassed wealth, grain, silver and gold. They will work at any occupation ordered by their śūdra master, become amiable towards him and flatter him.[20]

It is thus no wonder that orthodox brāhmaṇas viewed the middle and lower reaches of the Ganga River centred around the kingdom of Magadha as an impure region where the varṇa-based social order was breaking down.

The *Arthaśāstra*, which is said to have been written by Kauṭilya, the chief minister of the Mauryan dynasty that rose up in Magadha, takes the varṇa system as the ideal basis of society and lists the obligations of each varṇa. The obligations of the śūdra are described as 'service to the twice-born, occupations in the crafts and stage acting, and vārttā (engaging in economic enterprises)'.[21] The term vārttā is explained elsewhere as 'agriculture, herding and commerce',[22] which in all of the brāhmaṇa writings are the occupations of the vaiśya. The *Arthaśāstra* also actively urged the king to promote colonial and land reclamation projects employing the labour of śūdras. Such śūdra colonists were allowed to own the land they reclaimed for life.[23] This land was probably also inherited by the progeny of these colonists. Even though the provisions of *Arthaśāstra* resembles those contained in the *Dharmasūtras* concerning social discrimination against the śūdra, in contrast to the latter's clear intention of excluding śūdras from Aryan society, the provisions contained in the former, while discriminating against śūdras, at the same time take a position recognizing them as associate members of ordinary society. This way of thinking reflects clearly, like the Buddhist scriptures, the reality characterizing the region around Magadha.

The *Indika* of Magasthenes is a source material that tells us about Indian society around the time when the *Arthaśāstra* was written. According to the descriptions written by this Greek ambassador sent to the court of Candragupta, the first king of the Mauryan dynasty, seven kinds of castes existed in India at that time. Indians could enter only occupations within their own caste and were forbidden to marry outside caste lines.[24] The seven castes observed were: (1) philosophers (brāhmaṇas, etc.), (2) cultivators, (3) herders and hunters, (4) artisans and merchants, (5) warriors (kṣatriyas), (6) overseers or spies, and (7) high-level bureaucrats. Castes 3 and 4 were made up of a mixture of vaiśyas and śūdras. Magasthenes' descriptions, like Buddhist scriptures and the *Arthaśāstra*, are vague as to the distinction between the two lower varṇas and therefore show that differences existed between the ideal and real in the varṇa social order.

The Hindu Legal Codes

The theoretical basis of the four-varṇa system as described in the *Dharmasūtras* was systematized in the *Manu-Smṛti*, which was compiled between 200 B.C. and A.D. 200. This legal code, which from antiquity has been the most respected guide to Hindu social life, lays out in an even more substantive manner than the *Dharmasūtras* provisions about discrimination against the śūdra varṇa and its exclusion from Aryan society. For example, it is stated that the śūdra varṇa was created by God for the purpose of serving the brāhmaṇa[25] and that any wealth amassed by the former belonged to the latter.[26] There are many provisions set down for the purpose of excluding śūdras from places of Aryan religious worship. And concerning carnal relations or marriage between twice-born men and śūdra women, the *Manu-Smṛti* pronounces that 'from the moment of consummation they and all their progeny shall forever be of the śūdra varṇa' or 'be damned to hell'.[27] Heavy punishments, including sentences of death, were to be pronounced for śūdras violating the rights of higher varṇas,[28] and the king, in his position as the upholder of the state order, was strictly directed 'to ensure that śūdras stay in a servile position (dāsya) to the twice-born'.[29]

Despite the above principles of discrimination concerning śūdras, the *Manu-Smṛti*, like the *Dharmasūtras,* does take steps to make compromises with reality. There are purification rites for those polluted by contact with śūdras,[30] conditions under which food cooked by śūdras may be taken,[31] cases in which marriage to śūdra women can be permitted,[32] and exceptions to the rules in times of distress, like 'a brāhmaṇa in distress may take alms from anyone', and 'when life is endangered, it is permitted to take food from anyone'.[33]

The Hindu legal codes written after the *Manu-Smṛti* and the commentaries on them, which appeared from around the ninth century, continued to list the principles of śūdra discrimination and exclusion; but there are also items that describe the reality of enhancing unclarity of the distinction between the vaiśya and śūdra varṇas. For example, the *Yājñavalkya-Smṛti*, which was compiled between A.D. 100 and 300, has a provision allowing śūdras to engage in commerce.[34] On this provision the twelfth-century commentator by the name of Vijñāneśvara states that the obligations of the śūdra also include cultivation, herding and commerce in addition to service to the twice-born and entertainment.[35] Even the most strictly orthodox brāhmaṇas were forced to recognize the reality in the society around them. In other words, the concept of an 'Aryan (twice-born) society' that excluded śūdras from their ranks was disappearing due to the conceptualization of a 'Hindu society' that included śūdras as its general members, i.e. caste-Hindus.

Śūdras in Medieval Society

On his travels during the seventh century to the Indian subcontinent, Xuanzang writes:

> In India there are four castes: the pure and ascetic (brāhmaṇas), the nobility (kṣatriyas), the merchants (vaiśyas) and the cultivators (śūdras). Each of these castes forms an exclusive social group.[36]

Al-Bīrūnī, in the accounts of his travels to India in the eleventh century, also mentions the four-varṇa system, saying, 'great differences do not exist between the vaiśya and the śūdra'.[37] We have also seen above that a twelfth-century Indian commentator on Hindu law included the essentially vaiśya occupations of cultivator, herder and merchant within the obligations of the śūdra. In India today it is generally understood that the vaiśya is the varṇa of commerce and that agriculture belongs to the śūdra varṇa. From the record of Xuanzang, we may assume that such a division of labour between vaiśya and śūdra existed as early as the seventh century and has continued until the present day.

Under these circumstances, it was necessary for the orthodox brāhmaṇas to abandon their traditional ideas about the śūdra varṇa. What happened was that village-based brāhmaṇas began to conduct ceremonies, beginning with life-cycle and yearly rituals, for local śūdras and became dependent for their livelihood on the compensation received for these services. Therefore, a situation arose in which excluding śūdras from religious ceremonies in accordance with the traditional law codes would result in brāhmaṇas losing their means of livelihood. Brāhmaṇas, who were being so pressured to make concessions, finally compromised with reality by opening the *Mahābhārata*, the *Rāmāyaṇa* and the purāṇas, respected as holy Hindu scriptures, to śūdras. That is to say, śūdras were allowed to listen to the lessons taught by these scriptures from brāhmaṇas and attend ceremonies at which they could recite the holy mantras taken from them. However, only brāhmaṇas were permitted to preside over these rituals. In the midst of this evolution from Brahmanism to Hinduism, new mantras were given more importance over the Vedic mantras, and the religious discrimination against the śūdra almost lost effect.[38]

In the medieval period (from the sixth and seventh centuries onward), Hindu society (the four-varṇa-based caste-Hindu society), which accepted the śūdra as members, continued to develop; but in this process the number of untouchables excluded from the four varṇas increased. Many aspects of the social discrimination reserved for the śūdra in ancient Indian society were now transferred into the principles of untouchability.

UNTOUCHABILITY

The Origins

According to the Hindu law codes, the caṇḍāla, the representative of the untouchables of ancient times, was the progeny of a śūdra father and a brāhmaṇa mother, i.e. the offspring of the most condemned pratiloma marriage.[39] But this theory of the origin of the untouchables is the product of the varṇa conception of the orthodox brāhmaṇas and was not based on historical facts. Caṇḍālas came into existence around the end of the Later Vedic Era (1000–600 B.C.). During this era the Aryans, who had been mainly herders, advanced into the upper and middle reaches of the Ganga basin and formed an agrarian society. There is no doubt that the idea of the slaughtering of animals and related occupations being impure and forbidding contact with the people engaged in them did not arise from the customs and beliefs of pastoral life. There is a very close relationship between the establishment of untouchability and the formation of agrarian society. Also it seems that the general acceptance of ideas concerning the transmigration of the soul resulted in trends towards hatred against killing living things and eating the flesh of animals.

The Later Vedic Era was also a time when the brāhmaṇa secured the top position in society by virtue of their monopoly of the priesthood. A rough, primitive ideological distinction between purity and pollution developed to the point of fanaticism among the brāhmaṇas, who used such ideas to legitimize their supreme position by stressing their own purity and sanctity. This emphasis on purity gave rise to people on the opposite end of society who were considered to be impure. Then between the most pure brāhmaṇas and polluted untouchables were inserted the remaining three varṇas, ranked according to their level of purity.

During this era, regional states were formed in the upper and middle reaches of the Ganga River, going beyond the framework of tribal institutions. The kṣatriyas who ruled these states saw the advantages of incorporating the ideas propounded by the brāhmaṇas into their policies, thus contributing the political ingredient to the development of untouchability. That is to say, the existence of untouchables functioned to displace the dissatisfaction of the direct producers, vaiśyas and śūdras, within the varṇa-based society, thus ensuring a stable social order.

Since then, the untouchables have been placed outside of the framework of the varṇa social order and have functioned to cement class relations in that society in the form of groups ranked according to their level of purity (or impurity).

Most of the untouchables, or those inferiors equated with them, originated in tribal peoples carrying on hunting and gathering in the forests on the periphery of Aryan agrarian society. Some of these tribes adopted agrarian culture and were incorporated within the four varṇas.

But those who were not able to make this transition in lifestyle became objects of social discrimination, and were formed into groups that were obliged to play impure but indispensable roles in Aryan society. The name caṇḍāla was originally the name of one such indigenous tribe. Its first appearance in the source material occurred during the Later Vedic Era but was not equated with untouchability. As their untouchability developed over time, all people associated with their way of life came to be referred to as caṇḍālas. Some members of Aryan agrarian society were also added to their ranks by virtue of occupation, crime or vagabondage.

The Dharmasūtras, Buddhist Scriptures and the Arthaśāstra

The development of social inferiority in ancient India went through a complex process. References were made to the inferior classes by such general terms as antya or antyaja (the far end or lowest people) and bāhya (outcasts), although stratification existed among them, the lowest group containing the untouchables, or caṇḍālas. As early as the *Dharmasūtras*, the caṇḍālas were defined as 'people who will pollute the twice-born by either direct or indirect contact'. Any twice-born person who did come in contact with them would have to perform purification rites. Here is one example:

> Pollution will occur if these people are touched, conversed with, or even looked upon. In the case of such pollution, rites of purification must be performed. If the caṇḍāla was touched, you must bathe submerging the entire body; if conversed with, exchange words with a brāhmaṇa; if looked upon, observe the lights (sun, moon or stars).[40]

Closer contact, like intercourse with a caṇḍāla woman, required more difficult penances, including fasting.[41] Caṇḍālas, like śūdras, were completely excluded from the religious (Brahmanistic) practices of the twice-born.[42]

In Buddhist scriptures, people considered to be inferior to the śūdra are often referred to as caṇḍālas, nesadas, veṇas, rathakāras, and pukkusas. The four latter terms refer to groups of hereditary hunters, bamboo craftspeople, chariot-makers or wood-workers, and sweepers, who were not considered untouchables. In contrast, the caṇḍālas were considered untouchables like those mentioned in the *Dharmasūtras*. The members of varṇa society, especially those belonging to the upper strata beginning with the brāhmaṇa, were to take pains to avoid contact with caṇḍālas. In the Jātakas we see stories of the daughters of a brāhmaṇa and a wealthy merchant washing their eyes after looking upon a caṇḍāla;[43] a brāhmaṇa who was afraid of being caught downwind of one of untouchables;[44] and a brāhmaṇa who was so hungry that he ate food left by a caṇḍāla, then died from embarrassment.[45]

The caṇḍālas were segregated from the rest of the community, living in groups on the outskirts of cities and villages.[46] It goes without saying that their material lives were of the lowest standards in the society, and many became ill or crippled within such miserable living conditions.[47] As to their occupations, there were hunters, arrow-makers, and woodworkers among their ranks.[48] Here we can observe those who had not yet completely abandoned their traditional forest lifestyles. The tasks of executioner and disposing of dead animals were also caṇḍāla occupations, as were scavenging and earthworking.[49] Caṇḍāla women often worked side by side with their men in these occupations.[50] Buddhist scripture also mentions people among them who lived by acrobatic performances[51]and those who possessed special magical powers.[52]

Although the *Arthaśāstra* does not contain very many references to caṇḍālas, it does make clear that they are to be looked upon as inferior to the śūdra.[53] As a work of political theory, it proposes that caṇḍālas be employed in guarding the forests,[54] confirming that many caṇḍālas were forest people.

In the first section of this chapter, we established that the discrimination against śūdras was not as strict as what the *Dharmasūtras* advocated. On the other hand, there seems to be a common view of the caṇḍāla expressed in the *Dharmasūtras*, Buddhist scriptures, the *Arthaśāstra*, works of very different characters and purposes. This tells us that the discrimination described was actually implemented in the case of the caṇḍāla. Such discrimination continued to be mentioned in the writings throughout later generations.

Hindu Legal Codes

The *Manu-Smṛti* also tells of the existence of various people considered inferior to the śūdra. They are called apasadas (base-born) and are said to have originated in primary and secondary pratiloma intermarriages between varṇas.[55] What is being emphasized here is that the occupations of the apasadas must be those 'scorned by the twice-born varṇa'.[56] Among them the caṇḍāla is defined as 'the most debased men'[57] and is marked for the cruellest forms of discrimination.

The provisions set down in the *Manu-Smṛti* concerning the caṇḍāla first specify that they must reside outside of the villages and can interact only with members of their own group. They are to wear the clothing worn by the deceased, eat the food out of broken dishes laid on the ground for them by the twice-born, and wear personal ornaments of black iron. They may own dogs and donkeys, must always go about for the purpose of their work with special marks applied to their bodies, and are forbidden from walking in the villages or towns after dark. They are allotted such tasks as executing criminals and transporting the corpses of people with no kin.[58] There were also caṇḍālas who were engaged in hunting. The *Manu-Smṛti* says that the meat slaughtered by caṇḍālas is clean and may be cooked and eaten by twice-born varṇa,[59] suggesting that they would sell the game they hunted to village and town residents. Prohibition concerning contact with caṇḍālas is specified, as well as purification rites twice-born varṇas are to perform when such contact occurs,[60] in the same manner as the *Dharmasūtras*. Also, in times of distress when faced with starvation, it is not considered sinful to accept even the meat of impure animals polluted by the hand of a caṇḍāla.[61]

The provisions concerning caṇḍālas seen in the later Hindu law codes are not very different from those contained in the *Manu-Smṛti*; though for the first time there appears the term for untouchability, aspṛśya.[62] Also, the twelfth-century commentator Vijñāneśvara in his interpretation of the inferior people, antyaja, lists 14 representative castes including the caṇḍāla, and classifies them into two types depending on their levels of impurity.[63] Here we can observe the untouchability becoming more and more complicated.

The Chinese Buddhist priests who visited India describe in their itineraries the custom of untouchability practiced there. For example, at the beginning of the fifth century, Faxian writes:

> With the exception of the caṇḍālas, the people of this country do not kill living creature, do not drink intoxicating liquors, and eat neither garlic nor onions. The caṇḍālas are called sinners. They live segregated from the rest of society, and when they enter a city, they must sound an alarm by striking a piece of wood to warn everyone of their presence and enable the citizens to avoid running into them. . . . The caṇḍālas, fishermen, and hunters are the only sellers of animal flesh.[64]

The itineraries written by Xuangzang and Yijing in the seventh century tell us much the same.[65] According to the detailed account from the twelfth century by al-Bīrūnī, there were eight castes (fullers, shoemakers, acrobats, basket weavers, sailors, fishermen, hunters and cloth-weavers) called antyaja, who were considered inferior to the śūdra. They lived outside of the towns and villages where those of the four varṇas resided. There were four more castes, including the caṇḍāla, considered even more inferior. They were the entertainers, executioners and slaughterers, and the like.[66] These accounts of al-Bīrūnī show the same level of the development of untouchability as that discussed by Vijñāneśvara.

THE DEVELOPMENT OF UNTOUCHABILITY IN MEDIEVAL INDIA

There were three prominent differences between ancient untouchability as described above and the untouchability that has been recorded by modern and contemporary surveys. Firstly, in comparison to the many untouchable castes and large untouchable population in modern times, the people in ancient India who were considered untouchable, like the caṇḍāla, made up a very small portion of the sub-śūdra inferior people. Secondly, in ancient times, all types of inferior people, including the caṇḍāla, generally maintained their tribal organization and lived as fairly tight communities on the periphery of Aryan agrarian society. In contrast, in modern times people of the different untouchable castes live on the outskirts of each village as segregated communities. Finally, many untouchables in modern times not only engage in traditional occupations, but also work as farm labourer during the busy agricultural seasons. The caṇḍāla of ancient times did not directly participate in any facet of agricultural production.

What was the historical process in which such changes, which include an increase in the untouchable castes and in the total untouchable population, their diffusion into segregated communities around villages, and their participation in farm labour, came about? The problems involved in answering this question have yet to be clarified, but in the writings of the Hindu legal commentator and al-Bīrūnī mentioned earlier, we can say that such changes were already in progress during the eleventh and twelfth centuries. It would therefore be correct to understand these changes as part of the transition or evolution from ancient untouchability concentrated on the caṇḍāla to medieval untouchability, characterized by discrimination against many socially stratified castes scattered throughout the local region in segregated communities on the outskirts of agrarian villages. The following four points can accordingly be offered to explain what generally happened in such a transition.

To begin with, within the tribes who lost their hunting and collecting territories due to the expansion of agrarian society (with the śūdra as its major force of cultivators), there were those who could not make the transition to agriculture and were thus forced to make their livelihood on the periphery of agrarian society engaged in necessary tasks (often looked upon as too impure for the four varṇas to participate in) to supplement agricultural life.

Secondly, from the sixth and seventh centuries, characterized by the establishment of a feudal order based on the regional decentralization of political authority and the decline of urban commerce in favour of regional economies, village organization went through significant changes into strongly self-subsistent communities supported by many artisan and service-rendering castes. Within this process, some artisan castes broke up, and their members migrated to villages all over the region. The untouchable and other inferior groups living on the periphery of agrarian society were also caught up within this village reorganization, moving to the outskirts of individual villages and maintaining their tribal organization in the form of castes. Given the nature of the Indian climate, which is clearly divided into dry and rainy seasons, agriculture required the employment of large amounts of labour during fixed periods of time. During these times the labour of artisans and inferior castes was demanded in addition to the traditional services they provided.

Thirdly, the ideology of purity and pollution, which was developed by the religious leaders of Hindu society, the brāhmaṇa, contributed to the social stratification in villages organized according to many castes. Along with the development of this ideology, strata of inferior castes and artisans, who were previously not looked upon as ritually impure, were designated as untouchable. Moreover, stratification occurred among the old and new untouchable castes based on differing degrees of pollution, resulting in exclusionary behaviour among them.

Finally, the existence of untouchables functioned to reduce the tense relationships arising from inequality within the village community and brought about a certain amount of stability. This process of order and stability of the village community brought about the order and stability of the regional society and ultimately of the medieval state. Therefore, developments of untouchability were responses to the expectations of ruling classes and landlords. The role played directly or indirectly in the development of the untouchability during this time by the ruling classes on both the state and local levels was a very important one.

NOTES

1 The present paper is a shortened English translation of Chap. I (pp. 101–53), Chap. IX (pp. 299–338) and Chap. X (pp. 339–78) of Yamazaki's *Kodai Indo Shakai no Kenkyu: Shakai no Kozo to Shomin Kasomin* (*Society in Ancient India: The Social Structure and Middle/Low Classes*), Tokyo, 1986. The author owes much to the following studies.

P.V. Kane, *History of Dharmaśāstra*, 5 vols., 2nd edn., Poona, 1968–77.

R.P. Kangle, *The Kauṭilīya Arthaśāstra*, 3 vols., Bombay, 1960–65.

R.S. Sharma, *Śūdras in Ancient India*, 2nd. rev. edn., Delhi, 1980.

V. Jha, 'Stages in the history of untouchables', *Indian Historical Review* 2, no. 1 (1975), pp. 14–31.

Abbreviations:

Āp.: *Āpastamba Dharmasūtra*
Gaut.: *Gautama Dharmasūtra*
Vās.: *Vāsiṣṭha Dharmasūtra*
Baudh.: *Baudhāyana Dharmasūtra*
Manu : *Manu-Smṛti*
Yāj.: *Yājñavalkya-Smṛti*
Viṣṇu : *Viṣṇu-Smṛti*
Kāty.: *Kātyāyana-Smṛti*
Arth.: *Arthaśāstra*
VP.: *Vinaya Piṭaka*
DN.: *Dīgha Nikāya*
MN.: *Majjhima Nikāya*
SN.: *Samyutta Nikāya*
AN.: *Anguttara Nikāya*
Jāt.: *Jātaka*
Divyāv.: *Divyāvadāna* (Cowell and Neil, eds.)
Taisho: *Taisho Shinsyu Daizokyo* (*Taisho Tripiṭaka*)

2 *Baudh.* I, 10, 18, 5–6. Also, *Āp.* I, 1, 1, 6. *Gaut.* X, 56. *Vās.* II, 20.

3 *Gaut.* X, 57–59. Also, *Āp.* I, 1, 3, 41.

4 *Gaut.* X, 61–63; XVIII, 24.

5 *Gaut.* X, 31, 60.
6 *Gaut.* XII, 4–6.
7 *Gaut.* VIII, 18; X, 53, 64–65.
8 *Āp.* I, 5, 16, 22; I, 6, 18, 13; I, 7, 21, 17; II, 8, 18, 2. *Gaut.* IX, 11. *Vās.* X, 31; XIV, 4, 33. *Baudh.* II, 2, 3, 1; III, 6, 5; IV, 1, 5.
9 *Āp.* I, 6, 18, 33. *Gaut.* XV, 18. *Vās.* XIV, 11.
10 *Āp.* II, 10, 27, 9, 14–16. *Gaut.* XII, 1–3, 7. *Baudh.* II, 2, 3, 52.
11 *Baudh.* IV, 1, 5. Also, *Vās.* XIV, 33. *Baudh.* III, 6, 5.
12 *Āp.* II, 2, 3, 4–9.
13 *Baudh.* I, 8, 19, 2–6. cf. *Vās.* I, 24–27.
14 *Baudh.* II, 2, 3, 10. cf. *Gaut.* XXVIII, 39. *Vās.* XVII, 38–39.
15 *Gaut.* IV, 17, 27–28. *Vās.* XVIII, 1, 7. *Baudh.* I, 9, 17, 7.
16 *Gaut.* XII, 2–3. Also, *Āp.* II, 10, 27, 9. *Baudh.* II, 2, 3, 52.
17 *Āp.* I, 6, 18, 5–8, 14-15. *Gaut.* XVII, 4–6, 22–24.
18 *VP.* III, pp. 184–85; IV, pp. 80, 177, 272. *DN.* III, p. 82. *SN.* I, pp. 102, 166. *AN.* I, p. 162; III, p. 214. *Jāt.* III, pp. 194-95.
19 *MN.* II, pp. 152, 183–84; III, p. 169. *SN.* I, pp. 93–95. *AN.* I, p. 107; II, pp. 85–86; III, pp. 385–87.
20 *MN.* II, p. 85.
21 *Arth.* I, 3, 8.
22 *Arth.* I, 4, 1.
23 *Arth.* II, 1, 1–12.
24 J.W. McCrindle, tr., *Ancient India as Described by Megasthenes and Arrian*, Calcutta, 1960, Indian edn., pp. 38–41, 83–86.
25 *Manu* VIII, 413–14.
26 *Manu* VIII, 417.
27 *Manu* III, 15–17.
28 *Manu* VIII, 272, 279–82; X, 96.
29 *Manu* VIII, 410, 418.
30 *Manu* XI, 153.
31 *Manu* IV, 253.
32 *Manu* III, 12–13, 43–44.
33 *Manu* X, 102–8.
34 *Yāj.* I, 120.
35 *Mitākṣarā* on *Yāj.* I, 120.
36 T. Watters, tr., *On Yuan Chwang's Travels in India*, Delhi, 1961, Indian edn., p. 168.
37 E.C. Sachau, ed. and tr., *Al-Beruni's India*, Delhi, 1983, Indian edn., p.100.
38 P.V. Kane, *History of Dharmaśāstra*, vol. I, pp. 893–96;vol. II, pp. 155–59, 198–99; vol. V, pp. 920-30, 1641–42.
39 *Gaut.* IV, 17-18. *Vās.* XVIII, 1. *Baudh.* I, 8, 16, 8; I, 17, 7. *Manu* X, 12, 16.
40 *Āp.* II, 1, 2, 8–9.

41 *Gaut.* XXIII, 32–34. *Vās.* XX, 16; XXIII, 39–41. *Baudh.* II, 1, 2, 13–14; II, 2, 4, 12–13.
42 *Āp.* I, 3, 9, 14–18. *Vās.* XXIII, 33–35.
43 *Jāt.* IV, pp. 376, 390–91.
44 *Jāt.* III, pp. 232–33.
45 *Jāt.* II, pp. 82–84.
46 *Jāt.* IV, pp. 200, 376–77, 390; VI, p. 156.
47 *MN.* III, pp. 169–70. *SN.* I, pp. 93–95. *AN.* I, p. 107; II, pp. 85–86; III, pp. 385–86.
48 *Taisho* IV, p. 304. *Apadāna* II, p. 377.
49 *Taisho* IV, pp. 298, 352, 495.
50 *Jāt.* V, p. 429.
51 *DN.* I, pp. 6, 65. *Jāt.* IV, p. 390.
52 *Taisho* L, p. 139. *Jāt.* IV, p. 200. *Divyāv.* pp. 397–98, 612.
53 *Arth.* III, 7, 37; III, 18, 7.
54 *Arth.* II, 1, 6.
55 *Manu* X, 6–73.
56 *Manu* X, 46.
57 *Manu* X, 12, 16, 26.
58 *Manu* X, 51–56.
59 *Manu* V, 131.
60 *Manu* V, 85; VIII, 373; XI, 176, 179.
61 *Manu* X, 105–8.
62 *Viṣṇu* V, 104. *Kāty.* 433, 783.
63 *Mitākṣarā* on *Yāj.* III, 260, 265.
64 S. Beal, tr., *The Travels of Fah-hian and Sung-yum* , London, 1964, 2nd ed., p. 55.
65 T. Watters, tr., *On Yuan Chwang's Travels,* p. 147. J. Takakusu, tr., *A Record of the Buddhist Religion as Practised in India and Malay Archipelago by I-Tsing* , Delhi, 1966, Indian edn., p.139.
66 E.C.Sachau, *Al-Beruni's India,* pp. 100–2.

2

The Untouchables in Tamil Inscriptions and other Historical Sources in Tamil Nadu

NOBORU KARASHIMA

RESIDENTIAL AREA OF UNTOUCHABLES APPEARING IN CHOLA INSCRITIONS

Rajaraja I, the Chola king who ruled from A.D. 985 to 1016 extended his territory from the Kaveri delta to the extreme south of the Indian peninsula by conquering the Pandyan kingdom and also occupying the northern part of Sri Lanka, thus bringing to the Chola rule its most glorious period. He built in Thanjavur, the capital in the Kaveri delta, a magnificent Siva temple and granted to it a large number of villages scattered across his territory for the worship of Siva. Two continuous inscriptions (*SII*, ii, 4 and 5) dated to his twenty-ninth regnal year (A.D. 1014) and engraved on stone walls of the temple describe the grant by Rajaraja I of the revenue from 40 villages in Chola-mandalam, the heartland of the Chola empire. In the detailed description of the extent and composition of non-taxable lands in those villages, we find the reference to *tīṇḍā-chēri* along with other categories of residential area. *Chēri* in Tamil means 'street' or 'residential area', and the relative participle *tīṇḍā* means 'untouchable'. *Tīṇḍā-chēri* as a whole, therefore, means the residential area of the untouchables. Apart from references to some particular communities which are thought to be those of untouchables, this usage of *tīṇḍā-chēri* in the inscriptions of Rajaraja I seems to be one of the very few 'direct' references to 'untouchables' or 'untouchability' in Tamil inscriptions.

These inscriptions also give mention to *paṟai-chēri* as another residential area in a village. This means, of course, the residential area of the Paṟaiyas, the most well-known untouchable community in Tamil Nadu. In these long inscriptions, which describe the grant of 40 villages, following the eulogy (*meykkīrtti*) of the king in the beginning, there is the royal order that, for each granted village, the total extent of the village, the extent of non-taxable lands consisting of residential areas, temple sites, cremation grounds, and the like, and the amount of revenue accruing as tax from the taxable area, the extent of which is obtainable by deducting the extent of non-taxable land from the total extent of the village, should be recorded. Then follows, as per the order, the detailed description of the 40 villages in Chola-mandalam.[1]

Out of those 40 villages, the number of villages concerning which we are able to acquire sufficient information is 33, owing to damage to the stones, and there is reference to *paṟai-chēri* in some 20 villages out of those 33. This means, therefore, that not all the villages had *paṟai-chēri* within their bounds. However, the reference to *paṟai-chēri* in the royal order and its appearing in more than half of the granted villages may suggest a fair prevalence of *paṟai-chēri* in the villages in Chola-mandalam. On the contrary, reference is not made to *tīṇḍā-chēri* in the royal order, and moreover, even in the individual description of the granted villages, reference is made to it only in two out of the 33 villages which otherwise afford us ample information. The existence of *tīṇḍā-chēri*, therefore, does not seem to have been so common.

However, the relation between *tīṇḍā-chēri* and *paṟai-chēri* is not clear. If *tīṇḍā-chēri* and *paṟai-chēri* were not found together in one and the same village, we may presume that they were substantially the same and that the difference was only in name and usage. Actually, however, there existed *paṟai-chēri* in one of the two villages which had *tīṇḍā-chēri*. This suggests that they were different in substance too, though we do not know which particular community(ies) lived in *tīṇḍā-chēri*.

There is another rare reference to untouchables in an inscription of A.D. 1028 in the reign of Rajendra I found at Bahur near Pondicherry (*AR* 1976/77-191). In this inscription of a Brahmin settlement (*chaturvēdimaṅgalam*), it was decided that all of the local cultivators (*payir-cheyvār*), excepting the *tīṇḍāḍār* or untouchables, should contribute some compulsory labour annually for the desilting of the village tank.[2]

While these references to *tīṇḍā-chēri* and *tīṇḍāḍār* are rare direct references to 'untouchability' in Tamil inscriptions, references to *paṟai-chēri* or Paṟaiyas, or to some other communities which are later considered to have been untouchables or having a similar status, are found in other inscriptions also. Therefore, we shall examine below the case of Paṟaiyas and also that of Pulaiyas, another community of similar status. However, it is not clear whether the word Pulaiyar was used as the name of a particular community or as the general name meant for untouchables. According to Thurston and Hutton who identify Pulaiyar(n) with Cheruman,[3] Pulaiyar/Cheruman is the name of an untouchable community in Kerala, particularly in its northern part. Etymologically, however, this Tamil word means 'the lowest' or 'the polluted', and seems to have been used for the meaning of those referred to as untouchables. The usage in the *Periya Purāṇam* to be mentioned below may have been one such case.

SOCIAL POSITION AND PROFESSION OF THE PARAIYAS

First, I shall examine what social position Paṟaiyas occupied during the period from the Chola to the Vijayanagar empires. A thirteenth-century inscription of Tiruvottur (*SII*, vii, 118) in North Arcot District records the clash between the two brothers of a local chiefly family, which involved all the communities of the locality. In the inscription a great variety of communities is mentioned in this relation. The principle employed in enumerating those communities seems to have been from the top to the bottom in the caste (*jāti*) hierarchy, though confusion remains as to what extent adherence is made to this principle.[4] Nonetheless, the inscription mentions Paṟaiyas immediately after Pāṇar (bardic singers) and just before Chekkiliyar (leather workers). While we find further above the Pāṇar the names of Vēḍar (hunters), Uvachchar (drummers), Maṉṟāḍi (herders), Śiva-brāhmaṇar (temple priests), Kaikkōḷar (weavers), Vāṇigar (merchants), Cheṭṭigaḷ (merchants) and others in ascending order, Iṟuḷar (a tribe) is the last *jāti* below the Chekkiliyar.[5] From this, we can therefore ascertain that the social position of Paṟaiya lay close to the bottom in the thirteenth century.

Two fifteenth-century inscriptions from Tiruvaigavur (*AR* 1914-59) and Korukkai (*AR* 1917-216), both in Thanjavur District, which record the revolt of the lower communities of peasants, artisans and merchants against the government officers and landlords who oppressed them,[6] enumerate many communities. The order of enumeration seems to have again been vertically descending from the top according to the hierarchy of *jātis.* Above Paṟaiyas (*kaivvinai-paṟaiyar*) we find in ascending order the communities of watchmen, washermen, barbers, potters, goldsmiths, carpenters, blacksmiths, oil-merchants, weavers, merchants, and others, while below Paraiyas in descending order soldiers (Sārvakkārar) and toddy tappers (Īlampuñjai) only. This also confirms the very low social position held by Paraiyas in the fifteenth century.

The question then arises as to what profession Paraiyas were engaged in those earlier times? Concerning this point, several pieces of information are available in inscriptions and literature. In Rajaraja I's inscription referred to earlier, we find in the description of the twenty-eighth village the phrases 'southern *parai-chēri* of the Paraiyas who cultivate' and 'western *parai-chēri* of the Paraiyas who cultivate'. Since this is the only case in which we find this type of expression among the 33 villages, we are therefore not sure how commonly Paraiyas cultivated land. Conversely, however, we are able to glean from these phrases that Paraiyas were indeed engaged in cultivation to some extent. The Tiruvottur inscription refers in the passage of imprecation to 'Paraiyas who mow the grass for horses' (*kudiraikku-pullup-parikkira-paraiyar*). A twelfth-century inscription (*SII*, i, 64) refers to *(pa)rai-tari* in the enumeration of taxes, which may testify to the existence of Paraiyas who were engaged in weaving. *Parai-tari* is also mentioned in the Vijayanagar inscriptions of the early fifteenth century (*AR* 1918-91, 1937/38-490). Here it may be recalled that Paraiyas appearing in the above-mentioned Tiruvaigavur and Korukkai inscriptions are stated as 'craftsman Paraiyas' (*kaivvinai-paraiyar*).

The story of Saint Nandanar in the *Periya Purāṇam*, Saivite hagiology compiled by Sekkilar in the twelfth century, further supplements our knowledge. Nandanar, who lived in a Pulaiya hamlet attached to Adanur located close to the river Kollidam, was known for his deep devotion to Siva. For a long time he had been longing to visit the Nataraja temple in Chidambaram for the purpose of worshipping Siva in His dancing form. However, with the fear that his low-birth as a Pulaiya[7] would be a hindrance to his entering the temple, he postponed the trip continuously while taking the vow daily that he would go the next day. For this reason, he was also known as Tirunalaippovar (He who will go tomorrow). One day, however, he actually dared to start out for Chidambaram, his longing overwhelming his fear. On reaching his long-dreamed-of destination, he danced in ecstasy, but as he had feared, he was not allowed to enter the temple. He thus wept in despair outside the high wall of the temple, and then Siva Himself appeared before the temple priests and commanded them to light a fire and lead Nandanar through it into the inner sanctum. He walked unharmed through the flames and proceeded deliriously up to the image of Nataraja. Then, he disappeared under the raised foot of the dancing Siva.[8]

As to the duty Nandanar was required to discharge, it is said that he used to supply to the temple leather and leather straps for making drums, strings (guts) for lutes of various types and bezoar for the worship of the God of gods. The description of his village is as follows:

> The town of Ādanūr owed its great prosperity to its fertile fields and gardens, and had many tall mansions and a teeming population. In the outskirts of that town was a small hamlet of Pulaiyas studded with small huts under old thatches overspread by *śurai* creepers and inhabited by agrarian labourers engaged in menial occupations. In the thresholds of the huts covered with strips of leather, little chickens were seen moving about in groups; dark children who wore bracelets of black iron were prancing about, carrying little puppies whose yelps were drowned by the tinkling bells which girdled their waists.
>
> In the shade of the *marudu* trees, a female labourer (*uḻatti*) sent her baby to sleep on a sheet of leather; there were mango trees from whose branches drums were hanging; and under the cocoanut palms, in little hollows on the ground, tiny-headed bitches lay quiet after pupping. The red-crest cocks crowed before dawn calling the brawny Pulaiyar to their day's work; and by day, under the wide shade of the Kāñji tree spread the voice of the wavy-haired Pulaiya women singing as they were husking paddy. By the side of tanks full of warbling birds, the music of many instruments accompanied the drinking *fetes* of Pulaiya women who wore on their heads fragrant flowers and ears of paddy-corn, and who staggered in their dance as the result of increasing intoxication.
>
> In this abode of the people of the lowest caste (*kaḍaiñar*), there arose a man with a feeling of true devotion to the feet of Siva. He was the unrivalled Nandanar who inherited as his share communal service in the neighbouring township. . . . Depending for his livelihood on his share of the communal land, and following the profession that was his by birth, he used to supply. . . .[9]

Then, follows the description of the duty he discharged referred to earlier and the story of his going to Chidambaram.

The passage quoted earlier from the *Periya Purāṇam* suggests that the village land was assigned to Pulaiyas for cultivation for their own maintenance, and the word '*ulatti*' (female form of *ulavan̲* = cultivator) as applied to a Pulaiya woman also seems to associate Pulaiyas with cultivation, though it is not clear whether they were forced to cultivate land for the benefit of the higher caste people of the village. At any rate, their traditional work described here, at least for men, was related to working with leather. Other points of importance about this stroy are that the Pulaiyas were described as being the lowest (*kaḍaiñar*) on the social ladder and that they were regarded as being polluted. Though Nandanar was finally allowed to enter the shrine by the grace of the deity in this story, he was allowed in only after his purification by walking through flames.

UNTOUCHABLES AS SLAVES AS SEEN IN INSCRITIONS AND PALM-LEAF DOCUMENTS

I shall now examine Paṟaiyas and Pulaiyas as slaves (*aḍimai/aḍiyār*) appearing in the fourteenth-century Tamil inscriptions. One inscription from Tiruppalatturai (*SII*, viii, 590) in Tiruchirapalli District records the transfer of the *adiyārs* of Veḷḷāḷas and Pulaiyas. According to the inscription, a local magnate granted to a lady and her son pieces of land (nine and odd *vēli*) and a house, together with three Veḷḷāḷa *aḍiyārs* and seven Pulaiya *aḍiyārs*. It seems that the lady was a concubine of the magnate and the son was his son, and that the house was the one in which she gave birth to the son.[10]

The seven Pulaiyas, whose names were also recorded, were a family consisting of the parents, their daughter and four sons. They had been engaged in farm labour (*pāṭṭattil ninṟa*) in Nangaipuram before they were purchased by the magnate from their previous owner. This gives substance to Pulaiyas being objects of transfer. It may also be noted that the Pulaiyas in this case were Paḷḷas (see below) as the parents are mentioned as Paḷḷa and Paḷḷi. Another interesting aspect of this inscription, however, is that the Veḷḷāḷas, a superior caste, were also transferred as slaves from one owner to another.

Another inscription from Tirukkalukkundram (*AR* 1933-171) in Chingleput District records the sale of land (three and odd *vēli*), houses and slaves. Among the slaves there were three Veḷḷāḷas and 16 Paṟaiyas. In the latter case, the name of only their representative was given.[11] While in the case of Tiruppalatturai inscription it seems impossible for seven Pulaiyas to cultivate by themselves the land of nine and odd *vēli* it may have been possible in the case of the

Tirukkalukkundram inscription for 16 Paṟaiyas to cultivate the three and odd *vēli* of land. The Pulaiyas and Paṟaiyas appearing in these inscriptions seem to have been engaged not in leather working but in cultivation or in some other agricultural labour.

Lastly, I shall examine the conditions of the Paḷḷas by using for reference some palm-leaf documents of the nineteenth century, though the period of their appearance is much later than the Chola and Vijayanagar periods. Paḷḷas were a community who lived mostly in Thanjavur and Tiruchirapalli Districts and further south, being engaged mainly in agricultural labour. According to Thurston,[12] they were generally regarded the same as Paṟaiyas and were, therefore, compelled to live in the outskirts of villages. During the village survey conducted jointly by Indian and Japanese scholars in Tiruchirapalli District in 1979–81, some 64 palm-leaf documents were discovered from Nerinjalakudi village.[13] Seven out of those 64 documents record lease-deeds made by Paḷḷas.[14] The Paḷḷas living in Mandurai received on lease some land for cultivation from Ramachandra-rayar, a Maratha Brahmin landlord of the village, promising him to pay a fixed amount of crops (paddy) together with some other payments. The Paḷḷas are said to have lived in *paḷḷāḍi-chēri* (the residential area of Paḷḷa slaves), and to have been *paṇṇai-paḷḷaṉ* of the landlord who owned their houses too. The term *paṇṇai-paḷḷaṉ* is similar in purport to the term *paṇṇaìyāḷ*[15] mentioned in British records and later.

The fact that they received land on lease, the condition of which is stipulated in the palm-leaf documents, promising to pay a certain amount of crops and others to the landlord, may suggest that those Paḷḷas were actually 'tenants' and not 'slaves'. However, one document (No. 31) records clearly that the four Paḷḷas who appeared in the documents had been purchased together with families by Ramachandra-rayar as his *aḍimais* from their previous owner. Another document (No. 51) recorded that a Paḷḷaṉ of the *paṇṇai* of Ramachandra-rayar borrowed some money from the latter for the marriage of his son, under condition that his son and the son's family would become slaves of the moneylender and work on his farm (*paṇṇai-aḍichchu*).

In the beginning of the nineteenth century the Raiyatwari land-settlement was introduced in Tamil Nadu and the Slavery Abolition Act was enacted in 1843, which must certainly have effected some change in the conditions of the *aḍimai* and *paṇṇaiyāḷ* The records of their transactions examined earlier may have reflected to some extent the new situation which appeared in that century, but the conditions of the *paṇṇai*-Paḷḷas do not seem to have been much different from those of the Pulaiya and Paṟaiya *aḍiyārs* of the fourteenth century.

FOR FURTHER STUDY

The early conditions of the so-called untouchables have been elucidated ealier by examining Tamil inscriptions, a literary text and palm-leaf documents. We are able to ascertain, through this examination, several facts including the following three: (1) Certain communities were considered 'untouchable' during the Chola period, though we do not know the identity of those untouchables; (2) Paṟaiyas, who occupied the position close to the bottom of the social hierarchy, were engaged in an array of work such as cultivation, grass mowing, leather work and other handicrafts like weaving; and (3) Paṟaiyas and Pulaiyas were made slaves (*aḍimai*) and transferred from one owner to another, though Veḷḷāḷas were also transferred as slaves. In conclusion, although the conditions of the so-called untouchables do not seem to have changed much since the Chola period, further studies are necessary to better illuminate their conditions throughout the long history of south India.

Among any subsequent studies, suggested first is a thorough review of the Sangam literature. Though this may be somewhat difficult, the careful examination of Sangam texts from the foregoing perspective should be attempted. Second, besides the cases of Nandanar examined earlier and Tiruppan, another (Vaishnava) *bhakta* who was also not allowed to enter the temple, there must be some other important clues in the *bhakti* and other literature of the medieval period. A painstaking comparison of the findings from the Sangam, *bhakti* and other literature and from inscriptions would facilitate our comprehension to a greater degree about the emergence of, or changes in, the concept of untouchability in south India. The pertinent British administration records should also be explored in depth.[16] Furthermore, foreign observations such as those made by the Arab, Chinese and European travellers would also provide us with significant information.[17]

NOTES

1 For further information on these inscriptions, see N. Karashima, *South Indian History and Society: Studies from Inscriptions A.D. 850–1800*, Oxford University Press, Delhi, 1984, pp. 40–55.

2 This inscription was edited by M.D. Sampath in his article 'Bahur inscription of Rajendra-Chola I, Year 16' in K.V. Ramesh, S.P. Tewari and M.J. Sharma, eds., *Indian History and Epigraphy: Dr. G.S. Gai Felicitation Volume*, Agam Kala Prakashan, Delhi, 1990, pp. 87–91. The reason for excluding *tīṇḍāḍār* from the desilting labour is attributed by Sampath to the pollution *tīṇḍāḍār* would bring to the tank.

3 E. Thurston, *Castes and Tribes in Southern India*, vol. 2, Madras, 1909, pp. 45ff. and J.H. Hutton, *Caste in India*, 3rd edn., Bombay, 1961, pp. 78ff.

4 In some places names of *nāṭṭavars* are also inserted.

5 Immediately after this enumeration, however, it is summed up in the inscription as 'all the *jātis* including Andaṇaṉ (Brāhmaṇas), the first, and Arippaṉ (one who lives by sifting), the last'. The relation between Iṟuḷar and Arippaṉ is not clear, though Hanumanthan takes Arippaṉ to be 'one section of the Paṟaiyans'. K.R. Hanumanthan, *Untouchability: A Historical Study upto 1500 A.D. with special reference to Tamil Nadu*, Madurai, 1979, p. 163.

6 For the revolt and the communities, see N. Karashima, *Towards a New Formation: South Indian Society under Vijayanagar Rule*, Oxford University Press, Delhi, 1992, pp. 141–58.

7 Nandanar is generally regarded as a Paṟaiya, though he is described as a Pulaiya in the *Periya Purāṇam*, as the service-tenure land enjoyed by him is referred to as *paṟai-tuḍavai* (land of the Paṟaiya). Vidya Dehejia and Nilakanta Sastri also refer to him as a Paṟaiya. See notes 8 and 9.

8 Vidya Dehejia, *Slaves of the Lord: The Path of the Tamil Saints*, Delhi, 1988, p. 173.

9 K.A. Nilakanta Sastri, *The Colas*, 2nd edn., Madras, 1955, pp. 568–69.

10 N. Karashima, *Towards a New Formation*, p. 124.

11 Ibid.

12 E. Thurston, *Castes and Tribes in Southern India*, vol. 5, Madras, 1909, pp. 472ff.

13 The project 'Socio-cultural Changes in Villages in Tiruchirapalli District, Tamilnadu, India' organised by the late Prof. Tadahiko Hara of the Institute for the Study of Languages and Cultures of Asia and Africa, Tokyo.

14 The documents were edited and published by Y. Subbarayalu of Tamil University, member of the project, in his *Palm-leaf Records of the Tiruchirapalli District*, Thanjavur, 1991. The seven lease-deed documents are Nos. 38, 39, 41 and 46–49.

15 Paṇṇaiyāḷ is explained by H. Yanagisawa as 'an attached farm labourer' in his *A Century of Change: Caste and Irrigated Lands in Tamilnadu 1860s—1970s*, Delhi, 1996, p. 300.

16 Some preliminary discussion on this line is found in Hanumanthan, *Untouchability* and Michael Moffatt, *An Untouchable Community in South India: Structure and Consensus*, Princeton, 1979, pp. 32–58.

17 Mu-kua described as 'the lowest of men' in the section of Ko-chih (Cochin) of a fifteenth-century Chinese travels is thought to have been Mukkuvars in Kerala. Ma Huan, *Ying-yai Sheng-lan: The Overall Survey of the Ocean's Shores*, tr. and ed. J.V.G. Mills, Cambridge, 1970, p. 133.

3

The Chamars of South-eastern Rajasthan A.D.1650–1800[1]

MASANORI SATO

INTRODUCTION

Numerous village surveys have been conducted in connection with rural development in India since her independence, which has greatly contributed to throwing new light on the socio-economic life of the Chamars as well as other social groups. But no systematic studies of the Chamars have been done so far from the historical point of view, though there have been many historical studies referring briefly to the fact that they were engaged either in the traditional/hereditary occupation of disposing of dead animals and its related tasks as their main occupation or in agriculture along with their main occupation.[2]

This paper purports to elucidate the community structure of the Chamars, the way in which the state controlled them, and how much the solidarity of the Chamar community was affected by the state rule and the economic change through the analysis of the change in landholdings of some other social groups as well as the Chamars in south-eastern Rajasthan from the latter half of seventeenth century to the end of eighteenth century. The source materials utilised in this research paper are mostly the archival revenue records belonging to the erstwhile Rajput state of Kota preserved at the Rajasthan State Archives, Bikaner.

THE CHAMARS IN VILLAGE COMMUNITY

In general, an agricultural village of north India has been until quite recently a cluster of houses surrounded by fields, around which have lain wastelands or pasture lands forming the boundaries with the neighbouring villages. The houses with their garden lands of landowners descended from the first colonizers of the village or of people of high castes have been mostly clustered together in the centre of the village. The arrival order or the caste ranking of the people is considered to be factors to determine their location in the village from the centre to the outskirts.

The Chamars, one of the lowest castes, had to reside either in some blocks (*mohallas* or *pattis*) on the outskirts of the village or in their own hamlets away from the village. Thus, it can be said that the residential patterns in a village have been an indication of caste discrimination so far developed in history. This description may also have been true of that in south-eastern Rajasthan during the period under study.

The *Jama Bandhis* of village or *qasba* (town) of Kota State reveal that a tax called either *Agotri ka Hal* or *Poya ka Hal*[3] was imposed on those who held cultivated lands, while a hearth tax called *Kholheṛi*[4] was charged from non-agriculturists such as merchants, artisans and menials for doing traditional occupations. The Chamars were generally *Kholheṛi* taxpayers, but sometimes were taxpayers of *Agotri ka Hal* earning their livelihood by cultivation instead of doing their traditional occupations. However, there were some artisans and merchants on whom both taxes were imposed on the ground that they were engaged in agriculture as well as in their hereditary occupations, but this was rarely the case of the Chamars.

From the *Jama Bandhi* of village Kolana, *pargana* Baṛod for the year 1794 V.S. (A.D.1736–37),[5] we learn that *Kholheṛi* was levied from the Chamars at the rate of 12 annas per head (or per family),[6] while from two merchants eight annas and two Gujars nine annas per head, respectively. Besides these, there were one carpenter, one potter and one washerman in the village on whom *Kholheṛi* was imposed for doing their traditional occupations at the rate of 12 annas, respectively. From this we know that the lower castes of carpenter, potter and washerman were equally taxed at the same rate per head with the Chamars. We may thus say that the Chamars as well as lower castes were discriminated against in regard to taxation. However, we cannot say whether or not the Chamars were the heaviest taxpayers among the lower castes because we have only limited information on the taxation on these castes.

We may then ask how many Chamars or Chamar families there were in a village or in a *qasba* during the period under study. *Kholheṛi*, as stated earlier, was a hearth tax imposed on the head of family or house, which was symbolised by the hearth. It therefore appears relatively simple to arrive at the number of Chamars or Chamar families living in a village or in a *qasba* because we find mention of the names of Chamars as well as those of other castes in *Jama Bandhi* who paid *Kholheṛi*. Thus, in 1794 V.S., we find three Chamar families in village Kolana mentioned earlier. However, we have no idea of whether the family was a nuclear one or an extended one in the strict sense of the word and how many members comprised the family.

Moreover, the most common fact in history has been that the weak in a society like the Chamars sometimes did not appear on record because they were often regarded as subordinate members attached to a powerful family under the patronage of which they had come to exist. At present we must be satisfied with the fact that the number of Chamar families as well as that of other caste families are simply derived from that of *Kholheṛi* taxpayers of each caste or occupation appearing on the *Jama Bandhi*. According to the census of A.D.1901, the Chamars are said to have occupied from 8 to 10 per cent of the population of this region.[7]

In village Tekhṛa, *pargana* Kota, the *Jama Bandhi* records nine agriculturists and eight non-agriculturists in 1721 V.S. The latter consisted of two Chamars, two merchants, one Chhipa (calico printer), one potter and one Gujar with one carpenter from the nearby village Dewali working for the village as a *pahi* (non-resident).[8] From the *Jama Bandhi* of village Baṛodo-bujarkh, *pargana* Ghaṭi, we find there were thirty-three agriculturists, and six non-agriculturists (three Chamars, one carpenter, one Teli and one Gujar) in 1806 V.S.[9]

In the villages Tekhṛa (1721 V.S.) and Baṛodo-bujarkh (1806 V.S.) there were respectively 575 and 1,060 bighas of cultivated land. One-third of the cultivated land of village Baṛodo-bujarkh was cultivated by 15 agriculturists as landholders from *qasba* Chechat just next to its western border and the remaining two-thirds of that land by 18 agriculturists from village Baṛodo-bujarkh proper. Assuming that these 15 agriculturists from the *qasba* were supplied agricultural and allied services at the *qasba* by its artisans and menials, the remaining 18 agriculturists of village Baṛodo-bujarkh proper with its two-thirds of cultivated land would have been supplied by its 6 artisans and menials. Both the villages of Tekhṛa and Baṛodo-bujarkh would then have had the same number of 6 artisans and menials, respectively and also almost the same bighas of cultivated land only except for the 2 merchants of village Tekhṛa. On the other hand, the number of agriculturists of village Baṛodo-bujarkh proper would have been twice that of village Tekhṛa.

Similarly, in 1794 V.S. village Sagatpuro of *pargana* Nandgaon (Kota)[10] had 12 agriculturists with 685 bighas of cultivated land, which is almost the same size as that of the two villages mentioned earlier. However, it had 19 non-agriculturists, among whom there were really 15 Chamars with the remainder being 3 Kalalas (winemakers) and 1 carpenter. The existence of quite a number of Chamars in this village may suggest that they had some relationship with the winemaking of the 3 Kalala families.

Village Basai of *pargana* Sangod in 1786 V.S.[11] and village Dighod of *pargana* Nandgaon in 1789 V.S.[12] differed considerably from each other with regard to their caste-occupational structure, even though both of them were quite large villages and afterwards became *qasbas*.[13] Village Basai had 128 non-agriculturists among whom there were found to be 82 Chhipas and only 4 Chamars, whereas in village Dighod there resided 13 Chamars and no Chhipa among 61 non-agriculturists. From this we may say that there existed some villages noted for weaving connnected with the calico printing of village Basai located in its environs because this printing was closely related to weaving.

It can be said that the Chamars were found in almost every village and town throughout Rajasthan with only a regional difference in number, arising from its caste-occupational structure related to the structure of local industries. This begs the question of what the Chamars were doing for their living in the villages or towns.

We have seen above that a tax of *Kholheṛi* was imposed on the Chamars as well as non-agricultural social groups for doing traditional work. The Chamars were traditionally expected to remove dead cattle from the village, for which they were entitled to obtain them, tan leather from their hide, and manufacture leather goods. They were also responsible for making leather buckets, which were absolutely essential for agriculture, leather ropes, mats, bags and shoes and to supply them to the villagers.[14]

The Chamars also manufactured bridles, saddles, scabbards for swords and shields allied to their traditional work,[15] which were utilised by the state in supplying their *topkhanas* (arsenals) or *silahkhanas* (armouries). We learn from the records of 1806 V.S. that 35 bighas of land was granted to one Chamar and one carpenter respectively as remuneration for working at the state *topkhana*.[16]

It is a well-known fact that the Chamars were also engaged in agriculture as if it were their traditional occupation, though it is not known when they started this. In fact, during the period under review, they are often found to be agricultural labourers or sometimes land owners.

In the semi- or non-official records of village Birawda, *tafa* Baṛoda for 1806 V.S.,[17] we find mention of a tax that was levied on two Chamars for the production of tobacco and maize. Judging from the fact that both of them paid a tax imposed on their products without possessing any land, it seems that they farmed rather as tenants than as labourers. However, from the fact that they were also *Kholheṛi* tax-payers we know that they continued to follow their traditional occupation and to make their living by doing so.

The Chamar tenant farmers or agricultural labourers seldom appear on the official record of *Jama Bandhi* because a tax of *Agotri ka Hal* was generally charged from landowners or landholders, not from tenant farmers, much less from agricultural labourers. However, from *Jama Bandhis* we find that not a few Chamars were landowners or landholders making their living by agriculture. As mentioned earlier, some of them were granted lands as remuneration for their work at the state *topkhana*. They were generally given full exemption by the state from payment of *Agotri ka Hal* tax, so this is not the question at issue. The question with regard to Chamar landholders is taken up briefly here and in detail in a later section.

Besides the Chamars, there are numerous references showing that the artisans were also engaged in agriculture, sometimes exclusively as their sole means of subsistence and sometimes in conjunction with their traditional work. It can be said that some artisans were granted lands like Chamars by the village or local *zamindars* in reward for rendering their agricultural and allied services. A tax of *Agotri ka Hal* must have also been levied on them for their lands unless the transfer of land was authorised to be free from taxation by the state. Simultaneously artisans were given partial exemption by the government from paying a tax of *Kholheṛi*, mentioning that they were 'driving ploughs' (*hal chalo/hal joto*).

In the *Jama Bandhi* of village Ṭigari, *pargana* Kunḍi for the year 1730 V.S.,[18] it is mentioned that a Chamar called Dipo was one of eight landholders in the village. Further, from a document of 1766 V.S.[19] we learn that five Bohṛas[20] cultivated 40 bighas of land belonging to two Chamars in village Munḍana-bujarkh. The Bohṛas may have farmed it from two Chamar landholders for agricultural management.

The Chamars, like other lower social groups, were also appointed lower village officials of *balais*.[21] Chamar Parso was a *balai* of village Kasampura, *pargana* Mangrol in 1808 V.S. They functioned as messengers in taking letters and documents from the village headmen to *pargana* offices and neighbouring villages, helped revenue officials in measuring fields with carrying *ḍoris* (ropes or chains), and in serving government officials when they visited the village on tour. Such officials were authorised to obtain services from Chamars free of charge.

The *balais* received for their work many dues consisting of allowances either in kind or cash per plough, well or field, or in kind at every harvest. In addition to this, they were also given some money or goods by government officials as a token of favour for the services rendered to them during their stay. It seems that they obtained a considerable income through their work because they had to pay a tribute called *Balai ka Salina* twice a year.

Since *Balai ka Salina* and its amount are written almost in every *Jama Bandhi*, *balais* are generally found in every village. *Balais*' names never appear on the list of *Kholheṛi* but sometimes on the list of *Agotri ka Hal* in *Jama Bandhi*.[22] So they were sometimes landowners or landholders, some of whom may have been granted lands by village or village headmen. They were so extensively exploited privately as well as officially under the patronage of village headmen that they were regarded as village servants by the British colonial officers.[23]

In connection with their work in the village, Chamars were entitled to free entrance to *paḍat* (village wasteland). In this regard, *Chamara ka Paḍat* mentioned in *Jama Bandhi* as a commonage was enjoyed by them until quite recently. They were given the rights to gather cow dung, and cut grass and bush from the grazing grounds for fuel. It must be noted here that they continued to utilise the wasteland as a kind of common property which accordingly made up for their lack of income.

It is common knowledge that every village community did its utmost either to invite artisans or menials to settle down in the village or visit regularly for work from neighbouring villages or to encourage them to return to the village from where they came or migrated to another villages when the village community needed their services.[24] As with other artisans, so it was with Chamars who visited the village regularly from neighbouring villages for work essential to the life of the village community. In the record of *pargana* Sakhet for 1854 V.S.,[25] for example, we find that five *pahi* artisans from neighbouring villages and *qasbas* were visiting village Gundi to work regularly, among whom there was one Chamar of village Sohankheṛi.

However, it appears that there were very few Chamars who had come to settle down in the village for work, as shall be seen later, comparing with other artisans. However, it can be said that this was not of their own free volition but was the will of their caste community that they came to settle down in a particular village for the work which was portioned to them. The Chamars were forced to render *begars* (forced labour) by the state,[26] so their community must have been more strongly subjected to the rule of village communities which executed this on behalf of the higher authorities. This would also be true of other lower castes of artisans or menials on which *begars* were also forced. However, as far as Chamars were concerned, it can be easily understood that their very position made them all the more strongly subordinate to the organization of village communities.

COMMUNITY STRUCTURE OF THE CHAMARS

We know from *Jama Bandhis* that *chak* (village area) comprised *abadi* (habitation area), *hakkat* (cultivated land), and *biḍo* (cultivable wasteland) which came under cultivation only when it rained. *Paḍat/banjaṛ* (wasteland) lying beyond the village area was generally specially reserved under state control. When it was developed into *hakkat* or *biḍo*, it was incorporated into the village area, on which taxes were subsequently levied.[27] The commonage of the village *paḍat* was given to the Chamars on whom a tax of *Chamara ka Paḍat* was imposed except for only the grazing right which was granted to villagers on whom *charai* (grazing tax) was levied.

It must be noted that a tax of *Chamara ka Paḍat* has not appeared on every *Jama Bandhi* obtained so far. This does not mean that there might have been a village with *paḍat*, the commonage of which was not bestowed upon the Chamars. If there existed a village with *paḍat* of economic value, the commonage of which was not given to the Chamars, the state would have levied a tax on the villagers for the use of the *paḍat*, instead of leving *Chamara ka Paḍat*. Thus it seems that the village, whose *Chamara ka Paḍat* did not appear on its *Jama Bandhi*, was either a village without *paḍat* or a village with *paḍat* of no economic value for taxation.

In the *Parwana* of the Maharao of Kota for 1766 V.S. (A.D. 1708–9)[28] it is mentioned that Chamars Bhama, Lohtiya, Tila and so on (*wagar*) were exempted Rs. 10 out of Rs. 60 for payment of a tax of *Chamara ka Paḍat* and were requested to pay the rest in two installments in a year. It is very interesting to point out that the *Parwana* was addressed not only to Bhama, Lohtiya and Tila but also to some other Chamars whose names were not mentioned in the order with only the word *wagar* (*wagairah*) meaning 'and so on'.

Concerning a tax of *Kholheṛi* levied on the Chamars of village Kanwas, we know from the *Jama Bandhi* for 1780 V.S. that its tax-payers were nine, one of whom was called Tila. He is most probably the same person as that noted in 1766 V.S. The highest amount of the *Kholheṛi* paid by Isro was takas 31, with the next one respectively being takas 18 by Tila and Toro and the lowest one takas 4 by Padarath and Sawlo. Bhito paid takas 16 and Ramji, Pitho and Pemo paid takas 9 each. According to the *Jama Bandhis* of village Kanwas, of the number of the Chamars there were nine available taxpayers on the list of *Kholheṛi* in 1780 V.S., but this number increased to 14 in 1789 V.S. and to 15 in 1791 V.S. However, according to the *Jama Bandhi* of *qasba* (town) Kanwas for 1812 V.S., it decreased to 12, a reduction of 3, one of whom had run away from the then *qasba* Kanwas.[29]

In 1780 V.S., the state gave the *paḍat* of *qasba* Awan on *mukata* (contract) to Chamars Udo, Dilo, Toro and Jandiya on the condition that they had to pay the state Rs. 25 and Rs. 10 on each subsequent harvest respectively.[30] We can also find all their names on the list of taxpayers of *Kholheṛi* available in the *Jama Bandhis* of *qasba* Awan for 1789, 1791 and 1795 V.S. These *Jama Bandhis* mention that there were 15 Chamars in 1789 V.S., 16 in 1791 V.S. and 15 in 1795 V.S. in *qasba* Awan.[31]

Thus, we know that those four Chamars were in charge of payment of the tax of *Chamara ka Paḍat* of *qasba* Awan because the commonage of village/*qasba paḍat* was granted to the Chamars as a community and not to a Chamar individually. But on them the same amount of *Kholheṛi* tax was levied as that of other Chamar members of the *qasba* through the years of the *Jama Bandhis* concerned. However, in the *Jama Bandhi* for 1795 V.S., mention has been made about Chamar Udo who was exempted from payment of *Kholheṛi* tax in *qasba* Awan while being taxed in the nearby village Karodiya. He seems to have shifted his working place to village Karodiya from the *qasba* in 1795 V.S. or before.

As we have seen, the tax amount of *Kholheṛi* differed among the Chamar members of village Kanwas and *qasba* (town) Kanwas, whereas it remained exactly the same among the Chamar members of *qasba* Awan. From the difference in the tax amount among the Chamars of *qasba* Kanwas we may infer that the Chamar community of *qasba* Kanwas had just begun to develop some stratified internal structure. However, there were more than one Chamar representing the Chamar community for paying the tax of *Chamara ka Paḍat*, so we can safely say that its internal structure had not yet been fully stratified at the time. As we shall soon see, this view is also strongly supported by the fact that there existed some *Chamar panchas* (elders) and their *panchayat* (council) which functioned to maintain the community solidarity and protect their interests.

The documents of *Jama Farohi* of village Raipura and the related documents of *Likhtan(g)* of 1753 V.S. are those concerning the fines levied on offenders for their crimes by the state and/or the *panchayats*[32] of various social groups as well as the Chamars to which offenders belonged. However, we should not overlook the fact that offenders belonged not only to village Raipura but also to other villages under the jurisdiction of the former village. In particular, these offenders' crimes were principally theft, injury, murder, illegal marriage, adultery, killing cattle, and driving cattle into fields. Generally through *Farohi* documents we can not only get a glimpse of the rural and town life of the people but also an outline of the social organisation of *panchayat* of the various social groups and its workings.

We take a case of a Chamar widow of village Khangarpura who had illegal sexual relations with a Chamar of village Ghaṭi and was fined for her crime by the state as well as by her *Chamar panchayat*. The *Likhtan* was submitted to the state in 1753 V.S. by Chamar Chhitra of village Dhawad, father of the said Chamar widow, who pledged that the *paṭel* of village Raipura and the *panchas* of the Chamar community bore witness that he paid a fine of Rs. 4 to the *panchayat* and also a fine of *Chauthani*[33] (one-fourth) of Re. 1 as its surcharge to the state in place of his daughter. From this fact we know that the Chamars like other social groups had their own caste *panchayat* which dealt with matters and disputes among them. From the tax of *Chauthani* levied by the state, we also know that the state tried to utilise their caste *panchayat* to extend its authority to every individual member of the Chamar community.

Since there is no information available about the Chamar of

village Ghaṭi, with whom the said Chamar widow had illegal sexual relations, we presume that his village was not under the jurisdiction of the *paṭel* of village Raipura and also the *Chamar panchayat* concerned, but under the jurisdiction of another village/town and its relative *Chamar panchayat*. He seems to have also been fined by the state and his *Chamar panchayat*. However, it goes without saying that village Dhawad to which the said Chamar Chhitra, father of the said widow, belonged, was under the jurisdiction of the *paṭel* of village Raipura and the *Chamar panchayat*.

From other *Likhtans* written by members of other various social groups, we know that the villages under the jurisdiction of the *paṭel* of village Raipura and the *Chamar panchayat* were the same as those under the jurisdiction of the *panchayats* of other social groups as well as the *paṭel* of this village. Specifically, besides Raipura and Dhawad, these villages were Bandha, Gokulpura, Koṭha-baoṛi, Ḍorya-ka-kuwo, Gunda, Charan-baoṛi, Bara-bai, Pachpahar, Bugchach, Akawo, Mohanpura, which were situated in the south-western part of the present *tehsil* Laḍpura, to the south of the city of Kota. But we cannot confirm the location of some villages including village Raipura whose names are not available on the map of the Census Atlas of A.D. 1961. However, since we often come across the name of village Raipura in revenue documents of the period under study, it must thereafter have gotten its name changed.

The names of social groups, the *panchayats* of which put the same villages under their jurisdiction as that of the Chamars, were Telis (oilmen), Kalalas (winemakers), Gujars and Minas. However, it must be remembered that these village names and social group names have been obtained only from the *Likhtans* available, the description of which coincided with the contents of the documents of *Jama Farohi* of village Raipura in 1753 V.S., and that we lack many *Likhtans* which should have been attached to the said *Jama Farohi*. Assuming that such *Likhtans* were available, however, we may enumerate more names of villages and social groups which were to have come under the jurisdiction of village Raipura.

What is important here is that the Chamars were a social group having a socially well-organised network and group solidarity in a certain area consisting of several villages including some towns. They had their own caste *panchayat* consisting of elders who maintained group solidarity and internal order with the jurisdiction to hear cases and to settle disputes among the members. It thus follows from what has been said that the Chamars continued to maintain their communally organised structure in 1753 V.S., though it was exploited by the state in her attempt to rule over each individual of its membership. Unfortunately, we do not have any information about whether these elders were among those who were responsible for the payment of the *Chamara ka Paḍat* tax.

STATE RULE AND CHAMAR COMMUNITY

Generally speaking, tax or revenue administration of a state occupies one of the pivotal positions in the state policies for ruling people through its assessment, collection and distribution in money, goods and services. It is therefore very important to examine how the Chamars were ruled by the state through taxation. From the viewpoint of taxation as has been observed earlier, all the villagers or townsmen were divided into agriculturists and non-agriculturists from whom a tax of *Agotri ka Hal* and that of *Kholheṛi* were levied respectively for their work. They were thus ruled by the state through the *pargana* and town or village officials who functioned as assessors, collectors and distributors of these taxes.

Kheṛ Kharch is said to have been a military tax which was originally imposed on a defeated enemy, but actually it was levied by the state on its people residing in all of the communities of social groups including the Chamars living in villages as well as towns. Therefore, it was a military tax imposed on people under the pretext of protecting them from enemy attacks.[34]

The *Likhtan* of 1743 V.S. (A.D. 1685–86) submitted by *paṭels*, *paṭwari* (village accountant) and the farmers of village Khijuri mentions that Rs. 25 was collected from the village as *Kheṛ Kharch*. In *qasba* Kota, *Kheṛ Kharch*[35] was levied not only from the Chamars but also from all the communities of merchants, peasants, artisans and menials, as well as from *pargana* officials of *chaudhris* and *qanungos* and town officials of *paṭels* (heads of wards), *paṭwaris* and *balais*. A sum of Rs. 945 and annas 6 was collected as *Kheṛ Kharch* from 110 merchants of *qasba* Kota in 1743 V.S. and the amount per head ranged from Re. 1 at the lowest to Rs. 81 at the highest. But it is quite interesting to note that some *pargana* officials of *chaudhris* and *qanungos* paid Rs. 950 as their *Kheṛ Kharch*, which shows that their posts must have been quite profitable.

A sum of Rs. 17 was also levied as *Kheṛ Kharch*[36] on all the members of the Chamar community (*samast* Chamar) in *qasba* Kota. However, we have no idea whether *Kheṛ Kharch* was more heavily imposed on Chamars than on other social groups because we do not have enough information about the number of members of other social groups or of the Chamars.

Kheṛ Kharch was generally imposed on a village as a unit, while it is levied on every community of social groups in a *qasba*. Thus, we can understand how the state tried to extend its authority either over every individual in a village or over every individual of the community membership in a *qasba* by placing them at their own specific locality through taxation.

The documents of *Farohi* of *qasba* Kanwas for 1810 V.S. tell us that they collected a fine of Rs. 2 imposed on Chamar Rupo who had run away from the *qasba*, though they do not mention who paid it.[37] It must be his community of the *qasba* that paid it, however, because he was still on the run in 1812 V.S.[38]

From the *Farohi* documents of village Poholai-bujarkh in *pargana* Kota for 1743 V.S., we also know that some *jowar* (millet) was stolen from the threshing floor in the village, the responsibility for which was placed on the two grain watchmen of *balai* Hema and a *sansaṛi* (a village watchman whose name is not mentioned) who were fined Rs. 3 and Rs. 23 respectively. The former paid it, but the latter apparently ran away without paying the amount which was thereafter paid by the villagers.[39] This incident clearly shows that there existed the collective responsibility of villagers in matters of taxation and criminal law. We also learn from this that the state tried to perpetrate its authority on the village by exploiting the community pressure of the villages to conform.

The same may be true of the tax of *Chamara ka Paḍat* as has been observed earlier. Since all of the village was not provided with *paḍat* (wasteland), it must be considered that the exclusive right to utilise it was not only given to the Chamars of the village but also to the Chamars living in the surrounding villages without accompanying wasteland. It can be said that the priviledge was granted to the Chamars by the state with the intention, on the one hand, to keep them entirely under the state rule through their elders, and on the other, to keep them maintaining the community solidarity by making them aware that the *paḍat* was their common property.

We know from the documents of *Farohi* of village Raipura that *Chamar panchayat* had placed extensive areas under its jurisdiction.

More interesting are the contents of the *Likhtan* submitted by Chamar Chhitra of village Dhawad mentioning that the *Chamar panchayat* punished a Chamar widow, Chhitra's daughter, for her illegal sexual relations with a Chamar of village Ghaṭi by fining her Rs. 4, while the state imposed a tax of *Chauthani* (one-fourth of the fine) on her. In connection with this, we also know that the state punished not only the Chamars but also other members of various social groups for their crimes. What has to be noticed here is that the state imposed *Chauthani* on offenders for the purpose of not only punishing them for their illegal acts and increasing tax revenues but also of promoting the penetration of the state authority into every social group community as well as that of the Chamars and controlling its every individual member through its *panchayat*.

It may also be worth pointing out that the area under the informal or unofficial jurisdiction of the *paṭel* of village Raipura and every *panchayat* of some social groups as well as the Chamars coincided with the area under the official jurisdiction of village Raipura revealed from the *Farohi* documents of this village examined in the preceeding section. Thus, it can be said that the state tried to rule every individual member of each social group by putting the same area under the official jurisdiction of village Raipura after the model of the area under the unofficial jurisdiction of the *paṭel* of village Raipura and *panchayats* of some social groups. Therefore, it is through their *panchayat* that every individual member of the Chamar community was brought under the double or triple control of the state.

CHANGING SOCIAL STRUCTURE OF THE CHAMARS

We must discuss here what kind of changes were caused by the state rule and economic change in the internal social structure of the Chamars. In the *Jama Bandhi* of *qasba* Madhkargaṛh for 1806 V.S. (A.D. 1748–49) it has been mentioned that the *Chamara ka Paḍat* of the *qasba* was farmed out on *mukata* (contract) to Chamar Lalya, son of Chamar Kheta of the *qasba*, for Rs. 18 for one year in three installments.[40] Besides this, there are available both a *Parwana* of the Maharao of Kota and the *Likhtan* submitted to the state by Chamar Lalya.[41]

We do not know anything more about Chamar Kheta nor about Chamar Lalya written in the *Jama Bandhi*. However, this exhibits a striking contrast to the fact that there had been more than one *mukatedar* (contractor) of the *paḍat* so far and that only their names are mentioned in *mukata* documents without referring to their family relationship. This may suggest that some particular families had grown in importance among the Chamar community.

Unfortunately, there is no reference to Chamars of the *qasba* in the *Jama Bandhi* of 1806 V.S., but some Chamars except Chamar Lalya and his family must have lived there. In 1780 V.S., a sum of Rs. 28 and annas 13 was imposed on some Chamars in the *qasba* for the *Gharpati* (literally, a patriarch) tax, but the number of the Chamars is not mentioned in the documents. Judging from the amount of the tax, there must have been several Chamar families in the *qasba* in the period because a sum of Rs. 20 and annas 9 was imposed on 13 Khatis (carpenters), Rs. 6 and annas 2.5 on five houses of Luhars (blacksmiths), Rs. 25 and annas 3.5 on five houses of Kumhars (potters), Rs. 29 and annas 14 on 19 houses of Chhipas (calico printers), and Rs. 52 and annas 8 on 20 Telis (oilmen), along with other levies on others in the *qasba*.[42]

It must be noted in this *Likhtan* that the *Chamara ka Paḍat* of *qasba* Madhkargaṛh was farmed out (on *mukata*) to Chamar Lalya personally. As we have seen, *Chamara ka Paḍat* had so far been a common property of the Chamars living in the area concerned and had been farmed out (on *mukata*) to more than one Chamar representing the Chamar community, apart from how they shared the amount of the *mukata* among their members. Considering the fact that Chamar Lalya undertook personally the *Chamara ka Paḍat* of the *qasba* on *mukata*, it seems that the Chamar community, representatives of which had been so far entrusted with the joint care of the common property, had begun to sustain some internal change. This may have reflected some hierarchical structure of the Chamar community. In other words, it may have suggested that an influential or powerful family had risen up from the Chamar community.

Let us now discuss from a different angle the landholding and its change of the Chamars in view of that of other social groups, and the changing internal structure of the Chamar community. In the *Jama Bandhis*, we often come across the fact that there were not a few Chamars and other members of social groups who held cultivated land and practised agriculture. However, it is very difficult to obtain some *Jama Bandhis* of a particular village for a certain long period in order to trace the changing phases of their landholdings.

Here, however, in some of *Jama Bandhis* belonging to village

Manasgaon, we can trace the changes in landholdings of this village for comparatively a long period of 60 years. Village Manasgaon is an old village that can be traced back to 1691 V.S. to the extent that the records are available.[43] It lies 18 km north-east of the city of Kota and is situated on the east bank where Chambal River winds its way sharply. According to the land survey conducted by the Kota state in 1774 V.S., it was a large village with more than 5,000 bighas of cultivated land.[44] It may have been a village submissive to the state whose rule reached its every corner, however, because a lot of the village records are available.

As to the village records of village Manasgaon, there are its five *Jama Bandhis* available for the following periods of 1773, 1779, 1789, 1806 and 1814 V.S. In addition to these, we also have its revenue documents of 1839 V.S., a part of which has been lost.[45]

Table 1, prepared from the *Jama Bandhis* and other revenue documents of village Manasgaon, denotes several artisans and their landholdings in the village: a Chamar, a Chhipa (calico printer), a Luhar (blacksmith), a Teli (oilman) and a Tammoli (betel leaf seller). Besides these, there were carpenters, goldsmiths, potters, washermen and winemakers following their traditional occupations for some time during the period concerned.

The number of Chamars including Chamars listed in Table 1 appeared on the *Jama Bandhis* enumerates four in 1773 V.S., six in 1779 V.S., three in 1789 V.S., seven in 1806 V.S. and five in 1814 V.S. besides the two Chamars who had died and one who was on the run in 1789 V.S.

Chamar Chhitra is found as a landholder in the records of 1773, 1779, 1789 and 1806 V.S. His landholding decreased to 15 bighas in 1779 V.S. from 60 bighas in 1773. V.S. But it increased to 30 bighas in 1789 V.S. and then to 90 bighas in 1806 V.S. Assuming that Chamar Khemo was his son, his landholding then amounted to 105 bighas including Khemo's land in 1806 V.S. Chamar Soji, who had 120 bighas of cultivated land in 1814 V.S. may in fact have been another son of Chamar Chhitra. Chamar Khemo might have died shortly after 1806 V.S. because he never appears on any *Jama Bandhi* of the village except for the mention in 1806 V.S. From the revenue records of 1839 V.S., we find that there was no Chamar landholder in the village, and that Chamar Godho, the assumed son of either Chamar Khemo or Chamar Soji, had no landholding.

Table 1 Size of landholding of artisans and menials of village Manasgaon

Year (V.S.)	*Chamar*	*Chhipa*	*Luhar*	*Teli*	*Tammoli*
1773	Chhitra 60	Pathu 90	Nathu 120	Kilan 30	
1779	Chhitra 15	Pathu 90	Chhitra	Narhar 30	
1789	Chhitra 30	Pathu 94	Chhitra	Narhar	
1806	Chhitra 90 Khemo 15	Chhitra 90	Chhitra	Narhar	
1814	Soji 120	Harji 102	Bhopo		
1839	Godho		Kisno		(Lalu's widow)

Note: Figures (bighas) below each name denote the size of his landholding.

On the other hand, Chhipa Pathu continued to retain almost 90 bighas of cultivated land for a long period. In 1814 V.S. Chhipa Harji, possibly the son of Chhipa Pathu, added 12 bighas of cultivated land to his possession, but he must have left his traditional occupation and practised only agriculture because his name cannot be found among the list of *Kholheṛi* taxpayers.

Luhar Nathu was a large landholder, but we can not say anything about how he obtained his land in the course of his lifetime because we do not have any information concerning his landholding before 1773 V.S. All Luhars of Chhitra, Bhopo and Kisno, possibly descended from Luhar Nathu, left the practice of agriculture and followed the traditional occupation of smithery from 1779 V.S. onwards.

Teli Narhar may have inherited 30 bighas of cultivated land from Teli Kilan, the assumed father, but he must have lost all his possessions not long before he stopped doing his traditional work. He then left his village by 1814 V.S.

Tammoli Chhitra made his first appearance on the *Jama Bandhi* of this village in 1814 V.S. so he must have come to the village from outside. As he was not engaged in his traditional work, he may have purchased his 30 bighas of cultivated land for doing agriculture. In the *Jama Bandhi* for 1839 V.S. mention is made of Tammoli Lalu's widow, so the descendants of Tammoli Chhitra seem to have continued to live in the village after his death.

Obviously, it is very difficult to follow the change in landholding of each and every landholder who appeared in *Jama Bandhis*, but this is not our present purpose. It is sufficient for us to glean some idea of the general tendency toward change in landholding in village Manasgaon by examining the landholding of *paṭels* and any apparent change. However, *paṭelis* were not only inherited by their respective descendants but were also traded and partitioned as a family property. Thus it is also difficult to ascertain from whom they inherited *paṭelis* and with whom they had blood relationship because we can derive only their personal names with the official title of *paṭels* and the size of their landholdings from *Jama Bandhis*. Therefore, if we sum up all the landholdings of *paṭels* obtained from the *Jama Bandhis* of respective years and compare them, we shall then be able to have a glimpse of the change in landholding of *paṭels* in particular and consequently that of the village in general.

Table 2 thus indicates the number of *paṭels* and their total landholdings prepared from the *Jama Bandhis* and other revenue documents of village Manasgaon of the respective years. As is evident, there existed from four to eight *paṭels* during the period from 1773 to 1839 V.S., except that one *paṭel* may be missing from the *Jama Bandhi* for 1798 V.S. Thus, it can be said that the total landholdings of 1798 V.S. given in the table did not include his landholding. *Paṭels* range in the size of landholding from 60 to 180 bighas of cultivated land during the 1773 to 1798 V.S. period, but in 1806 V.S. one *paṭel* comprised an unusually large landholding of 420 bighas, while the other four were less than 100 bighas of land each. In 1814 V.S., the largest *paṭel* reduced his landholding to 370 bighas, while the other five amounted to less than 120 bighas each. We should note that in 1839 V.S. even the largest landholder among the *paṭels* had only 105 bighas of land and the total landholding of *paṭels* sharply decreased. It may be suggested from this that village Manasgaon underwent a predominant socio-economic change during the said period.

We can also confirm that this socio-economic change of the period was prevalent among the landholdings of merchants and the employment of *halis* (bonded agricultural labourers) by landholders. From the *Jama Bandhi* for 1773 V.S. we find two merchant names on

Table 2 Number of patels and their total landholding in village Manasgaon

Year (V.S.)	*Number of patels*	*Total landholding (bighas)*
1773	5	600
1779	5	630
1798	4	555
1806	5	694
1814	6	807
1839	8	379

the list of *Kholheṛi* taxpayers. But from 1773 V.S. on, neither their names nor any other merchants' names appeared on the lists of *Kholheṛi* in the *Jama Bandhis*.

However, we find some names of merchants in particular with extensive landholdings on the list of a tax of *Agotri ka Ḥal* in the *Jama Bandhis.* One of these had 240 bighas of cultivated land in 1773 V.S., which he increased to 500 bighas in 1779 V.S. and then to 570 bighas in 1789 V.S. Afterwards this landholding seems to have been divided among the two assumed descendants into 300 bighas and 216 bighas respectively in 1839 V.S.

Twenty-two *halis* in this village were registered in 1839 V.S. Seven of these were employed by the two merchants noted above, three by two other merchants, four worked at the state farm, another four cultivating 212 bighas of land held by a *khawas* (attendant to a prince), two by two government officers and the other two by two *paṭels*. As to their castes, there were fourteen Ahirs, four Dhakaṛs, one Jaṭ and three Brahmans. The former three belonged to agricultural communities of this region. We can not say for certain whether they were originally inhabitants of this village or outsiders. There were three Ahir landholders among the landholders in 1814 V.S. who had the same names as the three Ahir *halis* respectively. It is difficult to confirm this, however, because there was a 25-year difference between two of the *Jama Bandhis* and their names were very common for those days.

Concerning the *Panḍet* (Brahman) *halis*, all three of them were employed by two Bohoṛas (merchants). Two of them were among four *halis* employed by Bohoṛa Udo, a landholder of 300 bighas, and the other one was among three *halis* employed by Bohoṛa Nathu Ram, a landholder of 219 bighas. This suggests that even Brahmans could not escape from being reduced to poverty. In 1808 V.S. a Brahman (Baragaon) of *qasba* Sangod was fined Rs. 301 by the state for having sold the Vedas.[46] In view of the large landholdings by merchants, some artisan landholders and Chamar landholders, as well as the employment of not a few *halis* by village notables, it can also be confirmed that village Manasgaon witnessed a marked social and economic change during the period under review.

As seen in Table 1, Chamar Chhitra had been engaged in agriculture as well as followed his traditional occupation for a long time. But his descendant devoted himself to agriculture, giving up following his father's traditional occupation. This Chamar family is a good example of a family that incurred fluctuations in landholding and finally lost it during the period. The same observation can be applied to the families of Luhar, Teli and Chhipa, who lost all their landholdings by 1839 V.S.

We can find many artisans including Chamars who ran away from villages or towns during the period under study. This appears to have occurred first of all in towns rather than in villages in which they freed themselves from community pressures to conform and also found places in which to take refuge. Runaway from villages had begun to increase in greater numbers from around the end of the 1780s V.S. From village Manasgaon, a Chamar is also found to have run away in 1789 V.S.

Thus it appears that the Chamar community as well as the communities of other social groups had begun to go through the process of gradual disintegration. We can safely say that Chamar Lalya, for example, who had placed himself under *mukata* to the *Chamara ka Paḍat* of *qasba* Madhkargaṛh, was typical of the internal change of the Chamar community affected by the social and economic change of the period.

Let us finish this discussion by denoting an interesting fact as follows. From the *Taqsim* of *tafa* Bhaltha, *pargana* Barsana for 1780 V.S.[47] we learn that here was a village called Chamar-bhalthi, meaning a Chamar village established in *tafa* Bhaltha, which could have been named after its Chamar founders. There existed another village of Bhil-bhalthi in the *tafa* in the same year,[48] also meaning a Bhil village in *tafa* Bhaltha founded by the Bhils. But the *Taqsim* of *tafa* Bhaltha for 1811 V.S. tells us that the name of village Chamar-bhalthi was changed to village Rama-bhalthi, while that of village

Bhil-bhalthi was not changed. Although we do not know when and by whom the village name was changed,[49] we can readily note that it was a matter of 'discrimination' that the village name was changed from Chamar to Rama.

From the viewpoint of the internal structure of the Chamar community, we should not overlook the fact that there existed a village founded by Chamars. From the village name we can understand that the village was founded by a group of Chamars, and not by an individual Chamar. Is it then a coincidence that the name of the Chamar village was changed around the period when some Chamar communities started along the road to their gradual disintegration?

CONCLUSION

As mentioned, this paper has examined the community structure and the social organisation of the Chamars and has discussed the way in which the state tried to rule every individual member of the Chamar community. In this process the state adopted contradictory administrative policies to rule the Chamars, having tried, on the one hand, to maintain their community as a group with common property, and on the other, to dissolve the community by penetrating its authority to reach every individual Chamar member. In spite of these contradictory policies of the state, they seemed to have considerably influenced the Chamars' community structure and social relations.

Also analysed were the changing features of the landholding of merchants, *paṭels* and artisans as well as those of the Chamars, along with the existence of *halis* in village Manasgaon. Additionally witnessed was a remarkable change in landholding in the village which clearly shows that the Chamars' community structure and social relations were affected to a considerable degree.

Thus, the Chamar community seems to have started its decline toward disintegration under the state policies and under the influence of the prevailing socio-economic change of the period under study. Finally, although this paper has mainly dealt with the particular social group of the Chamars, we may say that some of the observations made thus far can also be readily applied to other social groups existing during this time period.

NOTES

1 When referring to the Rajasthani documents of the Kota Records available at the Rajasthan State Archives, Bikaner, the following abbreviations are used:
V.S.: Vikram Samvat
B.N.: Basta Number
Bh.N.: Bhandar Number

2 B.L. Gupta, *Trade and Commerce in Rajasthan during the 18th Century*, Jaipur, 1987, pp. 22, 24–25, 64. Dilbagh Singh, *The State, Landlords and Peasants: Rajasthan in the 18th Century*, New Delhi, 1990, pp. 28–29.

3 *Agotri* is said to be a cess which was paid by those who had wells in their fields. A plough (*hal*) pulled by two bullocks could cultivate 25 or 30 bighas of land in a season, so *Agotri ka Hal* may mean the area irrigated by wells. We do not know the meaning of *poya*, but *Poya ka Hal* is used in the same sense as *Agotri ka Hal*. B.N. Dhoundiyal, *Bundi: Rajasthan District Gazetteers*, Jaipur, 1964, p. 194.

4 *Kholheṛi* or *Kholṛi* is derived from *chulha* (hearth). It was also called *Jhunpri* or *Jhonpra* (a hut). *Jama Bandhi*, Mauza Tekhṛa, Pargana Kota, 1721 V.S., B.N. 1, Bh.N. 1. H.B. Abbott, *Report on the Revenue Settlement of Jhallawar*, 1885, p. 34.

5 *Jama Bandhi*, Mauza Kolana, Pargana Baṛod, 1794 V.S., B.N. 49/3, Bh.N.1.

6 B.L. Gupta, *Trade and Commerce in Rajasthan...*, p. 226.

7 *Imperial Gazetteer of India, Provincial Series, Rajputana*, Calcutta, 1908, rpt. New Delhi, 1989, pp. 34, 372, 391.

8 *Jama Kharch*, Mauza Tekhṛa, Pargana Kota, 1721 V.S., B.N. 1, Bh.N. 1.

9 *Jama Bandhi*, Mauza Baṛodo-bujarkh, Pargana Ghaṭi, 1806 V.S., B.N. 54, Bh.N. 1.

10 *Jama Bandhi*, Mauza Sagatpuro, Pargana Nandgaon, 1794 V.S., B.N. 49/3, Bh.N. 1.

11 *Jama Bandhi*, Mauza Basai, Pargana Sangod, 1786 V.S., B.N. 44/2, Bh.N.1.

12 *Jama Bandhi*, Mauza Dighod, Pargana Nandgaon, 1789 V.S., B.N. 46/2, Bh.N. 1.

13 Masanori Sato, 'The formative process of towns and market towns/villages in southeastern Rajasthan, A.D. 1650–1850', *Keizaigaku-Kiyo* (The Journal of Economics), (Asia University, Tokyo) 19, no. 2, (1995) pp. 5–10.

14 G.W. Briggs, *The Chamars*, Bombay, 1920, p. 56 and Appendix B, pp. 256–60.

15 B.L. Gupta, *Trade and Commerce in Rajasthan...*, pp. 24–25, 64.

16 *Jama Bighoṛi*, Pargana Nandgaon, 1806 V.S., B.N. 54, Bh.N. 1.

17 *Khata Zabti*, Mauza Birawda, Tafa Baṛoda, 1806 V.S., B.N. 54, Bh.N. 1.

18 *Jama Bandhi*, Mauza Tigari, Pargana Kunḍi, 1730 V.S., B.N. 2/3, Bh.N.1.

19 *Kagzat*, Mauza Mundana-bujarkh, 1766 V.S., B.N. 26/2, Bh.N. 1.

20 They belong to one of the chief cultivating castes in Chechat and Paṭan. See H.B. Abbott, *Report on the Revenue Settlement of Jhallawar*, p. 21.

21 *Farohi Peshkashi wa Nazarana*, Paragana Mangrol, 1808 V.S., B.N. 55, Bh.N. 1.

22 *Balai* Soji was a landholder of 60 bighas of land in village Manasgaon in 1806 V.S. *Jama Bandhi*, Mauza Manasgaon, Pargana Nandgaon, 1806, V.S., B.N. 54, Bh.N. 1.

23 M.S.D. Butler, *Final Report of the Second Settlement of the Kotah State*, Kotah, 1909, p. 47.

24 *Likhtan* in *Jama Bandhi*, Mauza Babli, Pargana Baran, 1784 V.S., B.N. 96, Bh.N.1. Masanori Sato, *Mugaru Ki Indo no Kokka to Shakai* (State and Society in Mughal India), Tokyo, 1982, p. 470.

25 *Kaṭta Mal Hasil*, Pargana Sakhet, 1854 V.S. B.N. nil, Bh.N. 16.

26 *Do Warki*, Qasba Chechat, 1839 V.S., B.N. 64, Bh.N. 1. *Parwana* from Maharao Shri Ummed Singhji to Karmandi Khan and Ujirkhan, Hawalgir-Subadars of Mukandgaṛh and Halkara of Darwaza ki Chauki, 1858 V.S., B.N. 72, Bh.N. 1.

27 120 bighas of *biḍo* indicated by two ploughs was incorporated into the land of village Manḍuheṛa in 1797 V.S. *Jama Bandhi*, Mauza Manḍuheṛa, Pargana Nandgaon, 1797 V.S., B.N. 112, Bh.N. 1.

28 *Parwana* from Maharao Shri Bhim Singhji to Chamar Bhama, Lohtiya, Tila and so on of village Kanwas, 1766 V.S., B.N. 26/1, Bh.N. 1.

29 *Jama Bandhis*, Mauza/Qasba Kanwas, Pargana Nandgaon, 1780, 1789, 1791 and 1812 V.S., B.Ns. 38/1, 46/1, 47/2 and 56/2, Bh.N. 1.

30 *Parwana* from Maharao Shri Durjan Salji to Chamar Udo, Dilo, Toro and Jandiya of Qasba Awan, 1780 V.S., B.N. 38/2, Bh.N. 1.

31 *Jama Bandhis*, Qasba Awan, 1789, 1791, 1795 and 1812 V.S., B.Ns. 46/1, 47/2, 50 and 56/2, Bh.N. 1.

32 *Likhtan* in *Jama Farohi*, Mauza Raipura, 1753 V.S., B.N. 14/1, Bh.N. 1. Concerning Chamar's *panchayat*, see G.W. Briggs, *The Chamars*, pp. 47–52, 71, 96, 157.

33 *Likhtans* in/and *Jama Farohi*, Mauza Raipura, 1753 V.S., B.N. 14/1, Bh.N.1.

34 James Tod, *Annals and Antiquities of Rajasthan*, edited with an introduction and notes by William Crooke, 3 vols., London, 1920, rpt. Delhi, 1971, vol. 1, pp. 197, 242. Badriprasad Sakariya and Bhupatiram Sakariya, eds., *Rajasthani-Hindi Shabd Kosh*, 3 vols., Jaipur, 1977-84, vol. 1, p. 294.

35 *Likhtan* written by *paṭels*, *paṭwari* and *kisanas* (agriculturists) of village Khijri in *Kheṛ Kharch Jama*, Qasba Kota, 1743 V.S., B.N. 5/4, Bh.N. 1.

36 Ibid.

37 *Farohi*, Qasba Kanwas, 1809–11 V.S., B.N. 56/1, Bh.N. 1.

38 *Jama Bandhi*, Qasba Kanwas, 1812 V.S., B.N. 56/2, Bh.N. 1.

39 *Jama Farohi*, Mauza Poholai-bujarkh, 1743 V.S., B.N. 5/3, Bh.N. 1.

40 *Jama Bandhi*, Qasba Madhkargaṛh, 1806 V.S., B.N. 54, Bh.N. 1.

41 *Parwana* from Maharao Shri Durjan Salji to Chamar Lalya, son of Chamar Kheta of qasba Madhkargaṛh and *Likhtan* written by Chamar Lalya, 1806 V.S., B.N. 54, Bh.N. 1.

42 *Gharpati ka Jama*, Qasba Madhkargaṛh 1780 V.S., B.N. 38/1, Bh.N. 1.

43 *Taqsim*, Pargana Kota, 1719 V.S., B.N. 1/1, Bh.N. 6.

44 *Taqsim*, Pargana Nandgaon, 1777 V.S., B.N. 1/2, Bh.N. 6.

45 *Jama Bandhis*, Mauza Manasgaon, 1773, 1779, 1789, 1806 and 1814 V.S., B.Ns. 31/4, 37/2, 46/2, 54 and 57/2, Bh.N. 1. *Bighoṛi Jamdari ki Jama*, Mauza Manasgaon, 1839 V.S., B.N. 64/3, Bh.N. 1.

46 *Farohi Peshkashi wa Nazarana*, Paragana Sangod, 1808 V.S., B.N. 55, Bh.N. 1.

47 *Taqsim*, Tafa Bhaltha, Pargana Barsana, 1780 V.S., B.N. 1/2, Bh.N. 6.

48 Ibid.

49 *Taqsim*, Tafa Bhaltha, Pargana Barsana, 1811 V.S., B.N. 3/2, Bh.N.6.

4

Ati Śūdra Castes in the Medieval Deccan[1]

HIROYUKI KOTANI

INTRODUCTION

This essay aims at shedding light on the reality of Ati Śūdra castes in the later medieval Deccan through the medium of Marathi public and private documents. Medieval Marathi documents cover chronologically from the fifteenth to the early nineteenth centuries and geographically the Western Deccan and Konkan to which the coverage of this essay also corresponds. More strictly, this essay focuses on the seventeenth and eighteenth century Deccan under the Maratha kingdom (Peshva government). Thus, the social life of Ati Śūdra castes under the Peshvas is the main theme of this essay.

DISCRIMINATION AGAINST ATI ŚŪDRA CASTES

The caste system is well known to be marked by severe discrimination against the Ati Śūdra castes. Although discrimination toward classes like the Caṇḍāla was widespread in ancient India, it does not seem likely that the members of these classes were grouped together to form a distinct social stratum (*varṇa*). Furthermore, the percentage of discriminated classes is considered to have been rather small in ancient India.[2] Conversely, in the medieval Deccan, discriminated castes were grouped together as Ati Śūdra and treated as a distinct social stratum. Moreover, the percentage of discriminated castes was also much higher than in ancient India. This means that the medieval discrimination which was quite different from its ancient predecessor was formed during this period. Nonetheless pinpointing the exact period of formation of this medieval discrimination is very difficult; the period between the eighth and twelfth centuries might reasonably well be presumed as being this formative era. We know, in fact, that Indian society in general began to change from the bottom in the seventh or eighth century, what is referred to as the post-Gupta period, and that this social transformation gave rise to the predominant features of medieval India such as the village community and the 'district (*pargaṇā*) community' by the twelfth century.

The shaping of medieval discrimination in the Deccan was also an unmistakable part of the general social transformation depicting this period, and, in particular, discrimination against Ati Śūdra castes in the later medieval Deccan was a direct development of this medieval system of discrimination.[3]

Sparś, Sparśāsparś and Saṁsarg

Contact with an Ati Śūdra was regarded as bringing impurity upon oneself and this impurity was considered to be transmittable from the person directly touched by an Ati Śūdra to other persons who happened to come into contact with him. Fundamentally then, what indeed did the word 'contact' (*sparś*, *sparśāsparś* or *saṁsarg* in Marathi) mean? Some examples may suffice.

In one instance, a Brāhmaṇa named Bajirav Moreshvar had stayed in the *vāḍā* of Anandrav Gopal Joshi with his family for four months. Afterwards, a *kuṇbīṇ* (female servant) of this family was found to be a woman of the Chambar caste. This meant that Anandrav, Bajirav and their families had become impure through contact (*saṁsarg*) with the *kuṇbīṇ* so that they had to undergo the following purification ceremony:

48 *prajāpatye* for each Brāhmaṇa,
24 *prajāpatye* for each woman,
24 *prajāpatye* for each Brāhmaṇa child,
4 *prajāpatye* for each Śūdra.
(1795. SPD XXXXIII-92)

In other instances there was a *baṭīk* (female slave) in the family of a Mamledar, Balaji Mahadev, who was a Prabhu by caste. As she was found to have committed *vyabhichār* (adultery) with an *Antyaj* (Ati Śūdra) man, she was regarded as having become as impure as an Ati Śūdra She had been working in the family for nearly two and a half years, sweeping, smearing the floor with a wash of cow dung, brushing kitchen utensils, cutting vegetables, making beds and engaging other duties. Thus, all of the members of this family had necessarily come into contact (*saṁsarg*) with her so that all of them were considered to have become impure. They were therefore ordered to undergo the following purification ceremony:

> 135 *prajāpatye* for the mother of the Mamledar,
> 270 *prajāpatye* for the Mamledar himself,
> 135 *prajāpatye* for the child of the Mamledar.

In practice, however, one *prajāpatyā* could be commuted for two rupees, with the money thus collected being distributed among Brāhmaṇas. In addition, as the house and the land on which the house stood was also regarded as impure, it had to be purified as follows:

> House land: To be dug up and purified by letting a cow walk on it,
> Earthernware and metallic utensils: To be purified by fire,
> Wooden floor and door: To be destroyed because it can not be purified.
>
> (1781-82. SSRPD VIII-1125)

These instances denote that contact with an Ati Śūdra did not necessarily mean bodily touch, but it included indirect contact (association) through living together in a same house. Indirect contact was termed *saṁsarg* in contrast with *sparś* or *sparśāsparś* meaning physical contact (cf. *Manu-Smṛti*, XI-176, 180–82).

Importantly as well, bodily touch with an Ati Śūdra was likely to occur in a crowded place like the pilgrimage centre of a sacred place.

A good example of this concerned Pandharpur on the river Bhima, a tributary of Krishna, situated nearly 300 km south-east of Pune which has remained the celebrated sacred place of Vithobha (Vitthara) where a great number of pilgrims gathered every autumn. They were known as the *vārkarī* and formed the main body of the Deccan *bhakti*. *Bhakti* was open to every man including Ati Śūdras, and even a Mahar saint Chokhamela had been enshrined in Pandharpur. Thus, a considerable number of Ati Śūdras (Mahars and others) joined these pilgrimages to Pandharpur. However, if an Ati Śūdra came near Vithoba Temple when it was jammed with pilgrims, bodily touch with him was quite likely to occur. Brāhmaṇas were so much afraid of this that they appealed to the government (Peshva government) to keep Ati Śūdras away from Vithoba Temple. The government resultantly decreed as follows:

> There is a stone image of Chokhamela to the north of Vithoba Temple and Ati Śūdras make their pilgrimage to it. The place neighbours the road frequented by pilgrims so that they happen to come in touch (*sparśāsparś*) with an Ati Śūdra. This is against (the *dharma* of) Brāhmaṇa. Therefore, Ati Śūdras should worship the image of Chokhamela by the side of the lump-pillar in front of Vithoba Temple or in the *mahārvāḍā*. Ati Śūdras must not approach Vithoba Temple itself. If they violate this edict, they must be punished.
>
> (1783-84. SSRPD VIII-1129)

As this case denotes, physical contact (*sparś, sparśāsparś*) with an Ati Śūdra was regarded as an incident to be avoided at all cost (cf. *Manu-Smṛti*, V-85). In villages where villagers knew each other well, physical contact with an Ati Śūdra was not likely to occur, of course, but in towns or at sacred places where unknown people gathered, the possibility of contacting physically with an Ati Śūdra was certainly not unlikely.

In Nasik, a Budhalkar (an Ati Śūdra caste, skinner) asked a barber (Nhavi) who was sitting on the river Godavari awaiting a guest to cut his hair. He did not inform the barber that he was a man of an Ati Śūdra caste as the latter did not ask him his caste. Just as the barber began to cut his hair, another member of the barber's caste happened to come along and told him that he should not have cut the hair of an Ati Śūdra. The barber who had thus made bodily touch with this Ati Śūdra was excommunicated from his caste. Having been embarrassed, the barber acknowledged his sin (*doṣ*) and asked the *dharmaadhikārī* of Nasik to make him free from his sin through an adequate ceremony (1795. ASS I-193).

Restriction of Dwelling Place

To prevent any physical contact with Ati Śūdras the places where they could dwell were restricted. In the medieval Deccan, these Ati Śūdra dwelling places were generally called *mahārvāḍā* and were situated just outside the village walls.

As a case in point, in the village Katraj (Karyatmaval District), for example, the homes of Mahars, Mangs and Chambars were thought to be neighbouring too near the village site (*pāṇḍhar*). It was therefore decided to destory and rebuilt their homes in a place more remote from the village site. The following sums of money were granted to them from the government for this relocation of their homes:

For Mahars (22 families): 207 rupees,
For Mangs (2 families): 14 rupees,
For Chambars (2 families): 30 rupees.

In addition, the government gave them in all 300 pieces of timber for rebuilding their houses (1789-90. SSRPD VIII-1142).

In another case, in the village Baner (Pune Province), the *mahārvāḍā* was situated to the east of the village wall. Through the *mahārvāḍā* a rivulet flowed where Mahars used to wash their skinned hides. When Shahaji, the father of Shivaji, came to hold this village as *jāgīr* his minister Dadaji Kondadev planned to draw water from this rivulet but so long as the Mahars continued to dwell there, water thus drawn could not be used. Thus, the *mahārvāḍā* there was destroyed and rebuilt on the opposite side of the village behind the shrine of Bairoba (SPD XXXI-65).

These cases demonstrate that the dwelling places of Ati Śūdras were occasionally changed to suit the needs of the village to which they were affiliated.

DUTIES AND PERQUISITES OF ATI ŚŪDRAS

In the medieval Deccan, many castes were classed as Ati Śūdra but the most numerous in number among them were Mahar, Mang and Chambar. Members of these castes who were incorporated into the village system of the division of labour (the so-called Vatan System) were respectively called Vatandar Mahar, Vatandar Mang and Vatandar Chambar. Although it is inopportune here to dwell on this Vatan System, in a word, this system constituted the most fundamental social relationship in the medieval Deccan which penetrated the village community as well as the district (*pargaṇā*) community. Notably, the *vatandārs* of the Ati Śūdra castes were an indispensable element of this system and included in the *bārā balute* (12 types of village servants).[4]

As a case pertaining to the perquisites of Ati Śūdras, a dispute broke out between Mahars and peasants cum Mangs in Parner District. The Mahars subsequently made the following appeals to the government:

1. When bulls and buffaloes (*bael va ḍhoren*) die in the village, it is the custom that we Mahars take their hides except for

those of the plough bullocks (*dhurecā bael*), even though the peasants have begun to dispute with us over this matter.

2. On the occasion of Dasarā, Mangs go about to every door asking for alms and we Mahars take *pāñc naivedya* (an offering) and *pāñc paise* (a money offering) but Mangs have begun to quarrel over this.
3. On the occasion of Polā, we Mahars take the offering offered to cows, but now Mangs say that they should take it.
4. When cattle of a Mang's house die, it is the custom that we Mahars take their hides and that Mangs should not interfere with this.
5. On the occasion of the *śānti* ceremony in Dasarā, we Mahars let a buffalo walk around the village boundary and we walk before it carrying a pot of *peḍhā* (sweetmeats) in hand. After the *śānti* ceremony is over, we Mahars take the buffalo and *peḍhā* but now Mangs are asking for a half of the *peḍhā*. Mangs must not be allowed to ask for this.
6. We Mahars take the offering offered to Jarimari (the *devī* of cholera) but now Mangs are making trouble over it and say that they should take it.
7. On the occasion of a marriage ceremony, the bridegroom of the Mahar caste rides on a horse and goes in the procession but the bridegroom of the Mang caste must ride on a bull. Now, Mangs are making their bridegrooms ride on a horse, so please order them to make their bridegrooms ride on a bull as in the past.

Receiving the appeal from the Mahars, the government conducted an inquiry, and the statement by the Mahars proved to be true. Therefore, a government order was issued to the district officials, *deśmukhs*, *deśpāṇḍes*, *pāṭīls* and Mahars of Parner and other districts to the effect that they had to behave in accordance with the long-standing custom and must not make trouble[5] (1776. SSRPD VI-816).

Disposing of the carcasses of dead cattle was one of the main duties of Vatandar Mahars and, in reward for this, they could take the hides of the disposed cattle except for those of plough bullocks which they had to hand over to the former owner of the cattle.[6] The first and fourth clauses of the above-cited document indicate that there were occasionally disputes between Mahars and peasants or Mangs over the right to the hides of dead cattle.

On the occasion of Dasarā, Polā and other festivals, it had been the custom to worship the *devī* by offering buffaloes or goats as a sacrifice.

Table 1 The Vatan System

Parganā			Parganā		
		Deśmukh			Sardeśmukh
	I	Deśpāṇḍe			Sardeśpāṇḍe
		Mhetar of each jāti		II	Sarpāṭīl
					Sarkulkarṇī
					Sarcaugula
Village			Market Town		
		Pāṭīl			Śeṭ
		Kulkarṇī		II	Mahājan
	I	Caugula			etc.
		Vatandār Kuṇbī			
		Bārā Balute	Fort		
					Sarnāik
		Vatandār Telī		II	Nāikvāḍī
	II	Vatandār Tāmbolī			Nāik
		etc.			

I Primary vatan II Secondary vatan

This ceremony was known as *śānti* and, especially on the occasion of Dasarā, the *śānti* ceremony used to be performed to pacify the *devī*. When cholera or other plagues broke out, the offering of sacrificed animals was also made to Jarimari, the *devī* of cholera, to pacify her anger. In the *śānti* ceremony Ati Śūdras, especially Mahars, played the leading role. In reward for this they had the right to take sacrificed animals, offerings and money offerings, after the ceremony was over. Disputes occasionally arose over this right between Mahars and Mangs. (The third and sixth clauses of the earlier-cited document.)

Disputes of a similar nature often occurred in various places. The headman (*mhetar*) of the Mahars of Karepathar District appealed to the government regarding the right to take the sacrificed buffaloes on the occasion of Dasarā:

> As the custom dictates, we make a buffalo walk around the village boundary and we walk before it with a pot of *peḍhā* in hand. After that we sacrifice the buffalo by the side of the house of *mulāṇā* (Islamic teacher) and skin the hide for making a drum. Mangs

> stretch the hide over the drum. When bulls, cows and buffaloes die in the families of Mang, we Mahars take their hides but now the Mangs say that they should take them (Otūrkar 77).

In another instance in the village Pargav (Karepathar District), a dispute between Mahars and Chambars broke out with regard to *pāñc naivedya* of Holī. The *pāṭīl* of the village gave the following evidence (1778-79):

> Since the time of my grandfather, *pāñc naivedya* of Holī had been given to the Chambars but at the time of my father Mahars began to quarrel over it. But even after that *pāñc naivedya* has been given to Chambars (Otūrkar 70).

Thus dispute over perquisites among various Ati Śūdra castes does not seem to have been a rare occurrence in the later medieval Deccan.

CASTE HEADMAN (*MHETAR*) AND CASTE-RANKING

In each village there usually dwelled several families of some Ati Śūdra castes, and each Ati Śūdra caste formed a tight-knit community within a district (*pargaṇā*) community generally composed of 50 to 100 villages which constituted a district (*pargaṇā* or *ṭappā*).[7] Each caste in the district community had its own headman (*mhetar*) whose duty was to represent the caste to the state and other castes. In reward for this, the caste headman had the right to take perquisites from caste members within the district community. His office was also a *vatan* to be held hereditarily.

The headman of the Chambar caste of Supe District presented himself at the office of Shahaji (the father of Shivaji) who held the district as *jāgīr* and made the following statement:

> Chambars of this district used to pay tax every year in kind using shoes and not in cash. However, this year officials did not take the shoes as tax and made us pay in cash by commuting a pair of shoes for one and a half ṭake. Owing to this we are now in a deplorable condition. Therefore, please take the tax in kind in the form of shoes as before and stop taking it in cash.

Shahaji acknowledged his statement as true and the following order was issued to the *kārkūn* of Supe District:

> It has been decided not to take the tax from Chambars in the form of cash. Therefore do not take even one rukā from them. Instead of it, take the tax in kind as before. . . . Order all Chambars of this district including Baramati to obey the headman Mal and if not, make them obey by force (MIS XX-12).

As this document shows, the headman of a caste played the role of representing the caste to the state (in this case, *jāgīrdār*) and of defending its interests for the discharge of which he could make the caste members obey him. The reason why the state (*jāgīrdār*) ordered the caste members to obey him was that tax from a caste was collected by caste headman so that for the state too it was necessary to support the authority of the caste headman over the caste members.

Perquisites of the headman of the Ati Śūdra castes were somewhat different from those of other castes. For example, perquisites of the headman of Mahars of Sasvad District were as follows:

1. Hooves and heads of cattle (*gurācā śīrā va khuravitā*)
2. *Polī* (plain wheaten cake) of Holī
3. *Taśrīf* (grant of a dress of honour) from the Government
4. *Nāikī* (*vatan* of *nāik*) of *ṭhāṇā* (soldier-police station)
5. Music (to be played in front of the house on the occasion of festivals)

(1657. SCS VII-43)

As mentioned before, one of the main duties of Vatandar Mahars was to dispose of the carcasses of dead cattle, and the 'hooves and heads' of cattle thus disposed of become the perquisite of the Mahar headman. The dispute arising between Mahars and Mangs over the right to take *polī* offered to the fire of Holī was already discussed. *Nāikī vatan* of *ṭhāṇā* was related to the military or police role of the Mahars. A certain portion of Mahars and other Ati Śūdra castes was posted in the station (*ṭhāṇā)* set up in the main town of a district as soldier-police. Their office was called *nāikī* and was a *vatan.* Ati Śūdra castes like the Mahar had been, in part, hillmen who had played a great role as a military force in the process of state building by Shivaji. *Nāikī vatan* of *ṭhāṇā* held by the Ati Śūdra castes was related to this character of these castes. (For further details, see below.)

In the medieval Deccan, there were various castes grouped together as Ati Śūdra but they were not on an equal footing with each other. The earlier-cited document regarding the dispute between

Mahars and peasants cum Mangs indicates that stratified caste-ranking existed even among the Ati Śūdra castes. Once again the last clause of the document runs as follows:

> On the occasion of a marriage ceremony, the bridegroom of the Mahar caste rides on a horse and goes in the procession but the bridegroom of the Mang caste must ride on a bull. Now, Mangs are making their bridegrooms ride on a horse, so please order them to make their bridegrooms ride on a bull as in the past.

The reason why a dispute occurred over this problem of on which animal the bridegroom of each caste was to ride was that the social status of a caste was indicated by the kind of animal on which the bridegroom of the caste rode. Specifically, the caste the bridegroom of which rode on a horse was considered to be higher in social (caste) ranking than the caste of which the bridegroom rode on a bull. Thus, Mahars claimed that they were higher in social (caste) ranking than the Mangs by saying that their bridegrooms rode on a horse while Mang bridegrooms were to ride on a bull. As stated before, this claim of Mahars was recognized by the government.

Social (caste) ranking among the Ati Śūdra castes was expressed in other forms too. In Pune and Junnar Provinces, a dispute broke out between the Chambars and Buruds (bamboo workers) over the problem of whether or not Chambars had to make shoes (*payepoś*) for Buruds. Finally, it came out that Chambars had not made shoes for Buruds in the past so that it was decided that from now on as well Chambars did not need to make shoes for them (1735. SPḌ XXII-306). This means that Chambars were regarded as being higher in social (caste) ranking than Buruds.

Social ranking between Ati Śūdra castes thus expressed in various forms accumulated and formed a social status chain like a staircase onto which all the Ati Śūdra castes were to be placed.

ATI ŚŪDRAS AND DEVI

Boundary Disputes

In the later medieval Deccan, boundary disputes between villages often occurred and on those occasions Vatandar Mahars played an important role. The boundary dispute between the villages Malshiras and Pisarven in Pune Province was very long-standing for example. In between, arbitration was tried several times but it took a long time to reach a final settlement.

This boundary dispute began in the early seventeenth century when the Nizam Shahi dynasty was under the sway of Malik Ambar. When the boundary dispute occurred, *pāṭīls* of these two villages asked Malik Ambar to intervene. Accordingly, it was decided that both parties were to go to Kasbe Harsul and undergo an ordeal (*divya*). The *huddedār*, *deśmukh*, *śeṭ* and *mahājan* of Kasbe Harsul gathered together in Kasbe Harsul and made preparations for the *divya*. However, the *pāṭīl* of Pisarven declared that there was no need for the *divya* since the rivulet which flowed from the direction of the village Tekavdi had served as the boundary between two villages and it continued to do so. Therefore, the government order was issued to the *kārkūn* to demarcate the boundary according to the statement of the *pāṭīl* of Pisarven.

With the *farmān* to this effect, both parties returned to their respective villages, but soon afterwards Pisarven began to make trouble again. This time the *pāṭīl* of Malshiras went to Pune and asked for arbitration. As a result, it was decided to resort to trial by *divya* at Vateshvar Temple in Kasbe Sasvad, and for this purpose the *kārkūn*, *deśmukh* and others were sent to Sasvad. The *vṛttidār* (Vatandar Mahar) Kaṇa bin Dhondi of Malshiras was to undergo the *divya*. All of them went to the disputed boundary, and according to the statement of the villagers of Malshiras, 27 boundary marks (mainly stones) were recorded down and soil of the boundary was gathered. Then all of them proceeded to Vateshvar Temple. The *divya* was to be done by using an anvil (*airṇī*). In the first place, a hand of Kana was cleansed and the characteristic points of the palm were noted down. Subsequently, Kana took up the red-hot anvil heated by charcoal in his hand and ran through seven circles drawn on the ground and threw the anvil onto a heap of hay. Kana's hand was then covered by a *khaletī* (*khalitā*, small bag or purse) and sealed. After three days all of them gathered again and unsealed Kana's hand to examine it. His hand turned out to not be burnt. Thus, it proved that Kana was successful in the *divya* and the boundary marks recorded down previously according to the statement of the villagers of Malshiras were acknowledged as being true.

This boundary dispute did not come to an end even with this trial though. Thereafter it became more complicated as the village Tekavdi was also involved in it. To bring this long-standing boundary dispute to a final settlement, the *nivāḍpatra* (deed of decision) of Peshva Bajirao was issued (1723-24. SGRAO Sanads and Letters II-39).

As this case indicates, a meeting of the district (*parganā*) community commonly known as *got* or *gotsabhā* with the attendance of local officials, *deśmukh*, *deśpānḍe*, *pāṭīl* and others was held when a boundary dispute occurred but it was not easy to reach an amicable decision even by its means. On such occasions, resort used to be made to the ordeal known as the *divya* for hearing the divine will. There were various types of *divya* but the most popular was the so-called *agni divya* to which was resorted in the above-mentioned case, and *ravā divya*. In the latter case, a small piece of iron called *ravā* was used. The *ravā* was put in a vessel filled with boiled oil and *ghī*. The man who was to undergo the *divya* put his hand into it and took the *ravā* out, and if his hand was not burnt he was proved to be successful in the *divya*.[8]

As stated ealier, on the occasion of the *divya*, Vatandar Mahars played an important role. The following is another case of this.

In the boundary dispute between Ghatan and Bhosar, the Vatandar Mahars of these two villages were to undergo the *divya* by hot anvil. At first, the nails of these two Mahars were pared and their hands were cleansed by soap and then the characteristic points of their palms were written down on a paper. Afterwards, their hands were sealed by *piśvyā* (*piśvī*, purse or small bag). The complainant (*agravāḍī*) village made leaves of *pīpal*, threads of *kovarī* (a kind of tree) and *dahībhāt* (mixture of curd and boiled rice) its witness. On the day of the *divya*, charcoal was brought from both the villages which was used to heat an anvil. The hands of the two Mahars were unsealed and then both of them were purified by ritual bathing. The Mahar of the complainant village touched the red-hot anvil first. Local officials and the other attendants put seven leaves of *pīpal*, threads of *kovarī*, 19 śer of *dahībhāt* and 9 śer of butter on his palm. And then his hand was sealed again. After three days, his hand was unsealed and examined. It came out that his palm was burnt and the inner side of his thumb was also blistered. On the other side, the hand of the Mahar of the defendant (*prativāḍī*) village was found to be clean. Thus, the Mahar of the defendant village was acknowledged as being successful in the *divya* and he walked on the boundary to determine it (SGRAO Sanads and Letters II-6).

As these cases denote, Vatandar Mahars usually played the role of undergoing *divya*. Why was it then that Mahars who were in everyday life discriminated against in various ways could play the role of hearing the divine will through *divya*? Who was the god whose will

Mahars asked to hear? He (or She) could not be an orthodox Hindu god under whose authority Mahars and other Ati Śūdras were discriminated against. Thus the only conceivable deity was a goddess called *devī*. In the understratum of Hinduism there existed the thick stratum of the animistic religious world that had not been totally assimilated into orthodox Hinduism. It might have been a pre-Aryan religious heritage rooted deeply into Indian soil, and the deity in this religious world was a goddess called *devī*. The divine ruler of the soil of the Deccan was not an orthodox Hindu god but a *devī* and the village boundary was also under the sway of *devī*. Therefore, the will of *devī* was requested in the case of boundary disputes.

Mahars and other Ati Śūdra castes, in general, were assumed to be *ādivāsī* who had been living in the Deccan from the pre-Aryan period. They had not been totally assimilated into the Aryan culture and still continued to retain their own peculiar culture. The reason why Mahars, who were counted in the class of Ati Śūdra, were called *bhūmiputra* might be attributed to the remoter memory that the Deccan was originally the land of Mahars.[9] Terefore, the *devī* who was ruling the soil of the Deccan was presumed to be, in origin, the goddess of Mahars. The fact that Mahars played the role of receiving the will of *devī* on the occasion of boundary disputes could be attributable to this reason.

Śānti

The religious ceremony known as *śānti* shows more clearly that the divine ruler of the soil of the Deccan was not an orthodox Hindu god but a *devī*. *Śānti* was performed on the occasion when plagues like cholera and smallpox broke out or extraordinary natural phenomena like earthquakes and thunderbolts occurred. These phenomena were considered to be caused by the *devī*'s anger so that the ceremony of *śānti* was performed to pacify this anger when these phenomena took place.

Even without the occurrence of extraordinary phenomenon, the *śānti* ceremony was performed as, so to speak, a yearly event on such festive occasions as Dasarā. In this ceremony of *śānti*, buffaloes or goats were sacrificed as offerings to the *devī*. In *śānti* Mahars and Mangs played a leading role as this ceremony belonged to the animistic religious world of *devī*. Then how in practice was the ceremony of *śānti* performed? A document relative to Kasbe Karad (1735-36) recorded the specific procedure of *śānti* as follows, which might refer to the ceremony of *śānti* on the occasion of Dasarā:

1. To walk around the village boundary while swinging *iraḍ* (pieces of wood taken from forest).
2. A Mahar proceeds with a pot of *peḍhā* in hand and a Mang follows him also with a pot of *peḍhā* in hand. All of them walk around the village boundary.
3. A buffalo decorated by turmeric and garland is to be made to walk around the village boundary.
   Iraḍ is held at the head of the procession, then the Mahar and Mang with pots of *peḍhā* in hand and then the buffalo walks around the village boundary.
4. A *rath* (float) made by the Sutar is decorated and drawn to the place of the Kumbhar. An idol of the goddess made from clay by the Kumbhar is put in the *rath* and drawn to a temporary *mandap* in front of the Hanuman temple with music. The idol of the goddess is installed in the *mandap* and the *rath* is cleansed and put by the side of the idol.
5. The Mahar worships the buffalo which has come to the *mandap* after walking around the village boundary. The offering and leaves of betel offered to the idol is to be taken by the Mahar and Mang.
6. The buffalo is taken before the idol and his head is to be cut a certain degree by the Mahar and then to be cut off by the Mang.
7. For three days the idol is worshipped. All the villagers, old and young, are to bring offerings to the idol.
8. Afterwards, the lump on the head of the buffalo installed in front of the idol is to be taken out and buried in the ground of the *pāṭīl* and *kulkarṇī*.
9. On the fourth day, the idol is to be brought to the village boundary and thrown out of the village. The *mandap* is burnt down.

(MIS XXII-215)

As this document denotes, an important part of the *śānti* ceremony was to walk around the village boundary in a procession. The *iraḍ* at the head of the procession might have relevance to animistic worship of the tree. While walking around the village boundary with a pot of *peḍhā* in hand, the Mahar and Mang threw *peḍhā* one by one out of the village, since evil spirits were assumed to go out of the village with the *peḍhā*.[10]

Thus, the important role played by Mahars and other Ati Śūdra castes in boundary disputes and *śānti* presents a striking contrast to the discrimination levelled against them in daily life.

ATI ŚŪDRA AND ĀDIVĀSĪ

Although Ati Śūdra castes were discriminated against in various ways in the later medieval Deccan, it would be improper or at least one-sided if we were to look upon them as deplorable beings only to be depressed. As mentioned earlier, they played an important role in the animistic religious world of *devī*. In other words, their existence was ambivalent in the sense that discrimination in everyday life and spiritual superiority in the animistic world counterbalanced each other in their very existence.

Moreover, Ati Śūdra castes, especially Mahars and Mangs, had a mode of existence which differed markedly from the one which the word Ati Śūdra tends to cause us to imagine. They had been, on the other hand, hillmen (*ādivāsī*) and often daring mountain soldiers. Shivaji, the founder of the Maratha kingdom, relied on them as military force especially in the earlier period of his state building.

Sarnāik and Nāik of Forts

In the Deccan, numerous forts (*gaḍ*) were built on the mountain tops. In each of these hill forts, some *nāiks* (the head of guards) and a *sarnāik* (the head of *nāiks*) were posted with tens of guards each. The *sarnāik* and *nāik* offices were *vatan* to be held by the hereditary patrimony of a certain family, though quite strange as it might sound.The fort was one of the most important power apparatuses of the medieval state. Accordingly, it would be rather difficult to understand the reason why the fort's *sarnāik* and *nāiks* were not appointed by the state under whose rule the fort was held. Yet the Vatan System which formed the backbone of the medieval society in the Deccan had penetrated so deeply into the power apparatus of the state that even the *sarnāik* and *nāik* offices had become *vatan*.

In the mountainous area of the Ghat, hillmen like Koli and Ramosi had been dwelling in great numbers. A large portion of Mahar and Mang whom we casually tend to regard as Ati Śūdra were also hillmen like them. The holders of the *vatan* of *nāik* were mostly those hillmen.

Purandhar had been an important fort situated nearly 20 km to the south of Pune whose *nāiks* used to be Kolis and Mahars. Around the end of the seventeenth century a dispute between the *sarnāik* of Purandhar, a Brāhmaṇa named Ganesh Nilkantrav, and *nāiks* of Koli and Mahar broke out. With regard to this dispute Nilkantrav made a statement to the government the substance of which is as follows.

Under the Bidar dynasty (in the late fifteenth century), since this area had been in a troubled condition, it was decided to build a fort here. Accordingly, the *deśmukh* of this district was dispatched for this purpose and succeeded in building Purandhar Fort. On him was bestowed the *sarnāik vatan* of this fort. To help him, a *nāik* with 60 guards and two other Koli *nāiks* with 15 guards respectively were also posted in it. Subsequently the Bidar dynasty collapsed, and this area was brought under the control of the Nizam Shahi. However, the Adil Shahi who had been a rival of the Nizam Shahi sieged Purandhar Fort, and Kolis, taking advantages of this, began to devastate this area. Therefore, Mahadaji Nilkantrav, the grandfather of Ganesh Nilkantrav, summoned the Kolis and bestowed on them the deed (*kaul*) to appoint them to the office of *nāik*. At the same time, as the bravery of Mahars had been well known in this area, Mahadaji bestowed a *nāik vatan* of Purandhar Fort on two Mahars with 40 guards each. After Mahadaji died, four of his sons quarrelled with each other and weakened as a result of which Purandhar Fort was captured by Shivaji. Thereafter, Ganesh Nilkantrav succeeded to the *sarnāik vatan* of Purandhar Fort, but Koli and Mahar *nāiks* had become powerful by then and often brought trouble to Ganesh. Ganesh therefore begged the government for arbitration (SCS I-92).

Purandhar Fort was brought under the control of the Mughals after Sambaji, the eldest son of Shivaji, had been captured and pitilessly killed by the Mughals on the river Bhima. But Maratha *sardārs* gathered under the banner of Rajaram, a half brother of Sambaji, began to counterattack the Mughals and tried to recapture the fort when Sarjarav Jedhe, the *deśmukh* of Rohidakhor, made it known to Rajaram that Kolis and Ramosis were eager to occupy it. In response to this, the *abhayapatra* (deed of security) of Rajaram was issued to order Kolis and Ramosis to occupy Purandhar Fort for a bounty in case success was met (MIS XV-352).

In 1747, when Madhavrao, the later Peshva, was born, ten *cāvar* (nearly 300 hectares) of land was granted to Kolis, Ramosis and Mahars of Purandhar Fort as tax-free land (SPD XXXI-182). As these documents indicate, *nāik vatans* of Purandhar Fort used to be held by Kolis, Ramosis and Mahars under whom many hillmen were posted as guards. *Nāiks* of Rohida Fort were also Mahars. In 1746, a dispute over the *nāik vatan* of this fort occurred. One party in this dispute, Khandnak Mahar, made a statement to the government in regard to this dispute. The purport of his statement is as follows.

Under the Adil Shahi and Nizam Shahi, the *nāik vatan* of Rohida Fort was held by an uncle of Khandnak's father and another Mahar. After both of them had died, Khandnak's father went to Raigad to see Shivaji at which time the latter bestowed on him the *sanad* (deed) of the *nāik vatan.* With the *sanad* of Shivaji, Khandnak's father returned to Rohida Fort and began to serve as the *nāik.* After his death, Khandnak succeeded to both the Mahar *vatan* of the village Karanjiye and the *nāik vatan* of Rohida Fort. As he had not previously been married, he then married a daughter of Bhojnak of Vadi (Utroli District). Thereupon, Bhojnak proposed to him to leave the Mahar *vatan* of the village Karanjiye to Bhojnak taking the *nāik vatan* of Rohida Fort himself as it would be difficult for him to discharge the duties of two *vatans* at the same time. Thereby a dispute between Khandnak and Bhojnak began (SCS III-609). Thus it is unquestionable that the *nāiks* and guards of the hill forts were mostly hillmen like Kolis, Mahars and Ramosis.

In the later medieval Deccan, however, these hillmen had already not been able to continue their own way of life in mountains free of any relationship with the settled agricultural society in the plain. For example, a portion of Kolis had been incorporated into the Vatan System of the village as water carriers. In some villages, those Kolis were counted as one of the *bārā balute* (12 types of village servants) (Otūrkar 139). A portion of Ramosis had become watchman of the village. When Kasbe Supe was infested with robbers, a Ramosi head watchman and three Ramosi watchmen were posted (1773-74. SSRPD VIII-954). There were three Vatandar Ramosis in the village Garade (Karepathar District) who watched the village gate (Otūrkar 78). In Kasbe Satara, there were 33 watchmen of the Ramosi and Mang castes whose charge was defrayed by the money collected from leading merchants of Satara (SSRPD VIII-958).

Thus hillmen like Kolis and Ramosis were living outside as well as inside the settled agricultural society and *nāiks* and guards of the hill forts were positioned exactly in between these two groups.

Mahars and Mangs whom we are accustomed to assume to be Ati Śūdra castes also had not been totally absorbed into the settled agricultural society. Even in the later medieval age a large portion of them were still hillmen, and in between the hill and village there were hill forts posted with Mahar and Mang *nāiks* and guards.

In principal towns of the Deccan there were *ṭhāṇās* (soldier-police station) posted with *nāik*. The office of *nāik* of *ṭhāṇā* was also a *vatan* whose holder was mostly Mahar. The Mahar who possessed the *nāik vatan* of the *ṭhāṇā* in Kasbe Paithan had the right to take numerous perquisites from the inhabitants of Paithan as well as merchants and others who brought commodities into the market of Paithan. The following are some of them:

1. Per one cart of brinjal, ten (śer) to the village watchman (*veskar*) and 15 (śer) to the Mahar.
2. Per one cart of sugarcane, ten (śer) to the village watchman and 15 (śer) to the Mahar.
3. Per one bullock-load of banana, seven (śer) to the Mahar.
4. Per one loom of Koshti (weaver caste), 5 rukā and a piece of cloth to be divided by the watchman and the Mahar.
5. Per one oil-press of Teli, half (śer) of the oil.
6. A Chambar is to give two pair of shoes to the Mahar per year.
7. A Dhangar is to give a goat on the occasion of Dasarā and two goats on the occasion of Divālī to the Mahar for sacrifice.

(MIS XX-174)

Thus it is brought to light that in the later medieval Deccan the so-called Ati Śūdra castes like Mahar and Mang assumed various modes of existence including that of hillmen, *nāik* and guards of hill forts or *ṭhāṇā* and village *vatandār* making it improper or at least one-sided to look upon them only as Ati Śūdras who were merely to be discriminated against.

Dispute between Mahar and Brāhmaṇa

Although Mahars in the later medieval Deccan functioned in various modes of existence, they did not form separate groups according to their respective mode of existence. On the contrary, all of them still held a strong nexus and acted in a body whenever any matters concerning them all occurred.

In 1784 Mahars of Paudkhor District appealed to the district official as follows:

It was the custom that Vatandar Joshi officiates as the priest at the marriages of us Mahars. In other districts too, a Brāhmaṇa is to officiate at the marriages of Mahars. However a dispute over the transaction (*deṇen gheṇen*) between us and Joshis arose and Joshis stopped officiating at our marriages. This state of affairs has been continuing for some 15 or 20 years. So we beg you to restore the matter as before, taking the custom of other districts into consideration.

Receiving the appeal, the district official made an inquiry and reached a conclusion that Vatandar Joshis were to officiate at the marriages of Mahars, and, as a matter of fact, Vatandar Joshis continued to officiate at the marriages of Mangs and others, making it improper for them to refuse to officiate at the marriages of Mahars only. Thereupon, the district official ordered Vatandar Joshis to officiate at the Mahar marriages (ASS I-74). However, the Vatandar Joshis of Paudkhor District refused to obey his order and presented a statement of the following purport to the government.

The offices of *joshi*, *upādye* and *dharmaadhikārī* of Paudkhor District had been *vṛtti* (patrimony) of their families. Although it was the custom that they did not officiate at the marriages of Mahars, Mahars began to complain in this regard to the district official. As a result, the district official ordered them to officiate at the marriages of Mahars merely on the ground that formerly the Havaldar of Korigad Fort had once made their uncle of 10 to 15 years old officiate at the marriage of a Mahar *nāik* of the fort since the priest of the Mahar caste (*meḍhyā* Mahar) had not been available.

Meanwhile, Mahars demanded Vatandar Joshis to officiate at their marriages on the ground of the order of the district official, but Joshis refused to do this. The district official thus levied a fine of 10 rupees and forced them to officiate. Thereupon Joshis presented a statement to the district official to the effect that they were to tell Mahars of the auspicious time for a marriage of the Mahars but not to officiate at the marriage. The district official did not acknowledged this, however, and confiscated their *vṛtti* saying that they must not officiate at the marriages of Śūdra castes either. Such being the case, Vatandar Joshis of Paudkhor appealed again to the government to intervene and order the district official to restore the *vṛtti* to them.

Receiving the appeal, the government conducted an inquiry and came to the following conclusion. It was not the custom for Vatandar Joshis to officiate at the marriages of Mahars. It might be the custom of some other districts but it was not the case in the Konkan. Here there was the Mahar priest (*meḍhe* Mahar) in the Mahar caste to officiate at their marriages. Joshis of Junnar too wrote to the government that Joshis did not officiate at the marriages of Ati Śūdras in Junnar as the priest of Ati Śūdra castes (*ḍhegomego*) was present and he officiated at their marriages. Formerly Mahars in the service of hill forts (*kilyāce cākarmāne*) and Mahars in the province (*prāntāntīl*), in all several thousand, had gathered together and caused a disturbance. They had appealed to the then ruler of the Deccan, Aurangzeb, to make Vatandar Joshis officiate at their marriages. But Aurangzeb had decided that Joshis were not to officiate at the Mahar marriages taking the long-standing custom into consideration. Even under the Mughal rule, the long-standing custom of the Hindus was respected so that it was very improper to make a new custom under the '*Svarājya*', abandoning the old. Therfore, the custom that Vatandar Joshis only officiate at the marriages of castes other than Ati Śūdra castes should have been respected.

According to this conclusion, a government order to the district official of Paudkhor District was issued to the effect that he must not force Joshis to officiate at the marriages of Mahars (SSRPD VIII-1132).

As this case shows, thousands of Mahars of various positions including *nāiks* and guards of hill forts and Vatandar Mahars of villages acted in a body to push their claim through. They failed, in the result, to accomplish this but nonetheless it is clearly evident here that Mahars of various circumstances struggled in a united front against discrimination.

CONCLUSION

The reality of Ati Śūdra castes in the later medieval Deccan which impresses us most strongly is the fact that their existence was ambivalent. They were discriminated against in various ways in daily life but at the same time they played an important role on the occasions of boundary disputes and the ceremony of *śānti*. They were *vatandārs* of villages but at the same time they were mountain soldiers and town police, with all of them still retaining a strong nexus with their fellow caste members in the hills. These facts clearly indicate the ambivalence of their existence. But, also at the same time, they were so deeply incorporated into the caste system that various castes assumed to belong to Ati Śūdra quarrelled with each other over the problem of social (caste) ranking among them. In this sense too, their existence was ambivalent.

NOTES

1 For reference to Marathi documents, the following abbreviations with Roman numerals denoting the volume number and Arabic numerals denoting the document number are used.

SSRPD: G.C. Vad, ed., *Selections from the Satara Rajas' and the Peshvas' Diaries*, 9 vols, 1905-11, Poona and Bombay.

SGRAO: G.C. Vad, ed., *Selections from the Government Records in Alienation Office Poona*,

1. *Kaifiats, Yadis, &c.*, 1908.
2. *Decisions from the Shafu and Peshva Daftar*, 1909.
3. *Sanads and Letters*, 1913.
4. *Treaties, Agreements and Sanads*, 1914.

SPD: G.S. Sardesai, ed., *Selections from the Peshva Daftar*, 45 vols, 1930–34, Bombay.

MIS: V.K. Rajvade, ed., *Marāṭhyāncyā Itihāsācin Sādhanen*, 22 vols, 1898–1919, Poona and Bombay.

SCS: Bhārat Itihās Saṁśodhak Maṇḍal, ed., *Śiva Caritra Sāhitya*, 13 vols, 1926–65, Pune.

ASS: Bhārat Itihās Saṁśodhak Maṇḍal, ed., *Aitihāsik Saṅkīrṇa Sāhitya*, 13 vols, 1934-67, Pune.

Otūrkar: R.V. Otūrkar ed., *Peśve Kālin Sāmājik va Ārthik Patravyavahār*, 1950, Pune.

2 G. Yamazaki, 'Social discrimination in ancient India and its transition to the medieval period', in this volume, p. 15.

3 Ibid., pp. 15–16.

4 H. Kotani, 'The Vatan-System in the 16th-18th century Deccan', *Acta Asiatica*, vol. 48, The Toho Gakkai, Tokyo, 1985. Reprinted in D. Jha, ed., *Society and Ideology in India: Essays in Honour of Professor R.S. Sharma*, New Delhi, 1996. A.R. Kulkarni, *Maharashtra in the Age of Shivaji*, Poona, 1969, pp. 24–55.

5 H. Fukazawa, *The Medieval Deccan: Peasants, Social Systems and States*, Oxford University Press, Delhi, 1991, p. 224.

6 H. Kotani, 'Conflict and controversy over the Mahar Vatan in the nineteenth–twentieth century Bombay Presidency', in this volume, pp. 110–11.

7 H. Kotani, 'The Vatan-System in the 16th-18th century Deccan', pp. 37–40.

8 V.T. Gune, *The Judicial System of the Marathas*, Poona, 1953, pp. 90–99.

9 S.M. Mate, *Asprṣṭāncā Praśna*, Pune, 1933, pp. 32–42.

10 H. Whitehead, *The Village Gods in South India*, Oxford University Press, 1916, pp. 46–53.

II

The Depressed Castes under British Colonial Rule

5

Introduction

Legal Status of the Depressed Castes under British Colonial Rule

HIROYUKI KOTANI

Under British colonial rule, various lawsuits were brought by native Indians into the law courts established by the British. The most difficult lawsuits for the British judges to decide were those pertaining to Hindu family law which included marriage, divorce, succession, heritage, adoption, guardianship and maintenance. These problems were not only intermingled with Hindu religion but were deeply related with the various customs of each castes which were quite unfamiliar to the British judges.

As if anticipating these difficulties, Warren Hastings, the then Governor of Bengal, made the following rule in 1772 when he introduced full-scale reforms in the judicial system for the first time in the history of British colonial rule in India:

> 23rd. That in all Suits regarding Inheritance, Marriage, Caste, and other religious Usages as Institutions, the Laws of the Koran with respect to Mahometans and those of the Shaster with Respect to Jentoos, shall be invariably adhered to; On all such Occassions the Mowlavies or Brahmins shall respectively attend to expound the Law, and they shall sign the Report & assist in Passing the Decree. (The Committee of Circuit's Plan for the Administration of Justice in Bengal, dated 15th August, 1772, in D.N. Banerjee, *Early Administrative System in Bengal*, vol. I, Calcutta, 1943, p. 667.)

'Shaster' (Shastra) referred to in this rule meant a series of classical law books written in Sanskrit amongst which the most important had been *Manu-Smṛti.* But in the medieval period (after the so-called post-Gupta period), these classical law books had become impractical for application to social problems so that commentaries of classical law books reinterpreted and readjusted to the reality of the medieval society and locality were prepared. Amongst these commentaries, the most influential was *Mitākṣarā,* a commentary on *Yājñavalkya-Smṛti*, which was composed in the Deccan under the Western Chalukya dynasty during the course of the early twelfth century. The so-called Shastra in the British judicial documents also included these medieval commentaries.

Although Hastings made it a rule to apply Shastra as such to lawsuits among Hindus and this rule was followed in British India at large, the rule was not easy to practise in a specific lawsuit because Shastra as such included various law books, classical as well as medieval, and there existed among them no concrete law system. Therefore, 'Brahmins' (Pandits) well versed in Shastra were posted in the Supreme Courts (King's Courts set up in the Presidency Towns of Calcutta, Madras and Bombay with jurisdiction over lawsuits among British citizens and among native Indians residing in the Presidency Towns) as well as in the Sadr Divani Adalats (East India Company's Civil Courts of Appeal with jurisdiction over lawsuits among native Indians residing in the areas outside the Presidency Towns called Mohassal). These Pandits were required to submit the 'Report' pertaining to the specific case known as Vyavastha to the courts.

In this process, the outline of Shastra as such had gradually become clear as a result of which the so-called Hindu Law was formed. The Hindu Law was, consequently, not the classical Brahmanical law itself. This was a law system based on the Brahmanical law but readjusted for the British judicial administration. In this sense, the Hindu Law was the law produced under British colonial rule for administrating jurisdiction over Hindu subjects. The Hindu Law as such established by the 1830s included only family law with the other laws like contract law being Anglicised.

This Hindu Law contained a kind of legal fiction. In it, Hindu society of the nineteenth century was presumed to be composed of four Varnas, namely Brahman, Kshatrya, Vaishya and Shudra in consequence of its being based on classical Brahmanical laws like *Manu-Smṛti*. In addition to this, the four Varnas were equated with castes so that Hindu society in the nineteenth century was assumed to be a 'Caste Society' to comprise four 'castes' by the Hindu Law. (The caste in its real sense, namely the social group known as *jati* in Indian languages, was called sub-caste in British administration documents.)

This legal fiction of the Hindu Law had a delicate relevance to the legal status of the depressed castes formerly known as the 'untouchables'. For one thing, the Hindu Law revived the classical distinction between the upper three Varnas (the so-called twice-born) and Shudra (the once-born) and all the castes other than those belonging to the twice-born were considered to belong to Shudra Varna because the Hindu Law did not recognize the existence of the 'Fifth Varna' being based on classical law books like *Manu-Smṛti* (X-4). Thus the depressed castes did not have a special legal status distinguishable from Shudra castes under the Hindu Law.

This legal fiction of the Hindu Law produced a queer result. Marriages among Hindus were usually conducted within the same caste (by British administration term, sub-caste), but according to the Hindu Law there existed only four 'castes' (in reality, Varnas) so that marriage, for example, between a man of a Shudra caste (sub-caste) and a woman of another Shudra caste was regarded as legitimate. Similarly, marriage between a man of a Shudra caste and a woman of a depressed caste became legitimate under the Hindu Law.

In one case in 1924, the Calcutta High Court pronounced the sentence of guilty on the accused in an adultery case. The accused was a man who had intercourse with a Dom woman. (Dom was thought to be a depressed caste.) This Dom woman had married a Kayastha man following the Hindu marriage ritual. (Kayastha in Bengal was considered to belong to the Shudra Varna.) In the trial, the accused claimed to be not guilty on the ground that marriage between a Shudra man and a woman of a depressed caste was not legal so that the charge of adultery could not be applied to the accused. The Calcutta High Court denied his plea by declaring that both Kayastha and Dom belonged to the Shudra 'caste' so that marriage between a Kayastha man and a Dom woman was legitimate. (51 C. 488, meaning the case reported in *Indian Law Reports, Calcutta Series*, vol. 51, pp. 488ff.) Similar marriages between a Shudra man and a woman of a depressed caste were decided as being legal by other High Courts like the Madras High Court also. (Manickam *v*. Poongavanammal, 66 M.L.J. 543, meaning the case reported in *Madras Law Journal,* vol. 66, pp. 543ff.)

These cases show that at least some women of depressed castes married Shudra men and that the High Courts regarded such marriages as legitimate under the legal fiction of the Hindu Law. If these judgements of the High Courts had had an effect on changing Hindu society in the direction of allowing intermarriage between a depressed caste and a caste other than the depressed, it would have diminished discrimination against the depressed castes. But in reality Hindu society in the nineteenth century did not change in this direction, and to the contrary, social discrimination against the depressed castes was covered under the legal fiction of the Hindu Law in the reference that there was no 'Fifth Varna' (cf. *Manu-Smṛti*, X-4).

An example of social discrimination against the depressed castes covered and kept intact by the legal fiction of the Hindu Law was the problem of 'temple entry' of the depressed castes. In 1908, the Legal Committee of the Privy Council decided in an appeal case from the Madras High Court that the custom of excluding a depressed caste from entry into a Hindu temple was legal. This was a suit brought against Shanars (Shanans) who forcibly entered the famous Meenatchi (Minakshi) Temple of Madura (Madurai) in a procession bearing torches and music. Shanans, traditionally palm distillers, were supposed to be a depressed caste but in the latter part of the nineteenth century they began to try to improve their social status by abandoning palm distilling and taking to other professions like trading. For the first time in 1874, they asked for the right to enter Minakshi Temple but were denied. After their sporadic attempts to enter the temple had failed, they decided to force their way into the temple on 14 May 1897. The hereditary trustee of the temple, the zamindar of Ramnadu, sued Madura District Court for a declaration that Shanans were not entitled to enter the temple, and an injunction to restrain them from so doing as well as compensation of Rs. 2,500 for the purification ceremony needed for the temple as it was considered to have been defiled by their entry. The Subordinate Judge of Madura who decided in favour of the plaintiff on the ground that entry of Shanans into the temple had been rejected by custom, said in the judgement as follows:

> Courts of Law have recognized and enforced customs of this character although they may be repugnant to generally received notions of what is just and proper. It is not for this Court to examine whether the doctrines or usages obtaining in a particular temple are defensible from a logical or equitable standpoint in the light of modern enlightenment and civilization. . . .

Against this judgement of the Subordinate Judge of Madura, Shanans appealed to the Madras High Court but their appeal was dismissed. Although they then appealed to the Pivy Council which functioned as the final tribunal for all of the appeals from the High Courts in India, the Legal Committee of the Privy Council affirmed the judgement of the Madras High Court. (31 M. 236, meaning the case reported in *Indian Law Reports*, *Madras Series,* vol. 31, pp. 236ff.)

As this case denotes, if a long ('immemorial') custom or usage to exclude depressed castes from entering a Hindu temple was proved to exist, then the law courts recognized and respected this custom or usage though it contradicted the legal fiction of the Hindu Law to deny the existence of the Fifth Varna. Thus, social discrimination against the depressed castes was kept intact in the name of custom and usage during British colonial rule.

This legal fiction of the Hindu Law became difficult to maintain in the course of time, however, and the British were forced to legally recognize the reality of Indian society, specifically, the existence of socially discriminated castes. The Government of India Act of 1919 enabled a new legal category of social stratum called the 'Depressed Classes' to be introduced. This legal category of the Depressed Classes comprised not only the depressed castes but the so-called tribes as well. Representatives of the Depressed Classes were appointed by the Governors of each State to the Legislative Council of the State giving rise to the problem of social discrimination against the depressed castes being discussed in the Legislative Council more often than before.

A great advance in this regard was the Government of India Act of 1935. This Act permitted the introduction of a new legal category of people called the 'Scheduled Castes'. In 1936, the castes which were to be included in this category of the Scheduled Castes were listed ('scheduled') in accordance with the Government of India (Scheduled Castes) Order of 1936. The castes listed on this Order corresponded for the most part to the depressed castes. For the Scheduled Castes, a preferential voting system was provided. This type of preferential treatment given to the Schduled Castes, popularly known as compensatory discriminaton, was fully developed after India gained its independence.

Thus, the specific legal status of the depressed caste was established by the 1930s, and special acts to secure their public rights also were passed by the State Legislative Council. One of the typical acts of this sort was the so-called Temple Entry Act passed by many States in the 1930s which provided the right of entry to Hindu temples to the Scheduled Castes.

6

The Untouchables and Economic Change in a Dry Village in South India[1]

TSUKASA MIZUSHIMA

DRY VILLAGE

An aerial view of the south Indian countryside in the monsoon season denotes a tremendous number of reservoirs overflowing with water. These reservoirs, called *eri* in Tamil, are one of the major irrigational sources in the region. The size of an *eri* is often as large as a football field or even several times more. In these cases, by utilizing the mildly undulating landscape, the people in the area built a bank, several metres high and a few hundred metres wide, in the lower part of the slope to construct these *eris*. Most of the villages in the area have one or two *eris*, and the stored water is used mainly for irrigational purposes.

Water which could fully fill the *eri* during the monsoon season, however, does not last long; it disappears in most cases after a few months. The emerging shallow bottom of the *eri* makes it clear that the quantity of stored water is deceptively little contrary to their huge size. The rest of the season leaves a savanna-like landscape covered by rocks and thorny bushes. With this precious, limited irrigational resource, many types of less water-consuming crops like *cholam*, *cumbu*, cotton, groundnut, gram, coriander, and others are grown in the area. More water-consuming crops like paddy and sugarcane are also grown in a very limited scale in areas having a comparatively stable irrigational source. Any such area without a perennial irrigational source is usually called as a dry (*punjai*) area.

Though south India (except Kerala) is categorized as a dry region as a whole, some parts are facilitated with a well-developed irrigational system. Rice cultivation, which produces a several-times larger output than do other millets and, therefore, can maintain a larger population, has been the preeminent choice not only for all south Indian dynasties but also for all south Indians. In this regard, their strenuous effort is evinced by the highly sophisticated irrigational system in the Kaveri Delta, where a dam called the Grand Anicut was constructed in the ancient period with river water being sub-distributed to a number of small tributaries. The grandeur of the system bespeaks the determination of ancient dynasties of south India to extend the production of their preeminent crop. An area featuring such a stable river irrigational system is called as wet (*nunjai*) area.

The difference in the irrigational condition has produced critical differences not only in agricultural activities but also in the village structures between the two areas.[2] Because of the high productivity of rice cultivation, the land in wet villages has very often been donated to the Brahmins or temples in the past. As the Brahmins are not engaged in agricultural operation, however, the donated land was left to be worked by the actual cultivators. In the course of time, a highly developed landlord-tenant system has thus been established, including the concept of absentee landlordism. Under the large landlords, the tenant cultivators engage in the agricultural operation and pay the rent to the former.

Conversely, the tenancy system has not developed in the dry areas. The typical agricultural management in the dry area is medium- to small-scale farming in which the landholder himself engages in the agricultural operation using family labour. Nor is the landholding structure in the dry area skewed to the extent observed in the wet area. Under the unstable condition of farming dependent solely on the ever-precarious rainfall, where many types of crops grow at different durations and where cattle herding is an important income source, dry farming requires the operator's intensive care and labour far more than does wet farming. Naturally the productivity is much lower. Thus, in most cases, both of these conditions have never allowed for the development of a tenancy system in the dry area.

The agricultural operation in the dry area is, however, not necessarily conducted solely by family labour. In many cases, agricultural labourers mainly comprising the untouchables are involved in the dry farming. In fact, villages in the dry area have a fairly good number of landless labourers.

Generally speaking, agriculture is a labour-intensive industry. Unless mechanized, the extent of cultivation possible by any one family is proportional to the family's available labour. In other words, the given technology determines the operational extent. If the operational extent is not proportional to the given technology, some 'unnatural' forces causing their disproportionate balance could be working. The tenancy system as observed in the wet area is one of such forces, as it enables the landlord to obtain produce simply by the land ownership. Farming operated by the landless agricultural labourers as observed in the dry area is another force. Such farming as operated by the tenants or by the landless labourers becomes possible only when some farmers are excluded from access to land ownership while the others monopolize land ownership. Both the wet and the dry areas thus have their distinctive landholding structures which have been historically developed in the past.

In this paper, I will take up a dry village I studied in the early 1980s to clarify the changing condition of the untouchables in the dry area in south India.

HISTORICAL CHANGE IN LANDHOLDING STRUCTURE

The studied village is located about 30 km north of Tiruchirapalli town, Tamil Nadu. The total number of households was 545 having a population of 2,245 at the time of my survey. The size of the village was around 4,000 acres, which was more or less the average size of the dry villages in the area.

The village level records started to be prepared from the early British period. The colonial government enforced the Raiyatwari Settlement in many parts of south India from the early nineteenth century. Under the presumed state ownership of land, land was demarcated into hundreds or thousands of small lots, each having a serial number, extent, tax rate, and assessment. The raiyat (farmer) who settled with the state to pay the assessment was considered to be the landholder, holding virtual ownership of the concerned lot. Those land lots on which no one agreed to settle were left as *tarish* (cultivable waste) until some raiyat took it over at a later stage. Settlement was to be renewed every 30 years according to the newly revised assessment rates.

The Raiyatwari Settlement was introduced in the studied area in the 1820s. The land record having the details of every lot, called as the Settlement Register[3], was accordingly prepared at the time of settlement. Unfortunately, though, the first set is not presently available. The oldest available set is the 1864 Settlement Register, followed by the 1898 and 1924 sets. Supplemented by a set of various

Table 1 Historical change in landholding classified by castes

	1864		1898		1924		1982	
	Acs.	%	Acs.	%	Acs.	%	Acs.	%
Total Extent	3707.4	100.0	4044.0	100.0	4046.9	100.0	4046.9	100.0
Occupied	1071.1	28.9	1808.0	44.7	2441.9	60.3	2620.2	64.7
Inam	78.3	2.1	39.0	1.0	36.9	0.9	36.9	0.9
Cultivable Waste	1744.1	47.0	1374.0	34.0	335.2	8.3	156.9	3.9
Unassessed					11.9	0.3	11.9	0.3
Poramboke	814.0	22.0	823.0	20.4	1221.1	30.2	1221.1	30.2
Reddiyar	823.4	77.6	1057.5	60.3	971.9	40.6	539.3	26.9
Gounder	2.3	0.2	35.6	2.0	276.3	11.5	369.2	18.4
Muttiriyan	81.6	7.7	294.6	16.8	383.3	16.0	441.5	22.1
Udaiyar	21.3	2.0	73.7	4.2	170.8	7.1	149.5	7.5
Untouchables	8.1	0.8	148.6	8.5	406.6	17.0	380.6	19.0
Pariah (Hindu)	(1.6)	(0.2)	(48.3)	(2.8)	(137.2)	(5.7)	(118.9)	(5.9)
Pariah (Christian)	(2.3)	(0.2)	(57.8)	(3.3)	(108.1)	(4.5)	(103.8)	(5.2)
Pallan	(2.8)	(0.3)	(22.5)	(1.3)	(84.9)	(3.5)	(86.8)	(4.3)
Sakkili	(1.4)	(0.1)	(20.0)	(1.1)	(76.5)	(3.2)	(71.1)	(3.6)
Muslim	20.1	1.9	11.5	0.7	66.5	2.8	39.4	2.0
Brahmin					3.3	0.1	4.7	0.0
Pandarum	4.1	0.4	0.7	0.0	6.2	0.3	35.5	0.2
Chettiyar					26.9	1.1	10.9	1.8

Ottan Chetti			10.8	0.6			0.0	0.5
Kal Ottan							17.6	0.0
Asari	13.7	1.3	28.3	1.6	17.6	0.7	2.8	0.9
Vannan			8.1	0.5	7.6	0.3	5.3	0.1
Pariyari					10.0	0.4	5.7	0.3
Vanniyar					5.2	0.2		0.3
Nayakkan	2.7	0.3	23.2	1.3	6.0	0.3		0.0
Pillai	0.8	0.1	3.9	0.2				0.0
Konar			13.2	0.8	10.1	0.4		0.0
Kusavan			24.6	1.4	6.0	0.3		0.0
Others					13.7	0.6		0.0
Unknown	82.8	7.8	17.8	1.0	6.6	0.3		0.0
Sub-total	1060.9	100.0	1753.4	100.0	2394.6	100.0	2002.0	100.0
Temple Inam	79.0		83.3		81.7		83.3	
Total	1139.9		1836.7		2476.3		2085.3	
Held by other villagers							571.8	

Note 1: Figures in the 1864, 1898 and 1924 columns include the land of landholders living in other villages.
2: Underlined figures in the 1982 column denote the land held by the landholders living in the studied village.

types of records currently used, however, the past changes in landholding of every lot and of every registered landholder from the 1860s onwards can be reconstructed. Accordingly Table 1 is prepared from these sets of records to show the changes in landholding classified by castes.

A look at the 1864 figures provides an interesting aspect of the landholding structure prominent in the village. Specifically, the Reddiyar caste held as much as three fourths of the owned land. At the time of the author's field study in the early 1980s there were more than 20 castes in the village. The Reddiyar's share in the total population was only 13 per cent. Gounders, Muttiriyans and the untouchables (Hindu and Christian Pariah, Pallan, and Sakkiliyan) occupied 15, 27 and 28 per cent of the village population respectively. The rest constituted 17 per cent.[4] Though these percentages in the 1980s cannot be simply applied to the 1860s, the near-monopoly of the Reddiyar in landholding remains distinctive.

Notably, however, it is in a sense unreasonable for the village land to be exclusively held by a single community under the Raiyatwari System. Under the system, the land categorized as 'cultivable waste' could have been occupied by anyone who proposed to pay the assessment upon it. In 1864, in fact, there still remained a fairly good proportion of uncultivable wasteland with one and a half times more than the occupied land or nearly one-half of the total village land still being categorized as cultivable waste. We may then ask how the exclusive land ownership of the Reddiyar could be established on such a scale.

Several interpretations can be given for this. From the Reddiyar's side there were some reasons for restricting other castes' landholding. Firstly, there was the lack of primogeniture rule in the inheritance rule. Land should be evenly divided among the male inheritors, so that in case there were five sons for two generations, the size of each holding becomes one twenty-fifth of the original holding. It was therefore essential for the Reddiyar to exclude others from land ownership and keep the land ready for occupation for their own members. Through this measure, the gap between the manageable size and holding size could be remedied, thus maintaining their unity and the leading status over others. The genealogical studies tracing the land transfer and inheritance patterns among the Reddiyar in the past hundred years or so find many instances of the acquisition of cultivable wasteland by the households whose holding fell below the viable size after inheritance.

The second reason was to secure the labour of other castes. As will be stated later, the Reddiyar have found it difficult to secure labourers in recent years because the other castes have acquired their own lands to operate. In this regard, it must have been essential for the Reddiyar to make other castes seek employment by excluding them from land ownership.

The third reason was to reserve the grazing ground for cattle herding. Because of these conditions the Reddiyar pressured other castes and monopolized village land even though access to land was institutionally provided to any one in the Raiyatwari System.

On the other hand, the non-Reddiyar castes had the following reasons for not owning much land. First, they could not afford to keep bullocks and ploughs, both essential for any agricultural operation. Second, they were engaged in some traditional occupation like shepherding. And finally, settled agriculture was not necessarily the objective for many of the villagers in those days. Migratory movements must have been more active than now under the previous more precarious conditions of agriculture.

Such a situation observed in the 1860s has, however, drastically changed since then. The share of the Reddiyar's landholding decreased around 20 per cent every 30 years to reach as low as 27 per cent by 1982. The untouchables and the Gounder, on the contrary, increased their share to 19 and 18 per cent respectively. The Muttiriyan, whose share was around 8 per cent in 1864, increased their share to 22 per cent.

I will now examine the causes leading to this change.

DEVELOPMENT SOURCES IN THE DRY VILLAGE

There were three sources of agricultural development in the dry village in the past. They were: (1) extension of cultivated area by bringing formerly unoccupied areas into cultivation, (2) intensification of land use by utilizing stored water, and (3) increase of productivity through the improvement of agricultural technology. As indicated in Table 1, the area under 'Cultivable Waste' occupied nearly one-half of the studied area in 1864. The area, however, greatly decreased since then, from 1,744 acres in 1864 to 1,374 acres in 1898, and to as little as 335 acres in 1924. The land left to be occupied at the time of the author's survey was rocky and barren, which seemed hardly possible for bringing into cultivation. In other words, the first source of extending the cultivated areas, or its possibility, disappeared in the early part of the twentieth century. The choice left to be taken since then has been to increase the unit productivity by intensifying land use and by improving agricultural technologies. Thus, as the rain-fed *eri* had its exacting limit, the intensive utilization of the groundwater resource came to be given the highest priority.

The studied village had two large *eris* as its irrigational source. Their storing capacity, however, was as small as a few months' use, so that only the lower area just below *erī*'s bank could be irrigated. What was significantly developed instead was well irrigation, which allows a more stable supply of water for a longer period. These wells usually take the form of an open well, which has a square shape around 10 m by 10 m in size and more than 10 m depth. Groundwater oozes out little by little through the cracks in and between rocks, and fills the well gradually. The village map prepared in 1892 gives the location of a total of 23 wells, concentrated near the habitation quarter and below the two *eris*. The former were probably for drinking purposes and the latter for supplementing *eri* irrigation. The number of wells steadily and greatly increased from the beginning of the twentieth century. The number of wells counted from the subsequent village maps, land records, and by lot-to-lot field survey revealed that as many as 207 wells were constructed by 1982. In the course of time, 34 wells were abandoned and filled in for some reason, so that 196 wells were existent. Among them, 35 wells were not in use for the reason to be stated later.

Technological progress was also witnessed in water-lifting from the wells. The oldest type of lifting implement is called the *mel-yatram* and was still in use in one of the village wells. It is a see-saw type of implement the end of which is tied with a rope on which is hung a leather bag. Labourers walk on the beam from one end to the other. The *mel-yatram* was followed by the *kabalai*, an epoch-making device in the sense that it was not operated by human labour but powered by bullocks. A pair of bullocks drawn by a labourer go up and down the sloped path pulling a rope connected to a leather bag via a wheel set at the edge of the well. Because of the precarious supply of electricity, the *kabalai* was still used in as many as 78 wells at the time of study. The work is, as can be well imagined, very simple and tedious. Only one acre of land can be irrigated with the *kabalai* through eight hours of work. This work used to be done by a *pannaiyal* or long-term attached labourer. The third type of device was the oil-engine pump. Though costly, it had been the most powerful equipment in use until the electric pump was introduced in 1970. There were 16 wells equipped with this oil-engine pump at the time of survey. The last and most popular type of equipment which started to be installed from 1970 was the electric pump when electrical connections were completed. In total, 79 wells were equipped with electric pumps.

The irrigated area had increased as well. The total cultivated area under irrigated crops was 120 acres in 1898, which increased to 215 acres in 1980. Though this rate of increase was not impressive, the villagers were clearly exerting their utmost effort to extend their irrigated area.

The intensive exploitation of the groundwater resource and its relative stability has enabled the introduction of improved agricultural technology. Not only the new types of irrigational facilities but also new varieties of crops, fertilizers, pesticides and other additives have been introduced. Though India has a long history of development in agricultural technology, it was the so-called Green Revolution that gave by far the most important impact. High-yielding varieties, chemical fertilizers, pesticides, and electric pumps were ushered together into Indian rural areas from the late 1960s. The studied village was also affected significantly when the village got electricity in 1970 and the actual installation of electric pumps became possible.[5]

AGRICULTURAL DEVELOPMENT AND LANDHOLDING STRUCTURE

The change in the three sources of agricultural development in the past was accompanied by the modification in the economic structure. The most important modification was found in the landholding structure as described earlier. The structural changes in agriculture and in landholding were interrelated as follows. The first important factor in this variation was well irrigation which made it possible to utilize irrigated land more intensively. Basically, a well makes it possible to irrigate land throughout the year, which provides greater stability, higher productivity, and higher profit than does rain-fed land. As stated previously, it was the Reddiyar who actively pursued this course. They gave priority to well-irrigated land and to the intensive agriculture accorded it. Instead of maintaining extensive but unstable dry land, they focused their future on the small but rich irrigated land. As one of its prominent results it became less important for the Reddiyar to keep the cultivable wasteland by rejecting others' access to it. It was at this stage when other caste members were given the chance to acquire land. Many of the land lots converted from cultivable waste to *patta* land (privately owned land) were found to be acquired by the members of other castes between 1864 and 1924 in the studied village. There were also many cases of land transfers from the Reddiyar to non-Reddiyar castes especially in the remote, barren areas within the village. Some Reddiyars must have disposed a part of their holdings to obtain funds for constructing the wells.

Another factor causing the Reddiyar to lose the incentive to maintaining their extensive holding was their departure from sheep and goat herding. The Reddiyar, a warrior cum agricultural caste who migrated from Andhra Pradesh several centuries ago with the advance of Vijayanagar rule to the south, were most probably engaged in mixed agriculture in which sheep and goat herding played an important role.

In the late nineteenth century, however, there occurred social movements, the so-called 'Sanskritization', in which every caste aspired to lift its social status above that of the others at the cost of some of their traditional customs. It was primarily motivated by the decennial population census operations in which caste ranking was attempted by using several indices. The important point was that shepherding was considered to be a somewhat degrading occupation. It seems the Reddiyar gradually eliminated shepherding from their farming. Because of the reason to be stated later, there occurred a revival of shepherding among the Reddiyar after 1970. Even then, however, the percentage of the Reddiyar households engaged in shepherding was only 10 per cent of the total at the time of the study. This figure contrasted greatly with the figure of 56 per cent among the Gounder households. Even so, it may be added that the total number of sheep and goats in the village decreased from 2,825 in 1898 to 1,635 in 1982. In a word, the incentive for reserving grazing ground for shepherding disappeared for the Reddiyar in the late nineteenth century.

The last but the most important factor was the loss of unity among the Reddiyar community. As was the case with any south Indian village, the studied village had sent many villagers to other villages, towns, or foreign countries. A demographic study of all the households in the village reveals that every caste sent a considerable number of people to other parts of the world as will be discussed later. The Reddiyar were no exception.

What was especially important in this regard was the disappearance of three out of four *kaniyatchikaran* families from the village. In pre-colonial south India, there operated a reproduction system designated by the author as the 'Mirasi System'. This system allocated a proportional share of the total produce to a particular role necessary to reproduce the regional society and maintained the people with roles as well. The reproductive spatial unit had been minimized to a village in the course of time and the village leaders had become in a sense owners of their own villages by the eighteenth century. These village leaders were called *kaniyatchikaran* (Tamil) or *mirasidar* (Persian) in the British colonial records. Genealogies indicate there existed four *kaniyatchikaran* families of Reddiyar in the studied village. They seemed to have played a leading role in the village and the surviving *kaniyatchikaran* family still performed symbolically the primary role in the village festival observed by the author, even though the family's landholding had been very much minimized at present. Other *kaniyatchikaran* families were, however, not traceable in the village. Such movement of the caste members as indicated by the *kaniyatchikaran* case operated in a destructive way on the unity among the Reddiyar, on their controlling power over other castes, and on their enforcement of exclusion of others from landholding.

On the other hand, the castes other than the Reddiyar have steadily increased the share of landholding. The same factors that reduced the Reddiyar's share worked in the opposite direction. Under the influence of Sanskritization, the shepherd castes like the Gounder tried hard to shift their main activity from shepherding to settled agriculture. (Note that they had virtually no land in 1864.) Non-Reddiyar utilized the opportunity to acquire the cultivable wasteland or the land sold by the Reddiyar. The result was that their increasing share amounted to as high as 70 per cent in 1982.

THE UNTOUCHABLES

The foregoing leads us to the question of how then the status and the orientation of the untouchables has been altered under such a structural change.

There were three untouchable castes in the studied village: the Pariah (Hindu and Christian), Pallan, and Sakkili. As is generally observed in south Indian villages, they lived in Paracheri (living quarter for the Pariah) located at the edge of the main habitation quarter and were completely segregated from villagers of other castes.

A look at the landholding share in Table 1 reveals a very interesting fact about their position in comparison to others. Though the untouchables' share was negligible in the oldest available record in 1864, they were not the exception. Other castes like Gounders suffered the same fate. It is sometimes argued that exclusion of the untouchables from the means of production has been the basic factor in the discrimination against them. This interpretation is too simple to accept, however, as is evidenced by the fact that their owned extent was actually larger than that of the Gounder in 1864. Nonetheless, it would be difficult to clarify the untouchables' problem unless a more composite approach were made.

The untouchables, whose share in the landholding was less than one per cent in 1864, drastically increased their share to nine per cent in 1898, to 17 per cent in 1924, and to 19 per cent at the time of the survey. In absolute terms, this was an increase from eight acres to 380 acres. Moreover, the studied village was not at all an isolated case. The same feature was observed in a nearby dry village studied by the author in 1979–80[6] and was confirmed by another extensive study of the area.[7]

Additionally, there were some factors peculiar to the untouchables other than the factors common to non-Reddiyar castes. Many of the untouchables were working as *pannaiyal* under the Reddiyar in the past. The *pannaiyal* engages in such agricultural pursuits as herding and *kabalai* work under his employer's supervision.[8] He is provided with daily food, a monthly allowance, and occasional gifts at the time of festivals like Pongal.

Such traditional employment relationship between the untouchables and the Reddiyar as symbolized in *pannaiyal* employment has undergone gradual change over the years. With the development of plantations in the tropical area from the latter half of the nineteenth century, the migratory movement of south Indians was greatly activated. Millions of labourers, many of them being the untouchables, emigrated to Ceylon, Burma, Malaya, and to other countries to seek employment.[9] Here, Tiruchirapalli was not exceptional and neither was the studied village. Genealogies show that there were totally 201 villagers born in the village who emigrated. Among them, 112 went to Ceylon and 34 went to Malaya. The opportunities suddenly opened to them greatly affected the traditional *pannaiyal*-type employment in the village. Those who returned were not only experienced in the new type of management in the estates but had also saved their earnings to invest in acquiring land. What was acquired was, then, not only the land lots but also their sense of self-respect and the first step to becoming independent from the centuries-long caste relationship.

The relation between the Reddiyar and the untouchables was further modified after 1970 when electric pumps were introduced and *kabalai* work was replaced. Because finding the labourers for the *kabalai* work, the sturdiest work in any agricultural operation, was no longer necessary since their wells were equipped with electric pumps, the Reddiyar dismissed them in many cases, which they have now come to regret as will be stated later.[10]

Thus, the untouchables who were deprived of their main employment in the village had to seek some other income source by themselves. What they found as an alternative was sheep and goat herding, which did not require much initial investment or skill to manage, and was profitable at the same time. Marketing was not difficult, either, as the village was located near Samayapuram, a well-known marketing centre. In addition, the meat consumption as well as its price was greatly enhanced as the Green Revolution progressed mainly because the non-vegetarian labouring castes in the wet villages along the Kaveri River very much benefited from it. In less than 10 years after the untouchables started shepherding, nearly 30 per cent of their households were found to be engaged in it. The income accrued from it was again invested in acquiring land, thus preparing a further step for strengthening their economic independence.

One of the results of such development was the difficulty for the Reddiyar in employing *pannaiyal* when they desperately needed it. The change between the employer and employee in the *pannaiyal* contract was observed in the nature of the cash advance. Some time in the past, probably in the early part of the twentieth century when more and more untouchables emigrated abroad, the advance system was started in the *pannaiyal* contract. Here, at the time a *pannaiyal* contract was made, a certain amount is advanced to the *pannaiyal*. The advance was to be repaid to the employer free of interest when the contract was terminated. This advance can be, in a sense, considered to have started as a measure to keep the labourers in debt bondage, and, in this regard, it is true that the system once served this purpose.

The nature of the cash advance has, however, witnessed dramatic change in recent years. The following case of the Pariah family will illustrate this point. The family had five male children and all except the eldest worked as a *pannaiyal*. The advance obtained through *pannaiyal* contracts was then used as the educational fund for the eldest, who eventually graduated from university and obtained a job in one of the leading banks in Madras by utilizing the reservation system for the Scheduled Castes. Though this case may not be a typical one, we can observe the determination of some untouchables in opening their own future by utilizing the given condition to their best. They were no longer people who were continuously oppressed and exploited.

Returning to the point, it became extremely difficult for the Reddiyar to acquire *pannaiyal* unless they offered a considerable amount in advance. Otherwise they had to acquire day workers in time of necessity. Actually, it became a daily routine for the Reddiyar to go to Paracheri early in the morning to seek workers for their fields during the peak agricultural season.[11]

NON-AGRICULTURAL EMPLOYMENT AND THE UNTOUCHABLES

Certainly, such trend as observed in the studied village will continue for some time, in which the untouchables are gradually increasing their landholding share. It does not, however, simply signify that their status is being lifted. For instance, the land lots owned by the untouchables were located far away from the habitation quarter and had a poor, barren outlook. Since this simple comparison in landholding may lead us to an improper conclusion,[12] I will explain the structure of non-agricultural employment to clarify this point.

There were many types of non-agricultural occupations in the village. Some of them were agro-based such as milk vending, tyre-cart transporting (using bullock cart equipped with rubber-tyres), and basket making. Washermen, barbers, carpenters, smiths, and temple priests belonged to the so-called service castes and were entitled to receive customarily fixed allowance from the concerned households in the village. There were also school teachers, medical practitioners, electricians, ice-bar sellers, tailors, and many other occupations. The proportion of the households having non-agricultural income was as high as one-quarter of the total households in the studied village.

What is to be noticed in non-agricultural occupations is the high correlation between the non-agricultural income level and the scale of operational landholding, caste, or both. If we exclude the tyre-cart transporters and the newcomers to the village, for instance, we can count 12 households engaged in non-agricultural employment while having more than 10 acres of operated extent (owned extent plus leased-in extent minus leased-out extent). Out of these, 10 households earned more than Rs. 400 a month from non-agricultural income sources. On the contrary, only four out of 78 households with less than 10 acres of operated land earned more than Rs. 300 a month. Caste origin also demonstrated a strong correlation. That is, seven out of 10 teachers (the best possible non-agricultural occupation found in the village) belonged to the Reddiyar caste.[13] The low-earning occupations like the milk-vendors or ice-bar sellers were mainly occupied by the Gounder and Muttiriyan. It was hardly possible for the untouchables to find a non-agricultural income source within the village.

More or less the same feature can be observed among the list of occupations of those moving out of the village. Most of the Reddiyar from the village were professionals or skilled workers working as lawyers, accountants, bank clerks, and other upper-skill occupations. Most of the untouchables, on the contrary, found work on the plantations.

This evidence clearly indicates that the Reddiyar's social position has never declined over the years despite their decreasing share in village land. With their historically accumulated wealth and their investment in education, they were positioned on a much higher social ladder than were others. A good contrast could be observed in the Gounder's orientation. The latter, which has increased the share in village landholding from 0.2 per cent in 1864 to 18 per cent in 1982, never showed any interest in education. A study of educational attainment of the respective castes in the village from the primary educational level clearly indicates that their drop-out rate from school was much higher than the Reddiyar or even the untouchables. As one of the 'Backward Classes', the Gounder was less privileged in the reservation system. As investment in their children's education cannot expect safe returns, they naturally put more emphasis in shepherding or acquiring more land. Such a course would definitely secure a much safer, surer future for them. They were in such a way exerting their utmost efforts to improve their position under the given conditions.

The untouchables, except the Christian converts, were offered more preferential privileges under the reservation system and seemed to have wider opportunities than others. Those who grabbed the opportunities were, however, still negligible. An insufficient network with the outside world, lack of accumulated wealth, poorer educational background, social prejudice and discrimination require a number of years to be rectified. Accordingly, they will still have to take the uphill road for the coming decades.

Insufficient employment opportunities in the village, which were worsened by the returning of village migrants to Sri Lanka at the time of the survey, pushed the villagers to take the negative choice. Thus, what many of the untouchable households had to resort to was the seasonal migration to the wet villages. Though it has a long history, the scale of seasonal migration was much more extended after the Green Revolution. Seasonal migration can be described as follows.

The paved road along the Kaveri River was often converted to a drying, threshing floor in the harvest season. Mixed into this scene was a number of labourers carrying huge bags on their heads. High-yielding varieties have a shorter duration, so that not only the output but also the double-cropped area increased. Generally speaking, wet villages are irrigated by the canals diverted from the Upper Anicut located in the upper part of Kaveri River. As the quantity of the canal water is limited, it fills the paddy fields little by little from the upper part of the area to the lower part over a period of many weeks. As soon as the water reaches their fields, people starts planting. The tight interval between the first crop harvest and the second crop planting makes it critically important to have sufficient labour at the correct timing. The labour demand in the wet villages thus attracted a large number of seasonal migrants from the dry villages.

These seasonal migrants from the villages usually made up a labour gang called Kottu which moved from the upper part of the river to its lower part following the flow of the canal water. Some of the villagers went as far as Thanjavur District. Though it was usually possible for migrants to commute to the working fields by bus, they rarely came home. They kept on working until they had saved a certain amount. Those bags the labourers carried on their heads contained such payment in kind.

The number of households sending seasonal migrants was 113 or around 20 per cent of the total village households. The participating households among the untouchables were 65 out of 135 households. The reason of their participation was simple: The acute labour demand in the wet villages offered two and a half times more wage than did the studied village. The instability of the agricultural condition and the insufficient employment opportunities in their own village was another factor. The economic status of the participating households was much lower than others too. Nearly 90 per cent of them held less than five acres of land. Their participating ratios in the respective spheres of agriculture, cattle herding, and non-agricultural activities were much lower than other households. Seasonal migrants cooked, ate, and slept under their emplyers' roofs in the working place. Some of the villagers spent nearly a half year in this way. This then was the opportunity offered to them.

FUTURE OF THE DRY VILLAGE AND THE UNTOUCHABLES

How can we then describe the future of the dry village and that of the untouchables? It was stated that the dry village had the three development sources in the past, namely the extension of cultivated area through the reclamation of the cultivable wasteland, the intensive land use through the exploitation of groundwater, and the improvement of productivity through technological progress. What the dry village in the area was facing at the moment was a situation in which these sources were dying out. As stated before, the extension of the cultivated area was already exhausted in the early twentieth century. Groundwater, which had been eagerly pursued in the past 100 years, was already experiencing serious constraints. Out of the 196 wells existent in the village, as many as 35 were no longer used. This was firstly because the number of wells reached the limit so that they could not store sufficient water for irrigation. Secondly there often occurred water disputes among the users of the same well. Notably, most of the wells constructed up until a few decades ago were jointly started by close kin. The increased water use of the high-yielding varieties and the unstable supply of electricity for electric pumps made it very difficult to use the well water jointly, leading to serious water disputes among the users. As a result, some of the joint wells were abandoned even if they were still usable. Other wells also had developed a low water problem, so that villagers started digging holes horizontally or vertically in the existing wells.

In any case, it was apparent that the groundwater resource had also reached its limit. However, there may still remain the further possibility of increasing productivity through technological improvement. As was observed in the Green Revolution, though, most new technologies presuppose stable irrigational facilities and therefore exhibit constraints, too. The unstable nature of agriculture still continued even after the Green Revolution. A typical instance was the drought year of 1980–81 when the cultivated extent in the village dropped from the preceding average extent of 2,200 acres to as low as 900 acres.

It was not only the dry farming that had limited prospects of further development. Cattle herding became extremely difficult because of the shortage of grazing ground. Villagers had to go to remote villages to buy fodder. If we were to give a livestock index of 10 points to a bovine and one point to a sheep or goat, the total points are found to have decreased from 13,125 in 1898 to 12,261 in 1924, and finally to 10,170 in 1982. Plantations which once absorbed many Indians into employment now give no further prospects. Seasonal migration to the wet villages may continue for some time to come until their work is replaced by mechanization. Whether or not the villagers can find any employment opportunities outside the village depends purely on the development of the Indian economy. In this regard, it was symbolic to find some villagers cutting trees along the roadside to sell. They were in a way cutting the very bottom of their life away.

Such features as described above signify that the chances given to the south Indian villagers have been and will remain absolutely insufficient. Their future prospect has been frozen with little opportunity for development. The ever-increasing population pressure upon land will no doubt further aggravate the situation. Under such a state of affairs, villagers will have to struggle hard with each other to gain a share of the limited choices according to their given circumstance. Not only the inter-caste disputes but also inter-intra family quarrels were not rarely witnessed during the study period. This then was the dry village I researched and where the untouchables were born to live.

NOTES

1 This article is based on my research paper titled 'Changes, chances and choices: the perspectives of Indian villagers', *Socio-cultural Change in Villages in Tiruchirapalli District, Tamilnadu, India, Part 2, Modern Period-1*, ILCAA (Institute for the Study of Languages and Cultures of Asia and Africa), Tokyo University of Foreign Studies, 1983. The research was conducted by a Grant for Scientific Research, Ministry of Education, Japan in 1981–82, for which I am grateful.

2 As to the wet villages in south India, see for instance Kathleen Gough, *Rural Society in Southeast India*, Cambridge, 1981 and *Rural Change in Southeast India: 1950s to 1980s*, Oxford, 1989; Haruka Yanagisawa, *Socio-economic Changes in a Village in the Paddy Cultivating Area in South India*, ILCAA, Tokyo University of Foreign Studies, 1985. Gough's works are about Thanjavur District and Yanagisawa's is about Tiruchirapalli District. As to the dry village, John Harriss conducted his

investigation in the North Arcot District. John Harriss, *Capitalism and Peasant Farming: Agrarian Structure and Ideology in Northern Tamil Nadu*, Oxford, 1982. A comparative study between the wet area and the dry area is found in Haruka Yanagisawa, *A Socio-economic Study on South India: Improving Status of the Depressed Class and the Changes in Rural Society* (in Japanese), Tokyo University, 1991; C.J. Baker and D.A. Washbrook, *South India: Political Institutions and Political Change 1880-1940*, London, 1975; D.A. Washbrook, *The Emergence of Provincial Politics*, Cambridge, 1976.

3 For various type of land records, see T. Mizushima, 'Village records on landholding in South India and ways for processing them', *Studies on Agrarian Societies in South Asia* 5, ILCAA, Tokyo University of Foreign Studies, 1980.

4 The basic source for south Indian castes is Edgar Thurston, *Castes and Tribes of Southern India*, 7 vols, Government Press, Madras, 1909.

5 A large body of literature is available on the Green Revolution. See for instance B.H. Farmer, ed., *Green Revolution? Technology and Change in Rice-growing Areas of Tamil Nadu and Sri Lanka*, London, 1977.

6 T. Mizushima and T. Nara, 'Social Change in a Dry Village in South India: An Interim Report', *Studies in Socio-cultural Change in Rural Villages in Tiruchirapalli District, Tamil Nadu, India 4*, ILCAA, 1981.

7 H. Yanagisawa and T. Mizushima, *Castes and the Structural Change in Land Ownership in South India in the Early Twentieth Century* (in Japanese), ILCAA, Tokyo University of Foreign Studies, 1988.

8 There are actually two types of *pannaiyal*. One is called as *periya* (big) *pannaiyal* who performs major agricultural operations like *kabalai* work. The other is called *chinna* (small) *pannaiyal* who engages in minor tasks like sweeping the cattle shed.

9 As to migration to Burma, Malaya, or Sri Lanka, see N.R. Chakravarti, *The Indian Minority in Burma*, Oxford, 1971; Kernial Singh Sandhu, *Indians in Malaya*, Cambridge, 1969; Dharmapriya Wesumperuma, *Indian Immigrant Plantation Workers in Sri Lanka: A Historical Perspective 1880-1910*, Vidyalankara Press, 1986.

10 Forty-three out of forty-four wells owned by the Reddiyar were installed with electric pumps at the time of the survey in 1982.

11 There were 21 *pannaiyals* from 17 households. Their composition was: untouchables, 8, Muttiriyan, 9, Gounder, 3, and Kal-Ottan (stone-cutter), 1. They were all from the households having less than five acres of operational holding or those with several male children. On the other hand, there were 15 households employing *pannaiyals*. Among them, the Reddiyar numbered 13, and the Gounder and Udaiyar one each.

12 If we look at the position of south Indian villagers as a whole, we may even maintain that they were totally left far behind in a harder, lesser circumstance from the rest of the world. What Gough asserted was that not only the lower castes but also the Brahmin could be placed at the lower side of the pyramidal structure if we consider the class structure on global level. See Gough, *Rural Society in Southeast India*.

13 The rest were two Pariahs and a Chettiyar (a vocational teacher).

7

Conflict and Controversy over the Mahar Vatan in the Nineteenth–Twentieth Century Bombay Presidency[1]

HIROYUKI KOTANI

INTRODUCTION

As mentioned in my foregoing essay in this volume, 'Ati Śūdra castes in the medieval Deccan', the Mahar Vatan in the medieval age had been a kind of hereditary patrimony to be safeguarded within the framework of social relations in the village community and district (*pargana*) community as well as the state power apparatus. Under British colonial rule, various types of *vatan* (hereditary patrimony) underwent divergent changes. Some types of *vatan* were abolished at an earlier stage, for example, while still some others were maintained tenaciously. It depended mainly on the necessity or expediency of British colonial rule and partly on the changing social relations within Indian society itself. What then was the destiny of the Mahar Vatan? The Mahar Vatan was one of the most tenaciously maintained *vatans* which was only to be abolished by the Bombay Inferior Village Vatan Abolition Act of 1958 after India gained its independence. This essay aims at clarifying the reason why the Mahar Vatan was maintained so persistently by tracing the conflict and controversy over it in the nineteenth-twentieth century Bombay Presidency.

VATANS IN THE EARLY ADMINISTRATIVE SYSTEM

Vatandars and the State

The Maratha kingdom (Peshva government) was overthrown by the army of the East India Company in 1818 and most of its territories, the so-called 'Conquered Territories' came to be incorporated into the

Bombay Presidency which formerly included only the narrow coastal areas of Gujarat and Konkan. The foundation of the administrative system of the enlarged Bombay Presidency was formed by the then Governor of Bombay, M. Elphinstone. He rearranged and consolidated regulations issued earlier by the Bombay government into 27 regulations promulgated at the same time on 1 January 1827. These 27 regulations were collectively known as the Elphinstone Code which formed the basis of the administrative system of the Bombay Presidency.[2]

In the Elphinstone Code, *vatan* was translated as the 'hereditary office' and allowed to continue to be enjoyed by the former holder. But the denomination of '*vatandar kunbi*' was discontinued so that the category of 'hereditary office' holders included only village establishments (*patel*, *kulkarni*, *balutedars* and some others) and district officers like *deshmukh* and *deshpande*. Bombay Regulation V of 1827, Chapter I, (I) provided a prescription of 30 years with regard to the immovable property which included 'lands, houses, hereditary offices, or other immovable property'. Thus, *vatans* (hereditary offices) were acknowledged as a kind of immovable property (*nibandha* in Indian terminology) by the Elphinstone Code.

However, the Bombay government did not deal with all *vatans* alike. It paid special attention to *vatans* which had a direct connection with the collection of taxes, especially land tax, and police administration in the village and district. In the Maratha administration, the Vatan System had had the twofold function of regulating the social relations within the village community and district (*pargana*) community as well as of substituting for the local administrative system of the state. Thus, *vatandars* had had the double standing as a member of the village and district establishment and as a local officer of the state. But all the *vatandars* did not share alike in this dual standing. *Vatandars* whose qualification as local officers of the state had been stronger than others were district officers like *deshmukh* and *deshpande* and village officers like *patel* and *kulkarni*. The Vatandar Mahar who had served as the assistant to *patel* in tax collection, the village police and other duties had had the standing of the 'inferior village officer'.

Thus, *vatans* to which the Bombay government as the successor state of the Marathas gave special consideration were those of district and village officers including the Vatandar Mahar whose knowledge of the district and village it had the intention to utilize for local administration at the early stage of British colonial rule.

The Bombay government defined *deshmukh* and *deshpande* as 'hereditary district officers' and *patel*, *kulkarni*, Vatandar Mahar and others as 'hereditary village officers'. Bombay Regulation XVI of 1827 provided the duties and powers of the Collector of which Chapters III and XVII-XXVII laid down rules regarding the 'hereditary district and village officers'. The duties and powers of the Collector with regard to the appointment and dismissal of the hereditary district and village officers were provided in Chapters XVII and XVIII which were later rescinded by Section I of Act XI,1843 of the Government of India to strengthen the powers of the Collector in this regard. Section II of the same Act provided the following provision:

> that all hereditary officers, of whatever denomination, belonging to, or employed in the management of the land revenue, or of the customs or town duties, or excise, or other revenue, or in the police, or in the civil administration of the country, shall render the usual services of their respective offices, as far as the same may be required by the collector, or other officer under whose control they may be placed by usage or the orders of Government.[3]

It follows that the Collector had the power to dismiss these hereditary district and village officers when he regarded their services as needless or useless. Thus, these hereditary district and village officers came to have strengthened their character as the local state officials under the control of the Collector than before, even though their offices were still hereditary.

Bombay Regulation XVI of 1827, XIX provided the duty of the Collector to keep records of the 'land and allowances attached to hereditary district or village offices'. The 'land' meant the service *inam* land of *vatandars* which was, as a rule, exempted from the payment of land tax, but in the usual cases, was made to pay a small sum known as *judi*. By Chapter XX of the same Regulation, the allowances and emolument attached to the hereditary offices were prohibited from leaving the family of the office holders. These provisions were aimed at eliminating any danger of the duties of these offices not being properly executed due to the transfer to others of the land or allowances attached to them. This land or allowances affixed to *vatans* had previously been able to be divided, transferred or sold as property under the Maratha administration. However, the Bombay government restricted this as far as the *vatan* of the hereditary district and village officers was concerned for the sake of ensuring efficient local administration through these hereditary officers.

Thus, under the early administrative system of Bombay based on the Elphinstone Code, *vatandars* closely connected with the collection of taxes and police administration were placed under the strong control of government as hereditary district and village officers. As a result, the Vatandar Mahar was also placed under the strong legal restriction as the most important inferior village officer.

Balutedars and Peasants

The regulations of the Bombay government, however, did not embody the power to regulate *vatandars* totally. As mentiond before, the Vatan System had had the twofold aspects of regulating the social relations within local communities and substituting for the local administration system of the state. The Bombay government paid attention only to the latter aspect of the Vatan System and its former aspect, that of regulating social relations within local communities, was left wholly uninfluenced by any legal control imposable by the Bombay government. Thus, relations between *vatandars* and peasants did not change even under the early Bombay administration because these social relations were set outside the legal restriction as private relations between private individuals. Under the Elphinstone Code system, the Vatan System was divided distinctly into two aspects, namely, the public aspect (relation between *vatandar* and state) and the private aspect (relation between *vatandar* and peasant) of which only the former was subject to the strong legal control exerted by the Bombay government.

In the village, *vatandars* other than *patel* and *kulkarni* were also known as *balutedars* or collectively, *bara balute*, meaning 12 earners of *balute* (a perquisite) in which were included artisan *vatandars* such as Lohar, Sutar and Kumbhar and service *vatandars* like Joshi, Nhavi and Parit as well as *dalit vatandars* such as Mahar, Mang and Chambhar.

What then was the relationship between these *balutedars* and peasants in the early administration of the Bombay government and how did it change in the course of time? These are questions examined hereafter through the medium of legal decisions passed by the Bombay Sadr Divani Adalat (up to 1862) and the Bombay High Court (from 1862 onward).

On 29 September 1840, the full bench of the Bombay Sadr Divani Adalat passed a decree on a case between Hunnappa, the Vatandar Lohar of the village Hosour, Dharwar Zillah and a fellow villager, Hunmunna. The plaintiff, the Vatandar Lohar sued for the payment of *balute* (a perquisite) for the year 1838 from the defendant which consisted of '11 phalies of jowaree and 1.5 ruts of kurbee'. The Munsif of Roan (Gondoo Temajee) held that the 'plaintiff, as the hereditary ironsmith of his village . . . was entitled, by the custom of the country, to receive from the defendant, a fellow villager, his bullootee hucks, whether the defendant employed the plaintiff as an ironsmith or not'. The defendant appealed to the Judge of the Zillah Court (J.A. Shaw) who reversed the decree of the Munsif on the ground that 'it rested with the Ryots whether they employed the Plaintiff as an ironsmith, and paid him his hucks or not'. The Zillah Judge did not acknowledge the obligatory character of the *balute* payment for the villagers. On this, the plaintiff asked the admission of a special appeal to the Bombay Sadr Divani Adalat which was subsequently allowed. In the hearing the Sitting Judge, G. Giberne, pointed out as follows:

> the Zillah Judge had taken an erroneous view of the subject, and that his decision tended to upset a custom universally acknowledged, and endangered the constitution and foundation of all village communities established from time immemorial.

The Sitting Judge, even though viewing this subject like this, still referred the case to the full bench of the Bombay Sadr Divani Adalat due to the importance of the subject for all of the *balutedars* and villagers. The full bench, consisted of three Judges including the Sitting Judge himself, confirmed the judgment of the Sitting Judge in favour of the plaintiff, the Vatandar Lohar of the village Hosour.[4]

As this was the decision of the full bench of the Bombay Sadr Divani Adalat, this judgement was treated as the precedent for binding the judgements on the similar cases to be filed in all of the courts in the Bombay Presidency. To put the purpose of the decision into a more general framework, this decision made it clear that the villagers (peasants) were obliged to pay the *balute haqqs* to village *balutedars* even though they did not request the *balutedars*' services. In other words, *balutedars* had the hereditary right to ask for the payment of *balute* irrespective of whether or not they rendered services to the villagers. This system of the division of labour within the village community was regarded as 'the constitution and foundation of all village communities from time immemorial' and respected as such by the Bombay Sadr Divani Adalat.

This standpoint was confirmed by yet another famous decision of the Bombay Sadr Divani Adalat in 1857. The Vatandar Joshi of the village Amberee, Krishnumbhut, sued for the payment of the equivalent sum of money which three villagers paid to the other Brahman whom they had asked to perform several ceremonies. In the judgement in favour of the plaintiff, the Bombay Sadr Divani Adalat pointed out as follows:

> Whether certain religious ceremonies, which are optional or others which are obligatory are performed, the person entitled hereditary right to perform them is entitled to be paid his fee, whether he performs them or not.[5]

Although this had been the fundamental line of the judgement of the Bombay Sadr Divani Adalat regarding the relationship between *balutedars* and peasants, it became more and more contradictory to the concept of freedom of the individual (freedom of contract) which the British had brought into India, and conflicts between *balutedars* and peasants began to occur more often than in the past.

The Vatandar Mahar being one of the *balutedars* had the right to receive the *balute* payment from peasants under the early administration of the Bombay government just like the Vatandar Lohar and Vatandar Joshi did. For the Vatandar Mahar, however, conflict with peasants was more likely to occur due to the peculiarity of his office. The major problem often responsible for conflict between Vatandar Mahars and peasants was the right to take the skins of peasant's dead cattle as mentioned in my foregoing essay (see pp. 59–60).

As an example, on 23 March 1849, the Bombay Sadr Divani Adalat decided not to admit the special appeal of Suntoo and three other Vatandar Mahars suing for their right to take dead animal skins. Suntoo and the others initially brought a suit for damages to the Munsif's court on the ground that Babajee and other peasants had made village Mangs skin their dead animals and appropriated the skins even though Vatandar Mahars had the right to take all the skins of the village's dead animals. The peasants argued that they had Vatandar Mahars skin the draught bullocks when they died in the village and deliver the skins to the former possessors of bullocks giving the fee of 5 seers (of grain) for bigger bullocks and 4 seers for smaller ones and that they made Mangs process the skins into ropes and other implements for agricultural purposes. They alleged that this had been the custom of the country by the time Vatandar Mahars began to reject delivering the skins of draught bullocks to peasants. Thus, they claimed, they were obliged to win Mangs over and made them skin their dead bullocks as a countermeasure to what Vatandar Mahars were doing. Therefore, it was against this action taken on the side of the peasants that Vatandar Mahars brought their suit.

The Munsif who tried the case decided in favour of the plaintiffs, Vatandar Mahars but in an appeal on this decision the Assistant Judge reversed it. The plaintiffs then appealed to the Zillah Judge who dismissed it. As a last resort, Vatandar Mahars prayed for the admission of a special appeal to the Bombay Sadr Divani Adalat which was admitted on the ground that the decisions of two lower courts were 'opposed to the usage of the country'. But in the hearing, it became clear that the plaintiffs (Vatandar Mahars as special appellants) did not object to the right of peasants taking back the skins of the draught bullocks, and peasants did not prevent the plaintiffs from conveying away the skins of other animals. The upshot was thus that there was nothing to adjudicate for the Bombay Sadr Divani Adalat.[6]

This conclusion exactly matches the decision of the Maratha (Peshva) government on the subject referenced in my foregoing essay in this volume. It had been the custom of the country since the Maratha period that the skins of dead draught bullocks belonged to their former possessors and that the skins of all other animals that died in the village went to Vatandar Mahars. This custom had been maintained by the decisions handed down by the Bombay Sadr Divani Adalat by the middle of the nineteenth century. In the second half of the century, however, this custom began to decay and a new custom that the skins of all dead animals were the property of the former possessors of the animals began to take shape.

In this regard, in a suit brought by two Vatandar Mahars of the village Bedzurgi, Bijaour Taluka, against two other fellow Vatandar Mahars of the same village concerning distribution of the perquisites of Mahar Vatan among them, the Bombay High Court pointed out as follows in 1870:

> it has been repeatedly decided in this court, in suits for proceeds of

> the carcasses of dead cattle between the Mahars and the ryot owners of the cattle, that the person who owned the cattle while alive has also a right to the property in the dead carcasses of such cattle, and may dispose of it to anybody he pleases.[7]

As this case denotes, in the course of the nineteenth century conflicts often arose between Vatandar Mahars and peasants over the problem of who should be awarded possession of the skins of dead cattle. In these cases, the parties to the conflicts frequently resorted to taking legal action. Through these actions a new precedent came to be consolidated in that the owner of the animal while alive was also the owner of the skin of the animal when dead.

Under British colonial rule, the relationship between *balutedars* and peasants began to change as one part of the general change in the framework of medieval Indian society, and this change was most prominently reflected in the conflict between Vatandar Mahars and peasants.

THE BOMBAY HEREDITARY OFFICES ACT AND ITS AFTERMATH

The Bombay Hereditary Offices Act of 1874

The Bombay Hereditary Offices Act (Bombay Act III of 1874) was an outcome of the policy of the Bombay government to readjust the concept of the hereditary office to the changing situation in the second half of the nineteenth century. The Bombay government had been trying to put the hereditary officers closely connected with tax collection and the village police under legal control, but the situation surrounding them began to change in the course of the nineteenth century.

One of the most important changes in local administration during this period was the dismissal of most *deshmukhs* and *deshpandes* (hereditary district officers) from their office through the procedure called 'commutation'. As a result of the Summary Settlement Act (Bombay Act II of 1863), it became possible to dismiss the *deshmukhs* and *deshpandes* of the Conquered Territories from their duties on the condition that a reduced rate of tax be levied on their *inam* land. This was because the establishment of the state administration system had made their services no longer necessary. The procedure of commutation of *deshmukh* and *deshpande vatans* was first started in the Southern Division (Southern Maratha Countries) by S.J. Gordon making it known as the Gordon Settlement. Since then, the process of commutation was extended to the Central and Northern Divisions also as a result of which this procedure was completed in 10 among 12 Collectrates of the Bombay Presidency by 1873. Thus, most *deshmukhs* and *deshpandes* had ceased to be hereditary district officers by the time the Bombay Hereditary Offices Act was enacted.

The first bill of the Bombay Hereditary Offices Act (Bill III of 1873) was introduced to the Bombay Legislative Council by A. Rogers on 23 July 1873. Declaring his bill being concerned only with the hereditary village officers, Rogers divided these officers into two distinct categories, *patel* and *kulkarni* on the one hand and inferior village servants represented by Vatandar Mahars on the other, to underscore the inherent problems of the respective categories. With regard to *patel* and *kulkarni* he indicated the principal problem to be that their duties were performed through the so-called rotation system in which each shareholder of the *vatan*, when the *vatan* was shared by several shareholders as was often the case, officiated by turns according to the share of each shareholder. Because of this rotation system, a shareholder of the *vatan* who was not deemed sufficiently competent to carry out the duties of the *vatan* happened to become the officiator of the *vatan*, thereby often inhibiting the efficiency of local administration. Thus, Rogers made it clear that his bill was aimed at abolishing the rotation system among shareholders of *patel* and *kulkarni vatans*.

With regard to the inferior village servants represented by Vatandar Mahars, Rogers indicated the principal trouble to be the disputes arising between Vatandar Mahars and peasants of which the main cause was the fee which Vatandar Mahars received individually from peasants. Rogers remarked as follows:

> our system of revenue surveying has rendered the registration of land so perfect that there is very little use for the service of some of these hereditary officers, that the villagers who have been in the habit of paying them with grains or some small perquisite now refuse to pay them anything at all; and it is suspected that the mhars, seeing no probability of recovering their rights, or what they imagined to be their rights, except by the expensive process of going to law, have resorted to the poisoning of cattle. This section [Section IV] will provide a simple means for remedying

> this state of affairs. By it a punchayet will be appointed, and the matters in dispute will thus be satisfactorily settled.[8]

Thus, troubles culminating in the poisoning of cattle of peasants by Vatandar Mahars made new legislation to regulate their relationship an urgent necessity.

Rogers's first bill met with strong opposition on the ground that it totally minimized the hereditary district officers attaching importance only to the hereditary village officers, and was consequently withdrawn. On 25 September, Rogers again introduced a renewed bill (Bill XII of 1873) with some amendment to his former bill to the Bombay Legislative Council. The main point of his amendment was to make it applicable to *deshmukhs* and *deshpandes* who still retained the office of hereditary district officer. The new bill was discussed and then passed as the Bombay Hereditary Offices Act of 1874 which was translated into Marathi, Gujarati and Kannada to make it thoroughly familiar to the Indian people.

The Bombay Hereditary Offices Act defined the hereditary office as follows:

> 'Hereditary offices' means every office held hereditarily for the performance of duties connected with the administration or collection of the public revenue, or with the village police, or with the settlement of boundaries, or other matters of civil administration. (Section 4)

By this definition, the only *balutedars* who were included in the category of the hereditary village officers were Vatandar Mahars and some other *balutedars* directly connected with tax collection, the village police and certain other duties. Thus, this act was not applicable to the other *balutedars* like Vatandar Sutars. Since enforcement of the Elphinstone Code, the Bombay government had been trying to divide various *vatandars* into two distinct categories, that is, *vatandars* who were closely connected with local administration and others who were not so, placing only the former under the strict legal control. In this historical context, the Bombay Hereditary Offices Act constituted the process of completion of this policy of the Bombay government. This Act was also inapplicable to *deshmukhs* and *deshpandes* whose *vatans* had been commuted by the Summary Settlement.

Section 15 of the Bombay Hereditary Offices Act provided the procedure of commutation by which the Collector could dismiss *vatandars* from their offices with the consent of *vatandars* under mutually agreed conditions. This procedure was also applicable to village *balutedars* but Section 16 of the Act provided that commutation of their *vatans* should not be 'held to affect any right of individuals or village communities to exact such service as may be customary from village servants who have been relieved by government of liability to perform such service to the State'. Thus, the procedure of commutation changed the relationship between *balutedars* and the state but not that between *balutedars* and peasants which had been left outside the concern of the state as a private social relation within their respective village communities.

The most important sections of the Bombay Hereditary Offices Act directly related to the inferior village servants were Sections 18 and 64. Section 18 stipulated the procedure to award disputes between the inferior village servants represented by Vatandar Mahars and peasants. The following were the main purposes of Section 18:

1. 'When all or any of the property of a village-vatan of lower degree than that of Patel and Kulkarni consists of a right to levy in money or kind directly from individuals', the Collector can constitute a *panchayat* of 5 men of whom 2 should be appointed by the villagers, another 2 by the *vatandars* and the *sar-panch* (headman) by the Collector to define the 'nature and extent of such right and of the duties to be performed'.
2. The decision of the *panchayat* 'shall be in accordance with the opinion of the majority of the punchayet. . . . In case the villagers or watandars fail to nominate members within seven days, the Collector shall appoint such members'.
3. 'In case the punchayet do not come to a decision within seven days from the appointment of sar-panch, the Collector may himself pass a decision.'
4. The decision of the punchayet or the Collector . . . shall be final and binding on all persons and classes.'

The purpose of this section was to relieve the civil courts from this kind of dispute between Vatandar Mahars and peasants by leaving it to the *panchayat* comprising the representatives of Vatandar Mahars and peasants or, in case of failure of the *panchayat*, to the discretion of the Collector.

Disputes concerning the perquisite of Vatandar Mahars so often occurred and went to law courts that the duties of Vatandar Mahar could not be performed properly. With this understanding foremost in mind, the Bombay government tried to devise a 'simple means for remedying this state of affairs'. This solution took the form of the *panchayat* provided in Section 18 of the Act. Specifically, this meant that the relationship between Vatandar Mahars and peasants had become too strained to be left outside the government concern as a private social relation within the village community.

Section 64 of the Act stipulated the registration of *vatandars* and appointment of the officiator among them with regard to *vatans* lower than that of *patel* and *kulkarni*. Clause (d) of the Section was 'to provide for and enforce the joint responsibility of the whole body for the neglect of duty or misconduct of any of their members or their representatives'. As to the 'misconduct of the whole body', it provided as follows:

> in cases where the crime of cattle poisoning is prevalent, with the sanction of Government, to attach, during the pleasure of Government the watans of the person whom he may have reason to believe to have been guilty of, or to have connived at, the commission of the crime.

As mentioned previously, Rogers noted the fact of cattle poisoning by Mahars when he introduced his first bill of the Bombay Hereditary Offices Act. However, Clause (d) of Section 64 which referred to cattle poisoning was inserted in his second bill in the course of discussion in the Council. F.S. Chapman summing up the purpose of the bill in the final discussion on 15 October 1874 remarked as follows:

> this principle of [joint] responsibility has been laid down for the first time in the case of the crime of cattle poisoning of which the mhars of the villages are often believed to be guilty, either from motives of revenge on account of non-payment of their dues, or in order to obtain the skins of the animals. This is a crime which is most difficult to detect and punish, and which entails the most ruinous consequences on the ryots. I believe the very guarded provision which we have made is most necessary, and I hope it may prove effectual.[9]

Thus, it seems that conflicts and disputes between Vatandar Mahars and peasants had risen to such a high pitch as to make poisoning of peasants' cattle by Mahars a frequent occurrence.

Disputes between Vatandar Mahars and Peasants

Here, the process of the intensification of tension between Vatandar Mahars and peasants is traced through the legal decisions handed down by the Bombay High Court concerning the Mahar Vatan. Section 18 of the Bombay Hereditary Offices Act provided a procedure for granting awards by a *panchayat* with regard to disputes between peasants and village *vatandars* lower than *patel* and *kulkarni*. Still, however, some law suits were brought to civil courts based on various causes of action or misunderstanding.

In 1885, four Vatandar Mahars of a certain village in Belgaum District sued five Vatandar Mangs and ten peasants of the same village for proclaiming a declaration to Mangs to the effect that the right to take *aya* (a perquisite) which wrongfully had been given to Mangs by the peasants belonged to Vatandar Mahars and an injunction against the peasants to the effect that they should not give *aya* to Vatandar Mangs. In opposition to this allegation, Vatandar Mangs claimed that they were also *vatandars* of the village and performed the duties concomitant to their *vatan* so that they had the same right as that of Vatandar Mahars to take *aya* from villagers. The peasants contended that Vatandar Mangs had the same right to take *aya* as Vatandar Mahars with some peasants giving it to Vatandar Mahars and some others to Vatandar Mangs. The Judge in the first instance held that Vatandar Mangs were intruders of the right of Vatandar Mahars and that Vatandar Mahars were entitled to the relief claimed. From this decree, the defendants appealed to the District Court of Belgaum on the ground that this suit was not cognizable for the civil courts under the provisions of the Bombay Hereditary Offices Act. The District Judge held that the suit was barred under Section 18 of the Act which provided a *panchayat* as a means of giving awards in cases of disputes of this kind and reversed the decree of the lower court. Standing against this decree, the plaintiffs appealed to the Bombay High Court which confirmed the decree made by the District Judge.[10]

This dispute seemed to take place owing to the action of peasants to exclude Vatandar Mahars from their office by taking Vatandar Mangs to their side when tension between Vatandar Mahars and peasants heightened. The remarkable point of this decision reached by the Bombay High Court was that not only disputes between Vatandar Mahars and peasants but also those between Vatandar Mahars and Vatandar Mangs were held to be awarded by a *panchayat* or at the discretion of the Collector. This must have been due to the understanding of the Court that the main confrontation was between Vatandar Mahars and peasants involving Vatandar Mangs as the secondary participants. As mentioned in my foregoing essay printed in this volume, the confrontation between Vatandar Mahars and peasants cum Vatandar Mangs had been rather the usual pattern of contention since the Maratha period.

In 1892, all of the peasants of the village Chinchodi, Ahmadnagar District, decided to remove Vatandar Mahars from providing the services for the village and villagers and to employ Mangs in their place. In 1894, after two years had passed under this state of affairs, a meeting of peasants was held at the house of the *patel* to consider the restoration of Vatandar Mahars to their duties. It was therefore agreed in the meeting that the latter should be restored to their office on condition of payment of Rs. 300 supposed to be for the repair of village temples. This payment was, in fact, the fine for suspected poisoning of certain cattle by Mahars during the period of suspension of their services. Vatandar Mahars also agreed with this condition and paid the sum to the *patel* through a village *vani*.

Thus Vatandar Mahars were to be restored to their office but only after the *patel* was prosecuted under Section 161 (bribery) of the Indian Penal Code (Act XXXXV of 1860) on his receiving this Rs. 300 from Vatandar Mahars. The reason for his prosecution was that as it was a part of the *patel*'s performance of official duties as a superior to restore Vatandar Mahars to their office, the *patel* who took Rs. 300 for this restoration was therefore considered to have committed the crime of bribery. Against this judgement, the *patel* and villagers contended that they had excluded Vatandar Mahars from their 'private services' to the villagers and not from their 'public services' as the hereditary village servants. And this time, they restored Vatandar Mahars to their 'private services' so that this did not comprise the performance of official duties by the *patel* even though he took part in the restoration of Vatandar Mahars. In the Bombay High Court, the *patel* was subsequently sentenced to pay a fine of Rs. 10 on the ground that Vatandar Mahars' 'public services' and 'private services' could not be distinctly separated and, in fact, that the *patel* had removed Vatandar Mahars from the essentially public function of carrying the village revenue to the District Office during the period of suspension. Thus, a reconciliation between Vatandar Mahars and peasants through the payment of Rs. 300 by the former was broken.[11]

In 1911, a dispute between Vatandar Mahars and peasants in the village Peth, Satara District, again involved Mangs of the village. Vatandar Mahars alleged that peasants of two hamlets (branch villages) of Peth had given the skins of dead animals to Mangs intruding on the rights of Vatandar Mahars. On this allegation,Vatandar Mahars asked for an award of the Deputy Collector of Satara District who ordered a Mamlatdar to inquire into the case and submit a report to him. The Mamlatdar asked for the Deputy Collector's sanction to constitute a *panchayat* for the award which was given. He appointed his Head Karkun as the *sar-panch* and ordered both parties to nominate two *panchs* respectively. The Vatandar Mahars nominated them but the peasants rejected their nomination. Resultantly, the Mamlatdar nominated the *panchs* himself. On 22 January 1912, the *panchayat* awarded in favour of Vatandar Mahars, and the Deputy Collector approved the award and ordered the Mamlatdar to take action in accordance with the award. But the legality of this procedure was examined in the civil courts and, in the end, the Bombay High Court decided the award as invalid on the ground that the procedure for making the award did not substantially comply with the provisions of Section 18 of the Bombay Hereditary Offices Act.[12]

This case clearly denotes that the system of granting awards by a *panchayat* as spelled out in Section 18 of the Act did not function satisfactorily.

TOWARD THE ABOLITION OF THE MAHAR VATAN

Discussions in the Bombay Legislative Council

In the 1920s, various demands brought forward by Vatandar Mahars were being discussed more often than before in the Bombay Legislative Council. Initially, the Council started with a small number of members as a kind of advisory body of the Governor of Bombay, but in the second half of the nineteenth century and the early part of the next, the Indian Councils Act was revised several times through which the Legislative Council of each of the Presidencies or States was enlarged to include Indian members recommended from various bodies. Through the Government of India Act of 1919 (the so-called Montagu-Chelmsford Reform), representatives of the 'Depressed Classes' which included the depressed castes formerly known as the untouchables as well as tribes, were nominated to the Legislative Assembly of the Centre and the Legislative Council of each of the Presidencies or States. In the case of the Bombay Presidency, two members of the Depressed Classes were nominated by the Governor of Bombay. In January 1921, the first session of the new and enlarged Bombay Legislative Council commenced in which representatives of the Depressed Classes took their seats for the first time in the history of the Bombay Legislative Council. This resulted in the demands of Vatandar Mahars being discussed in the Council with ever greater frequency.

On 26 February 1923, D.D. Gholap presented a resolution to the Legislative Council which was very implicative though very short: 'That this Council recommends to the Government the commutation of the Maharki vatan.'[13]

Gholap was a veteran leader of the Mahar community and as such became the first member from the Depressed Classes to be nominated to the Bombay Legislative Council. The 'commutation' referred to in his resolution, as an administrative term, meant the procedure for relieving hereditary officers from their duties in return for enhancement of tax levied on the lands which had been held by them as the service *inam* lands that had been the tax-exempt or priviledged tenure. But what Gholap asked for was to relieve Vatandar Mahars from their duties on condition that the full assessment be levied on the Mahar Vatan lands the same as on the *raiyatwari* lands of peasants. On Mahar Vatan lands only a small sum called *judi* had been levied formerly. This procedure of relieving *vatandars* from duties was, in administrative terms, known as 'resumption' and not 'commutation' as a government member pointed out in the discussion. The 'resumption' meant the procedure to resume the *inam* lands which had been exempt from land tax or held on a nominal levy paid to the government as ordinary *raiyatwari* land under full assessment. The difference between commutation and resumption was that, in the case of commutation, a reduced rate of land tax was still levied on the commuted lands.

Gholap explained the reason of his presenting the resolution as follows:

> There is a tendency to be seen in all parts of the Presidency on the part of the ryots to say 'Mahars are Government servants, why should we pay them for nothing?' On the other hand, Government had declared that the Mahars are not full-time and salaried servants of Government, and that they do not come within the category of Government servants. But what is the real fact? The Mahars are not Government servants, neither do they serve the ryots: they serve the village officers and their relatives in the name of public business, rather than the Government. . . . They are

engaged day and night in doing the private work of the *patel* and *talati*, being under their influence.[14]

Gholap cited his personal experience as an example that Vatandar Mahars were busily involved with the private works of the *patel* and *kulkarni*. In 1910, Gholap was in his village as his high school was on vacation when the *patel* of his village called for his father, a Vatandar Mahar of the village. As his father was busy with sowing in the field at that time he presented himself to the place of the *patel*. The *patel* ordered him to cut bamboos and carry them to his relative's place in a village nearly eight miles' distance. Bamboo was urgently needed for the Dasara festival to be held in the evening of that particular day. Accordingly Gholap hurried along a hilly road with his friends shouldering a bundle of long bamboo. But as it got dark halfway to the village, he missed a step and tumbled down from the edge of the road, badly injuring himself.[15]

As this personal experience denotes, it was very difficult to separate the public duties of Vatandar Mahars from the private service asked for by the *patel* and others. Beside, Vatandar Mahars were ordered to serve at any time, day or night, so that for them the concept of working hours was not applicable. Further, not only Vatandar Mahars themselves but their family, wives and sons, were compelled to work. This state of affairs had made the life of Vatandar Mahars a very difficult one. Gholap finished the explanation of his resolution with the following remarks:

> The Vatandar mahars are now quite tired of it and there is no resource left to them to defend themselves against their miserable state except the commutation of their watans. Government have commuted the kulkarni watans of about 7,000 villages in the Central and Southern Divisions alone. Also a native state in the Deccan has commuted the Maharki watan by which the Mahars of that state are more happy than they were before. On the same basis, I beg to urge upon the Government the necessity of the commutation of the Maharki watan, as it is found that the duties of the Mahars, as part-time village servants, are too laborious, that their remuneration for these services is too low, and that the numbers generally requisitioned by the village officers to do the duties are too large.[16]

The commutation of the Kulkarni Vatan mentioned here by

Gholap was the policy of the Bombay government carried out rather forcedly in the closing decades of the nineteenth and early part of the twentieth centuries. Vatandar Kulkarnis were dismissed from their hereditary offices and replaced by *talatis* who were employed by the government without hereditary rights. By this time, as the existence of hereditary officers like Vatandar Kulkarni had become undesirable even for local administration, the Bombay government endeavoured to get rid of them by means of commutating their *vatan*. It thus seems that due to a misunderstanding, Gholap referred to the commutation of the Kulkarni Vatan as a boon to them since a majority of Vatandar Kulkarnis complained about it.

Gholap also mentioned the commutation of the Mahar Vatan in 'a native state in the Deccan'. He indicated the princely state of Kolhapur where Shahu II, a famous leader of the Non-Brahmin Movement in the Deccan, abolished the Kulkarni Vatan in 1913 and then in 1918 relieved Vatandar Mahars from their duties on the condition of levying the full assessment on the *inam* lands of Vatandar Mahars. Thus by this time, the Vatan System had begun to change in various aspects and from various causes leaving only the Mahar Vatan maintained intact under British colonial rule.

Gholap's resolution aimed at calling attention of the members of the Bombay Legislative Council to these points. His resolution was supported by many Indian members of the Council but was ultimately withdrawn in the face of stiff opposition from government members. The causes of opposition were, first, that the enforcement of the commutation of the Mahar Vatan must be 'forcing upon the Mahars a policy which will be extremely hard to a majority of them', and, second, that if the commutation of the Mahar Vatan were to be carried into effect, the government would have to employ a great number of 'stipendiary servants' to replace Vatandar Mahars, which would be quite difficult for the government to accomplish due to the financial stringency prevailing at the time. Of these causes, the first was, to some degree, grounded since a certain portion of Vatandar Mahars objected to the abolition of the Mahar Vatan. The second cause meant that the Bombay government confessed inadvertently that they had been making Vatandar Mahars work for a very undervalued rate of payment. This financial concern continued to be the greatest cause of opposition to the commutation of the Mahar Vatan.

In the new session of the Bombay Legislative Council beginning in February 1924, R.S. Nekaljay played an active part as a representative of the Depressed Classes. On 24 July of the same year, R.S. Nekaljay and several other members asked questions such as the following, regarding the Mahar Vatan:

> Nekaljay: (a) Will Government be pleased to state whether they are aware of several resolutions passed at public meetings of the depressed classes requesting Government to grant an immediate increase in the monthly salary of every watandar Mahar in the Presidency? (b) Will Government be pleased to state the duties which a watandar Mahar is required to perform in a village and his working hours?
>
> [Government]: (a) Yes. (b) The principal duties of Mahars are to watch boundary marks and village office (chavdi); to carry Government letters and remittance to the taluka treasury, to sweep the village roads, to keep an eye on all Government property, trees, etc., to serve as a village guide and to help Government officers passing through the village, and to obey the orders of village officers in the discharge of Government duties. The Mahars are not full-time servants of Government and therefore no working hours have been fixed in their case.
>
> R.D. Shinde: Is it not a fact that all these multifarious duties take up the whole day?
>
> [Government]: No; I don't think so.
>
> M.D.Karki: Are they to watch the boundary marks of every village occupant?
>
> [Government]: Yes; I believe so.
>
> S.S. Dev: If the boundary marks are to be watched by them, will it not require their attention for full 24 hours?
>
> [Government]: I do not think boundary marks easily disappear, so I do not think it requires full 24 hours' attention.
>
> S.S. Dev: Are they to keep their eyes on the trees for 24 hours?
>
> [Government]: During the time they are awake I think they have a chance of keeping an eye on them.[17]

Through discussions it became clear that even the government did not grasp the exact extent of the duties of Vatandar Mahars as the government corrected its answer by admitting that the watching of boundary demarcating lands of peasants was not a duty of Vatandar Mahars but that of the peasants themselves.[18]

Nekaljay presented various resolutions concerning the Mahars or the Depressed Classes and demanded that the government seek a solution to the problems pointed out in his resolutions. On 14 August

1925, he presented a resolution to the effect that: (1) 'a limited number of watandar Mahars should be kept in each district of the presidency and that they should be paid at the rate of Rs. 15 rising to Rs. 20 per month', and (2) 'the inam lands at present held by watandar Mahars in the various districts should be continued free of assessment to the present holders in return for the long and meritorious services rendered to government by them and their ancestors'.[19] The second demand meant that Vatandar Mahars should retain their *inam* lands as tax-exempt lands even though their services were done away with. Thus, Nekaljay demanded a much more favourable dealing for Vatandar Mahars than the 'commutation' ('resumption') of the Mahar Vatan demanded by Gholap.

In a resolution also presented on 4 November 1925, Nekaljay asked the government to institute a semiofficial committee to inquire into the problems concerning Vatandār Mahars and Dheds of Gujarat.[20] Nekaljay also presented another resolution asking the Bombay government 'to recommend to the Imperial government to make necessary provisions as early as possible to form a full Mahar battalion or a Mahar company in each of the Indian regiments'.[21] As I mentioned in my foregoing essay in this volume, Mahars well acquitted themselves as daring mountain soldiers and played an important role in the state building by Shivaji, making many Mahars recruited even in the early stage of British colonial rule. But by the end of the nineteenth century, recruitment of Mahars was suspended probably under the influence of the 'Martial Races' theory. During World War I, recruitment of Mahars was resumed due to the strained military conditions, but with the termination of the War this practice was again suspended. As the case of the father of Ambedkar indicates, improvement of the social status of Mahars largely depended on one's military career, so that the demand for resumption of recruitment was strong among Mahars.

On 5 November 1925, Nekaljay presented another resolution to the Bombay Legislative Council:

> The Council recommends to the Governor in Council to prohibit by law the practice prevailing among certain classes of eating the flesh of dead animals keeping intact the right to take out the skin of dead animals.[22]

Nekaljay had already presented a resolution of the same purpose on 15 August 1925 focusing mainly on Mahars. As mentioned in my foregoing essay, Mahars not only skinned the dead animals but made use of their flesh as food. By this time, however, a strong argument was put forward that the 'eating of the flesh of dead animals' was the cause of discrimination toward Mahars. For this reason, Nekaljay presented a resolution recommending that the government prohibit by law the eating of the flesh of dead animals..

All of the resolutions presented by Nekaljay were withdrawn or voted down except one concerning the recruitment of Mahars. However, it should not be underestimated that the problems regarding Mahars or the Depressed Classes were discussed in almost all sessions of the Bombay Legislative Council. It must have been on this groundwork that Ambedkar was able to play an active role as the representative of the Depressed Classes in the new session of the Bombay Legislative Council beginning in January 1927.

Ambedkar in the Bombay Legislative Council

B.R. Ambedkar was nominated as the representative of the Depressed Classes of the Bombay Legislative Council in 1927. He focused his activities in the Council toward the revision of the Bombay Hereditary Offices Act for improving the living conditions of the Vatandar Mahars. Ambedkar introduced a bill (Bill XII of 1928) to amend the Bombay Hereditary Offices Act on 19 March 1928. The 'statement of objects and reasons' of his bill ran as follows:

1. To make better provision for the remuneration of the officiating watandars.
2. To allow commutation of watans of inferior hereditary village servants.
3. To provide for the conversion of Baluta into a money cess.
4. To allow the holder of inferior watan to free himself from the obligations to serve the ryots.
5. To define the duties of officiating watandars.[23]

This order of the 'objects and reasons' is somewhat confusing. To rearrange them, they can be divided into two parts. The first part constitutes the second clause that demanded the commutation of *vatans* and the second part relates to the first, third, fourth and fifth clauses for improving the lives of *vatandars*. These two parts constitute separate and parallel demands.

Ambedkar made the concept of 'freedom of contract' the leading principle of dealing with the problems of Vatandar Mahars:

> What my bill aims at is freedom of contract; if the ryots do not want to employ the Mahars, they ought to have perfect liberty not to employ them, and if the Mahars do not want to serve, the Mahars should have perfect liberty not to serve.[24]

On this principle, he wanted to revise the Bombay Hereditary Offices Act in the dual direction of improving the conditions of Vatandar Mahars who wished to be relieved from their duties as well as of those who wished to remain in the Vatandar Mahar office. Thus, he intended to meet the demand of the former category of Vatandar Mahars through the commutation of the Mahar Vatan (the second clause of his bill) and of the latter category through the first, third, fourth and fifth clauses of his bill.

With regard to the commutation of Mahar Vatan, Ambedkar's bill proposed to insert a provision of the following purpose to Section 15 of the Act. If 'the whole body of representative watandars or a majority of them' agreed, they could be 'relieved of their obligations to perform such services in perpetuity' by a written application to the Collector, and in that case they should be 'entitled to retain possession of the lands held by them if they agree to pay full survey assessment on such lands'.[25] This was, in essence, the same as the purpose of the resolution presented by Gholap.

The ground for opposition by the government to the commutation of the Mahar Vatan was the financial stringency as was the case with Gholap's resolution. J. Ghosal, the Commissioner of the Central Division, estimated the cost needed for the commutation of the Mahar Vatan as follows. Roughly there were 10,000 villages in the Central Division in which there were in all nearly 50,000 officiating inferior village servants. This number could be reduced to the absolute minimum of 24,000 by replacing them with stipendiary servants. The cost needed to pay this number of stipendiary servants was about Rs. 2,900,000 at the rate of Rs. 10 per month per person. On the other hand, financial gains of the commutation of the Mahar Vatan constituted the balance (in administrative terms, *nuksan* meaning the loss) between the full survey assessment on Mahar Vatan lands and the *judi* formerly paid by Vatandar Mahars. This balance was estimated to be only Rs. 500,000. Thus, for the commutation of the Mahar Vatan a new financial burden of Rs. 2,400,000 was needed in the Central Division alone which only had to be met by levying a new cess on the lands of 'poor agriculturists' or by government finance. This burden was too heavy for the agriculturists as well as, it turns out, for the government.[26]

Regardless of the accuracy of his estimate, the point was that the government itself acknowledged the fact that it had been paying only Rs. 500,000 for the services of Vatandar Mahars estimated to cost Rs. 2,900,000 if performed by stipendiary servants.

The Bombay government was, however, not favourably disposed to giving up its right to get this free service from Vatandar Mahars. As this fact indicates, the Mahar Vatan represented something like a miracle for the government. Thus, it was quite natural that Gholap, Nekaljay and Ambedkar repeatedly demanded the commutation of the Mahar Vatan.

However, Ambedkar was largely mistaken if he expected to be able to relieve Vatandar Mahars from their services to the village community or villagers by the commutation of the Mahar Vatan. As mentioned before, the commutation would serve to change the relation between *vatandars* and the state alone. To alter the relation between *vatandars* and the village community or the villagers, however, Section 16 of the Act had to be amended, but Ambedkar's bill did not include a provision for this amendment.

With regard to the demands of Vatandar Mahars who wanted to remain in the office of Vatandar Mahar, Ambedkar's bill proposed the revisions of the following purposes to the Bombay Hereditary Offices Act corresponding respectively to the first, third and fourth clauses of his bill.

1. 'To make better provision for the remuneration of the officiating watandars', the transfer of Mahar Vatan lands must be nullified even though it took place before the enforcement of the Bombay Hereditary Offices Act to cope with the situation that many Mahar Vatan lands were transferred into the hands of money lenders.

In the discussion held by the Council, strong opposition was put forward that it should entail a loss only to the present landholders after several transfers of the lands. Ambedkar himself was forced to acknowledge this.

2. 'To provide for the conversion of Baluta into a money cess', the Government should levy a money cess corresponding to *balute* along with other taxes and deliver it to Vatandar Mahars since *balute* taken directly from the villagers by Vatandar Mahars has been the main cause of the disputes between these two parties.

In the discussion, it was argued that this procedure was too much trouble for the government and too heavy a burden for the villagers.

3. 'To allow the holder of inferior watan to free himself from the obligations to serve the ryots', it is expedient to separate the portion of the money cess which is supposed to be the reward for the services to the village community or villagers from that portion which is supposed to be the reward for rendering services to the state and to relieve Vatandar Mahars from rendering services to the village community or villagers on condition that the former portion of the money cess be relinquished by Vatandar Mahars.

In the discussion, an argument was put forward against this action that it was not practicable due to the difficulty of separating the two portions of the duties of Vatandar Mahars.

Thus, Ambedkar's concrete proposals met with strong opposition. Furthermore, Ambedkar was criticized that he himself contradicted his own principle of 'freedom of contract' by keeping the interests of Mahars alone in mind without giving any attention to the interests of the villagers. Ambedkar himself conceded to this criticism.

Despite the strong opposition and criticism, however, Ambedkar's bill was referred to the Select Committee. It was the general procedure of the Council to refer the bill to the Select Committee when agreement had been reached on the main portions of the bill but the details were yet to be scrutinized. However, in the case of Ambedkar's bill, even agreement with the main portions of the bill had not been reached. Yet in spite of this, his bill was referred to the Select Committee on his approval that he would accept even a modification of the principle of the bill as a result of the discussion.[27] The Select Committee comprised 15 members which, besides Ambedkar, included government members such as three Division Commissioners and Indian members like S.K. Bole and P.G. Solanki. The Select Committee was to submit a report to the Council by the beginning of June 1929.

However, as this procedure of referring his bill to the Select Committee was too exceptional to produce a satisfactory result, Ambedkar was finally obliged to withdraw it. Thus, the first endeavour of Ambedkar to improve the life conditions of Vatandar Mahars through the revision of the Bombay Hereditary Offices Act ended in failure. Subsequently, Ambedkar again introduced a bill of a similiar purpose to the Council in 1937, but under the stringent situation prevalent just before World War II he was compelled to suspend his activities. Thus, the problem of the abolition of the Mahar Vatan was carried over to the post-independence period.

CONCLUSION

On 15 August 1947, India gained its independence though in the form of the Partition. On 29 August of the same year, the Drafting Committee of the Constituent Assembly started to function with Ambedkar as its Chairman. On 26 November 1949, the Constitution of India passed the Assembly and came into force on 26 January 1950 of which Article 17 provided the abolition of untouchability. In 1955, the Untouchability (Offences) Act was enacted to put into practice the constitutional abolition of untouchability. In line with this overall movement against social discrimination after gaining independence, the Mahar Vatan was at last abolished by the Bombay Inferior Village Vatan Abolition Act of 1958.

NOTES

1 In this essay, technical terms of Indian languages are printed in italics without any diacritical marks while proper nouns, like the name of persons, castes or offices, are printed in initial upper case letters. In the case of quotations, original texts are preserved without any alteration or correction.

2 For the Elphinstone Code, see R. Clarke, *The Regulations of the Government of Bombay in Force at the End of 1850 to which are added, the Acts of Government of India in Force at That Presidency*, London, 1851.

3 This Act is not the Act of the Bombay government but of the Government of India. The Presidency governments were deprived of the legislative right by the renewed Charter Act of 1833. The legislative right of the Presidency governments was restored by the Indian Councils Act of 1861.

4 *Reports of Civil Cases Determined in the Court of Sudder Dewanee*

Adawlut of Bombay 1840 to 1848, compiled by A.F. Bellasis, 1850, pp. 8ff.

5 *Cases Disposed of by the Sudder Dewanee Adawlut of Bombay*, vol. IV, 1857, compiled by James Morris, 1857, pp. 111ff.

6 *Selected Decisions of the Court of Sudder Dewanee Adawlut of Bombay*, Part II, 1848–1850, compiled by James Morris, 1852, pp. 68ff.

7 *Reports of Cases Decided in the High Court of Bombay*, vol. VIII (Appellate Civil Jurisdiction), 1871, pp. 28ff.

8 *Proceedings of the Council of the Governor of Bombay*, 1874, vol. XII, p. 94.

9 *Proceedings of the Council of the Governor of Bombay*, 1874, vol. XIII, p. 56.

10 Parsha *v.* Lagmya, 13 B. 83. (*Indian Law Reports, Bombay Series* is commonly abbreviated as B. with the volume number before B. and the page number whence the case starts after B. Therefore, 13 B. 83 denotes the case reported in *Indian Law Reports, Bombay Series*, vol. 13, pp. 83ff.)

11 Imperatrix *v.* Appaji, 21 B. 517.

12 Mahadu *v.* Krishna, 47 B. 95.

13 *Bombay Legislative Council Debates*, vol. VIII, 1923-2-26, p. 369.

14 Ibid., p. 370.

15 Ibid., p. 371.

16 Ibid., p. 373.

17 *Bombay Legislative Council Debates*, vol. XII, 1924-7-24, pp. 291–92.

18 *Bombay Legislative Council Debates*, vol. XVII, 1926-2-26, p. 370.

19 *Bombay Legislative Council Debates*, vol. XV, 1925-8-14, p. 1383.

20 *Bombay Legislative Council Debates*, vol. XVI, 1925-11-4, p. 739.

21 Ibid., 1925-11-5, p. 783.

22 Ibid., p. 770.

23 *Bombay Legislative Council Debates*, vol. XVIII, 1928, Appendix 17, p. 1084.

24 Ibid., 1928-8-3, p. 718.

25 Ibid., Appendix 17, pp. 1082–83.

26 Ibid., 1928-8-3, p. 723.

27 Ibid., 1928-8-4, p. 791.

III

Liberation Movements of the Depressed Castes

8

Introduction

Circumstances Surrounding and Problems Underlying Liberation Movements of the Depressed Castes

MASAO NAITO

Article 338 of the Indian Constitution which came into effect in January 1950 stipulates that the President is to appoint 'a Special Officer for the Scheduled Castes and Scheduled Tribes' whose duty is 'to investigate all matters relating to the safeguards provided for the Scheduled Castes and Scheduled Tribes under this Constitution and report to the President upon the working of those safeguards'. Needless to say, the term 'Scheduled Castes' mentioned here was initially adopted by the Government of India Act, 1935[1] and afterward by the Constitution of independent India to enable certain preferential treatment to be offered to people who were commonly called 'untouchables' or 'depressed classes'. Ordinarily, however, the term 'harijan', meaning 'son of god', initially used by Mahatma Gandhi during his anti-untouchability movement spearheaded in the 1930s, has been preferred for quite some time, and more recently 'dalit', a Marathi (or Hindi) word equivalent to 'depressed', has come into more frequent use.

According to the above-mentioned provision stated in the Constitution, L.M. Shrikant was appointed Commissioner for Scheduled Castes and Scheduled Tribes in November 1950 and submitted the first report of the commission in July 1952, in the introduction of which he stated:

> A remarkable change is coming over public feeling and untouchability has during the last thirty years received a death blow, from which it will never recover, through the Herculean efforts of Mahatma Gandhi to fight the demon of untouchability. The movement started by Mahatma Gandhi is still continuing.[2]

The statement reflects an air of optimism and elation and a naive feeling of laudation to the Father of the Nation in the post-independence days. But, ironically in a sense, the succeeding volumes of the Commissioner's yearly report continue to publicise not only the constructive achievements brought about for the uplifting of Scheduled Castes and Scheduled Tribes in many fields but also the realities of various discriminatory practices still persisting doggedly in many parts of India.

Moreover, we know through various newspaper articles that the number of more brutal atrocities inflicted upon the depressed (dalits) than those incidents mentioned in the Commissioner's annual reports rather increased after the independence. To cite a few instances, some Brahman landlords of Keelavenmani Village in Thanjavur District, Tamil Nadu, attacked and burnt alive more than 40 persons from families of Scheduled Caste agricultural labourers by using hired goondas in December 1968,[3] and a group of high-caste landlords of a village in Gaya District, Bihar, slaughtered 10 Scheduled Caste peasants in December 1991.[4]

One of the more prominent characteristics of these atrocities committed against Scheduled Caste members is that besides caste problems some sort of economic factors involving land or wages can be distinctly observed to underlie these incidents. This can be said to be rather a new tendency after the independence. As may be well imagined, however, there is no end to the examples that could be cited of straightforward exclusion of and discrimination against Scheduled Castes.

It was once the usual practice in most Indian villages for caste Hindus to prohibit untouchables from entering Hindu temples and utilising common wells, and the elimination of this form of discrimination was one of the important goals to be achieved for anti-untouchability movements in the pre-independence period. But even at present, five decades after the independence, almost the same situation remains in various parts of India.[5]

According to an extensive survey conducted in four districts of Marathwada, Maharashtra State, in May 1991, dalits are not allowed to enter Hindu temples in 75 out of a total of 95 villages surveyed and in 81 villages they cannnot go into the houses of upper castes. Furthermore, the burial grounds of dalits and caste Hindus are separated from each other in all of these villages.

The report cites many instances where dalits have been insulted, beaten up and socially boycotted by upper-caste villagers if they tried to enter a temple. Such incidents also add to the deplorable misery predominant in Maharashtra which claims to be a 'progressive' state, blessed by a succession of great leaders of social reform and the anti-untouchability movement like J.G. Phule and B.R. Ambedkar, and suggests that constitutional equality exists merely on paper.[6]

This state of affairs, however, does not mean that the history of the anti-untouchability movements launched by many individuals and organisations since the pre-independence period can be interpreted as a record of failures though undeniably there have been and continue to be many difficulties underlying this problem. There is no doubt that one of the main factors behind these atrocities perpetrated against Scheduled Castes by caste Hindus in independent India has been the latter's jealousy of and resentment toward various preferential measures extended to the former and economic and social improvements enjoyed by some members of Scheduled Caste communities. Moreover, the endeavours of Scheduled Caste groups to arouse self-awareness as 'dalits' among their fellow members and to organize themselves politically sometimes exacerbated a sense of crisis among caste Hindus and drove them to trample the efforts of the former.

We certainly cannot neglect the fact that in many parts of rural India, as in the aforementioned case of Marathwada, the majority of Scheduled Caste inhabitants have to face appalling poverty as landless agricultural labourers under the situation where land reforms are not being effectively formulated and implemented. At the same time, we can also note that the rate of literacy among the whole of the Scheduled Caste population now exceeds 37 per cent and that the arising new middle class in their communities has been the result of the reservation policy for them in education and employment following the independence.[7]

Of interest is the fact that most members of the Bahujan Samaj Party (BSP) which emerged in 1984 are principally from this very stratum. The party demonstrated its expanded strength in the assembly elections of November 1993 in the northern states and joined the state government of Uttar Pradesh led by the Samajwadi Party (SP) which is mainly backed by the rural backward castes. After breaking with the SP, the BSP singly formed the state government in June 1995 with the support of the Bharatiya Janta Party (BJP) from outside the cabinet, whose withdrawal of support to the BSP led its retreat from the cabinet in October 1995.

Though the question emerges concerning BSP's alliance with a reactionary and communal party like the BJP, the emergence of the BSP as a party representing the political aspirations of the Scheduled Caste masses is of no less historical significance. In Maharashtra also it is reported that various dalit parties and groups are now trying to merge into a unified force.[8] This state has a long history of post-independence anti-untouchability agitations fomented under the leadership of the Republican Party of India established in 1957 according to the last wishes of Ambedkar and the Dalit Panthers formed in 1969 by a radical group of young dalits. These parties, however, could not bring about effective results for the emancipation of the whole dalit community because of the frequently occurring factional conflicts and divisions.

A strong solidarity among these dalit forces which is now being sought will not only strike a blow against the strategy of the caste-Hindu-led political parties to appease Scheduled Castes as a 'vote bank' but also offer a good chance to reflect on the anti-untouchability movement anew along the ideals of Ambedkar. Maharashtra is also known as the birthplace of the 'Dalit Sahitya'. This new genre of literature created by dalits, both male and female, has played an important role in opening up a new arena in the history of the dalit liberation movement through the candid expressiveness of every kind of inequality and injustice surrounding these writers. Moreover, its influence has been spreading beyond the boundary of languages per se.

There is no gainsaying that the present stage of the anti-untouchability movement is still fraught with many difficulties. The drastic land reform is only one of the prerequisites essential to the economic improvement of conditions for agricultural labourers the majority of whom are Scheduled Castes.[9] Moreover, as has been mentioned earlier an important problem at issue is how the movement will be confronted with the reality of economic and social stratification among Scheduled Caste communities.

Political parties like the BSP in Uttar Pradesh which has recently extended its influence also confront some notable problems such as the meshing of interests with the OBC forces, the rapid expansion of cooperation with other similar parties and organisations in the areas beyond the 'Hindi Belt' of north India, the strengthening of the organisation without the need for retaining it under the limited leadership, and how its relationship will develop with the movement of adivasis (Scheduled Tribes).[10]

NOTES

1 It was in the Government of India (Scheduled Castes) Order, 1936, enacted in April 1936 according to the Government of India Act, 1935, that the province-wise list of names of 'scheduled' castes was publicly announced for the first time.

2 L.M. Shrikant, *Report of the Commissioner for Scheduled Castes and Scheduled Tribes for the Period Ending 31st December, 1951,* Govt. of India Press, New Delhi, 1952, p. 2.

3 Initially most of the newspapers reported the incident in Keelavenmani as a clash between peasants led by the Communist Party of India (Marxist) and those opposing them [*The Statesman* (Weekly), 28 Dec. 1968]. But as its background became gradually clearer, the relationship between Scheduled Caste agricultural labourers demanding a wage increase and upper-caste landlords suppressing this demand rose to the surface.

4 On the night of 23 Dec. 1991, 10 Scheduled Caste (harijan) landless agricultural labourers were murdered in two villages of Gaya District, Bihar, by a group calling itself the Savarna Liberation Front. Here also of note is that there was animosity among upper-caste gentry against harijan peasants who went on strike for higher wages (*The Times of India*, 30 Dec. 1991,.3 Jan. 1992). After this another incident happened on 13 Feb. 1992, in a different village of the same district in which harijan supporters of the Maoist Communist Centre killed 37 caste Hindus. This was reported to be done in revenge for the previous murders (*The Times of India*, 14 Feb. 1992, R.R. Lal, 'Exploding caste volcano in Bihar', *Illustrated Weekly of India,* 29 Feb.–6 March 1992, pp. 8–11).

5 The Dalit Panthers, a radical dalit group in Maharashtra, includes in its programmes the demand for permission for dalits to draw water from the public wells (Barbara R. Joshi, ed., *Untouchable: Voices of the Dalit Liberation Movement*, London, 1986, p. 146).

6 *The Times of India,* 3 Sept. 1991. Almost the same is reported in the states of Tamil Nadu, Rajasthan and Gujarat as well (*The Times of India,* 15 Sept. 1991).

7 M. Raman and Z. Agha, 'Dalits: A new assertiveness', *India Today,* 30 April 1994, pp. 28-29.

8 *The Times of India*, 26 Dec. 1995.

9 *The Times of India,* 5 Sept. 1991, V.R. Mani, 'Political steps needed to liberate Dalits', *The Times of India*, 14 Nov. 1991.

10 T. Horimoto, 'Politicisation of Scheduled Castes in independent India', in M. Naito, ed., *Anti-Untouchability Ideologies and Movements in Modern India* ('Caste System and the Depressed' Series, vol. 3, in Japanese), Akashi Shoten Publishers, Tokyo, 1994, pp. 357–58.

9

Some Aspects of the Tiyyas' 'Caste' Movement with Special Reference to British Malabar

TOSHIE AWAYA

INTRODUCTION

In his autobiography, Cherukat (1914–76), the Malayalam writer from South Malabar, narrates an interesting episode. Although he belonged to the high caste called Pisharodi (one of the temple service castes, Ambalavasis), he had a Tiyya friend named Chami. One day in the 1920s, he first heard the name of Sri Narayana Guru (1854/56–1928) from this friend. This guru preached that there was only one god and had constructed temples more magnificent than the one in Cherukat. (Cherukat is the place name as well.) According to Chami, he was superior to Sankaracharya. Guru's first disciple was Chinna Swami—Kumaran Asan (1873–1924) was known by this popular name. Chinna Swami was a noted poet as well. Chami predicted that caste 'pollution' would disappear in future. When Cherukat was told that this guru was a Tiyya, he burst into a laughter with the remark 'a Tiyya Swami!'. Undaunted, Chami questioned whether such an ignorant who did not know about Guru or Chinna Swami deserved to be called 'Thampuran' (honorific term used by an inferior while addressing a superior caste). Thus, Cherukat borrowed Kumaran Asan's works from Chami.[1]

Sri Narayana Guru and Kumaran Asan are well-known figures in Kerala modern history. The former was a spiritual leader of the Tiyyas' 'caste' movement and the latter was one of the great trio in Malayalam modern poetry and the first General Secretary of the Sri Narayana Dharma Paripalana Yogam (Association for the Protection of the Dharma of Sri Narayana, hereafter Yogam). The Yogam was founded in 1903 with Narayana Guru as its President.

There is no wanting of the scholarly studies on the many

movements claiming to address the needs of particular 'castes' in different places throughout India. Among these, Tiyyas' movement has continued to attract considerable interest of the scholars. These studies to date have generally focused on analyzing Guru's religious and social ideas and the development of the Yogam. Consequently, the area covered by these studies tends to be Travancore State.[2] For, apart from the fact that Guru was from Travancore, the influence of the Yogam was most felt in that area and its activities were to a great extent framed by the socio-political conditions prevalent there.[3] For instance, at the end of 1915 out of the 1,299 members of the Yogam, only 138 and 74 were from Malabar and Cochin, respectively.[4]

There is no doubt that from the very start the Yogam aimed at organizing the Tiyya population scattered over Kerala. Its annual conferences presided over by Tiyya notables from different localities were held in various places across Kerala. However, Malabar Tiyyas not only regarded the Yogam as 'a sabha of southerners'[5] but also they tried to build their own independent organization.

Considering such a background, this chapter intends to focus on the thus far relatively neglected Tiyyas' movement in British Malabar. By so doing, an attempt is made to bring to light the down-to-earth level of Tiyya activities which have not been dealt with in previous studies. Further, by examining the British-ruled area, where the nationalist movement had a profound impact unlike in the Native States, we are able to historicize the Yogam's role in the Travancore region.

KERALA SOCIETY AND THE TIYYAS

Occupying about 20 per cent of the whole population, the Tiyya was the largest 'caste' community among the Hindus in Kerala State (see Table 1 and 2).

Nobody would expect that such a large body, which counted more than 15 lakhs of people in the early twentieth century, could be a homogenous entity. In fact, reference was made to them in various ways in Kerala. Whereas one of the appellations, 'Tiyyas', is used throughout in this essay (except when talking exclusively of the Travancore case)[6] since they were most commonly known in the Malabar area, 'Ezhavas' was the most familiar name in Travancore State. 'Chogans' or 'Chovans' were the other appellations in use. Even in Malabar, they were known as 'Ezhavas' in the Palghat area.

Table 1 Population and area of Malabar, Chochin and Travancore

	Area (sq.mi.)	*Population*	*Hindus (%)*	*Christians (%)*	*Muslims (%)*
Malabar	5,794	3,015,119	66.5	1.8	31.6
Cochin	1,362	918,110	67.1	25.4	7.0
Travancore	7,594	3,428,975	67.0	26.4	6.7

Source: *Census of India, 1911*.

Table 2 Tiyya population in the three areas

	% of the total population	*% of the Hindu population*
Malabar	25.2	37.7
Cochin	22.7	33.9
Travancore	15.9	23.8

Source: *Census of India, 1911*.

The community was divided into many sub-castes. The 1891 census report entered 'Tiyyas' and 'Ezhavas' separately in the category of toddy drawers, and counted 19 sub-castes in the former group and 12 in the latter.[7] As to the law of inheritance, North Malabar Tiyyas (as well as Central Travancore Ezhavas) followed the matrilineal law (Marumakkatayam) and South Malabar Tiyyas the patrilineal (Makkatayam). There were no inter-marriages between them until recently. The marriage between a North Malabar Tiyya woman and a Tiyya man from the South (in 1903) was of sufficient interest as to be reported in the newspaper.[8] The marriage metwork was also narrow. A small episode in the autobiography written by a North Malabar Tiyya woman, who married in the beginning of this century, confirms this. According to her story, she suffered considerably since the bride procession leading to the bridegroom house was not supposed to use any vehicles.[9]

Cocoanut cultivation as well as toddy tapping was considered to be their hereditary occupation. Yet, it is foolhardy to think that more than 15 lakhs of people all laboured under this profession. According to the Madras census of 1901, 10 per cent of the 280,000 Tiyya labouring population were engaged in this 'hereditary' occupation (this number involves Tiyyas only), while 70 per cent were agriculturists.[10]

Tiyyas were heterogeneous in economic as well as in social status. It is true that most of them were sub-tenants or landless labourers—usually working under the higher-caste landholders of Brahmans and Nayars. Yet, there were wealthy landowners among them. For instance, out of 1,079 principal landholders, who were in the possession of more than 100 pieces of land within one revenue village (amsam), Logan reported in the 1880s that eight were Tiyyas. In Travancore State also, among those landholders who paid more than Rs. 100 land revenue in the beginning of this century, eight Tiyyas were included.[11] Tiyyas were found in other occupations such as commerce and weaving as well. Not a few Tiyyas who were specialists in traditional Ayurvedic medicine and astrology were conversant in Sanskrit literature, which is normally regarded as the purview of the higher castes.[12]

Concerning the social hiatus, it should be mentioned that Ezhavas in the Palghat area were considered lower than other Tiyyas.[13] Status consciousness at that time is clearly evident from the following incident. When Dr. Pulpu (1863–1950) conveyed his idea of organizing the Tiyyas, C. Krishnan was doubtful of its success, because, in his opinion, the North Malabar Tiyyas looked down upon those from the south.[14] Thus, Innes was right when he said that 'their status varies widely in different parts of the country'.[15]

In the caste hierarchy in Kerala, the Tiyyas were placed under Nayars and artisan castes. Since the Nayars were recognized as the 'Sudra', the Tiyyas accordingly belonged to the 'avarna', that is, outside the varna system.[16] There were, however, other much lower castes such as Cherumas, Pulayas, Parayas and Nayadis. Compared with those castes, the Tiyyas boasted of having a high social status. Today, in fact, they are not included in the 'Scheduled Castes'.

'Theendal' was a peculiar and notorious custom prevailing in Kerala. Gundert's Malayalam Dictionary (1872) defines it as 'atmospheric pollution (Nayadi at 72 feet, Pulayan at 64, Kanisan 36, Mukuvan 24,...)'. Distance pollution, to which it is usually referred, means that a low-caste person pollutes a higher caste not only by touch but by approaching him within the specific distance. For instance, a Nambudiri Brahman and a Nayar were required to take a bath to purify themselves when a Tiyya happened to approach them within 36 and 12 feet respectively.[17]

Yet, here again a local variation affected the rigidity of this custom. There seems to have been no such distance pollution with the North Malabar Tiyyas.[18] And it must be borne in mind that the Tiyyas themselves demanded that the lower castes should keep a proper distance from them.

As a corollary to the Theendal custom, the lower castes were not allowed to enter the temples frequented by savarna 'castes' and were restricted in their use of the passages near those temples. At a certain point on the roads leading to the temples stood the notice boards or stones, which marked the maximum point to which the 'Theendal jatis' could approach. If they saw someone of higher caste coming along the same road, they were supposed to step aside for them. Hence, the Vivekananda's often cited statement that 'these Malabaris are all lunatics, their homes so many lunatic asylums, and that they are to be treated with derision by every race in India until they mend their manners and know better'.[19]

The lower castes including the Tiyyas appear to have suffered from caste discrimination more severely in the Native States (Travancore and Cochin) where the governments tried to bolster their rule by representing themselves as a protector of Hindu orthodoxy.[20] In Travancore State, public educational institutions were closed to the Ezhavas even in the 1870s. Public jobs being restricted to the higher castes, the first two graduates from the Ezhava community had to seek employment in Mysore State and the British India respectively.[21] These two were brothers, the younger being Dr. Pulpu who was to be responsible for founding the Yogam.

Though the famous 'Malayali Memorial' submitted to the Travancore government in 1891 mainly reflected the complaint among the Nayars against the non-Malayali Brahman-controlled administration, it pointed to the Ezhavas' predicament as well. It stated that 'there are no Ezhavas who are getting monthly salary of more than Rs. 5 in the Travancore administration'.[22] Even at the turn of the century, non-Hindus and avarna were not employed in the Travancore revenue department. The only reason for that was that the officials of that department had to deal with the temple properties. It was in 1922 only after the success of the movement of the Civic Rights League, the main organizers of which were the Christians, that this obstacle was removed by the temple properties being separated from the control of the revenue department.[23]

There was no caste-based discrimination in British Malabar so far as the appointments in government service were concerned. On the contrary, the Malabar Tiyyas could be proud of the fact that their community produced the first Deputy Collector as a Malayali in the

Tabel 3 Tiyya population, literacy, and English knowledge

	Population	*Literacy (%)*	*English knowledge*
Malabar	760,970	9.1 (16.5)	3,443 (3,053)
Cochin	208,453	8.2 (15.5)	290 (280)
Travancore	46,265	10.1 (18.6)	1,441 (1,359)

Table 4 Nayar population, literacy, and English knowledge

	Population	*Literacy (%)*	*English knowledge*
Malabar	412,102	26.1 (41.9)	6,113 (5,095)
Cochin	121,206	27.1 (41.3)	2,981 (2,551)
Travancore	592,489	24.5 (40.7)	5,446 (5,088)

Note: Figures in the brackets are regarding the males.
Source: *Census of India, 1911.*

1850s.[24] Muliyil Krishnan, B.A., B.L. from Cannanore was appointed as a Malayalam teacher earning Rs. 30 per month before becoming a Malayalam Professor at Madras Presidency College.[25] In the field of education, they were not excluded from the public institutions. It is true that Zamorin College in Kozhikode did not accept Tiyya students until 1920. Yet, they could have recourse to Mission College. More than half of the students of Kozhikode Mission College in 1914 were Tiyyas.[26] As Tables 3 and 4 show, the male literacy rate among them was 16.5 per cent, which was higher than the average of the Madras Presidency. Although they lagged behind the Nayars in education, more than 3,000 Tiyyas had a working knowledge of English.

Articulate members were in evidence in the areas of law and the local boards/municipalities. For instance, whereas Oyitti Krishnan, B.A., B.L. (d. 1915)[27] was elected as Chairman of Kozhikode Municipality four times, Kottiyath Krishnan, B.A., B.L. (1878–1939) was the Mayor of Tellicherry for a long time. Both were lawyers. Murkoth Kumaran, B.A. (1874–1941), who earned his name in the field of Malayalam literature and journalism, was a member of Tellicherry Municipality (19 years) as well as the Malabar Educational Board (9 years).[28] 'Mitavadi'[29] C. Krishnan, B.A., B.L. (1867–1938), was also active in Kozhikode Municipality, Malabar District Board and Madras Council as a nominated member.

Jeffrey's study on Travancore State pointed out that the trade in cocoanut products in which the Tiyyas were deeply involved, developed from the late nineteenth century. 'Exports of coir, the rot-resistant fibre of the cocoanut husk, used for making ropes and mats, rose from Rs. 9.27 lakhs in 1871 to Rs. 26.22 lakhs in 1891.' As to toddy and arrack trade, it more than doubled between 1860–80.[30] It would be hasty if we were to assume that these expansions in trade resulted in benefiting every Tiyya. Most of the profits must surely have gone to the intermediaries. Yet, it is quite possible to surmise that such a trend benefited some of the Tiyya community and that the same picture can be applied to the Malabar Tiyyas. In fact, Murkoth Ramunni, Kumaran's father, was an influential figure in the toddy trade of North Malabar.[31]

The Tiyyas' 'caste' movement was born in a heterogenous community with such minorities experiencing gradual upward mobilization. Its leadership was, as we find in other 'caste'/nationalist movements, commanded by the intellectuals among the Tiyyas. It was they with their English knowledge who keenly followed the census reports and ethnological publications. Moreover, it was they who realized their superiority in numbers and tried to create a united community regardless of the vast differences in evidence among them. The Tiyya 'caste' was not a given but rather an entity to be created.

AGENDA OF THE TIYYAS' 'CASTE' MOVEMENT

Critique of the Caste Discrimination

Gradually Tiyya intellectuals began to regard as humiliating the various caste usages, particularly 'Theendal', which must otherwise have been followed for ages as natural. It is doubtful they suffered from 'Theendal' in their daily lives, for they not only mingled rather freely with higher castes as members of local boards or other committees, but they, as lawyers or officials, sometimes acted as superior to the Nayars or Brahmans. This was especially so in the case of Malabar Tiyyas. Even 'Mitavadi' Krishnan, however, who employed a Nayar at his office,[32] had a bitter experience during his student days in Madras of being excluded from the mess for the 'savarna' students.[33] Whatever their personal experiences, *Mitavadi* was always replete with attacks leveled against caste discrimination. Its brunt was directed to the notice boards prohibiting the use of roads by 'Theendal jatis' and the discriminating policy of the State governments regarding admission to the public institutions.

A further edge was added to these attacks by referring to the fact that the converts from the lower castes became free from such disabilities, demonstrating the irrationality and arbitrariness of Theendal usage.[34] *Mitavadi* gave space to any kind of protest lodged against such discrimination. Pulayas' movement was thus welcomed and encouraged.[35] Reporting the racial problem and protest movement in America, Booker T. Washington's autobiograhy was recommended.[36]

The challenge against the existing caste order, the symbol of which was the foundation of the Yogam in 1903, aroused strong reaction from upper castes, especially Nayars. Nayar-Ezhava friction initiated just after the foundation of the Yogam, and spread from Kollam (Quilon) to northern Travancore.[37]

Apart from this, court cases and violent incidents continued sporadically. These were provoked by the defiance or negligence of the custom on the side of Tiyyas, like passing through the forbidden roads, being enraged by the traditional cry 'Ho, ho' (which was used by upper castes to demand that Theendal jatis step aside), or approaching the temple processions too closely.

As far as we can judge from the pages of *Mitavadi*, these incidents occurred more frequently in the Native States.[38] But one of them took place in Malabar and the principal actor was 'Mitavadi' Krishnan. Tali Temple in Kozhikode, which belonged to the Zamorin, was the centre of this drama. In November 1917, Thorne, Managing Collector of Zamorin's estate, put up notice boards on the road near Tali Temple. On that day, Krishan along with his friend Manjeri Ramayyar passed along that road and informed Thorne that they had done so.[39] Afterward, somebody defiled one board with tar, and someone else pulled the board up and threw it into the tank.[40] Without any action being taken on the Zamorin's side, this incident was remembered as a victory for the Tiyyas. These facts show that the criticism of the caste system was not entirely confined to journalism but was also demonstrated in action.

Tiyya intellectuals never failed to raise their voice against the caste discrimination experienced by their caste members. Considering that 'one caste (jati), one religion, one god for man',[41] a famous teaching of Sri Narayana Guru, was a favourite cliche that Tiyya intellectuals often held up as an antithesis aganst the caste order, we may therefore ask what their stance was in relation to the same discrimination practised toward those castes ranking below them. It is true that they not only drew attention to the injustice suffered by them but also took up the issue of discrimination based on birth. They made a plea to their fellow caste members to treat the lower-caste people with equality. This issue was, for instance, taken up seriously by K. Ayyappan (1889–1968), the Tiyya leader from Cochin State. His organization, Sahodara Sangham,[42] celebrated its first anniversary by burning a Rakshasa (implying the caste system) in effigy and propagated commensality with Pulayas in pursuit of rooting out the caste order.

Their efforts along this line, however, seem to have been comparatively effete or sometimes confronted the opposition from within their own community. It was before the Guruvayur Satyagraha (1931–32), the Temple Entry Proclamation of the Travancore government (1936)[43] and the Madras Legislation of the same nature (1938), that community temples constructed by the Tiyyas were thrown open to the Pulayas.

Yet, that was not accomplished without some difficulty. A Tiyya temple in Trishur (Trichur), consecrated by Guru in 1916, was open to the Kammalas (artisan caste), but not to the Pulayas. The latter were allowed to proceed up to a certain point.[44] Jagannatha Temple in Tellicherry is another case in pont. According to Murkoth Kumaran, there arose a dispute among the Tiyyas regarding the admission of the Pulayas to the temple. Failing to arrive at the agreement, Guru's intervention was sought. Though Pulaya devotees were allowed to worship at the fixed place for some time, after a few years, several influential Tiyyas refused them again. Whereas chagrined Pulayas boycotted the temple, the Tiyya youth held a meeting in protest. Such a situation again required Guru's mediation.[45] Another Tiyya temple in North Malabar is said to have been made open to the lower castes in 1932.[46]

K. Ayyappan and his comrades were excommunicated for a time on account of their commensality activities. Furthemore, Ayyappan earned the unenviable nickname 'Pulayan Ayyappan'. *Mitavadi* reported this excommunication case with some regret, though it did not particularly recommend engaging in the commensality activities.[47] Criticizing the discrimination based on birth was indispensable in order to bolster their demand for equality. Yet, their criticism appears to have been less consistent when it was directed toward the discriminatory attitude of their own community.

Reform of the Customs, Education and Economic Improvement

These issues of reforming the customs, education and economic improvement are to be considered together since these were inseparatively related to each other through education as the binding centre. Apart from the critique of caste discrimination, the necessity of spreading education among the community occupied a primal place in the discourse and activities among the Tiyya intellectuals of the time. When *Mitavadi* invited the opinions from the Tiyya notables the best way to ensure the community's progress, they invariably emphasized education as the most appropriate measure. It may be noted that the respondents were officials and professionals themselves. Its editorials and letters from the readers also often dealt with the same topic. The interest in education was further underscored by such information as reporting the results of various examinations and appointments/promotions in government service. The information carried about marriages and deaths mostly concerned officials and professionals. Here, it is interesting to note a certain usage of adding the titles to the personal names, like Muliyil Krishnan Munshi and Kanpotu Tahsildar.[48]

The emergence of a new category of notables who achieved their position based on their acquired education and English knowledge-related occupation explains such emphasis on encouraging education in the Tiyya movement. This category sometimes overlapped with the old type notables, but sometimes stood in opposition to it.[49] One reader of *Mitavadi* wrote 'Nowadays only the opinions of those who have a couple of letters after their names (that is, B.A., B.L., etc.) are regarded as valuable, so I am trying to become one'. This letter was wholly supported by another reader.[50]

At the core of the Tiyyas' movement were those who held such a value in common. For them, becoming educated was the fastest possible route to social mobility on the private level. At the same time, producing as many educated Tiyyas as possible was considered as the best route to the community reform, the result of which was a resolution of caste disabilities. Their attempts to reform age-old customs were connected with their goal to spread education among them. The usages they tried to reform or suppress were almost the same as those at which the educated Nayars were aiming, that is, the Marumakkatayam law of inheritance, Talikettu (Tali-tying ceremony the girls went through before puberty), Thirandukuli (ceremony for the first menstruation), and Pulikudi (ceremony taken place during pregnancy). The women's dress and accessories were also scrutinized by the educated. These ceremonies and customs were regarded not only as disgraceful and meaningless, but also as a waste of money which should have better been spent on education and the maintenance of a life-style agreeable to the new notables.[51]

The ultimate goal, viz., education, forced the educated Tiyyas to reflect on the economic problems facing Tiyya commoners. Without their ecomonic betterment, they had neither a slight chance to get an education nor the possibility of bringing forth the self-respect essential to protest against caste-related injustice.

Their concern with the tenancy problem is especially important in the history of the peasant movement in Malabar. The fact that most Tiyya commoners were tenants (often with inferior rights) pressed the Tiyya intellectuals to advocate the tenants' interests. For instance, the Tiyya organization in Tellicherry submitted a petition to the Madras Governor visiting there, demanding that a permanent occupancy right should be endowed to cultivating tenants.[52] Though he was a landower, C. Krishnan presided over a tenant conference.[53] The principal members of the Kurumbranad Tenant Association founded in 1921 were Tiyyas and its secretary was a Tiyya teacher.[54] It may be noted that it was Kottiyath Krishnan who represented the tenants' interests in the Malabar Tenancy Committee set up in 1927. Furthermore, Murkoth Kumaran and C. Krishnan attended the round-table conference organized by the Madras Governor in 1930 as representatives of the tenants. It could be said from these facts that the Tiyya leaders contributed to furthering the tenancy movement in a great way. Of specific note is that though the tenancy movement in the 1920s reflected mainly the interests of upper-strata (usually non-cultivating) tenants, the Tiyya leaders' concern was directed toward the less-privileged tenants.[55] We could thus suggest that their stance conditioned by the Tiyya commoners' interests helped to broaden the scope of the 1920s tenancy movement.

Toddy tapping and sales was another important economic activity of Tiyya commoners. The phenomenon of Sanskritization has been pointed out in a number of movements among lower castes. And temperance was one of the criteria of that phenomenon. Seeing that many Tiyyas were dependent on liquor-related activities, we may ask how the Tiyya leaders came to deal with this problem. This became all the more complex when Sri Narayana Guru preached 'Do not make, give, or drink spirits'.[56] It cannot be denied that in the course of the

Tiyyas' caste movement temperance was encouraged.[57] Yet, it is doubtful that Tiyya leaders thought it advisable or possible for the Tiyyas enmasse to leave their toddy making occupation.[58] Their efforts were rather prominent in drawing the government's attention to the complaints of the toddy tappers about the abkari policy. They did deplore the fallacy of competiton in the auctions for licenses, but their concern was not so much about principle as it was about the financial loss they suffered. Additionally, it was sometimes asserted that their low social status did not necessarily derive from their traditional occupation of toddy tapping.

Communal Representation

To understand the emergence of caste-based associations, 'Cambridge School' scholars emphasized that the caste categories were rather arbitrarily constructed by the colonial government and that the caste associations were deployed by the caste big men to pursue their own political ends.[59]

In the course of the Tiyyas' caste movement, the demand for communal representation constituted the area where their argument would to some extent be applicable. For it was along the lines of gaining some reservation or consideration for the Tiyyas as a 'caste' in the field of education, government service, and seats in the elected bodies that the Malabar Tiyya leaders continued to think and attempt to organize themselves outside the Yogam. This was considered necessary because the Yogam's demand for communal representation was directed toward the Travancore government. In 1917, just before the Montagu-Chelmsford Reform, Tiyya petitioners demanded of the Madras Governor when he visited Malabar that they be given reserved seats. *Mitavadi* repeatedly complained about the absence of Tiyya representatives in the Council.

Thus, in a sense, Tiyya leaders had several points in common with the Justice Party that claimed to represent 'non-Brahmans' interests. Yet, the fact that in Malabar the most influential 'non-Brahmans' were the Nayars prevented them from joining the Justice Party wholeheartedly. Some of the leaders seem to have had the idea of allying with the Nadars or Billavas, who occupied a similar position in the caste order outside Malabar.[60] In the end, however, they were not successful in their endeavour to gain communal representation unlike the Ezhavas in Travancore State.[61]

TIYYA ORGANIZATION AND SRI NARAYANA GURU

Community Temples

In 1888, Sri Narayana Guru consecrated a Siva temple at Aruvippuram in south Travancore. This act was against the tradition, according to which the right of temple consecration was the monopoly of the Brahmans. Since that first consecration, it is said, Guru installed images in as many as 64 temples.[62] These images were not of local gods and goddesses but those of the Sanskrit pantheon such as Siva and Subramania. Discouraging animal sacrifices and offerings of toddy, he introduced a Brahmanical form of worship, for the performance of which Tiyya priests were trained.

Rendering the constructions and management of community temples the principal means for organizing the Tiyyas is one of the characteristics of the Tiyyas' movement. As the Yogam itself developed from the managing committee of Aruvippuram Temple, the same type of committees of each area became the bases not only through which to organize the local Tiyya populace but also to spread the new ideas of reform among them. Among the prominent members of these committees were local notables espousing reformist ideas. To give an example, the managing committee of Jagannatha Temple in Tellicherry, called Gnanodaya Yogam, had Kottiyath Ramunni, father of Kottiyath Krishnan, as its first President. The figure responsible for constructing Sreekanteswara Temple in Kozhikode was Kallingalmadattil Rarichan Mooppan, a famed landowner and the father-in-law of C. Krishnan.

Here, it would serve us to review some of the activities related to these temples. Besides organizing annual festivals, Gnanodaya Yogam tried to attract people to Jagannnatha Temple from Kottiyur Temple, which was one of the most popular places for pilgrimage among Tiyyas.[63] The festival of Sreekanteswara Temple in 1915 was organized by dividing the Kozhikode Taluk into 10 divisions with a manager, who was to assume the leadership for collecting money to finance the festival. And each division was responsible for a particular day during the festival.[64] Also resorted to was 'pidiyari', the customary way to collect money through giving up one day's grain. 'Pidiyari' was the method used at the time of construction of a Tiyya temple in Trishur.[65] During the festivals, such meetings for reforms were commonplace. Some temple committees even aimed at starting a scholarship for higher education.[66]

The inspiration for utilizing the temples for various community programmes might have derived from the functions played by churches among the Christians,[67] who were on their way toward the economic advancement especially in the Native State. Additionally, not only had the 'tara' organizations, the traditional caste self-governing bodies, become weakened,[68] but their functions did not always fall in line with the aspiration of the new Tiyya leaders. Kottiyath Krishnan once declared that the existing caste organizations whose main concern was to maintain caste rules were not suitable for unifying the Tiyyas.[69] To those who were attempting to unite the Tiyyas on a higher level, such a decision by the tara leaders (tarayil karanavars) that the artisan Tiyyas were not recognized as being equal to other Tiyyas was irritating indeed.[70]

In witnessing this change over to the worship of the orthodox Hindu gods and Brahmanical rituals, we could interprete this as being another example of Sanskritization. Yet, at the same time we should not overlook the element of defiance against the caste order in the act of constructing the parallel temples. In fact, Murkoth Kumaran found a denial of the Brahmanical authority in Guru's consecration of Siva temple at Aruvippuram.[71] Moreover, it is to be acknowledged that in the course of the construction and management of the community temples, the focus was not so much on Sanskritization as on caste unity and reform. Some presidential speeches at the early Yogam conferences show that there was a certain amount of doubt among the Tiyya intellectuals with regard to the meaning of temple construction, for some sections considered it to be promoting idolatry and irrationality. The reply to such doubts was generally given by way of pointing out the role of temples in encouraging the unity and in propagating reform.[72]

Tiyya Intellectuals and Narayana Guru

The principal accomplishment in constructing community temples was organizing local Tiyyas. At worst, the management of the temples could possibly cause factional strifes among the leaders. On the other hand, propagation through journalism catered to a limited literate circle only. The unique role played by Narayana Guru must be considered against this background. As the episode mentioned in the beginning of this chapter shows, it was the reputation of Narayana Guru as a Tiyya 'saint' that reached even less-educated Tiyyas.

Guru was an indispensable link between the educated Tiyyas and the Tiyya masses. The question arises then as to how the latter perceived their guru. Among the numerous Guru biographies, Murkoth Kumaran's is famous. What is interesting about his work is that one-seventh of more than 400 pages speaks of the miraculous power of Guru. His power was said to be manifested in his ability, for example, to read minds, cure diseases, and reform drunkards. One person, who visited Kerala around 1915, reported on the myth being created centring on Guru. It was said that, for instance, one of the Guru's followers told him that Guru could be present at different places at the same time.[73] *Mitavadi* also carried a news item without accompanying comment that a Christian youth suffering from the disturbances caused by a pishachi (evil spirit) was cured after his visit to Arvippuram Temple.[74] It seems safe to assume that Guru's image among the masses was not far from the one commonly found among them about 'saints' with great power. To them, Guru did not really epitomize a reformer as such.[75]

The Tiyya intellectuals reacted in varied ways to such myth-making. Even though he noted some reservation for accepting every story, Murkoth Kumaran tried to justify it by proving that the Yoga experts in fact possessed real power. (See the first chaper of his book on Yoga.) K. Ayyappan, on the other hand, criticized the trend to deify Guru in 1920.[76] While Kumaran's biography was acclaimed at the time of its publication, its second chapter dealing with Guru's power was considered dispensable by some circles.[77] Whatever each intellectual's attitude, what was common is that they all understood Guru's great influence well enough to use it for mobilizing the Tiyya masses and justifying their particular reform programmes. For instance, when Ayyappan was excommunicated on account of his commensality with Pulayas, he obtained a verdict from Guru that 'whatever their religion, dress, or language, jati being the same (as mankind), it does not matter to inter-marry or inter-dine' and silenced his opponents.[78] Even P. Achuthan (1883–1938), one of few Tiyya leaders who participated from the beginning and remained in the Congress movement, appealed in the name of Guru, saying that joining in the Civil Disobedience Movement was exactly what Guru taught.[79]

Guru's name was thus a valuable instrument for promoting Tiyya unity. His birthday was celebrated throughout Kerala, the reports of which were notable items in *Mitavadi* as well as *Vivekodayam* (the organ of the S.N.D.P. Yogam). The fact that he was invited as a celebrated guest to the Nayar conference[80] confirmed that his fame was beyond his particular caste. Moreover, Tiyya intellectuals repeatedly emphasized the universality of Guru's teaching. Yet, Narayana Guru remained nothing more than the Tiyyas' guru ('kula-guru' was a term often used), unlike, say, Ramakrishna Paramahansa or Vivekananda. It is therefore ironical that by utilizing Guru at every possible opportunity, as a symbol of Tiyya unity or as an authority to justify their opinions, Tiyya intellectuals made Guru their 'kula-guru'.

TIYYAS AND THE INDIAN NATIONALIST MOVEMENT

It was not until the early twentieth century that the Congress movement took root in British Malabar. Though the educated Malayalis were paying due attention to it (Indeed, some individuals attended the annual conference of the Congress.), Malabar became politicized only after Besant's Home Rule League had spread there. The first political conference was held in Palghat in 1916.

In the 1920s to 1930s, the reaction of Tiyya intellectuals to the nationalist movement was generally negative. *Mitavadi*'s critical editorials about the demand for self-government by the Home Rule League as well as the Congress are typical examples.[81] Ashes of the same journal are said to have been sent to C. Krishnan, the editor, from the nationalists.[82] Their argument is a familiar one found in other non-Brahman or lower-caste movements in different areas. They asserted that those who were demanding self-government were the Brahmans and other higher castes and that they neglected the issue of caste discrimination. To them self-government meant nothing but being ruled by the higher castes. Only under British rule could they enjoy equality and freedom. 'The victory of self-government is not ours', *Mitavadi* concluded.[83] On 28 October 1917, a meeting held at the Tiyya temple in Palghat made it clear that they would not get involved in the Home Rule movement. One Nayar, who attempted to make a speech supporting self-government, was thrown out of the meeting.[84] In March of the following year, another meeting took place against self-government in which more than a thousand Tiyyas attended.[85] Murkoth Kumaran criticized P. Achuthan who participated in the third Malabar District Conference. Kumaran made a comment on Achuthan later as a person who 'advocating nationalism on the side of savarna, criticized the Tiyyas' unity as communalism and obstructed (their) advancement'.[86]

It would be hasty, however, to conclude that the Tiyyas' movement was completely isolated from the nationalistic trend. It would be of benefit to try to locate such places where both the Tiyya and nationalist movements met despite considerable friction, which is essential to understanding the history of the nationalist movement in Kerala and to making corrections to the Congress-centred historiography. I shall thus hereafter point out the exchanges and reinterpretations of the important vocabulary as well as ideology between the two movements.

The transformation of the term 'passive resistance' is one such interesting case. *Mitavadi* had been approvingly reporting from the early period about Gandhi's activities in South Africa.[87] At the same time, the same magazine made it a point to contrast his protest against racial prejudice with the higher-caste nationalists' neglect of the question of caste discrimination. After his return to India, Gandhi's intervation in the textile factory workers' strike in Ahmedabad and the no-tax movement in Gujarat were also covered.[88] Thus, *Mitavadi* contributed greatly to enhancing Gandhi's fame. *Mitavadi*'s estimation, however, changed dramatically after Gandhi joined and took the leadership of the Congress movement since Gandhi's stance opposing British rule and upholding the varna system was not acceptable.[89] K. Ayyappan was also critical of Gandhi. Specifically, he asked why Gandhi did not call such Indians 'satans', who were treating the Parayas and others as less than animals, though he fought against the British government, calling them 'devil'-like and cruel. Neither a Gandhi nor a Malaviya comprehended the evil of caste discrimination, he said.[90]

Nevertheless the value of 'satyagraha' as a political weapon invented by Gandhi was not lost on the Tiyya intellectuals, who innovatively deployed it against caste discrimination. At that time, the incident of Tiyya pupils being compelled to leave the school after the members of the Cochin royal family began to attend the same incited much criticism among the Tiyya intellectuals. In October 1918, the 'Passive Resistance League' was set up at the meeting held at Paran Hall in Kozhikode. At this occasion, P. Achuthan, a Congressman, and T.K. Madhavan (1885–1930) stood on the same platform.[91] One of the resolutions passed at the meeting declared that they would not retain the 'Theendal' practice against the lower as well as higher castes. The later history of this league is not tracable, but most probably it had become defunct. We know at least, however, that out of the fund set up by one of the resolutions Rs. 200 was utilized for fighting the case, which originated from caste friction in Tannisherry (Cochin State). And a pamphlet emerged which appealed for offerings not to be made to such temples that denied entrance to the Tiyyas.[92] Thus, Tiyyas' 'Satyagraha' was directed to an object different from that of the Congress. Nevertheless, this could be viewed as one of the routes that led to 'Satyagraha', Congress's distinguised political style, becoming popularized among the sceptical Tiyyas.

As the Tiyyas reinterpreted and adopted 'satyagraha', the Congress drew inspiration from the Tiyyas' movement. To the point, the Malabar District Congress organized two temple satyagrahas, Vaikkam and Guruvayur, not merely because they followed the Congress' general anti-untouchability policy. It would be more correct to say that these satyagrahas were conceived owning to persistant criticism aired by the Tiyyas. Reference had already been made to the issue of temple entry in the presidential address (though the president was not a Tiyya) at the Tiyya conference of 1917 held in Kollam. In December of the same year, C.V. Kunhu Raman (1871–1949) elaborated on this in his article in the *Desabhimani.*[93] It is well known that T.K. Madhavan, the editor of the same paper and the Organizing Secretary of the Yogam during the 1920s, was the main proponent for passing the temple entry resolution at the 1923 Kakinada Congress Conference and became one of the leaders of the Vaikkam Satyagraha.[94] Even before that, he had stepped into the road near Vaikkam Temple and reported it to the official.[95] Again in 1922, K. Ayyappan made public his intention to enter the prohibited area. In fact, some Tiyyas actually did so.[96] Furthermore, the notice boards near Vaikkam Temple prohibiting approach of the lower castes had been made an issue in the *Mitavadi* in early 1919. *Mitavadi* also suggested boycotting the Guruvayur festival.[97] Thus, the stage for Congress-led temple satyagrahas had already been prepared in the course of the Tiyyas' movement.

ISSUE OF CONVERSION AND THE 'SWATANTRA SAMUDAYAM' (INDEPENDENT COMMUNITY) MOVEMENT

Mass conversion to Buddhism of the Maharashtra Mahars led by Ambedkar[98] was prompted on the belief that so far as they remained within Hinduism they could not attain equality. In Kerala, since the beginning of the nineteenth century, the Protestant missionaries succeeded in gaining a good many converts, especially among the lowest ranking castes. It is well-known that a sort of mass conversion among the Shanars (Tamilian toddy tapper caste) of southern Travancore led even to the confrontation between the Nayars and Christian converts.

The Tiyyas were benefited considerably by the schools run by missionaries, which were often free. Seeing the Tiyyas and Shanars ranked similarly in the caste hierarchy, missionaries expected a large-scale conversion of the Tiyyas, though this did not materialise.[99] The relation between the missionaries and Tiyyas, however, was not confined to the field of education alone. Not only did some Tiyyas, such as Muliyil Krishnan's uncle, become Christian, but there were Tiyya intellectuals as well who advocated conversion to Christianity. A case in point is Potteri Kunhambu (1857–1919), a lawyer practising in Cannanore. He recommended conversion to Christianity at the end of the nineteenth century. His novel, *Sarasvati Vijayam* (1892), is the story about a Cheruman. While he is almost killed by the manager of a Nambudiri landlord, this Cheruman is luckily saved by a missionary. After receiving an education, he becomes a judge. The story climaxes in the scene in which the Nambudiri landlord confronts the Cheruman judge. The story additionally included a sub-plot about a Nambudiri woman, who is also protected by a missionary, being excommunicated as punishment for her adultery. Though the main point of this novel was to criticize the caste system and to advocate the necessity of education, it was considered to be propagandist literature catering to the missionaries' interests.[100]

According to Jeffrey, 'From 1934 to 1936 calls for conversion became an almost daily occurrence in the vigourous Travancore vernacular press.' At that time the Yogam was generally interested in Christianity and C.V. Kunhu Raman was one of the advocates for conversion.[101] It seems that Jeffrey places greater emphasis on the aspect of this conversion move as a 'threat' to the higher castes. In the prevailing Travancore conditions, where the Christian population numbered almost one third and was burgeoning, Tiyyas' mass conversion could indeed have been a 'threat' perceived to both the government and higher castes. In fact, the Temple Entry Proclamation of 1936 appears to have been propelled by the 'threatening' mass conversion, which helped to break apart the conversion movement.[102]

We would be premature, however, to simply be content to dismiss

Tiyyas' idea to leave Hinduism as a political maneuver to push their more 'mundane' ends. Rather we must look into the intellectual sphere of the educated Tiyyas, in which their urge for emancipation was always in motion.

Mitavadi of February 1917 carried an article by Sivaprasada Swami, in which, reflecting on his Yogam activity, he deplored its results. He complains 'how many temples, Sanskrit schools, yogams, or ashrams were started, what names or dresses were adopted, how respectable character was nourished, so far as we remained within Hinduism, we who were born to a depressed class, would remain depressed'. In his letter to Narayana Guru, he also commented that the more Guru spread the Vedic teaching, the more caste consciousness became strengthened. And he advised that Guru should start a new religion, preferably such a religion as Buddhism which negated the jati distinctions. His inclination to convert to Buddhism was also implied.[103] This letter brought about a controversy surrounding the conversion. It preceded by a few decades Ambedkar's conversion to Buddhism.[104]

This is not the first time Buddhism was presented as an antithesis to discriminatory Hinduism by Tiyya intellectuals. Their concern with Buddhism had formerly appeared in various forms throughout their movement. For instance, in explaining the prevailing conditions of the Tiyyas, they often looked into the history of Buddhism in Kerala. They asserted that because of the Tiyyas' alleged commitment to Buddhist teachings even after the coming of Brahmans to Kerala, their social status was pushed down to the lower rung of caste hierarchy.[105] Seen in this light, their low social status presently held could be reinterpreted as a result of the Tiyyas' heroic resistance of the past against unegalitarian Hinduism.

As a poet, Kumaran Asan found the themes for his works in Buddhist stories especially in his poetry with its poignant criticism of the caste system. *Chandalabhikshki* (Untouchable Nun, 1923) and *Karuna* (Compassion, 1925) are two examplary cases.[106] Latent in the background could have been Asan's view that after Buddha 'there has not appeared great men who fought against the jati (caste system) and won the victory'.[107] He also translated Edwin Arnold's *Light of Asia*[108] into Malayalam, published under the title Sri Buddha Charitam (Life of Buddha).[109]

Madras Mail, the English daily from Madras, reported in the mid-1920s of the interest in Buddhism among the Tiyya leaders.[110] Yet, mass conversion into Buddhism was not organized by these leaders, except in such isolated cases as C. Krishnan's actual conversion. The main reason for this could be their fear of causing a split among the Tiyya masses, as Asan's criticism of C. Krishnan typically reveals. First of all, it was considered unlikely to succeed in mobilizing the Tiyya masses on account of Narayana Guru's stance on the conversion problem. He, truly as a follower of Advaita, maintained that 'whatever is one's religion, it is sufficient that man be good'.[111] Besides, economic consideration might have had its share in making their choice. For, unlike conversion to Christianity, they could not hope to be the recipients of much financial aid should they converted to Buddhism.[102]

Their interest in Buddhism nonetheless cannot be taken lightly when we view the later history in which many Tiyyas became attracted by socialism and communism. For instance, C. Krishnan not only appreciated Buddha's egalitarian teaching, but also his understanding of Buddhism was characterized by his emphasis on its rational and ethical aspects. The preface to *Light of Buddhist Teaching* (1929) written by Krishnan denoted the difference between Buddhism and other religions: 'What is of importance in Buddhism is the principle as to how we have to lead a life as a human being. . . . Without trying to atone for our sins by prayers and rituals or by giving money and food to the deities and priests, Buddhism taught us to endeavour to lead a pure life with good deeds.'[113] According to him, it is not proper to call Buddhism 'religion'.[114] We see here that C. Krishnan's concept of Buddhism was of a highly humanistic nature in the sense that it does not seek the exemplary behaviour and redemption in some absolute and unhuman authority.

As seen in the political sphere in Kerala as well as in India as a whole, ideological conditions among Tiyya youths became radicalized in the 1920s to 1930s. In 1925, the first meeting of 'rationalists' was held at the Advaita Ashram established by Narayana Guru in Alwaye.[115] It was in 1929 that a Malayalam magazine called *Yuktivadi* (Rationalist) was started with K. Ayyappan as its editor. He had coined the famous slogan 'No jati, no religion, no god, for man'.[116] In the 1930s, the 'Swatantra Samudayam' movement came into being the centre of which was 'All Kerala Tiyya Yuvajana Sangham'.[117] The primal message of this movement was represented by E. Madhavan's book, *Swatantra Samudayam* (1934).[118] He asserted that religion had given to man nothing but harm. It blocked the progress of education and science, surpressed freedom of thought, and caused wars. So far as Hinduism was concerned, it made the position of women unbearable, and to top it all, it could not be separable from the evil practice of caste discrimination. The Hindu temples were a hotbed of superstition and discrimination, and causes of waste of money and time. Uplifting of the untouchable or reforms of Hinduism promoted by Gandhi and others was a fake. Did Gandhi ever commend the inter-caste marriage and commensality which are essential to destroy the caste system? Tiyyas should declare that they are not Hindus but an 'independent community' and that without converting to any religion, they should opt for atheism. It may be noted that he referred to revolutionary Russia as a model of ideal society. His emphasis was laid on the economic reconstruction of the whole socicty.[119] For him and his associates who thought Hindu temples were disseminating only superstitions, temple entry was a negligible issue. In fact, around 1936, the secretary of Kozhikode Tiyya Yuvajana Sangham published a pamphlet in which he regarded the temple entry movement by the Congress as propaganda for election purposes. He denounced the issue of temple entry itself as meaningless, for its underlying aim was to preserve Hinduism intact.[120] The report of the 32nd Yogam conference (1935) tells us that at the 'Swatantra Samudaya Darbar' held in Chertala, a 'Five Year Plan' was prepared to transform the Tiyyas to 'Swatantra Samudayam'.[121]

C. Krishnan, who had written the foreword to E. Madhavan's book, presented an interpellation to the Madras Council, when the same was banned.[122] Krishnan was one of the founders of *Yuktivadi*[123] as well. Seen in this way, we can locate Krishnan's interst in Buddhism not in the process toward the world of 'Swatantra Samudayam', where religion was rejected, but rather in the same framework as an ideological choice. It may be noticed that E. Madhavan mentioned C. Krishnan as the 'father' of the 'Swatantra Samudayam' movement.[124] A similar trajectory of thought can be detected in R. Sugatan (1901–70), a Travancorean, who was to become a leader of the trade union and communist movement. He, with his associates, set up an organization called the 'Buddha Mission' in his native place, Alappula (Alleppey), and became a Buddhist. (Sugatan was his name after his conversion, his original name being Sreedharan.) His group is said to have read and discussed *Light of Asia* and *Sri Buddha Charitam*.[125]

It would be obvious that the conversion to Buddhism, the *Yuktivadi* and 'Swatantra Samudayam' movements cannot be understood merely as threats to the upper castes. Rather, we should consider these varied trends as delineating a certain stage in the ideological development of the Tiyyas' critique of the caste system. These trends were not unrelated to the Yogam. On the contrary, advocates of each trend nursed their idea while getting involved in the Yogam, and expected the Yogam to adopt their stance.[126] Finally, when the Yogam, especially its top leadership, remained immersed in the political squabbles, some portion of these trends merged in other political forces such as socialism or communism.

CONCLUSION

From the construction of community temples to their denial or from the deification of Narayana Guru to atheism, the Tiyyas' movement subsumed varied trends and changed its character over the course of time. Under such circumstances, it was the presence of Narayana Guru that served to retain the ambience of Tiyya unity. On the organizational level, the Yogam, like the Congress, provided a focal point where contradictory ideas and activities competed against each other for salience. Although British Malabar Tiyyas tried to set up another independent organization, they failed to do so. It seems to be only in the 1940s that the Yogam took root in Malabar.[127] Even then, that root was rather feeble at best.[128]

There are several reasons for the weakness of the Tiyya organization to hold firm in Malabar. First, in Malabar the Tiyyas did not suffer from caste discrimination so far as the fields of government service and education were concerned, which was a glaring issue in the Native States. Second, unlike in the limited area of the Native States, there was no scope for forcing the Madras government to admit communal representation for each caste such as the Tiyyas. Finally, in Malabar the Tiyyas' movement was challenged by the nationalist movement which was weak and late-coming in the Native States. By the time Malabar subscribed to the influence of the Yogam, the political scene in Malabar had already been very much radicalized and the Tiyyas themselves were the main body supporting this political picture.

In concluding this chapter, some comments are appropriate on the approach to the caste movements of the 'Cambridge School' scholars. Their arguments are no doubt important in drawing our attention to the arbitrariness of the construction of the caste category and in disclosing the caste leaders' political opportunism. Yet, much would be missed if we were to attribute every activity and statement of the caste leaders to some political end. Even if their primary object were to obtain power for themselves, the impact of these movements cannot necessarily be confined to their intentions alone. Furthermore, the very way the movements were organized was conditioned by the economic and social fabric facing the caste commoners and their concerns. In the case of the Tiyyas, the fact that the Tiyyas intellectuals took up the issue of caste discrimination and the tenancy problem gave impetus to Kerala society as a whole, the meaning of which was far beyond some Tiyya intellectuals' speculation. C. Kesavan (1891–1969), who was a General Secretary of the Yogam and in the end became a Minister of the State Congress Government, could be regarded as a typical example of those utilizing a caste organization for their personal political ends from the Cambridge School's point of view. Yet, by so doing we overlook the meaning of the fact that he used to refer to the messages of 'Bagavan Karl Marx'.[129] Thus, in sum, there remain many questions to be explored regarding the relations as they unfolded between those 'caste' leaders and the masses they sought to guide.

NOTES

1 Cerukat, *Jivitappata* (Mal.), Pattambi, 1974, pp. 91–92.

2 Before the formation of Kerala State, the Malayalam-speaking area was divided into three political entities: British Malabar and two princely states, viz., Travancore and Cochin.

3 For the history of the S.N.D.P. Yogam, see P. S. Velayudhan, *S.N.D.P. Yoga Caritram* (Mal.), Ernakulam, 1978. This volume was published at the time of the Platinum Jubilee of the Yogam. A selected bibliography of the studies on the S.N.D.P. is as follows: G. Rajendran, *The Ezhava Community and Kerala Politics*, Trivandrum, 1974; Robin Jeffrey, 'The social origins of a caste association, 1875–1905: the founding of the S.N.D.P. Yogam', *South Asia*, no. 4, 1974; P. Chandramohan, 'Popular culture and socio-religious reform: Narayana Guru and the Ezhavas of Travancore', *Studies in History*, n.s. 3, no. 1, 1987; Cyriac K. Pullapilly, 'The Ezhavas of Kerala and the historic struggle for acceptance in the Hindu society', *Journal of Asian and African Studies*, XI, nos. 1–2, 1976; T. M. Thomas Isaac and P. K. Michael Tharakan, 'Sree Narayana movement in Travancore, 1888–1939', *Centre for Development Studies Working Paper*, no. 214, Trivandrum, n.d.; Shoji Ito, 'Religio-social movement in modern Kerala: with special reference to the Ezhava caste' (in Japanese), *Shiso*, no. 651, 1978; Dilip M. Menon, *Caste, Nationalism and Communism in South India: Malabar 1900–1948*, Cambridge, 1994; do., 'Limitations of equality: shrines and politics in Malabar, 1900–1923'

in Peter Robb, ed., *Dalit Movements and the Meanings of Labour in India*, Delhi, 1993. The last two are exceptional in the sense that they focus on the Malabar area.

4 *Mitavadi*, vol. 4, no. 6, June 1916, p. 10.

5 Ibid., vol. 6, nos. 1–2, Jan.–Feb. 1918, p. 40, no. 12, Dec. 1918, p. 37, vol. 5, no. 3, Mar. 1917, p. 7. See also Rajendran, *The Ezhava Community and Kerala Politics*, p. 34 and K. Gough, 'Village politics in Kerala II', *Economic Weekly*, Feb. 27, 1965, p. 417.

6 Transliteration is quite troublesome at best. So far as the Malayalam terms (personal as well as caste names) in the text are concerned, those forms usually used in English publications are followed.

7 *Census of India*, 1891, vol. XIV, Madras, Table XVI–A.

8 *Malayala Mamorama* (Mal.), vol. 1, comp. by Murkkottu Kunnappa, Kottayam, 1973, pp. 280–81.

9 C.K. Revati Amma, *Sahasrapurnnima* (Mal.), Kottayam, 1977, p. 155.

10 *Census of India*, 1901, Madras Pt. II, Table XVI. According to the Travancore census of 1931, the Ezhavas engaged in toddy drawing was less than 4 per cent. See Velayudhan, *S.N.D.P. Yoga Caritram*, p. 323.

11 *Malabar Special Commission*, *1881–82*, *Malabar Land Tenures*, vol. 1, Madras, 1882, paras. 232, 241. Velayudhan, *S.N.D.P. Yoga Caritram*, p. 7.

12 K.M. Nayar, *Muliyil Krsnan* (Mal.), Calicut, 1931.

13 C.A. Innes, *Madras District Gazetteers: Malabar*, Madras, 1951 (1st pub. 1908, ed. by F. B. Evans), p. 124.

14 K.R. Acutan, *C. Krsnan* (Mal.), Kottayam, 1971, p. 48.

15 Innes, *Madras District Gazetteers: Malabar*, p. 124.

16 The upper castes such as the Brahmans and Nayars were referred to as 'savarna'.

17 The information is not uniform as to the prescribed distance. For instance, 24 Malabar feet (about 19 feet) is given in C. Achuta Menon's *The Cochin State Manual*, Ernakulam, 1911, pp. 195–96. See also J. H. Hutton, *Caste in India*, 4th edn., Bombay, 1963 (1st pub. 1946), pp. 79–82.

18 Innes, *Madras District Gazetteers: Malabar*, p. 124.

19 *The Complete Works of Swami Vivekananda*, vol. III, Calcutta, 1955, pp. 294–95.

20 It is well known that Marthanda Varma (1729–58), the Travancore Raja, donated his whole territory to the deity of Sri Padmanabhaswami Temple and took an oath to rule the country as a servant of that deity.

21 Robin Jeffrey, *The Decline of Nair Dominance: Society and Politics in Travancore 1847–1908*, 2nd edn., New Delhi, 1994, pp. 129–31. Travancore government's replies to the petitions of Dr. Pulpu's brother can be seen in Velayudhan, *S.N.D.P. Yoga Caritram*, pp. 27–29.

22 Ibid., appendix 5.

23 Jeffrey, *The Decline of Nair Dominance ...*, p. 234.

24 E.K. Krishnan, 'A brief account of the late Churia Canaran, Deputy Collector', *Malabar Quarterly Review*, 3, no. 3, 1904, pp. 209–20.

25 Nayar, *Muliyil Krsnan*.

26 *Mitavadi*, vol. 1, no. 3, Mar. 1914, p. 25.

27 He married Muliyil Krishnan's daughter.

28 For the details of his life, see the biography written by his son. Murkkottu Kunnappa, *Murkkottu Kumaran: Jivacaritram* (Mal.), Kottayam, 1975. See also K. P. Kesava Menon, *Samakalinaraya cila Keraliyar*, vol. 2 (Mal.), Kottayam, 1974. Swami Guruprasad, *Sri Murkkottu Kumaran* (Mal.), Tellicherry, 1941.

29 A journal with the same name was first published from Tellicherry in 1907/8 with Murkoth Kumaran as its editor. It was, however, discontinued after two years. The name was taken from the 'Moderates', one of the two groups in the Congress after its split.

30 Jeffrey, *The Decline of Nair Dominance ...*, pp. 126–28.

31 Kunnappa, *Murkkottu Kumaran*, p. 2.

32 Acutan, *C. Krsnan*, p. 61.

33 G. Priyadarsanan, ed., *S.N.D.P. Yogam Platinum Jubilee Souvenir* (Mal.), Quilon, 1978, p. 486.

34 It is doubtful that the ex-'avarna' could gain relief from the stigma of Theendal so easily after conversion. See Jeffrey, 'The social origins of a caste association, 1875–1905 ...', p. 42. *Madras Mail*, 14 Apr. 1925, p. 4.

35 No substantial studies on Pulayas' movement have been done thus far. 'Cochi Pulaya Mahasabha' was founded in 1913. T. H. P. Centarasseri, *Ayyankali* (Mal.), Trivandrum, 1989, p. 113. Jeffrey refers to 'Pulaya Samaj' organized in 1903. Robin Jeffrey, *Politics*, *Women and Well-being: How Kerala became 'a Model'*, London, 1991, p. 109. It is not certain whether this is the same organization as the 'Hindu Pulaya Samajam' mentioned in *Mitavadi*, vol. 5, no. 8, Aug. 1917, p. 35. Ayyankali (1863–1941), the Pulaya leader, organized the Sadhu Jana Paripalana Sangham (1907). The membership of this organization was not confined to the Pulayas. See ibid. and *Ayyankali natattiya Swatantrasamarannal* (Mal.), compiled by T. H. P. Centarasseri, Calicut, 1991.

36 Incidentally, this book was one of the textbooks used in secondary high schools in Travancore. Jeffrey, *Politics*, *Women and Well-being ...*, pp. 66–67.

37 Velayudhan, *S.N.D.P. Yoga Caritram*, pp. 147–52.

38 *Mitavadi*, vol. 3, no. 11, vol. 5, nos. 1, 2, 5, 8.

39 Ibid., vol. 5, no. 11, Nov. 1917, pp. 6–7, 53. It should be noted that Kesava Menon mentioned his name and Madhavan Nair along with Ramayyar as the persons who accompanied C. Krishnan. Kesava Menon, *Samakalinaraya cila Keraliyar*, p. 39.

40 *Mitavadi*, vol. 5, no. 12, Dec. 1917, p. 7.

41 This word appears in his poem composed in 1914. *Sri Narayana Guruvinte sampurnna Krtikal*, comp. and commented by T. Bhaskaran, Calicut, 1985, pp. 487–90.

42 He was known as 'Sahodaran Ayyappan' after this organization and his Malayalam journal, *Sahodaran*. See M. K. Sanu, *Sahodaran Ayyappan* (Mal.), Kottayam, 1989.

43 Robin Jeffrey, 'Temple-entry movement in Travancore, 1860–1940',

Social Scientist, 4, no. 8, 1976. The proclamation of the same nature was made by Cochin State in 1948. P.K.K. Menon, *The History of Freedom Movement in Kerala*, vol. II, Trivandrum, 1972.

44 *Mitavadi*, vol. 4, no. 10, Oct. 1916, p. xx. Though this decision sounds half-hearted, it was much praised in the papers.

45 Murkkottu Kumaran, *Sri Narayana Guruswamikalute Jivacaritram* (Mal.), Calicut, 1971 (1st pub. 1930), pp. 275–76. Yet, by the time this book was written (1930), the temple had been thrown open to the Pulayas.

46 K. Gopalankutty, 'The Guruvayur Satyagraha, 1931–2', *Journal of Kerala Studies*, XIII, pts. 1–4, 1981, p. 51. Gopalankutty regards this as an effect of the Satygraha.

47 *Mitavadi*, vol. 5, no. 10, Oct. 1917, p. 4.

48 Kunnappa, *Murkkottu Kumaran*, p. 249.

49 It is said that K. Ayyappan, the first Tiyya B.A. in Cochin State, was called Ayyapan B.A. as if the degree were part of his name. Murkot Kunhappa, *Sree Narayana Guru*, New Delhi, 1982, p. 55. Elsewhere E.K. Ayyakutti is mentioned as the first B.A. in Cochin. Acutan, *C. Krsnan*, p. 104.

50 *Mitavadi*, vol. 5, no. 2, Feb. 1917, p. 55, no. 4, Apr. 1917, p. 49.

51 Cf. Lucy Carroll, 'Swami Shivagan Chand, Kayastha conference organizer', *Indian Economic and Social History Review*, 12, no. 3, 1975.

52 C. Govindan Nair, *The Malabar Tenancy Act, 1930*, Madras, 1931, p. 49.

53 Acutan, *C. Krsnan*, chap. 10.

54 *Report of the Malabar Tenancy Committee, 1927–28*, vol. II, Madras, 1928, Evidence, Tellicherry, no. XX.

55 Toshie Awaya, 'Situating the Malabar Tenancy Act, 1930' in P. Robb et al., eds., *Local Agrarian Societies in Colonial India: Japanese Perspectives*, London, 1996.

56 Kumaran, *Sri Narayana Guruswamikalute Jivacaritram*, p. 286.

57 On an individual level there were those Tiyars such as C. Krishnan and Murkoth Kumaran who were for temperance, and the S.N.D.P. Yogam under the leadership of T.K. Madhavan included temperance in its programmes during the 1920s. See P.K. Madhavan, *T.K. Madhavante Jivacaritram* (Mal.), Kottayam, 1986.

58 A speech by Murkoth Kumaran at the death of Kottiyath Krishnan. This document was provided by the late Murkoth Kunhappa.

59 A.D. Washbrook, 'The development of caste organisation in south India, 1880–1925' in C.J. Baker and D.A. Washbrook, *South India: Political Institutions and Political Changes 1880–1925*, Delhi, 1975.

60 A speech by Murkoth Kumaran. There was an opinion among the Nadars that they should ally with the Tiyyas. However, this was opposed on the ground that the Tiyyas were below the Nadars with respect to both social status and wealth. R.L. Hardgrave Jr., *The Nadars of Tamilnad: The Political Culture of a Community in Change*, Bombay, 1969, p. 178.

61 Rajendran, *The Ezhava Community and Kerala Politics*, p. 43.

62 Chandramohan, 'Popular culture and socio-religious reform ...', p. 62. The number presented by Kunhappa is more than 30 including the ones

located in Tamilnadu and Sri Lanka. Kunhappa, *Sree Narayana Guru*, p. 26.

63 *Report of the Malabar Tenancy Committee*, p. 373.

64 *Mitavadi*, vol. 3, no. 1, Jan. 1915, p. 34.

65 Ibid., vol. 4, no. 11, Nov. 1916, p. 30.

66 Ibid., vol. 2, no. 9, Sept. 1914, p. 24.

67 See the leader of the first issue of *Mitavadi*.

68 K. Anandan, *Kerala Caritra Nirupanam* (Mal.), Cannanore, 1935, p. 139.

69 *Mitavadi*, vol. 5, no. 7, July 1917, pp. 36–44.

70 Ibid., vol. 8, no. 4, Apr. 1920, pp. 1–2.

71 Kumaran, *Sri Narayana Guruswamikalute Jivacaritram*, p. 130.

72 N.K. Damodaran, ed., *S.N.D.P. Yogattile Addhyaksa Prasamgannal* (Mal.), Trivandrum, 1982.

73 *Mitavadi*, vol. 3, no. 2, Feb. 1915, p. 8(b).

74 Ibid., vol. 5, no. 1, Jan. 1917, p. 58.

75 K.C. Govindan notes the childhood experience of his meeting Guru. Asked by Govindan about Guru, his mother answered he was 'God's representative'. K.C. Govindan, *Memoires of an Early Trade Unionist*, Trivandrum, 1986, p. 2. This is not to say that the 'intellectuals' should be assumed to be 'immune' to the belief in saints' miraculous power. See Tapan Raychaudhuri, *Europe Reconsidered: Perceptions of the West in Nineteenth Century Bengal*, Delhi, 1988.

76 G. Priyadarsanan, ed., *Sahodaran enna Viplavakari* (Mal.), Kottayam, 1989, p. 154.

77 Kumaran, *Sri Narayana Guruswamikalute Jivacaritram*, p. v.

78 Sanu, *Sahodaran Ayyappan*, pp. 70–71. It is interesting that the opponents of Ayyappan also tried to justify their action in the name of Guru. Ibid., pp. 68–70.

79 Menon, *The History of Freedom Movement in Kerala*, p. 204.

80 *Mitavadi*, vol. 4, no. 10, Oct. 1916, p. iii. Sivaprasad criticized all speakers who referred to Guru as the leader of the 'Tiyyas'. See also Murkkottu Kunnappa, *Malayala Manorama* (Mal.), vol. 2, Kottayam, 1988, p. 229. At least two Nambudiris, viz., V.T. Bhattatiripad and Lalitambika Andarjanam, recorded Guru's name in their autobiographies as a person whose teachings or words impresssed them. V.T. Bhattatirippattu, *Karmmavipakam* (Mal.), Trichur, 1988, p. 162, Lalitambika Antarjanam, *Atmakathaykku Oramukham* (Mal.), Trichur, 1979, pp. 28–30.

81 Kesava Menon, one of the earliest Congress leaders in Malabar, testified that *Mitavadi* had represented Tiyyas' political stance against the nationalist movement. M. Gangadhara Menon, *Malabar Rebellion 1921–22*, Allahabad, 1989, p. 490. Incidentally, Paran Square owned by C. Krishnan in Kozhikode is called 'the venue of activity of the reactionaries' in Menon, *The History of Freedom Movement in Kerala*, (p. 144), which is the work of a very much Congress-centred nature.

82 Acutan, *C. Krsnan*, p. 142.

83 *Mitavadi*, vol. 5, no. 10, Oct. 1917, p. 2.

84 Ibid., vol. 5, no. 11, Nov. 1917, pp. 34–37.
85 Ibid., vol. 6, no. 3, Mar. 1918, p. 59.
86 Kunnappa, *Murkkottu Kumaran*, p. 20.
87 *Mitavadi*, vol. 1, no. 5, Dec. 1913, pp. 140–41.
88 Ibid., vol. 6, no. 4, Apr. 1918, p. 3, vol. 6, no. 5, May 1918, p. 6.
89 Ibid.,vol. 8, no. 11, Dec. 1920. pp. 14–19.
90 Priyadarsanan, ed., *Sahodaran enna Viplavakari*, pp. 159, 161.
91 *Mitavadi*, vol. 6, no. 11, Nov. 1918, pp. 5–8, 30–32.
92 Ibid., vol. 6, no. 12, Dec. 1918, p. 51, vol. 8, no. 5, May 1920, p. 38.
93 The original is cited in Madhavan, *T.K. Madhavante Jivacaritram*, pp. 81–86.
94 Ibid., chaps. 9 and 10. T.K. Ravindran, *Eight Furlongs of Freedom*, New Delhi, 1980, chap. 2.
95 Jeffrey, 'Temple-entry movement in Travancore ...', p. 13.
96 Ravindran, *Eight Furlongs of Freedom*, pp. 44–45.
97 *Mitavadi*, vol. 7, no. 3, Mar. 1919, p. 106, vol. 6, no. 12, Dec. 1918, pp. 24–26, 52.
98 Gen'ichi Yamazaki, *Indian Society and neo-Buddhism: Personality and Thought of Ambedkar* (in Japanese), Tokyo, 1979.
99 D.B. Forrester, 'The depressed classes and conversion to Christianity, 1860–1960' in G.A. Oddie, ed., *Religion in South Asia*, 2nd and enlarged edition, New Delhi, 1991, pp. 82–84. Jeffrey, 'Social origins ...', pp. 47–48.
100 Potteri Kunnampu, Sarasvativijayam in George Irubayam, ed., *Nalu Novalukal* (Mal.), Trichur, 1985.
101 Jeffrey, 'Temple-entry movement in Travancore ...', p. 22. It should be mentioned that Kunhu Raman showed considerable interest in Buddhism as well. See, *C.V. Kunnuramante tirannetutta Krtikal* (Mal.), vol. 1, Kollam, 1971. pp. 45–46, 71, 100.
102 Ibid., pp. 21–22. Jeffrey, 'The decline of Nair dominance ...', pp. 117–18, 236.
103 *Mitavadi*, vol. 5, no. 2, Feb. 1917, p. 32.
104 Cf. Eleanor Zelliot, 'The psychological dimension of the Buddhist movement in India' in G.A. Oddie ed., *Religion in South Asia.* For the history of pre-Ambedkar Buddhist movements, see Adele Fiske, 'Scheduled caste Buddhist organizations' in J. Michael Mahar, ed., *The Untouchables in Contemporary India*, Tucson, 1972.
105 Pullapilly, 'The Ezhavas of Kerala and the historic struggle ...', p. 30, K. Anandan, *Kerala Caritra Nirupanam*, pp. 47, 82. It does not seem to be uncommon among the 'untouchable' intellectuals to explain the degradation of status by way of connecting it with the Buddhist background. See, for instance, Ambedkar, *The Untouchables: Who were They and why They became Untouchable?*, New Delhi, 1948.
106 P. K. Parameswaran Nair, *History of Malayalam Literature*, New Delhi, 1967, pp. 192–95. K. Ramachandran Nair, ed., *Selected Poems of Kumaran Asan*, Trivandrum, 1975, pp. 5–51.
107 *Mitavadi*, vol. 5, no. 5, May 1917, p. 15.
108 Sir Edwin Arnold, *Light of Asia*, Boston, 1879.

109 While serialized from 1915 to 1924, it was not completed. K.M. George, *Kumaran Asan*, New Delhi, 1972, p. 79.
110 *Madras Mail*, 11 Feb. 1925, p. 6, 14 April 1925, p. 4.
111 Kumaran, *Sri Narayana Guruswamikalute Jivacaritram*, p. 295.
112 *Kumaran Asante Gadyalekhanannal* (Mal.), vol. II comp. and ed. by N. K. Damodaran, Trivandrum, 1982, pp. 300–13. Damodaran, ed., *S.N.D.P. Yogattile Addhyaksa Prasamgannal*, p. 147.
113 Acutan, *C. Krsnan*, pp. 236–37.
114 C. Krishnan, 'Bhuddhabhiksukkal verum Samudayikasusrusakanmar' (Mal.) in *Mahabodhi Souvenir*, Calicut, 1964, p. 26.
115 Issac and Tharakan, 'Sree Narayana movement in Travancore, 1888–1939', note. 36.
116 K. Ayyappan, *Sahodarante Padyakrtikal* (Mal.), Kottayam, 1981 (1st pub. 1934), pp. 28–30.
117 This was founded at the conference held at the end of July 1933. Velayudhan, *S.N.D.P. Yoga Caritram*, pp. 321–32.
118 Born in Vaikkam in 1903 and educated up to matriculation. Jeffrey, 'Temple-entry movement in Travancore...', p. 21.
119 E. Madhavan, *Swatantra Samudayam* (Mal.), Trivandrum, 1979 (1st pub. 1934). His idea is obviously far from Narayana Guru's. He claimed, however, that 'if Guru's great precept, one jati, one religion, and one god, were interpreted correctly, it means no jati, no religion, and no god'. Ibid., pp. 108–9. We perceive here the same attempt to enlist Guru's authority for justifying his idea. Yet, he adds further that 'if Guru's opinion were mistaken, what is wrong if we say so?' pp. 110–11.
120 Kunnappa, *Malayala Manorama*, vol. 2, pp. 262–66. See also *Mathrubhumi*, 17 Dec. 1933, p. 6.
121 Velayudhan, *S.N.D.P. Yoga Caritram*, p. 332.
122 Acutan, *C. Krsnan*, p. 203. *Madras Legislative Council Debates*, vol. 77, p. 493.
123 C.K. Gangadharan, 'Izhavarum yukutivada prasthanavum' in Priyadarsanan, ed., *S.N.D.P. Yogam Platinum Jubilee Souvenir*.
124 Madhavan, *Swatantra Samudayam*, p. 206.
125 Putuppalli Raghavan, *Sukhav Sugatante Jivacaritram* (Mal.), Trivandrum, 1979, p. 28.
126 For instance, at the July 1933 meeting, the demand was raised that the Yogam should declare Tiyyas were not the Hindus. Velayudhan, *S.N.D.P. Yoga Caritram*, pp. 321–32.
127 Ibid., CL XIII.
128 Gough reported the cases of Yogam's institutions being hijacked by the communist Tiyyas. Gough, 'Village politics in Kerala II', p. 419. See also her 'Palakkara: social and religious change in central Kerala' in K. Ishwaran, ed., *Change and Continuity in India's Villages*, New York, 1970.
129 C. Acuta Menon, *Smaranayute Etukal* (Mal.), Trivandrum, 1975, p. 102.

10

Anti-Untouchability Ideologies and Movements in Maharashtra from the Late Nineteenth Century to the 1930s

MASAO NAITO

INTRODUCTION

In this essay I examine some of the important social and political ideologies and movements that attempted to resolve the problem of untouchability in some way or other, particularly referring to Maharashtra where well-known anti-untouchability struggles had been waged. After the advent of British rule many schools of thought appeared whose main targets were the 'evils' within Hindu society such as discrimination against women and caste prejudices. Christian missionaries and Indian social reformers played important roles in the diminishing of this discrimination.

In modern Maharashtra Balshastri Gangadhar Jambhekar, Lokahitawadi (Gopal Hari Deshmukh) and Dadoba Pandurang Tarkhadkar were the forerunners of the social reform movement. But we cannot deny the fact that it was only after Jotirao Govindrao Phule that the movement aiming at abolishing caste discrimination and untouchability with certain clear ideas and organisation started. By establishing the Satyashodhak Samaj (Truth-seeking Society) in 1873, he challenged and attacked the Brahmanical ideology and caste system which had fettered the low castes and untouchables (Shudra-Atishudra) for a long time. Though Phule's organisation could not retain a strong and stable basis during his own times partly because of its revolutionary radicalness, he was recognised as the 'Mahatma' who sought to improve lower-caste farmers and untouchables as a whole socially, economically and ethically and also who tried to spread education among women and depressed people to eradicate the discrimination levelled against them.

A successor to Phule's movement in the twentieth century was Shahu Chhatrapati of the princely state of Kolhapur who was geneaologically related to Shivaji, the founder of the Maratha kingdom. Though Shahu did not abandon his status as a ruler under British paramountcy and his rivalry against Brahman bureaucrats and priests was well-known, he helped promote the low-castes' movements by appointing young activists to the office of his government irrespective of caste origin or stratum and also made a considerable effort toward abolition of discriminative customs and practices against the untouchables and toward furthering their education and employment in his own state. He extended his support, financial as well as moral, to a variety of groups and individuals outside the state, one distinguished recipient of which was B.R. Ambedkar.

In the late 1920s when the non-Brahman movement was gathering momentum, two young radicals, K. Jedhe and D. Jawalkar, entered the arena. In line with the young generation of Marathas they led active movements against the Brahman ascendancy, and at the same time they took part in movements led by Ambedkar demanding the opening of public places and institutions to untouchables. But most of the Maratha activists who took the place of the political leaders of Maharashtra, mainly Brahmans, in the process of the Gandhi-led national liberation struggle drifted away from the movement to fight against untouchability. It may safely be said that in 1932 when Keshavrao Jedhe formally joined the Indian National Congress, the Maratha-dominated non-Brahman movement in Maharashtra was finally alienated from the anti-untouchability cause.

In the 1920s–30s there appeared two different types of anti-untouchability movement, one being the 'harijan' movement led by Gandhi and another the 'dalit' movement headed by Ambedkar. While Gandhi himself and his caste Hindu disciples, who were no doubt keen on abolishing untouchability, were unfavourable to the autonomous movement of the untouchables (harijans) themselves and emphasised that high-caste Hindus' cooperation or rather their initiative was of primary necessity, Ambedkar demanded the liberation of the depressed (dalits) from the caste discrimination not as a gift by the others but as their human right. Therefore, unlike Gandhi who sought 'hriday-parivartan' (return to conscience) of the discriminating caste Hindus but not a political settlement of untoubhability, Ambedkar aimed at a comprehensive measure of liberation including even enforcement by laws. Needless to say, there were many ordinary active workers particitating in the movements who wavered between these two great personalities.

MODERN MAHARASHTRIAN SOCIETY AND DEVELOPMENT OF CASTE MOVEMENTS

Caste relations and untouchable castes in Maharashtra

Notably, the politics of modern Maharashtra has usually been related with three main caste groups, that is, Brahmans, Marathas and Mahars, and the political problems there have more often than not come to the fore as conflicts either between Brahmans and Maratha-dominated non-Brahman caste groups or between caste Hindus and Mahar-dominated untouchable caste groups.[1] Though this generalisation appears to be oversimplified, we cannnot deny that it presents a salient aspect of the characteristics of the Maharashtrian society.

In Maharashtra, as in other parts of India, however, the social life of the people was and also continues to be more directly restricted by the customs and practices of smaller communities, jatis or dnatis. Iravati Karve, a prominent sociologist, characterises a jati as a group 'in which there is marriage only among members of the group (endogamy), that used to be spread over a contiguous small area, the members of which generally had one or more interconnected occupations, and that used to have a rank relative to all similar groups'. Also according to her, there were over two hundred jatis in each linguistic region.[2]

Brahmans occupying less than four per cent of the total population of Maharashtra had obtained an important position with economic, political as well as socio-cultural privileges, under Peshwa rule and also under British rule since the early nineteenth century. Among the main Brahman sub-castes in Maharashtra mentioned in the caste census, Chitpavans or Konkanasthas whose ancestral place is said to be the coastal area of Konkan and Deshasthas, meaning people of the Deccan (Desha), who are believed to be the first Brahman settlers here,[3] played more significant roles in the political history of Maharashtra.

Marathas classified as 'intermediate' in the caste census of 1931 were and still are the most numerous caste group in Maharashtra. E.V. Enthoven, who was directly associated for a long time with the census surveys in the Bombay Presidency and the author of the classical book,

The Tribes and Castes of Bombay, mentions that the word Maratha covers the following three classes:

> Marathas proper, the chiefs, landowners and fighting Marathas of the Deccan and Konkan, claiming Kshatriya rank, eschewing widow remarriage and socially superior to the cultivating classes, from whom, however, in places [*sic*] they will take girls in marriage, Maratha Kunbis or cultivators, also known as Kulvadi, and Maratha occupational castes such as Kumbhar, Lohar, Mali, Nhavi and so on.

He also mentions the common belief in Maharashtra that there is little or no difference between Marathas and Kunbis.[4] Malis (gardeners) listed in the third category are considered to have been originally Kunbis who took to gardening, and by degrees formed a separate community.[5] They used words like phul (flower), jire (cumin seed) or halad (turmeric) as their sub-caste name according to the crop they cultivated. Under Maratha rule they prospered by supplying flowers, fruits and vegetables to towns like Pune and, even after the British replaced it, they continued their development and formed a conspicuous community. They showed great concern in the diffusion of education and through it produced many social activists. One of the most distinguished among them is J.G. Phule whose thought and activities will be studied hereafter.

Most of the occupational castes listed by Enthoven except Malis and some others were usually thought of as being separate from Maratha-Kunbis. But these artisan castes were closely tied with cultivators (Maratha-Kunbis) under the watan system which characterised the agrarian society of Maharashtra. The remuneration by crop, cash or a piece of land paid for services which were offered to cultivators by patil (village headman), kulkarni (village secretary) and village artisans or servants was balute, and the right to obtain it was called watan. Hereditary succession to watan among the family actually means 'an occupation as family property', and a watandar (watan-holder) was considered to be exclusively entitled to this occupation.[6] People who received balute by offering services to agriculturists were classified into 12 caste groups. These groups which were generally called bara balutedars were Sutars (carpenters), Lohars (blacksmiths), Chambhars (leather workers), Mahars (village servants), Kumbhars (potters), Parits (washermen), Nhavis (barbers), Mangs (rope makers), Joshis/Bhats (astrologers/genealogists), Mulanas (superintendents of mosques), Guravs (temple watchmen) and Kolis (water drawers).[7] Most of their services were essential to the everyday life of village farmers but there frequently occurred trouble concerning the payment of balute.[8]

Of the bara balutedars, Mahars, Mangs and Chambhars were ranked as untouchables. The residing area of these castes, called, for example, Maharwada, was in most cases located outside of the villages. The largest group among these untouchable castes was that of Mahars and it is said that there were almost no villages in Maharashtra in which there were no Mahars.[9] The services they were requested to do for villagers were enormously diverse. In his detailed study on the social structure of Maharashtrian villages, T.N. Atre points out that at least 18 kinds of duties were imposed on Mahars, which included calling landholders to pay the land assessment, watching the thrashing places, cleaning the front of the village office and village gate, and removing dead bodies of animals left on the road.[10] Besides these, however, Mahars had the one more important duty of watching the boundary as the designated authorities of all boundary matters, which is said to demonstrate the fact that they once owned much of the land in the village.[11] As we shall see later, it can be said that because unlike other balutedars they did not have any specific skills with which to provide their livelihood, many Mahars joined the army under British rule or left their villages for neighbouring towns and cities to get jobs, and this historical situation gave the community a certain peculiar socio-economic status. B.R. Ambedkar, whose thought and activities are one of the main topics of this article, was from none other than this community.

The second largest untouchable community in Maharashtra was that of Chambhars, equivalent to Chamars in north India.[12] They also called themselves Charmkars, 'charm' meaning skin or leather, and, as their traditional occupation, produced and mended leather shoes, sandals and leather bags for drawing water from wells. But as the work of skinning and tanning was done by Dhors and other castes, Chambhars claimed a higher status among untouchable castes, and their economic position and literacy were also usually higher than those of others.[13] Mangs, also called Matangs, were found to reside throughout almost all of Maharashtra but not in particularly large numbers anywhere.[14] Traditionally, they produced and sold different kinds of ropes, bamboo baskets, and the like for farmers.

Besides these, the censuses listed some other depressed classes, none of which, however, were numerically large. One more aspect to be noticed about the untouchable caste groups in Maharashtra is, as pointed out time and again, that there existed mutual animosity and discriminatory feelings against each other. Among those castes mentioned earlier, for example, there was a sort of hierarchy in which Chambhars claimed the top of the list with Mahars, Mangs, Dhors and Bhangis below them claiming a higher position than others.[15] V. R. Shinde, a social worker to whom I will refer later, notes his bitter experience that in a free boarding house in Pune built for untouchable students by the government of Bombay, Mahar and Chambhar students opposed each other in demanding a separate cook from their own community.[16] Even after India's independence, a village survey reported that Chambhars claiming a higher status themselves refused to mend the shoes of Mahars and Mangs and that a Chambhar who tanned hide was excommunicated from his community. In another village, Mangs who were engaged in the work of carrying dead bodies of animals and also of tanning, but unlike Mahars did not eat dead flesh, considered themselves higher in rank than Mahars. The same survey report gives us an example of the intense rivalry dividing Mahars and Mangs seeking social superiority: In a marriage ceremony of a villager, a Mang, who was served food after a Mahar rejected taking it, and another Mahar preceded by a Mang also did not receive food.[17] This sort of mutual hostility very seriously annoyed many of the leaders of the anti-untouchability movements.

Pre-history of Non-Brahman Movement in Maharashtra

One of the most conspicuous aspects in the modern history of Maharashtra and Tamil Nadu was the non-Brahman, practically anti-Brahman, movement which incorporated not only religious, social and economic spheres but also the various forms of political agitation for power. Though there are arguments as to why this particular movement was seen in these areas only, it cannot be denied that most of the social, economic and political privileges had been placed in the hands of small caste groups occupying only three to five per cent of the society for quite some time.

Even at the time of Shivaji, the founder of the Maratha kingdom, who appointed men from a variety of castes to his officialdom, many Brahmans occupied important administrative posts like the clerkship and others which necessitated some specific degree of learning and knowledge. In north India, most of the court clerks were from Muslim or Kayastha communities.[18] After the rule of the Peshwa, a Chitpawan Brahman, was established, the concentration of power in the hands of Brahmans increased more strikingly in the court. The city of Pune, for example, became somewhat akin to a Brahman centre because the government served them lavishly with dakshina (monetary gift) and food.[19] In villages, their economic and social privileges were also strengthened.[20]

The Peshwa government in Pune ended with the third Maratha War with the East India Company's army in 1818. Though initially Mountstuart Elphinstone, the Commissioner of the Deccan (1818–19) and the Governor of Bombay(1819–27), and his successors tried not to bring about radical changes in the social and religious life of the populace from the viewpoint of law and order, they gradually began to institute the establishment of the new legal and administrative system suitable for the smooth colonial rule.[21] The collapse of Peshwa rule generated a blow to Brahmans who had enjoyed privileges under it and drove them, especially Chitpawans, toward the cities in search of a job. They showed great interest in acquiring an English education introduced from the 1830s and, by adapting themselves to the new colonial order, steadily obtained the jobs and positions produced anew under British rule. By and large this process might have been the case with colonial India as a whole but the Maharashtra's case was significant as Shankarrao Deo, a Gandhian political leader, mentions that 'while in north India many non-Brahmans formed a middle-class as professionals like lawyers, doctors, and teachers since the early period, here in Maharashtra Brahmans monopolised most of these positions'.[22] Temple, the Governor of Bombay in the 1870s, also refers to the situation of Maharashtra:

> in Bengal, Brahmin influence was moderated by the trading and literary castes; in the North-Western Provinces by the Rajputs and Muslims; and in Bombay, by the Parsis and Jains; in Maharashtra and South India, Brahmin influence was absolute with the other castes in a position of almost total subservience.[23]

After the British came to power in Maharashtra, Maratha-Kunbis, who were farmers and also warriors in times of war during the Peshwa period, concentrated on agriculture. With the result of the new land settlements introduced by the British administration, some of the farmers (Kunbis) accumulated capital. These rich farmers then excavated wells to irrigate their fields for producing more profitable food grains and cash crops such as rice and sugarcane.[24] And with the rapid progress of the commercialisation of agriculture, many from the Mali community also made a fortune by supplying city dwellers with vegetables and fruits.

NON-BRAHMAN MOVEMENT AND ANTI-UNTOUCHABILITY MOVEMENT

Anti-casteism of Mahatma Phule

In Maharashtra some non-Brahman castes, especially the Maratha-Kunbi caste groups, had started to claim their higher status in the caste hierarchy even before the British came to power in this area. And in the latter part of the nineteenth century they established their strong social status vis-à-vis the Brahman caste groups.[25] Out of this situation aroused the so-called non-Brahman movement, one of the earliest and most distinguished ideologues of which was Jotirao Govindrao Phule (1827–90).

Phule, called respectfully 'Mahatma' or 'Jotiba' in a familiar way by his contemporaries, belonged to the Mali caste, the name of the sub-caste being Phul Mali or Kshatriya Mali. The family moved to Pune during his grandfather's generation and his father was successful in managing fruit, vegetable and flower shops in the city in addition to farming in the suburbs. After graduating from a primary school of Marathi, Jotirao continued his learning in a Scottish mission school and an English school managed by the Bombay Government from 1841 to 1847. It seems that there he experienced his mental awakening through encounters with Christianity and books like Thomas Paine's *Rights of Men* which opened his eyes to the new European ideas. Later he highly evaluated these educational institutions managed by the mission and the government in his writings.[26]

But almost at the same time, Jotirao had to recognise another reality. He was deeply humiliated when in a marriage procession of his Brahman friend he was condemned by an orthodox Brahman as a 'Shudra' violating a caste rule by walking along with Brahmans and had to leave the procession on the way. He also came to know that untouchables were required to walk the streets of Pune with a pot hanging from his neck for spitting and was prohibited to walk in the early morning or late evening so that their shadow might not be cast upon Brahmans.[27] These incidents and experiences engrained in him great indignation against the Brahmanical ideology dominating every sphere of the society and also against poverty and mental slavery among low-caste communities and urged him to launch a battle to eradicate such evil customs in Hindu society.

Though coming a little after Bengal, Maharashtra had also produced pioneers of the social reform movement by the middle of the nineteenth century when Phule started his public activities. Balshastri Gangadhar Jambhekar (1812–46) publishing the *Darpan*, the first Marathi newspaper in 1832 and Govind Vitthal Mahajan (1815–1900) publishing the *Prabhakar* and other magazines attacked a variety of social prejudices and ignorance among Hindu masses and insisted on the necessity of the social reforms. Dadoba Pandurang Tarkhadkar (1814–82), a reformist from the lower caste, appealed for the destruction of the caste system. In Pune, Lokahitawadi (Gopal Hari Deshmukh 1823–92) in serial articles of Shatapatren published in the *Prabhakar* called out, especially to Brahmans, to abandon social evils like the caste system and to open their eyes to modern learning and new ideas. Many of these reformers were financially assisted by Nana Jagannath Shankarsheth (1803–65), a millionaire from the Sonar caste in Bombay, under whose auspices Phule also set to work.[28]

With the founding of a school for low-caste girls in Pune in 1849 as a start, he centred his energy on the education of non-Brahman children including untouchables as well as Muslims. He was among those who established a society aiming at promoting the education of Mahar and Mang children in 1852. Hereafter I will follow his thought on social matters, particularly on caste and untouchability.

Among Phule's early writings *Brahmananche Kasab* (English title given by author himself being *Priestcraft Exposed* but literally meaning Cleverness of Brahmans), written in the pawada (ballad-like poem) style in 1869, is noticeable because many important subjects he was to discuss in his later works were mentioned in it. In the short preface he gives the direction of the contents of this booklet:

> Before Brahmans came to exercise authority over Hindusthan, who ruled this holy land and how and where? How are those Brahmans who captured this country, enslaved those defeated in the war, forced many of Maha Aris (Mahars–author) to wander from place to place and let all other Maha Aris fall into hell, tormenting these people even now? This is a pawada which refers to these matters.[29]

He starts by explaining how Kshatriyas, original inhabitants, under the aegis of Bali Raja were conquered by invading Aryans. According to him, the Aryan conquerors, who were none other than Brahmans, enslaved indigenous Kshatriyas and ranked them as Shudras. So-called untouchables were also included in this category. Some people who lost the valorous fighting with Parashuram, a king of Brahmans, came to be called Mangs and Maha Aris (brave enemies, that is, Mahars) and were degraded to the status of the untouchable.[30] Though this was a novel explanation of the origin of low castes and untouchable castes in Maharashtra, the extent of his interest in and sympathy with them can be proved by the fact that he presented this booklet 'to Kunbis, Malis, Mangs, Mahars with the greatest affection'.[31] He hereafter called untouchables 'Ati-Shudra' and non-Brahman masses as a whole 'Shudra-Atishudra'. In the remaining eight chapters of the booklet he describes in simple but bitter terms how Brahman priests, astrologers and physicians interfered with every field of social and religious life of the ordinary people and robbed them of properties and money in every possible way, which is to be one of the important themes in his later writings.

Another of his books, *Gulamgiri* (Slavery), as known from its English subtitle 'In the Civilised British Government under the Cloak of Brahmanism', shows his great expectations of British rule as sponsors of the social reforms on the one hand and his harsh censure of the die-hard oppression against the low-caste people on the other. This book was 'dedicated to the good people of the United States as a token of admiration for their sublime disinterested and self-sacrificing devotion in the cause of Negro Slavery; and with an earnest desire, that my countrymen take their noble example as their guide in the emancipation of their Shudra Brothers from the trammels of Brahmin thralldom'.[32] Referring to inherent human rights in the introduction he writes:

> Though God gave Shudras, Ati-Shudras and others the right to enjoy equally all the things in the world which he created, Bhats (Brahmans) rejected this right of all and placed themselves at the topmost status in the false books they forged in the name of God.[33]

In more than half of the 16 chapters of this book he gives a detailed description of the process of invasion and conquest of indigenous Kshatriyas by Aryans (Brahmans) which were mentioned in

Brahmananche Kasab earlier. He also submits a theory that Brahmans created jatibhed (caste discrimination) in order to subjugate indigenous people permanently. Noticeably here he argues that non-Brahman Shudras (Kunbis, Malis, etc.) were also responsible for the origin of untouchability because they accepted the notion implanted by Brahmans that Mahars and Mangs who fought most valiantly and underwent the most severe revenge by Brahmans should not be even touched.[34]

Contrary to his expectations that the advent of British rule would bring caste discrimination to an end, in reality Brahmans held a variety of powers in their hands under the new circumstances. Though he attributes a part of this responsibility to the British administration or some of the British administrators, he appeals to them for the diffusion of education among the lower castes and for the opening of new jobs and positions to them for their social and economic improvements. In the latter half of the book he presents examples of social and economic monopolies by Brahmans in colonial India and requests the colonial authorities to redress the evils thereof on the one hand and encourages his Shudra and Ati-Shudra brethren to receive a good education while the British stayed in India for the purpose of exterminating their ignorance and prejudices and for breaking away from the yoke of slavery of Brahmanism.[35]

His other writings worth taking notice of are *Shetkaryacha Asud* (Cultivator's Whip-Cord) written in 1883 and *Sarvajanik Satya Dharmpustak* (Real Religious Book for the Public) in 1891. In the former he gives us clear ideas of the situation of his contemporary farmers who were annoyed and plundered by Brahmans in the name of religion on every occasion from birth until death. The latter one, covering almost all aspects of human life such as life and death, felicity, morality, marriage, production, sexual relations, and caste relations, teaches readers the values of the equality of both sexes, the respect of other person's rights, the esteem for labour, the negation of idol worship and other duties considered important for human beings. Though there was a marked influence of Christianity prevalent in these items, which are rather commonplace if viewed from today's criteria, we can find very clearly Phule's intention to emphasise the importance for farmers to transform themselves spontaneously in opposition to the Brahmanical ethical code which controlled the whole society. For example, his consistent attitude in rejecting every form of discrimination can be observed in such excerpts as 'You should not regard others as hereditary slaves according to books full of falsehoods written in olden days' and 'You should not disdain the works of Chambhars and others but assist them'.[36]

Phule founded the Satyashodhak Samaj (Truth-seeking Society) in September 1873 and became president and treasurer himself. The aim of founding this society is given in its report for the first two years:

> To free Shudras from subjugation to Brahmans, Bhats, Joshis, Upadhyas and so on, to give an understanding of the real right to Shudras whom they have been disdaining and exploiting nonchalantly for a thousand years on the basis of their crafty books, or in other words, to liberate these Shudras from the false and self-interested books of Brahmans prescribing religious and everyday affairs through good education and learning, a group of some educated Shudras established this society on September 24, 1873. In this society the discussion on political matters is completely prohibited.[37]

As shown in the society's rule which emphasises ideas like the heavenly father or humanly brotherhood and accepts no intermediary between God and human beings, the spirit of the society was markedly influenced by Christianity through the medium of Phule.

In the initial stage its weekly meetings put stress on the matters deeply concerned with everyday life of the ordinary farmers like the holding of marriage or remarriage ceremonies without Brahman priests, the abolition or celebration sans Brahmans of festivals such as Ganesh-chaturthi and the stoppage of fasts or food serving to the Brahmans on specific days. These activities and the contents of his writings given above show that Phule's sense of values with anti-Aryan and anti-Vedic substance was a challenge to the existent Hindu society and culture.[38] But this radicalness seems to have deprived popular support from ordinary members and farmers and very few people conducted ceremonies without the presence of Brahmans.[39] This anti-Vedic standpoint characteristic of Phule was nearly forsaken by his successors of the non-Brahman movement with the conspicuous exception of B. R. Ambedkar.

Though the society made some compromises now and then, it extended its activities gradually. The list of the activities included promotion of studies on comparison between Indian and foreign agriculture and technical improvements of the former, preparations for founding night schools for farmers, assistance of school fees to children of poor families, application for exemption of tuition on behalf of poor candidates for engineering colleges and activation of debates on the evils of caste discrimination and idol worship and so on.[40] In 1877 the society,started publishing its weekly bulletin, the *Din Bandhu* (Friend of the Poor).

The society's membership consisted of those not only of the Mali caste but of Maratha-Kunbi or artisan castes and even Mahar, and though many members of Pune and Bombay were rich merchants and contractors, many others of various professions like doctors, clerks and students were also included.[41] Some aspects common to many of them were that while they obtained a respectable social and economic place in the local circle in some way or other, they were given a lower ritual status as Shudras in the caste hierarchy by Brahmans, and they could not gain access easily to the advantages exclusively enjoyed by Brahmans in the local institutions of British administration. For them a broadly-based organisation was essential to extricate themselves from the adverse circumstances and to claim vociferously their rights equal to those of Brahmans.[42] Phule was not negative to their aspirations altogether but his fundamental principle to protect the interests of low-caste peasants was maintained. He contributed to the improvement of education and welfare of low-caste people from the later 1870s until the early 1880s as an appointed member of Pune Municipality Assembly and as a witness before the Indian Education Commission appointed by the Government of India (popularly known as the Hunter Commission) in 1882.

It was also during this period that he drew water and ran it to the fields from Khadakwasra Dam the construction of which he himself joined as a contractor and initiated several experiments to improve the cultivation of fruits and vegetables such as mosambi (sweet orange) and cauliflower. The earlier-mentioned *Shetkaryacha Asud* was one of the most remarkable outcomes of the same period.

Phule assisted in fomenting an agitation of peasants in Junnar Taluk of Pune District in 1884. That year he and his society gave vehement support to small farmers and tenants who together with Teli and Sonar artisans submitted a memorandum to the Government of Bombay demanding the protection of peasants from tyrant Brahman landlord-moneylenders. Countering these landlord-moneylenders by rejecting the Brahmans' function in marriage and other rituals and refusing to cultivate their lands for one year, the peasants continued their agitation. This was finally settled by the compromise reached between the Government, landlord-moneylenders and the peasants through Phule's mediation.[43]

Though the organisation of the Satyashodhak Samaj was small, it seems that it was not always managed under a well-coordinated leadership. For example, Narayan Meghji Lokhande (1848–1907), who founded the first factory labour union in Bombay and made great efforts to improve working conditions of low-caste labourers there, had a very different opinion from that of Phule. Krushnarao Bhalekar (1850–1910), one of Phule's cooperators joining him since the foundation of the society and once the editor of the *Din Bandhu*, also disagreed with him regarding the management of the paper and Phule's status in the organisation. Finally in 1884, Bhalekar left the society and organised the Din Bandhu Sarvajanik Sabha. Though Phule was a celebrity in Pune, the society he founded had already lost its vigour in the latter half of the 1880s. In his last days he faced economic adversity and died poor in November 1890.

Even though Phule was not successful in his lifetime in establishing a stable organisation for a movement to realise his ideals, he did leave a clear framework of anti-untouchability and anti-casteism as a legacy for the next generation. One of the most important aspects of his heritage is that he placed untouchable castes on an equal footing with other non-Brahman castes and gave pivotal significance to the work of abolishing discrimination against them.

Gopalnak Vitthalnak Warangkar, known to be the first Mahar to submit their demands publicly, came into contact with Phule while stationed in Pune as a soldier of the Indian Army. Retiring from the military service on a pension in 1886, he started a struggle with caste discrimination by publishing a pamphlet *Vital Vidhvansana* (Abolition of Untouchability) in 1888.[44] In 1894 he submitted a petition to demand the reopening of the recruitment of Mahars in the Indian Army which was suspended a year before. In the petition he criticised caste discrimination and untouchability as shown in suspension of recruitment of Mahars vehemently but the demand for Mahar recruitment was fulfilled only in 1942.[45] Another Mahar leader, Shivram Janba Kamble, who is said to have been attracted by Phule's activities and writings since his childhood, convened a large meeting of Mahars of 51 villages to appeal to the Government for Mahar recruitment in the Indian Army and police and for the diffusion of education among Mahar children.[46] Kamble later became an important co-worker of Ambedkar.

Non-Brahman Movement and Anti-Untouchability Movement in Maharashtra

As the national movement started gathering momentum in many parts of India in the early twentieth century, the colonial authorities responded to this with different kinds of policies from those of the former days and the situation of colonial India underwent remarkable changes. In Maharashtra, which exhibited radical national struggles together with Bengal and Panjab at that time, for example, there appeared strong caste movements opposed to the old Brahman authorities and privileges. In this section I examine the thoughts and activities of certain leaders who played an important role in these movements and also their stance concerning the problem of untouchability.

SHAHU CHHATRAPATI

The spirit and programmes of the Satyashodhak Samaj were succeeded and partly extended by Shahu Chhatrapati Maharaj (1874–1922) of Kolhapur, a princely state of a little more than 3,000 square miles in southern Maharashtra. Like all other princely states in India the royal family of Kolhapur genealogically connected with Shivaji was also loyal to the British colonial power after the Mutiny (1857–59). Shahu himself very strictly prohibited anti-British nationalist activities led by B.G. Tilak (1856–1920) in the state and this raised considerable tension between the Kolhapur state and nationalist forces.[47]

Important posts of Kolhapur administration were almost compeletely monopolised by Brahmans and even in 1894, 10 years after Shahu's coronation, 60 out of 71 bureaucrats were Brahmans.[48] In 1902 he issued an order that 50 per cent of the state's officialdom be assigned to those from low castes. This order was not implemented soon,[49] partly because the literacy of Brahmans accounting for about three per cent of the total population of the state was 80 per cent while that of all other castes was only 10 per cent.[50] Besides, in Kolhapur, there was a longstanding feud, called the Vedokta Prakaran, between the royal family who claimed Kshatriya varna and Brahman priests who denied this.[51] The Brahman forces were thus considered to pose a serious obstacle both to Shahu and to the society, and maintaining opposition to them inevitably remained one of his biggest tasks throughout his life.

In 1911 he assisted young non-Brahman officials like Bhaskarrao

Jadhav and Anna Babaji Latthe to found the Shahu Satyashodhak Sangh. Declaring their firm resolution to be successors to Phule's movement they devoted their energies to the diffusion of education among Maratha and low-caste children and the foundation of hostels for students from untouchable castes. Shahu also supported the publication and spread in his state of newspapers propagating non-Brahman ideology such as the *Jagruti* (Awakening) and the *Vijayi Maratha* (Victorious Marathas) which was published in Vadodara (Baroda) and Pune respectively. They performed rituals like the shravani (sacred thread) ceremony along with the recital of Vedic hymns by Maratha priests.[52]

With changes in the British policy in India brought about during World War I, the non-Brahman movement faced quite a new aspect. Expectations for larger participation in the legislative and executive councils aroused by the announcement of E. Montagu, the Secretary of State for India, of August 1917 and the Montagu-Chelmsford Reforms of 1918, gave this movement a salient political tinge. In Madras the South Indian Liberal Federation, founded as a 'Dravidian nationalist' organisation in 1917 and commonly known as the Justice Party, manifested its vehement anti-Brahman stance. Encouraged by this movement in south India which demanded the enlargement of political rights for non-Brahmans, Latthe and others founded the Brahmanetar (Non-Brahman) Association in 1920. This society soon started its political activities and Shahu supported the move to demand separate electorates for non-Brahman castes in the provincial legislative council of Bombay Province.[53] These developments were desirable also for the colonial authorities who expected the emergence of parties conforming to the government's policy other than the Indian National Congress. Thus the non-Brahman movement in Maharashtra which declared a profound attachment for Phule's ideals became rapidly politicised.

In the meantime reforms of some old caste traditions were effected in the state, one of which was the abolition of the watan system. Shahu discarded the post of kulkarni (village script) who held considerable influence in rural society and set up new positions for non-Brahmans including untouchables. In 1918 he ordered the abolition of the watan (balute) system, by which he liberated balutedars from services to the villagers. More importantly he showed considerable interest in the emancipation of Mahars, the most depressed under the watan system.

At the first Deccan Untouchables Conference held at Mangao in Kolhapur in March 1919 with B.R. Ambedkar, then professor of

Sydenham College in Bombay, as president, Shahu mentioned the abolition of Mahar watan. In his speech he stated that Mahars should abandon their watan worthy of only a small piece of land and meagre grain and leave the village to get a new job outside. As Mahars were hesitant to give up their land, he finally declared that land already held by them would be recognised as ordinary taxable land and that their services for village farmers would be abolished.[54] Though with this Mahar watan did not come to a complete end, Mahars at least were given the option to free themselves from slavery.

Shahu also took a firm stand on the treatment of untouchable castes. He had already opened officialdom in his state to them and in January 1919 he issued an order to every department of the government to promote them in the same way as caste Hindus. The quota of seats was allotted for them even in the Kolhapur Municipality, in which a young Chambhar assumed the office of chairman. Moreover, untouchability regarding water pipes, places for drawing water and public institutions like lodgings and hospitals was abolished, and schools meant only for untouchables were closed. Some educated untouchables were registered as lawyers in the state. On the occasion of the first Akhil-Bharatiya Bahishkrut Parishad (All-India Depressed Classes Conference) held at Nagpur in May 1920, Shahu proclaimed his decision to issue a sanad (royal order) for assurance that Mahars, Mangs and others could get any jobs they wanted.[55] It was also in this very year that Shahu formed a close relationship with Ambedkar who started his first newspaper, the *Muknaik* (Voice of the Dumb People), and left for London for study with the financial support of Shahu.

The standpoint of Shahu, however, differed from that of Phule on one very important point: While Phule categorically disapproved the Vedic values as being essential for the caste system and untouchability, Shahu attached great importance to the Vedic authority under the influence of the Arya Samaj which attracted him since 1902. He adhered to the Vedic rituals, for which he created the Maratha priesthood and its religious authority (Kshatra Jagatguru) on the one hand[56] and he did not abandon idol worship which the Arya Samaj rejected on the other.[57] His stance on approving the distinction among castes while arguing for abolishing untouchability was not common with that of Phule.[58] It is rather difficult to explain these seemingly contradictory aspects of his thought and behaviour, but the following citation from the Memoirs written by A.B. Latthe, one of his loyal co-workers seems very suggestive:

> He was essentially a rationalist but even rationalism was to him a creed. Everything, even religion itself, was to his mind an instrument. The main principle of his life was the practical interests which he set about to achieve with all the energy and all the resources which he could command.[59]

Shahu was from time again described or criticised as 'a conservative reformer' who did not express interest in the democratisation of his princely state as a whole[60] and as 'a compromise between conservative and Satyashodhak ideologies'.[61] As mentioned before, his loyal approval of the colonial rule and opposition to the nationalist movement are also debatable matters. But we cannot deny the historical meaning that, as one of the few leaders who tackled vigorously the prospects of social and economic improvements of untouchables in the process of the non-Brahman movement, he supported and encouraged many young untouchable workers including Ambedkar both inside and outside his state.[62]

VITTHAL RAMJI SHINDE

Though it may be somewhat inconsistent to include Vitthal Ramji Shinde (1873–1944) in the list of workers attempting to promote the non-Brahman movement, there is no denying that he was also one of the successors to Phule's ideology in the sense that he carried on a campaign for abolishing caste as a challenger to the Vedic and Brahmanical authorities.

Shinde was born of a Maratha farming family in a small princely state not far from Kolhapur. Though his family faced abject impoverishment because of his father's unemployment and loss of agricultural land, he managed to graduate from Fergusson College in Pune with a scholarship and enter University of Bombay to get his LL.B. in 1899.

In the meantime, he was drawn to the Indian National Congress and also came into contact with the Prarthna Samaj in Bombay, a social reform organisation which was founded in 1867 with the influence of the Brahmo Samaj in Bengal and led by outstanding Brahman intellectuals such as M.G. Ranade, R.G. Bhandarkar, N.G. Chandavarkar at that time. Like its unitarian Bengali counterpart the Samaj propagated worship of one God, negation of idol worship, abolition of child-marriage and absurdity of caste.

While in the university Shinde received a unitarian missionary scholarship of the Samaj to study at Manchester Theological College in England for two years from 1901. On this occasion he was given generous financial support by Sayaji Rao, Maharaja of Baroda.[63] Soon after returning from abroad with a religious liberal outlook he was appointed as a missionary by the Samaj and held this post for seven years. But while discharging his duty he felt dissatisfied with the Samaj whose activities were restricted to the upper levels of society only and his interest moved gradually toward the role of untouchable activists like Kamble.

In October 1906 he and his fellow activists established the Depressed Classes Mission Society of India. The list of its office-bearers included persons like S.R. Lad who once worked under Phule. The ultimate purpose of the mission was to abolish untouchability, but Shinde emphasised the necessity of the elimination of caste distinction by the united efforts of all groups seeking the abolition of untouchability. He also urged that the activities only in the fields of education and employment would not be able to elevate untouchable communities as a whole and that the movement should not be limited to the individual or community level but should be extended to the national level as well. He tried to influence not only untouchables and caste Hindus but also British officials, which had some effect on an educational policy prescribed for untouchables of the Government of Bombay. The daily tasks of the mission included management of boarding schools and free hospitals and in these they sought to do away with mutual discriminative consciousness through united operations of untouchables and caste Hindus.[64] The society helped forcefully the movement to revive the recruitment of untouchables in the army which had been launched by Walangkar and Kamble.[65] With financial aid from the rulers of Mysore and Indore and other princely states[66] this move spread to the larger cities of Bombay, Madras and the Central Provinces.

In 1908 Shinde published an article titled 'Bahishkrut Bharat' after his continuous studies on the history of untouchability. Whether intentionally or accidentally, Ambedkar adopted this title meaning 'Untouchables in India' for his newspaper started in 1927. In the first part of the article Shinde expressed his fundamental position in unequivocal words:

> Wherever and to whomever exorbitant social expulsion was inflicted in the history of human beings on this earth, if there is any

> which had been executed from olden times and now pervades over the whole land, it is this horrible social expulsion of castes deemed mean in the land of India. Indians, do let this vicious and sinful expulsion of our own brethren come to an end.[67]

The article refers to the origin of untouchability in India and examples of discrimination in brief and also discusses on the effects brought about to Indian society. His studies including this were later collected in one book, *Bharatiya Asprushyancha Prashna* (1933), in which after describing the history of untouchability and the religious and social conditions of almost all main untouchable castes in India he gives us a very detailed explanation of Mahars in Maharashtra, especially their position in Maharashtrian agrarian society including Mahar watan. It is of interest that in this he supports a theory that the original inhabitants of Maharashtra were those like Mahars and Mangs who were robbed of their rights by Marathas and Brahmans who came there in later periods.[68]

Interested in the Satyashodhak Samaj movement started by Phule, Shinde attended a convention of the Satyashodhak Sangh founded in 1911 by Shahu and Jadhav every year. But the difference of opinion between him and Sangh leaders was so great that in the 1916 convention, though elected its chairman beforehand, his invitation as chairman was cancelled since Jadhav, Latthe and others were against it.[69] They could not accept Shinde who negated the Vedic values as the basis of the caste system on the one hand while he argued for cooperation even with Brahmans who shared the same purpose with them on the other.[70] From Shinde's side he disliked the attitude of the Non-Brahman Party opposing the nationalist movement and co-operating with the colonial authorities.[71]

Since his founding the mission, Shinde appealed time and again to leaders of the Indian National Congress to tackle the problem of untouchability. However, the Congress, which had, from the beginning, maintained the policy of not discussing religious and social matters in its sessions, turned a deaf ear to his appeals. But the expectations among the depressed classes for larger participation in politics awakened by the 'Montagu Declaration' in 1917 elicited their strong demand to send their representatives to the legislative council, which in the end caused the Congress to adopt a resolution on the abolition of untouchability at its session in December 1917 for the first time.[72] Encouraged by this, Shinde organised the Akhil-Bharatiya Asprushyata

Nivarak Parishad (All-India Conference for Abolition of Untouchability) in Bombay in March 1918, in which Tilak and other Congress leaders also participated. In a speech supporting a resolution for the abolition of untouchability in the conference, Tilak, though regarded as an adamant opponent of the social reforms, pointed out that there was no scriptural authority in untouchability, that 'the house of god is closed to no one. I don't recognise anyone trying to close this door as god', and that 'I think the evil custom of untouchability must be extinguished'. Even some of the newspapers known as being anti-Tilak set a high value on this speech.[73] But when requested to sign a declaration stating that participants in the conference would not observe untouchability in their own daily life and would make every personal effort toward its abolition on a social level, Tilak rejected the signing of it on the spot as he was disuaded from doing so by his Brahman followers.[74] This event much disillusioned Shinde in Tilak and in the Congress as well. In fact, Ambedkar called this Bombay conference a farce and criticised Tilak severely.[75]

In January 1919 when the Reforms Committee (Franchise), commonly known as the Southborough Committee was set up under the new Government of India Act, 1919, Shinde was also invited to give evidence before it on behalf of his mission. He and two other representatives of Mahars, Ambedkar and G.A. Gavai, demanded separate electorates for the depressed classes. Though it seems that Shinde thought of a co-option of appointment of the depressed classes' representatives by elected members of the legislative council, he argued for five elected members from the depressed classes in the legislative council of Bombay in writing. Referring to the enlargement of the franchise for the depressed classes, he proposed that qualifications for election be an income of more than Rs. 144 per annum and an education over the fourth standard of government-approved schools.[76] Ambedkar emphasised that the depressed classes were naturally entitled to separate electorates already given to Muslims and also that the depressed classes would be represented by their own community members.[77] He and other depressed class leaders denounced Shinde's proposal for electoral qualifications as being too high for them and he and his mission were severely criticised on this point in the first Akhil-Bharatiya Bahishkrut Parishad held in Nagpur on 30–31 May 1920.[78]

Ultimately the political reforms under the Government of India Act, 1919 supplied the depressed classes with only one appointed seat.

Though Shinde tried to get this seat on behalf of them, this post was filled by D.D. Gholap, a Mahar activist who was editor of the *Muknaik* started by Ambedkar. From this period onward the confidence in Shinde among the depressed classes faded rapidly. In the *Muknaik* during the years of 1921–22 many complaints arouse from the Mahar students living in the mission's boarding schools about food and the like. Not a few of them attacked his arrogance.[79] Increasing dissatisfaction over his leadership in the mission itself caused him to retire from it in 1923 and from the next year he served as a missionary of the Brahmo Samaj until he died in 1944.

Shinde can be placed on the same level as social reformists of the late nineteenth and early twentieth centuries as far as his moderate reformist stance is concerned. There was an insurmountable wall between him and Ambedkar who was strongly fixated on the solution of the problems of untouchables on their own initiative. But we know that many Mahar activists like Shankarrao R. Kharat, one of Ambedkar's young cooperators, paid the highest respect to Shinde. In his well-written history of the liberation movements of untouchables, *Asprushyancḥa Muktisangram*, Kharat confesses that he was greatly impressed by Shinde's remarks on the occasion of a temple liberation movement at Pune in 1929, that is, 'If India advances for independence with untouchability remaining intact, it will not only be a crisis for the world but also a direct challenge to god.'[80]

KESHAVRAO JEDHE

Keshavrao Jedhe (1896–1959) was one of the most important leaders not only of the non-Brahman movement but also of the political history of modern Maharashtra as a whole. His family was directly descended from Kanhoji Jedhe, distantly related to Chhatrapati Shivaji, and considered to be on a higher rank even among the 96 distinguished Maratha families (assal Maratha). The Jedhes made a fortune through management of a bottle factory which Marutirao Jedhe, Keshavrao's father, started at the end of the nineteenth century. Their residence, built in 1914 and commonly called Jedhe Mansion, soon became the unofficial headquarters of the non-Brahman movement in Pune and was frequented by Shahu and other leaders.[81]

After leaving Fergusson College in mid-course in 1918, Keshavrao joined the All-India Maratha League which his elder brother Baburao and others founded as a base of the non-Brahman movement. Shinde also visited Jedhe Mansion often and strongly impressed Keshavrao who did not agree with the programmes of Shinde's mission but vehemently supported his activities of abolishing untouchability. In 1918 Keshavrao took part in the Akhil-Bharatiya Asprushyata Nivarak Parishad in Bombay as a volunteer and this was his first experience of public work.[82] At that time there were many non-Brahman activists in Pune who were interested in the movement in Kolhapur but gradually became skeptical of its pro-British stance. Shahu was also among those who were criticised by the Brahmanetar Sangh (Non-Brahman League) founded on the initiative of the Jedhe brothers at Jedhe Mansion in December 1920.[83]

The Jedhe name was reported from time to time in newspapers since the controversy over a Shivaji mela (festival) began. This festival was initially planned by Shahu and other rulers of Baroda and Gwaliyar to heighten the prestige and unity of the Maratha community. But as they invited European and Brahman guests and requested the attendance of the Prince of Wales who visited India at that time, Jedhe and other young Maratha activists launched a movement to organise their own mela. After Shahu, a pivotal person among the rulers, died in 1922, Jedhe and his co-workers held a Chhatrapati mela, which was coupled with the Ganeshotsav (Ganapati festival). The public Ganapati festival was originally organised by Tilak in 1893 to encourage the masses to join the nationalist movement and was thereafter managed mostly by Tilak's followers. Therefore the seizing of control of this festival meant for non-Brahman activists an acquisition of their symbol as well as the enhancement of their voices in the political field. Finally this competition was won by the Jedhe group in 1927.[84] During this period Jedhe met a talented young man named Dinkarrao Jawalkar (1898–1932) who was active in Kolhapur. Though their partnership did not last long, the combined name Jedhe-Jawalkar marked an important page in the history of the non-Brahman movement in Maharashtra.

In 1925 Jedhe was elected a member of Pune Minicipality Assembly. But at that time non-Brahmans were still a minority group in the assembly. In September the same year he proposed a bill to open public wells and water pipes in the city indiscriminately to untouchables, which was voted down by a majority group mainly comprising Brahman members commonly known as the Tilakites. Another bill to erect a bronze statue of Phule was also rejected. It was also in the same year that a booklet titled *Deshache Dushman* (Enemies of the Country) came out with Jedhe as publisher and Jawalkar as author. With the opening sentence 'Enemies of the Country, Tilak and Chiplunkar. Clever leaders of the poor and helpless world',[85] the booklet hurled a thoroughgoing criticism against these two great thinkers of modern Maharashtra as representative ideologues of Brahmanical dominance. The bellicosity of the words used in it can be easily imagined by the fact that the republication of this booklet was not possible until 1984 and its republished copies suffered public book burning in 1991.[86] Jedhe, Jawalkar and others concerned were charged by Tilak and Agarkar families and sentenced to paying a fine and imprisonment. They immediately appealed to the high court and it was Ambedkar, a barrister and a member of the Bombay Legislative Council at that time, who went forth to defend them after all other lawyers refused their defence. The result was that all were declared not guilty except that Jawalkar was indicted on other charges.[87]

Jedhe and Jawalkar actively took part in the so-called Mahad Satyagraha which was launched at Mahad in Colaba District under the leadership of Ambedkar in 1927. The purpose of this satyagraha was to materialise the resolution already adopted in the Bombay Legislative Council in 1924 to enable those who were deemed untouchables to use public reservoirs, schools and charity lodges. In March people of depressed classes held a huge meeting to demand the opening of the Chavdar Tank. They then marched on the tank and drank water there, at which point they were attacked by caste Hindus and many were injured. Jedhe and Jawalkar went to Mahad and participated in a large-scale agitation which Ambedkar started in protest against this violent action. They issued statements of fiery tone in one of which, dated June 19, they proposed an action plan: to carry out satyagraha completely in a non-violent way, not to include any Brahmans in the satyagraha, to march on the reservoir with flags of Hindu dharma and drink water there in groups of 15 hundred, and for non-Brahman brethren to take part in the struggle to do away with untouchability, a stigma of Hindu dharma. They also appealed to non-Brahman leaders to take a firm stand without delay.[88]

Though accepting their proposals on the whole, Ambedkar disagreed with them in excluding all Brahman elements indiscriminately from their agitation and emphasised the necessity to make a distinction between Brahmanical ideology and individual Brahmans free from it. Jedhe and Jawalkar were then requested by Ambedkar to make a speech, in which they praised Ambedkar's act of burning *Manu-smruti*. Whereas a neutral statement was issued by non-Brahman leaders that they would not obstruct the depressed classes' endeavours to win human rights, there were few activists like Jedhe and Jawalkar among them who positively supported this agitation.[89] They were involved in other anti-untouchability agitations such as temple entry movements at Parvati Temple of Pune in 1929 and also at Kalaram Temple of Nashik from 1930 to 1935.[90]

Besides these two activists we must mention here Shridharpant Tilak, the second son of Lokmanya Tilak, who sympathised deeply with Ambedkar's cause. His contact with Jedhe's group started from around 1926. In September 1927 when a Krishna mela procession organised by people of various castes including untouchables was interrupted by the police, he approved of the procession coming into his residential compound, the Gaekwadwada located at Sadashiv Peth known as a Brahman residential area in old Pune.[91] In April 1928 he opened at his residence a Pune branch of the Samaj Samta Sangh (League for Social Equality) founded by Ambedkar the year before. Jedhe was one of its executive members. Though the main programmes of the league were only to hold meetings for discussion of social questions like caste discrimination and to sponsor saha-bhojans (eating together) of all castes including untouchables, the setting up of its branch at the very centre of the Brahman residential area was a shocking event in Pune.[92] Ambedkar who visited the Gaekwadwada with his co-workers in Bombay to attend its inaugural meeting told in deep emotion:

> There is no doubt that Shridharpant showed great courage by supplying the League with its field of action and supporting the principle of equality. If this duty is discharged with diligence continuously, people will say that he has accomplished a thousand times as an important work than his father. Standing at LokmanyaTilak's residence, I have no intention to criticise him. Everyone will agree that he displayed great courage in the political field. But there is also no doubt that he did not fulfill his responsibility for social matters.[93]

But longstanding discord with the trustees of the Kesari office and family matters drove him to killing himself in May 1928. Some time later the *Bahishkrut Bharat*, a newspaper published by Ambedkar, carried an article referring to Shridharpant's contributions which cited a part of his letter addressed to Ambedkar just before his suicide. It says, 'I am going to the feet of Lord Krishna to present the grievances of untouchable castes to him. I hope our agitation will achieve a complete success.'[94]

As mentioned earlier there were divisions among non-Brahman forces and the conflict became more intense especially concerning the attitude toward the Indian Statutory Commission, commonly known as the Simon Commission, which was appointed by the British government in 1927 to prepare for the future revision of the government of India Act. Jedhe's group argued for its boycott and the conservative group was in favour of it.

At that time Jedhe and his co-workers spent a long time in discussing whether or not they should join the Indian National Congress. Jedhe himself, without deciding on this, participated in the Non-Cooperation Movement, known as the Salt Satyagraha, under the leadership of Mahatma Gandhi, and was arrested in March 1930. Feeling fully assured of Gandhi's leadership he made up his mind to be a member of the Congress after being released the next year. By 1932 the leadership within the Maharashtra Congress organisation had shifted from the so-called Tilakites headed by N.C. Kelkar to a Gandhian group led by Shankarrao Deo, which was strengthened by the entry of Jedhe and his Maratha following. But since then positive participation of the non-Brahman forces in the anti-untouchability movement rapidly disappeared from the arena partly because the Congress almost completely entrusted this responsibility to the Gandhian 'harijan' movement and also because the new movement led by Ambedkar became more and more active.

DALIT MOVEMENT

Bhimrao Ramji Ambedkar

As has already been presented, with the appearance of Bhimrao Ramji Ambedkar (1891–1956), the history of the liberation movement of untouchables in Maharashtra entered a completely new dimension. While taking over the pioneering having been done by Walangkar and Kamble hailing from his own caste, Mahar, Ambedkar played a unique and important role in awakening people treated as untouchables to a sense of duty to free themselves from the yoke of slavery and to make redress of their grievances as an essential problem to be solved in modern India.

SOME ASPECTS OF AMBEDKAR'S MOVEMENT

Since an early stage Ambedkar showed great zeal for the abolition of Mahar watan. As described in the first section Mahar watan meant an entitlement to a small quantity of grain or a fragment of land traditionally given to Mahars who rendered a variety of services including those very loathful to caste Hindu villagers. This watan legislated by the colonial government in the Bombay Hereditary Offices Act, 1874, was part of Mahars' livelihood but at the same time it was regarded as 'visavya shatakatil gulamgiri' (slavery in the twentieth century)[95] which shackled them to the lowest status in the agrarian society. By citing three reasons, Ambedkar argued that there was no other way except abolishing their watan: firstly, Mahars had lost their sense of self-respect because of watan; secondly, aspirations of Mahars to work in other field of society had been washed away because of watan; and thirdly, Mahars could not hope for their self-reliance and improvement in life as long as they continued to depend on watan.[96]

In the problem of Mahar watan Ambedkar saw some symbolic meaning for the Mahar's improvement such as economic status connected with land and social status. Though his interest in the abolition of Mahar watan went back to the 1910s, he was greatly influenced by Shahu's efforts to abolish it. After gaining a seat in the Bombay Legislative Council in 1926 and especially from 1928 when he submitted a bill on watan (Hereditary Offices Act Amendment Bill) for the first time, this was one of the biggest subjects retaining his interest until the end of his life. It was only in August 1959, almost 12 years after India's independence, that his purpose was fulfilled by the enforcement of the Bombay Inferior Village Watan Abolition Act of 1958.

Assisted by caste Hindu activists, untouchable leaders tackled the problems of drawing drinking water and entry into Hindu temples since the earlier period. They were taken up in provincial legislative councils, which adopted a resolution to end their social disabilities. The satyagraha launched in Mahad in 1927 to demand the implementation of the resolution by opening the Chavdar Tank to untouchables made Ambedkar's name known to the whole of India, but as well, it cannot be denied that this satyagraha invited the animosity and vigilance of many caste Hindus. Faced with violent acts of caste Hindus toward participants of the agitation, he had to accept arbitration of the Collector and call a halt to it, but he also confessed that he did not think that the purpose of their movement could be fulfilled soon.[97] Actually, after the Congress won the provincial assembly elections in 1937, a bill to abolish the diabilities of untouchables related to the use of public tanks and wells, and roads and other transportation facilities was introduced in the Bombay Legislative Assembly to which Ambedkar was also elected as a member. However, the enactment of law did not effect a real solution to the problem.[98]

As for the temple entry movements of untouchables, the satyagrahas of Vaikkam (1924–25) and Gurvayur (1932) launched with the support of Gandhi in south India were well known.[99] But Gandhi was rather negative toward other satyagrahas which the untouchables tried to organise on their own initiative.[100] Ambedkar, on the other hand, took the lead in his first temple entry movement at Ambadevi Temple in Amravti of Vidarbha in August 1927 when the Mahad satyagraha was still under way. Thereafter Parvati Temple of Pune and Kalaram Temple of Nashik were selected as stages of the movement in 1929 and 1930 respectively. Like the movement demanding the opening of tanks, these were also aimed at winning equal rights for untouchables. However, when explaining the reason for selecting Nashik, for example, he said that if they were allowed to enter a temple deeply connected with Ram, one of the most popular gods of Hindus, it would denote a change of their minds and would be the first step in the solution of the untouchability problem.[101] In this period Ambedkar seems to have thought about something akin to 'hriday-parivartan' (return to conscience), a favourite idea of Gandhi who would be a target of his harsh criticism in later years.

Though the satyagraha of Pune was fought on a large scale with the support of some cooperative Brahmans, Marathas and non-Mahar untouchable workers and that of Nashik was continued for five long years, their demands could not be met. This failure deeply disappointed Ambedkar and led him to declare at Yeola in Nashik in October 1935 that though he was born to be a Hindu, he would not die as a Hindu.[102] In 1938 when the Harijan Temple Worship Bill was introduced in the Bombay Legislative Assembly, he and two other members of the depressed classes not only refused to join a select committee[103] but also eschewed even to speak on the subject in the assembly.[104] His decision of abandoning Hinduism and to convert to another religion would have been strengthened gradually through these processes.

I believe it was probably in a memorandum submitted to the Reforms Committee (Franchise) and in an interview of his in January

1919 that Ambedkar made his first political statement. On this occasion, as mentioned earlier, he intensely demanded for the depressed classes the setting up of separate electorates. Here, interestingly enough, he connected the representation of the depressed classes with the principle of self-determination argued by many politicians after World War I and regarded them as two different expressions of the same conception.[105] As the Government of India Act, 1919 did not approve separate electorates for the depressed classes, the debate continued for some years to come but opinions among depressed class leaders were divided between separate electorates and general electorates with reserved seats for them. In a report submitted to the Simon Commission in 1927, Ambedkar himself argued for universal suffrage and general electorates with reserved seats for the depressed classes, which he later withdrew.[106]

The situation changed, however, when the Congress adopted the resolution of 'purna-swaraj' (complete independence) in its Lahore session in December 1929 and started the second Satyagraha Movement under Gandhi's leadership in March 1930. As the anti-British struggle led by the Congress was gathering momentum in this way, Ambedkar, who harboured a distrust of the reformist attitude of Gandhi and the Congress concerning social matters, was obliged to place the depressed classes' distinct interests to the fore. So at the Round Table Conference held in London in October 1930, he again demanded serarate electorates for the depressed classes.[107] In the conference to which the whole world was attentive he claimed that the depressed classes, regarded as an integral part of Hindu society, had actually a separate existence just like other communities in India such as Muslims but were given discriminative treatment not shared by any other community.[108] When he had a talk with Gandhi in August 1931 for the first time in Bombay, he emphasised the distinct position of the depressed classes and their initiative in the movement and did not yield a single point to Gandhi for whom it was beyond question that harijans (untouchables) formed an indivisible portion of the Hindu society.[109]

A clash between Gandhi and Ambedkar was observed again in the second Round Table Conference started in September 1931 in which the former participated as the representative of the Congress. Raising a question as to who would represent untouchables, Gandhi claimed that he would top the poll if this was put to a referendum of untouchables. He also criticised the classification of Scheduled Castes (untouchables) as a separate class in the census and stood against serarate electorates for them. In the last words of his argument, 'Those who speak of the political rights of untouchables do not know their India, do not know how Indian society is today constructed, and therefore I want to say with all the emphasis that I can command that if I was the only person to resist this thing I would resist it with my life.'[110]

After no conclusions came out of these Round Table Conferences, British Prime Minister Ramsey MacDonald announced the 'Communal Award' in August 1932 which approved separate electorates for the depressed classes. Gandhi who was imprisoned after the suspension of the satyagraha wrote in a letter to MacDonald dated 9 September 1932, 'I sense the injection of poison that is calculated to destroy Hinduism and do no good whatever to the Depressed Classes'[111] and started his 'fast unto death' on 20 September. Ambedkar pressed by public opinion quite bitter to him was in the end compelled to accept the 'Poona (Pune) Pact' which would shelve the separate electorate for the depressed classes.[112]

The pact by which the depressed classes were to get more reserved seats than were to be made available by MacDonald's Award, did not mean victory to either side.[113] Rather this whole event more embittered the confrontation between these two leaders and made the alienation of their agitations for the abolition of untouchability from each other decisively unavoidable.

CASTE GROUPS' RESPONSE TO AMBEDKAR'S MOVEMENT

By what has so far been mentioned, it is clear that Ambedkar's basic principle was to consider placing untouchables themselves in the seat of primary responsibility for the anti-untouchability movement. In the aforementioned conversation with Gandhi in 1931 Ambedkar said in an emphatic way, 'If untouchability is to be abolished, it will be done by the efforts of none but untouchables.'[114] Important to be noticed together with this point is that he laid stress on the importance of self-identity among untouchables. In the *Bahishkrut Bharat*, a newspaper started by Ambedkar in 1927, there appeared many articles infused with such tone, one of which was titled as 'Asprushya ki Purvasprushya' (Untouchable or Ex-Untouchable). In this short article Ambedkar asserted that the use of the term 'purvasprushya' (ex-untouchable) instead of 'bahishkrut' (depressed) or 'asprushya' (untouchable) was a cunnning practice of caste Hindus and stressed that untouchables should fight against caste Hindus with a strong consciousness that untouchability was not a past phenomenon yet and that they were still untouchables.[115]

Though the present author has not clarified if Ambedkar ever used the term 'dalit' (depressed) which has been in general use in the radical liberation movements of Scheduled Castes in contemporary India, he was consistent in placing self-identity of the depressed at the basis of their movement. Ambedkar, however, did not reject the participation of caste Hindus including Brahmans in the movement altogether. As shown in the preceding pages, he emphasised the necessity of differentiating as clearly as possible between Brahmanical philosophy and individual Brahmans.

Shripad Mahadev Mate (1886–1957), a writer residing in Pune and affiliated with the Hindu Mahasabha, was one of those activists severely criticised by Ambedkar, though he advocated the necessity of improving the life of untouchables, particularly that of Mahars. From Ambedkar's viewpoint, however, the policy of the Mahasabha to agree to the abolition of untouchability on the one hand but to argue for the continuation of the caste system itself on the other was not acceptable, and the opinion of Mate that privileges for untouchables were more generous under the Peshwa's rule than in the British period was rather dangerous.[116] Ambedkar was enraged when Mate issued a statement in which he denied that violent actions were committed against participants of the movement by caste Hindus.[117] Ambedkar advised his followers not to be a party to divisive activities of deceitful persons by reporting an episode reported by one of his friends who visited Mate's house in which untouchable guests could not enter rooms other than one meant for them only, and when a caste Hindu visited his house while they were still inside, Mate himself went out to talk with his newly coming guest.[118] As for the Hindu Mahasabha, Ambedkar also criticised Vinayak Damodar Savarkar (1884–1960), who was to be the most prominent leader of the orga-nisation, for encouraging the building of temples meant only for untouchables as it would delay formulating the solution to the problem.[119]

Practically, there were only a few cases of Brahmans who gave willing cooperation to Ambedkar's movement. Having already mentioned Shridharpant Tilak, another example is that of Narhar Vishnu Gadgil (1896–1966), one of the top leaders of the Congress organisation in Maharashtra and a minister of the post-independence Nehru cabinet, who took part in the temple entry satyagraha of Parvati Temple in Pune.[120]

What Ambedkar actually thought about the depressed castes themselves as primary promoters of the anti-untouchable movement is an important subject of concern. At the start of this essay, I pointed out that there was a mutual animosity and discrimination among such untouchable castes of Maharashtra as Mahars, Mangs, and Chambhars. Though each of these communities was not completely homogeneous and their behaviour could not always be judged on the basis of caste, a serarate sense of self-awareness and discrimination among themselves vis-à-vis other caste communities was quite strong. In this vein, a letter from a reader to the editor of *Bahishkrut Bharat* in May 1929 sounded a warning to untouchables about their mutual discrimination with each other saying that Mahars regarded Mangs as inferior to them and Mangs placed Bhangis on a lower status than theirs before Ambedkar launched his movement, and even now most Chambhars treat other untouchable castes as their inferiors.[121] Therefore, as easily imagined, active members of Ambedkar's organisation were predominantly from the Mahar community and support from other caste groups was very much limited. Moreover, it must also be noted that even in the Mahar community there appeared such an activist as G.A. Gavai from the Vidarbha area who was educated in the Shinde's mission and formed a group opposed to Ambedkar.

One of the most sensitive problems that bothered Ambedkar was how to form and maintain a united action with Mangs whose antagonism to Mahars was well-known. But in 1927 when he appealed to Mang inhabitants to participate in the temple entry movement in Amravti, he was disappointed with their response that they were unwilling to abandon their traditional practices.[122] K.K. Sakat, an influential Hindu Mahasabhaite Mang leader deeply connected with above-mentioned Mate, attacked the Brahmanya (Brahmanness) of Mahars who, according to Sakat, regarded Mangs as inferior and prohibited them from entering Mahar's temples. In response to this, Ambedkar admitted the necessity of reforming 'evil' customs of Mahars on the one hand and criticised the similar attitude of Mangs toward Mahars and also the Hindu Mahasabhaite stance of Sakat subservient to Mate and other Brahman leaders on the other.[123] It was again Mang leaders that took a strong stand against the direct action at the temple entry satyagraha of Parvati in Pune in 1929.[124]

Chambhars who considered themselves to be higher than Mahars in social status also did not easily rally to Ambedkar's flag. In a meeting held during the Mahad satyagraha in 1927, one Chambhar participant stated that Ambedkar took account of the interests of Mahars only and neglected those of others. The feeling behind this statement is considered to have been held more or less in common among non-Mahars because people knew that Ambedkar was pouring much of his energy into the abolition of Mahar watan at that time. In reply, he emphasised that their movement was aimed at improving all untouchable communities as a whole and assured the audience that he was ready to concede his position at any time to a more competent leader from the Chambhar community.[125] During this period he continued to appeal to his Chambhar fellowmen to join him in the struggle to regain their humanity at all costs.[126]

Along this line, I shall later take up one Chambhar worker, P. N. Rajbhoj, who actively cooperated with Ambedkar without exhibiting a narrow-minded community consciousness.

AMBEDKAR AND NATIONALISM

Here it is necessary to examine how Ambedkar related his movement of liberating the depressed classes with the Indian national struggle with which almost the whole of India was involved.

In evidence taken before the Southborough Committee in 1919, Ambedkar stated that as the political movement gathered momentum, the social reform movement died down and also that the Congress organisation was largely composed of men who were by design political radicals and social conservatives.[127] This opinion basically remained unchanged even after the new era was ushered in under Gandhian leadership. In particular, he was deeply distrustful of Congress' want of zeal in tackling the duty of eliminating discrimination against the depressed classes comprising one fourth of the population and in launching a radical movement on a national level.[128]

But Ambedkar's distrust of the Congress does not mean that he did not take up the issue of political independence from the colonial rule. In the presidential address of the first session of the All-India Depressed Classes Conference held at Nagpur in August 1930, his basic stance of furthering the national independence movement connected with the pursuit of social equality was clearly in evidence. First, he posed one question that was looming on the horizon at that time, 'Is it possible for the peoples of India to become one united self-governing community?' After referring to examples of Latvia, Rumania, Lithuania, Yugoslavia, Estonia and Czechoslovakia which, with all their difference of race, creed, language and culture, came into being as self-governing states after World War I, he asserted that the case of India which was regarded as a helplessly heterogeneous country was not more bewildering than those countries.[129] He admitted that 'the system of self-government itself has been the cause of unification of many a people who in its absence would have remained as discordant and as distinct as they were in the original condition'. But turning to India which 'did not recognise the hard facts of its society', he thought it deplorable that 'the strings of political power will be in the hands of the ambitious members of the upper strata of Indian society drawn from the high-placed, well-educated and opulent castes, that is, in the hands of the aristocracy of wealth, education and social standing'. Though he agreed with the Congress that no country was justified in ruling over another, at the same time he never failed to add 'that the proposition (of the Congress–author) does not end there and that it is equally true that no class is good enough to rule over another class'.[130]

Ambedkar then pointed out that a variety of political programmes of the Congress including the Nehru Committee's Report in 1928 had not guaranteed the fundamental rights of the minorities, especially of the depressed classes, and demanded a reasonable share of political representation for them. But here, without sticking fast to the scheme of separate electorates, he argued for that of joint electorates with reserved seats together with adult suffrage 'so that we may thereby minimise such influence as the majority community may happen to cast in the election of our representatives'.[131] In the latter part of his speech, he maintained that while generally people of India remained subject to the miserable poverty under 'the costliest government' of the British Raj, it was the depressed classes who were most directly suffering from the poverty, and appealed to them that 'it is only in a Swaraj constitution that you stand any chance of getting the political power into your own hands without which you cannot bring salvation to your people'. Though he admitted that Swaraj, the idea of getting the political power, was a peculiar apparition to some people and might remind them of 'the tyrannies and oppressions and injustices practiced upon them by their fellow-countrymen', Ambedkar assured the audience of his firm conviction:

> If you will for one moment forget the past and visualise the Swaraj of the future with its wholesome devices to protect the masses from classes you will find that far from being a weird apparition it

> is going to be a system of Government in which you yourselves stand the chance, other things being equal, of being amongst those who will be installed as the political sovereigns of this country. Do not be obsessed by the past. Do not be swayed by fear or favour from any quarters in making your decision. Consult your best interests and I am sure you will accept Swaraj as your goal. [132]

Lastly, mentioning the civil disobedience movement of Gandhi, he asserted that he was opposed to that movement because he was convinced that the question was not whether his movement was right or wrong but whether it was opportune and consistent with the safety and security of depressed classes' interests, and in fact he thought it extremely inopportune.[133]

Ambedkar to whom nationalism and agitation for rights of untouchables were not contradictory to each other participated in activities of the legislative council which the Congress boycotted tactically. In that sense his political stance can be recognised as one similar to those of Gopal Krushna Gokhale (1866–1915), Motilal Nehru (1861–1931) and Chitt Ranjan Das (1870–1925) who were called the moderates or parliamentarians.

Pandurang Nathuram Rajbhoj

Chambhars form the second largest community among Scheduled Castes (untouchables) in Maharashtra. Therefore it evokes somewhat of a strange impression that their existence went rather unnoticed in the history of the anti-untouchability movement in Maharashtra while Mahars played a conspicuous role in it. [134] As a matter of fact, this caste group as a whole showed very little interest in Ambedkar's movement. One of the exceptional cases, however, was that of Pandurang Nathuram Rajbhoj (1906–86). I believe that a glance at his philosophy and behaviour will bring us a somewhat different image of the movement from that which we have formed only through Ambedkar and his Mahar co-workers.

Rajbhoj was born to a comparatively prosperous Chambhar family that followed the traditional business of leather working and also cultivated hereditary land in a small village of Nashik District. Among Chambhars his family belonged to a sub-caste of pious Vaishnav Harli which eschwed the custom of meat-eating. According to Enthoven, Harlis did not mend the shoes of the 'impure' castes, such as Mahars and Mangs, which Chevlis, another meat-eating sub-caste of

Chambhars, did.[135] The family being economically well-off, little Rajbhoj was not discriminated openly against in the village. But after experiencing discriminatory treatment like prohibition from drinking water together with caste Hindu boys and cleaning forced on Chambhar boys, he decided to leave school.[136] He got a job at a Taluk Magistrate's office, where he was ordered to work outdoors separately from ordinary officials and so abandoned it in protest against this treatment.[137]

He went to Pune in 1919 and after graduating from New Marathi School at the age of 18, he got a job as a petty official and at the same time joined the Asprushya Nivarak Mandal (Untouchability Abolition Society, founded in 1917) headed by Shripad Mahadev Mate who taught him at New Marathi School. The main purposes of the society were, among others, to make temples open to untouchables and to found schools for their children. On one occasion when Rajbhoj was appointed as a secretary of a conference of Chambhars organised on the initiative of the society in 1926, he had a chance to observe minutely the lives of untouchable families. While referring to Rajbhoj as one of Mate's collaborates, Ambedkar who censured the latter severely at that time, thought highly of this young activist for not being thoroughly obedient to his ex-teacher.[138] It was the Mahad Tank Satyagraha in 1927 that gave Rajbhoj a complete turnabout. As a satyagrahi he witnessed the vigorous resistance of caste Hindus and had to remain in a dispensary for 15 days because of a serious injury inflicted on him by a farmer. This was the first ordeal he experienced in obtaining the right just to drink water.[139]

In 1928 he started the *Dalit Bandhu* (Friends of Untouchables), his first newspaper. It is probable that the term 'dalit' was used for the first time as the name of a newspaper or a periodical.[140] Though initially the main interest of this paper was centred on discusions about problems and reforms within the Chambhar community, it gradually broadened its outlook to socio-economic conditions of untouchables as a whole.[141] In the same year, he obtained a seat allotted to the depressed classes in Pune Municipality Assembly. During this election campaign, B.R. Ambedkar spoke highly of Rajbhoj as a person suitable for doing the work of the assembly in all senses.[142] He served his term actively untill 1932 tackling such problems as the housing for untouchable residents and their use of public water service. He was also a member of the education committee of the city. In 1932 he became a secretary of the Pune branch of the Samaj Samta Sangh founded by Shridharpant Tilak and it was there that his direct association with Jedhe and Ambedkar started.

Rajbhoj participated in the Parvati Temple Entry Satyagraha in 1929. In submitting a notice addressed to the temple trustees demanding to open the temple for untouchables, an arrangement was made to put on the notice the signatures of representatives of three main untouchable castes, that is, S.J. Kamble from Mahars, K.K. Sakat from Mangs and Rajbhoj from Chambhars.[143] Of these, however, Sakat left the front before the satyagraha began. In November 1929 when satyagrahis started walking in line toward the temple on the hill-top, caste Hindus violently attacked them. Rajbhoj was among the wounded who were carried into hospitals. Finally in September 1932, the committee of the temple proposed a compromise that untouchable devotees be allowed to see and worship the images of gods from staircases specially built for them, which could by no means satisfy the participants of the movement.[144] Rajbhoj also took part in the Nashik Satyagraha which was launched in February 1930 under the strong leadership of Ambedkar and experienced his first arrest and imprisonment.

In 1931 a meeting of the Bombay Province Charmkar Parishad (Chambhar Conference) was held at Nashik with Rajbhoj acting as chairman. The purpose of this meeting was primarily to work out the Chambhars' position with consideration given to the proposed second Round Table Conference that year in which both Ambedkar and Gandhi were to participate. Representing an opinion quite common among the majority of the Chambhar community that the scheme of separate electorates would be advantageous only to Mahars, Rajbhoj insisted on the necessity of reserved seats in legislative bodies not only for the depressed classes as a whole but also for Chambhars independently. He expressed his dissatisfaction that though the Chambhar community had a population of more than two lakhs in Bombay Province only which was several times bigger than that of other communities like Europeans, Anglo-Indians or Sikhs the protection of whose rights the government was considering, the protection of rights of Chambhars was never discussed. He then referred to the intra-caste problems of Chambhars and requested his caste fellows especially to make every effort to stamp out such 'evil' habits as drinking and the use of opium and mutual distinction or discrimination among sub-castes. He said that the extinction of untouchability would be possible only if they themselves would practise good behaviour within their community, gain a deep understanding of the heart of caste Hindus, and obtain their own rights through 'true satyagraha' instead of confronting them with forcible acts.[145] Here it is evident that this perspective about how untouchability should be abolished is obviously more similar to that of Gandhi.

His association with Gandhi started from around 1932 when Gandhi declared that he would resort to fasting unto death to be commenced from 20 September in protest to the British Prime Minister's 'Communal Award' which approved separate electorates for the depressed classes. Rajbhoj's first letter to Gandhi dated 15 September 1932, concerned itself with this matter. In this letter he called for Gandhi's approval for the Rajah-Munje Pact, which was signed in March the same year by M.C. Rajah, a Tamil untouchable leader, and B.S. Munje, a Maharashtrian leader of the Hindu Mahasabha, to propose the scheme of general electorates with the reservation of seats for the depressed classes. The letter states:

> They (Depressed classes–author) fear that without reserved seats their interests will not be safeguarded nor are their fears, we submit, ill-founded. They certainly wish that nothing in the proposed constitution should be done which shall widen the existing gulf between the higher castes and depressed classes as separate electorates would certainly do, but at the same time they also wish that some provision be made for safeguarding their interests which have good need to be safeguarded.
>
> We think that statesmanship lies in harmonising these two views (concerning the position on franchise–author) and submit that the Rajah-Munje Pact has successfully harmonised them. If, therefore, you declare your readiness to assent to this Pact, most of those who have stood aloof from it or have joined the Separatist's move will come over to the Rajah's party. . . . We, therefore, request you most humbly to make this declaration at a very early date and thus save the Hindu Religion from disruption and the country from the terrible strain which your proposed fast will put upon it.[146]

But Gandhi replied to it in the negative in a letter to Rajbhoj dated 20 September the date to start his fast, saying:

> If you will not resent my saying it, I would like to say that as I am a 'touchable' by birth, I am an 'untouchable' by choice. . . . It was that dual capacity that has compelled the fast. Looking at the

> matter in this light I must say that I am not in love with the idea of statutory reservation. Whilst it is not open to the same objection that separate electorate is, I have not a shadow of a doubt that it will prevent the natural growth of the suppressed classes and will remove the incentive to honourable amends [*sic*] from the suppressors. What I am aiming at is a heart understanding between the two, the greatest opportunity of repentance and reparation on the part of the suppressors. I am certain that the moment is ripe for the change of heart among them. I would therefore favour widest [*sic*] possible franchise for the suppressed and establish a convention between the two sections for securing proper election of representatives of the suppressed. . . . If I get the opportunity, I should certainly try to create public opinion among the suppressed against statutory reservation.[147]

After this, Gandhi's fast produced an acute political tension in the whole of India, which led to the agreement of the 'Poona Pact' to assure the depressed classes of reservation of seats instead of separate electorates. The name of Rajbhoj was also found in the 24 signatories of the pact.

A week later, on 30 September the All-India Anti-Untouchability League was established with Ghanshyamdas Birla, as president, and A. V. Thakkar, as secretary. It was soon renamed the Harijan Sevak Sangh (HSS, Servants of Untouchables League) and its branches were set up at many places of the country. Initially, the name of Ambedkar was included among members of the organising committee and the central board of the league. But soon after, unsatisfied with saliently Gandhian philosophy which infiltrated into this organisation, he left it. After the founding of the HSS Gandhi began to use the term 'harijan' (son of god) instead of 'untouchable' or 'depressed', and on 11 February 1933 when still staying in prison, he started an English weekly, the *Harijan*, under the editorship of Ramchandra Shastri. Ambedkar who was requested by Gandhi to contribute a message for the first issue of the new weekly sent the following short statement dated 7 February instead to clarify his position vis-à-vis Gandhi:

> The Outcaste [*sic*] is a bye-product [*sic*] of the Caste-system [*sic*]. There will be Outcastes as long as there are castes. Nothing can emancipate the Outcastes except the destruction of the Caste-system. Nothing to save Hindus and ensure their survival in the coming struggle except the purging of the Hindu Faith of this odious and vicious dogma.

Refuting this statement, Gandhi defended his attitude toward caste and untouchability:

> Untouchability is the product not of the caste system, but of the distinction of high and low that has crept into Hinduism and is corroding it. The attack on untouchability is thus an attack upon this 'high-and-low'ness. The moment untouchability goes, the caste system will be purified, that is to say, according to my dream, it will resolve itself into the true Varna-dharma, the four divisions, each complementary of the other and none inferior or superior to any other, each as necessary for the whole body of Hinduism as any other.[148]

Here we can see very clearly the difference of opinion regarding untouchability and the caste system itself between these two eminent leaders of their respective anti-untouchability movements.

During this period Rajbhoj became more interested in Gandhi and his mission and in 1933 joined the Sabarmati Ashram of Gandhi in Amdavad (Ahmedabad) and stayed there for a few months. But when Gandhi came to know that Rajbhoj was working in the HSS, he was advised to stop his activities in the HSS, which, Gandhi emphasised, was an organisation meant for savarnas (caste Hindus) who repented of discrimination against harijans and so could not be predominantly manned by harijans.[149]

After this, in March 1935, Rajbhoj founded the Bharatiya Dalit Seva Sangh (All-India Untouchables Service League) at Kanpur in northern India with other harijan leaders like R.L. Vishvas. Rajbhoj and Jagjivan Ram, a leader of Chamars of Bihar, as secretaries of the sangh, campaigned in many places in Bengal, Bihar, Bombay, the United Provinces and the Central Provinces to organise various untouchable caste groups, but without a firm financial foundation their sangh could not last long.[150]

In 1936 when the holding of the first elections to the provincial legislative assemblies under the Government of India Act, 1935 was announced, Ambedkar formed the Independent Labour Party to gain seats for the depressed classes. Nine out of its candidates were from Mahars and one from Mangs. Rajbhoj founded the Independent National Harijan Party in the same year, and put up three candidates, all Chambhars including himself, two of whom were elected though he himself lost.[151] As the result of the election, the Indian National Congress came to power in Bombay Province and the Congress ministry enacted a few laws related to the improvement of the depressed classes' status, which were never materialised. Rajbhoj who had placed some hope on the provincial Congress ministry was disillusioned by this. Also dissatisfied with the HSS being unprepared to accept untouchable members in its leadership, he even called for a boycott of the HSS's conference to be held in June 1936. Moreover, he sent a letter to Gandhi asking for his directions to reorganise the HSS, to appoint harijan ministers in the provincial cabinet, and to implement strictly the laws enacted by the Congress government concerning the open use of temples, hotels, wells and the like, which all fell on deaf ears.[152]

Rajbhoj, disappointed with Gandhi, was again drawn toward Ambedkar and joined his Independent Labour Party in 1940. As for Ambedkar, discontented with the status of the depressed classes mentioned in the 'Cripps Plan' of March 1942, he convened a Delhi meeting of leaders of the depressed classes for their unity in March followed by the large-scale All-India Depressed Classes Conference in Nagpur in July 1942, where the founding of a new party, the All-India Scheduled Castes Federation (SCF), was declared. Its executive committee held in September adopted a party constitution and there Rajbhoj was elected general-secretary of the SCF.[153] Though the SCF played no significantly decisive role in the political process during the period between World War II and the partition of India in 1947, Ambedkar took office as a Law Member in the Governor-General's Executive Council, and Rajbhoj concentrated himself in uplifting political consciousness among the depressed classes through activities in the SCF.

In the first general elections following the independence in 1951–52, while Rajbhoj, standing for the Lok Sabha under the SCF banner, was elected a member of parliament, Ambedkar, also from the SCF, was defeated. Subsequently, differences between the two concerning management of the organisation and party programmes gradually widened and in1955 Rajbhoj left the party and joined the Congress. But next year he was converted to Buddhism with Ambedkar and other co-workers and since then serving as the president of the All-India Buddhists Association he continued his efforts to organise 'neo-Buddhists' who after their conversion to Buddhism were deprived of privileged treatment guaranteed for Scheduled Castes by the constitution to regain it.[154]

While as evident from what we have seen above, the stance of

Rajbhoj on caste discrimination and its elimination was rather more similar to that of Gandhi, he had always to be conscious of the existence of Ambedkar as the leader representing the voices of untouchables as a whole. It can be easily imagined that there might have been many such activists like him who wavered between these two distinguished leaders of marked individuality. Though most probably Rajbhoj might have been subjectively above the sense of distinction and discrimination among untouchable castes like Mahars, Mangs, Chambhars and the like, he had to face a narrow-minded caste-oriented consciouness linked with tradition or some practical interests among Chambhars whose die-hard antagonism toward Mahars continued to harass Ambedkar throughout his movement.

CONCLUDING REMARKS: AMBEDKAR AND GANDHI

The anti-untouchability movement in Maharashtra started in the beginning as one of several programmes of the social reform movement launched by organisations like the Satyashodhak Samaj of J.G. Phule. Thereafter the non-Brahman movement took over its purpose to some degree but when the Maratha-dominated non-Brahman political ascendancy became the main object of the movement, the cause of the abolition of untouchability gradually began to disappear from the arena. But almost at the same time a liberation movement was commenced by the depressed classes themselves.

As to the largest mass organisation in British India, the Indian National Congress, it continued the tradition since its establishment in 1885. We are reminded that Allan Octavian Hume, one of the most important founders of the body, was very much anxious that the Congress should steer clear of social questions which he knew to be highly controversial,[155] and that Dadabhai Naoroji in his presidential address to the Congress session in 1886 appealed to the audience:

> We are met together as a political body to represent to our rulers our political aspirations, not to discuss social reforms, and if you blame us for ignoring these you should equally blame the House of Commons for not discussing abstruser problems on mathematics or metaphysics. But, besides this, there are here Hindus of every caste, amongst whom, even in the same province, customs and social arrangements differ widely, —there are Mohammedans and Christians of various denominations, Parsis, Sikhs, Brahmos and what not— men indeed of each and all of those of numerous

> classes which constitute in the aggregate the people of India. How can this gathering of all classes discuss the social reforms needed in each individual class? What do any of us know of the internal home life, of the customs, traditions, feelings, prejudices of any class but our own? How could a gathering, a cosmopolitan gathering like this, discuss to any purpose the reforms needed in any one class? Only the members of that class can effectively deal with the reforms therein needed. A National Congress must confine itself to questions in which the entire nation has a direct participation, and it must leave the adjustment of social reforms and other class questions to class Congresses.[156]

Though it is obvious that Dadabhai as well as Hume did not have the problem of untouchability in mind when they referred to social reforms and that the Congress was indifferent altogether to any social matters, it also cannot be denied that the organisation entrusted activities for untouchability problems to Gandhi and his HSS supported by many humane volunteers.

Gandhi himself consciously alienated his own social reform programmes, commonly known as constructive programmes including harijan works, from movements for national freedom and economic emancipation of the country. The HSS mainly aimed at promotion of education among harijans, management of boarding houses for harijan youth and training of tannery, shoe-making, tailoring and weaving and the like, but it evaded its commitment to economic problems such as the elimination of poverty. The second annual report of the HSS for the year 1933–34 asserts that 'The disease of poverty is an all-India ailment and is by no means peculiar to Harijans, though sometimes observed in a virulent form among them. The economic field is vaster and far more complicated than the educational field.' As to begging or veth (forced labour) which was quite often inflicted on the depressed classes in many places, the report says that it 'stands partly for a social disability, but mostly represents an antiquated system of customary payment in kind. . . . Nor is the evil peculiar to Harijans or the insuperable concomitant of untouchability.'[157] Moreover, as mentioned earlier with reference to Rajbhoj, the HSS was defined by Gandhi as an organisation of caste Hindu penitents and so not to be predominantly manned by harijans. Harijan workers were requested to devote their energy to promoting cleanliness and hygiene, to improving the method of carrying on what were known as unclean occupations, such as scavenging and tanning, to giving up carrion and beef as well as intoxicating liquors, and to abolishing untouchability among themselves.[158] Gandhi also advised Rajbhoj in an interview with him in November 1932 that the chief goal was to create favourable local public opinion toward harijans by nurturing a conciliatory attitude.[159]

Obviously, Gandhi's expressed point of view was far from being close to the political philosophy of Ambedkar whose object was to win human rights for the depressed through 'organisation, education and agitation' and not through a philanthropical way.[160] The untouchability problem was saliently an ethical and religious one for Gandhi[161] who treated it as a matter entirely unpolitical and concerned with the conscience of individuals. Thoroughly contrary to him, Ambedkar tried to politicise it to the utmost and to emphasise its economic aspects as well.[162] It was because of this basic attitude that he was deeply interested in reform of the election system and adhered to the demand of separate electorates for the depressed classes time and again. He also tackled the problems related to land such as the abolition of the khoti system, an old landlordism commonly seen in coastal Konkan,[163] and of Mahar watan. In a conference held in July 1942 where the foundation of the SCF was decided he proposed a resolution to build independent villages to be colonised by the depressed classes to realise their overall and dramatic uplifting.[164] The proposition that economic problems were deeply rooted in matters concerning untouchability was never raised from Gandhi's side or from the Congress during the nationalist movement.

As Gandhi thought of all Hindus as one monolithic community with untouchables as its indivisible part, so Ambedkar considered that all untouchable communities having broad differences of traditional occupations and socio-economic interests could be united into one homogenised community through movements. Actually many ardent young activists from a variety of untouchable castes participated in his movement but his aspirations were to face great hardship as we have seen already. Thus, shouldering the same cause of anti-untouchability considerably differing agitations were embroiled after the mid-1930s. However, we cannot help agreeing with Eleanor Zelliot when she writes:

> The paths of Gandhi and Ambedkar, while they often diverged, ultimately converged, forcing on the Indian conscience the problem of untouchability as an issue of national concern.[165]

NOTES

1 A.G. Kulkarni, 'A Study of Political Parties in Maharashtra: With special reference to the period 1947–1962' (Ph.D. dissertation to University of Poona, 1968), pp. 56–57.

2 Karve here calls our attention to her giving only very salient features that are needed for the understanding of Maharashtra's social structure without mentioning certain well-known exceptions, and the exception to the exceptions. (Iravati Karve, *Maharashtra: Land and Its People*, Maharashtra State Gazetteers, Bombay, 1968, p. 83)

3 R.E. Enthoven, *The Tribes and Castes of Bombay*, vol. 1, Bombay, 1920, p. 144.

4 Ibid., vol. III, pp. 8–9.

5 Ibid., vol. II, p. 422.

6 H. Fukazawa, *Study on Socio-Economic History of India* (in Japanese), Tokyo, 1972, p. 329.

7 T.N. Atre, *Gao-Gada*, Mumbai, 1959 (3rd edn., 1st edn. in 1915), pp. 9, 31. The list of bara balutedars is not always the same. Atre himself mentions Sonar (goldsmith) and Chaugula (assistant to patil) instead of Mang and Mulana in another part of his book (ibid., p, 10).

8 Ibid., pp. 68–73.

9 Karve, *Maharashtra*, p. 32. Karve also refers to an old saying that Maharashtra means where the Mahars reach. [Karve, *Marathi Lokanchi Sanskruti*, Pune, 1962 (3rd edn.), p. 122.]

10 Atre, *Gao-Gada*, pp. 34–35.

11 K.R. Hanumanthan, *Untouchability: A Historical Study upto 1500 A.D.: With Special Reference to Tamil Nadu*, Madurai, 1977, pp. 94–95. The author of the book refers to examples of the Mahars of Maharashtra and the Paraiyans of Tamil Nadu. In the case of the Mahars the fact that they were also known as 'bhumiputra' (son of the land) may demonstrate their relationship with the land. (Enthoven, *The Tribes and Castes...*, vol. II, p. 401)

12 But it is also pointed out that the Chamars in north India, mostly leather workers but in many cases field servants also, were rather similar to the Mahars of Maharashtra in their structural position. (B. Patankar and G. Omvedt, 'The dalit liberation movement in colonial period', *Economic and Political Weekly*, Annual Number, Feb. 1979, p. 410)

13 M.G. Bhagat, *The Untouchable Classes of Maharashtra*, rept from *The Journal of the University of Bombay*, vol. IV, Part I, July 1935, p. 11.

14 Karve, *Maharashtra*, p. 33

15 S. Ghugare, *Renaissance in Western India: Karmveer V. R. Shinde*, Bombay, 1983, p. 77.

16 V.R. Shinde, 'Asprushoddharachya margatil dhonde' (Feb. 1923), *Bharatiya Asprushyatecha Prashna*, Mumbai, 1976, pp. 273–74.

17 V.M. Dandekar and M.B. Jagtap, *Maharashtrachi Gramin Samajrachna*, Pune, 1957, pp. 54–56.

18 M.S. Gore, *Non-Brahman Movement in Maharashtra*, New Delhi, 1989, p. 5.

19 M.P. Mangudkar, *Mahatma Phule ani Satyashodhak Chalwal*, Pune, 1965 (2nd edn., 1st edn. in 1954), p. 7.
20 Ravinder Kumar, *Western India in the Nineteenth Century*, London, 1968, p. 44.
21 B.R. Sunthankar, *Nineteenth Century History of Maharashtra*, vol. 1 (1818–57), Pune, 1988, pp. 18–27.
22 Shankarrao Deo, *Daiv Deten pan Karm Neten* (Autobiography), Pune, 1976, p. 74.
23 Richard Temple, *Man and Events of Time*, London, 1882, pp. 459–60 (cited in R. Suntharalingam, *Politics and Nationalist Awakening in South India*, Jaipur, 1980, p. 7).
24 R. Kumar, *Western India*..., pp. 298–99.
25 R. O'Hanlon, *Caste, Conflict and Ideology: Mahatma Jotirao Phule and Low Caste Protest in Nineteenth-Century Western India*, Cambridge, 1985, pp. 40–49.
26 J.G. Phule, *Shetkaryacha Asud* (1883) in Y.D. Phadke, ed., *Mahatma Phule Samagra Vangmaya*, Mumbai, 1991 (5th edn.), pp. 264–65.
27 D. Keer, *Mahatma Jotirao Phooley: Father of Our Social Revolution*, Bombay, 1964, pp. 17–18.
28 P.B. Kulkarni, *Nana Shankarsheth Yanchen Charitra*, Mumbai, 1959, pp. 438 –39.
29 J.G. Phule, *Brahmananche Kasab* (1869) in Y.D. Phadke, ed., *Mahatma Phule Samagra Vangmaya*, p. 89.
30 Ibid., pp. 90–91.
31 Ibid., p. 86.
32 J.G. Phule, *Gulamgiri* (1873) in Y.D. Phadke, ed., *Mahatma Phule Samagra Vangmaya*, p. 114.
33 Ibid., p. 130.
34 Ibid., pp. 137–38.
35 Ibid., pp. 173–86.
36 Ibid., p. 500.
37 J.G. Phule, *Pune Satyashodhak Samajacha Report* (1877) in Y.D. Phadke, ed., *Mahatma Phule Samagra Vangmaya*, p. 195.
38 S. Joshi and K.S. Raman, 'Jotirao Phule: an incomplete renaissance', *Economic and Political Weekly*, 25 May 1991, p. 1325.
39 R. O'Hanlon, *Caste, Conflict and Ideology*, pp. 248–49.
40 *Satyashodhak Samajache Tisrya Varshik Samarambhachi Hakigat* (1876) in Y. D. Phadke, ed., *Mahatma Phule Samagra Vangmaya*, pp. 209–14.
41 R. O'Hanlon, *Caste, Conflict and Ideology*, pp. 246–49.
42 Ibid., pp. 249–50.
43 Ibid., pp. 278–80.
44 B.R. Sunthankar, *Maharashtra 1858–1920*, Bombay, 1993, p. 186.
45 Eleanor Zelliot, *From Untouchable to Dalit: Essays on Ambedkar Movement*, New Delhi, 1992, pp. 91, 213.
46 Shankarrao R. Kharat, *Asprushyancha Muktisangram*, Pune, n.d., pp. 197–201.
47 This interesting and important subject is closely studied by Y.D. Phadke

in his book, *Shahu Chhatrapati ani Lokmanya*, Pune, 1986.

48 Ibid., p. 20.

49 A.B. Latthe, *Memoirs of His Highness Shri Shahu Chhatrapati Maharaj of Kolhapur*, vol. I, Bombay, 1924, pp. 154–55.

50 Chandra Y. Mudaliar, 'The non-Brahman movement in Kolhapur', *Indian Economic and Social History Review*, vol. XV, no. 1, Jan.–March 1978, p. 8.

51 A.B. Latthe, *Memoirs...*, vol. 1, p. 185–208.

52 Ibid., vol. II, p. 377.

53 Y.D. Phadke, *Keshavrao Jedhe*, Pune, 1982, p. 7.

54 In a letter addressed to Ambedkar almost about the same period Shahu wrote: 'About 100 to 150 Mahars live on a land of 16 to 20 acres. This small land is again divided into two to four aras (one ara being equal to 30 square metres–author). Five or six aras of land is not enough to fill their stomachs. And their family is fastened tightly to this land of six aras. Besides, people are compelled to work for peasants in the name of balutes. Village officers like patils and kulkarnis force them to offer services for their families at very meagre remuneration.' (Y.D. Phadke, *Shahu Chhatrapati ani Lokmanya*, p. 272.)

55 A.B. Latthe, *Memoirs...*, vol. II, pp. 501–2.

56 Ibid., pp. 505–31.

57 Ibid., p. 490.

58 M.S. Gore, *Non-Brahman Movement...*, p. 59.

59 A.B. Latthe, *Memoirs...*, vol. II, p. 491.

60 D.B. Rosenthal, 'From reformist princes to co-operative kings', *Economic and Political Weekly*, 19 May 1973, p. 907.

61 G. Omvedt, *Cultural Revolt in Colonial Society: The Non-Brahman Movement in Western India 1873–1930*, Bombay, 1976, p. 136.

62 Latthe and Jadhav who led the non-Brahman movement with Shahu in Kolhapur were not so interested in concrete programmes and activities of anti-untouchability. Latthe, for instance, was negative to saha-bhojan (eating together with untouchables on the same table) programme on the excuse that it might endanger the non-Brahman movement. (Y.D. Phadke, *Shahu Chhatrapati ani Lokmanya*, p. 192.)

63 Shinde himself described the process of decision of his studying abroad and support of Maharaja in his autobiography. (V.R. Shinde, *Majhya Athavni ani Anubhav*, vol. I, Pune, 1940, pp. 181–84.)

64 S. Ghugare, *Renaissance in Western India*, pp. 81–83.

65 Ibid., pp. 86, 91.

66 C.B. Khairmode, *Dr. Bhimrao Ramji Ambedkar: Charitra* (hereafter, *Charitra*), vol. I, Mumbai, 1968, p. 229.

67 V.R. Shinde, 'Bahishkrut Bharat', *Bharatiya Asprushyancha Prashna*, Mumbai, 1976 (1st edn. in 1933), p. 185.

68 Ibid., p. 152.

69 S. Ghugare, *Renaissance in Western India*, p. 53.

70 Ibid., p. 54.

71 Y.D. Phadke, *Shahu Chhatrapati ani Lokmanya*, p. 212.

72 S.R. Kharat, *Asprushancha Muktisangram*, pp. 16–18.

73 C.B. Khairmode, *Charitra*, vol. I, pp. 246–52.
74 S. Ghugare, *Renaissance in Western India*, pp. 95–96.
75 B.R. Ambedkar, 'Evidence before the Reforms Committee (Franchise)' cited in C. B. Khairmode, *Charitra*, vol. I, Appendix, pp. 132–33.
76 V.R. Shinde, 'Evidence before the Reforms Committee (Franchise)' cited in V. R. Shinde, *Asprushatecha Prashna*, pp. 327–28.
77 C.B. Khairmode, *Charitra*, vol. I, pp. 126–27, 141.
78 Ibid., pp. 280–81.
79 Ibid., vol. II, pp. 36–45.
80 S.R. Kharat, *Asprushancha Muktisangram*, pp. 11–12.
81 Y.D. Phadke, *Keshavrao Jedhe*, pp. 3–7.
82 Ibid., pp. 9–10.
83 Ibid., p. 18.
84 Ibid., pp. 39–43, 57.
85 D. Jawalkar, *Deshache Dushman*, in Y.D. Phadke, ed., *Dinkarrao Jawalkar Samagra Vangmaya*, Pune, 1984, p. 82.
86 *The Times of India*, 2 Aug. 1991.
87 Y.D. Phadke, *Keshavrao Jedhe*, pp. 77–82.
88 *Bahishkrut Bharat*, 1 July 1927 [*Dr. Babasaheb Ambedkar ani Asprushyanchi Chalwal Abhyasachi Sadhne*, vol. II, Mumbai, 1990 (hereafter *AACAS*), pp. 58–59].
89 Y.D. Phadke, *Keshavrao Jedhe*, pp. 97–100.
90 Ibid., pp. 139–40.
91 *Bahishkrut Bharat*, 30 Sep. 1927 (*AACAS*, pp. 104–5).
92 C.B. Khairmode, *Charitra*, vol. II, pp. 255–56.
93 Y.D. Phadke, *Keshavrao Jedhe*, p. 101.
94 *Bahishkrut Bharat*, 4 Jan. 1928 (*AACAS*, p. 212).
95 Shankarrao R. Kharat ed., *Dr. Babasaheb Ambedkar Yanchi Atmakatha*, Pune, 1987, pp. 71–78.
96 B.R. Ambedkar, 'Mahar ani tyanche watan', *Bahishkrut Bharat*, 16 Sep. 1927 (*AACAS*, pp. 99–100).
97 *Bahishkrut Bharat*, 3 Feb. 1928 (*AACAS*, pp. 157–61).
98 A Bill No. xvi of 1939 (A Bill to provide for the Removal of certain Disabilities of Harijans), *Bombay Legislative Assembly Debates, 1939*, vol. 5, Bombay, 1939, pp. 3161–91; Text of Bill, pp. 3683–85. Independent Labour Party led by Ambedkar was opposed to this Bill as they regarded it as devoid of what they demanded.
99 Cf. S.R. Venkataraman, *Temple Entry Legislation Revised*, Madras, 1946, T.R. Ravindran, *Vaikkam Satyagraha and Gandhi*, Trichur, 1975, etc.
100 In 1932 when the temple satyagraha was going on in Nashik, Gandhi advised P.N. Rajbhoj, an untouchable leader, and his followers to concentrate themselves on movements initiated by caste Hindus and not on their own. (*The Collected Works of Mahatma Gandhi*, vol. LI, Ahmedabad, 1972, p. 404.)
101 S.R. Kharat, ed., *Dr. Babasaheb Ambedkar Yanchi Atmakatha*, pp. 89–90.
102 Ibid., p. 95.

103 *Bombay Legislative Assembly Debates,* 1938, vol. 2, 1938, p. 613.

104 Ibid., p. 915. After the Bill was passed, K.M. Munshi of the Congress Government of Bombay who was asked about the number of temples opened for harijans (untouchables) as of February 1939, reported to the assembly that 142 out of the total 39,744 temples among which 5,207 were managed by office-bearers were actually opened for them. It was also reported that no temples were opened in Gujarat from where Gandhi himself came. (*Bombay Legislative Assembly Debates*, 1939, vol. 6, pp. 57, 193–97.)

105 B.R. Ambedkar, 'Evidence before the Reforms Committee (Franchise)', *Dr. Babasaheb Ambedkar: Writings and Speeches*, vol. I, Bombay, 1979, p. 270.

106 B.R. Ambedkar, 'Report on the Constitution of the Government of Bombay Presidency (1929)', in *Dr. Babasaheb Ambedkar: Writings and Speeches*, vol. II, Bombay, 1982, pp. 335–37.

107 *Round Table Conference: Proceedings of the Sub-Committee, No. III (Minorities)*, 1930, in ibid., p. 533.

108 Ibid., p. 503.

109 S.R. Kharat, *Dr. Babasaheb Ambedkar Yanchi Atmakatha*, pp. 132–36. Incidentally no part of *The Collected Works of Mahatma Gandhi* nor the entry made for the day (14 August 1931) in the diary of Mahadev Desai, Gandhi's personal secretary, refered to this talk.

110 *Round Table Conference: Proceedings of the Federal Structure Committee and Minorities Committee*, 1931 (*Dr. Babasaheb Ambedkar: Writings and Speeches*, vol. II, p. 663).

111 Pyarelal, *The Epic Fast*, Ahmedabad, 1932, p. 111.

112 As to the detailed description of this process, see B.R. Ambedkar, *What Congress and Gandhi Have Done to the Untouchables*, Bombay, 1945 and aforementioned Pyarelal's *The Epic Fast.*

113 Eleanor Zelliot, 'Congress and the Untouchables, 1917–1950' in R. Sisson and S. Wolpert, eds., *Congress and Indian Nationalism*, Berkeley, 1988, p. 190.

114 S.R. Kharat., *Dr. Babasaheb Ambedkar Yanchi Atmakatha*, p. 135.

115 'Asprushya ki purvasprushya', *Bahishkrut Bharat*, 4 Jan. 1929 (*AACAS*, p. 215).

116 'Mate Mastarancha nava shodh', *Bahishkrut Bharat*, 1 Feb. 1929 (*AACAS*, p. 230).

117 'Nyayamurti Jativar Gele', *Bahishkrut Bharat*, 1 July 1927 (*AACAS*, p. 49).

118 'Matyanchya Asprushyata Nivaranatil Karsthan', ibid., p.230.

119 'Asprushyakarita khas devalay', *Bahishkrut Bharat*, 12 April 1929 (*AACAS*, p. 263).

120 N.V. Gadgil, *Pathik* (Atmakatha), vol. 2, Pune, 1964, pp. 218–21.

121 S.D. Darbari, 'Bahishkrutatil Brahmanya', *Bahishkrut Bharat*, 31 May 1929 (*AACAS*, p. 277).

122 'Jyacha Nishchay jhala nahi tyachi vat pahat basnyas kay hasshil?', *Bahishkrut Bharat*, 30 Sep. 1927 (*AACAS*, p. 104).

123 'Vichar karal tar kalel', ibid.

124 C.B. Khairmode, *Charitra*, vol. III, Bombay, 1964, pp. 289–90.
125 Dhanajay Kir, *Dr. Babasaheb Ambedkar*, Bombay, 1966, p. 88.
126 'Sandhyakalchi Chambharwadyatil sabha', *Bahishkrut Bharat*, 3 Feb. 1928 (*AACAS*, p. 167).
127 B.R. Ambedkar, 'Evidence taken before the Reforms Committee (Franchise)', *Dr. Babasaheb Ambedkar: Writings and Speeches*, vol. I, p. 263.
128 S.R. Kharat, *Dr. Babasaheb Ambedkar Yanchi Atmakatha*, p. 81.
129 H.N. Mitra, ed., *The Indian Annual Register*, 1930, vol. II, Calcutta, 1931, pp. 367–68.
130 Ibid., pp. 368–69.
131 Ibid., pp. 369–71.
132 Ibid., pp. 372–73
133 Ibid., p. 374.
134 E. Zelliot, *From Untouchable to Dalit: Essays on Ambedkar Movement*, New Delhi, 1992, p. 106.
135 R.E. Enthoven, *The Tribes and Castes of Bombay*, vol. I, pp. 263–64.
136 G.B. Nirantar et al., eds., *Shri Bapusaheb Rajbhoj: Jivan va Karya*, Pune, 1956, pp. 1–5.
137 Ibid., pp. 6–7.
138 'Nyayamurti Jativar Gele', *Bahishkrut Bharat*, 1 July 1927 (*AACAS*, p. 49).
139 G.B. Nirantar et al., eds., *Shri Bapusaheb Rajbhoj*, pp. 16–17.
140 According to H. Nirmal, ed., *Dalitanchi Niyatakalike*, Pune, 1987., It seems there was no newspaper or periodical to whose name the word 'dalit' was prefixed before Rajbhoj's paper.
141 Ibid., p. 85.
142 'Pune Municipalitychi niwadanuk va asprushyanche umedwar', *Bahishkrut Bharat*, 3 Feb. 1928 (*AACAS*, p. 161).
143 G.B. Nirantar et al., eds., *Shri Bapusaheb Rajbhoj*, p. 19.
144 Ibid., p. 39.
145 Ibid., pp. 56–62.
146 Ibid., Appendix, pp. 3–4.
147 *The Collected Works of Mahatma Gandhi*, vol. LI, Ahmedabad, 1972, p. 111.
148 *Harijan*, 11 Feb. 1933.
149 Letter from Gandhi to Rajbhoj, 31 Aug. 1934 (*The Collected Works of Mahatma Gandhi*, vol. LVIII, Ahmedabad, 1974, p. 383). It is sometimes pointed out that at least in the anti-untouchability movement Gandhi was 'paternalistic' in not regarding the initiative of harijans (untouchables) as primarily important for their emancipation and instead regarding the cooperation of upper-caste Hindus to be essential for it. [For example, P. Bidwai, 'Relevance of Ambedkar: Modernity and pseudo-Gandhians', *The Times of India* (Bombay edition), 5 May 1995.]
150 G. B. Nirantar et al., eds., *Shri Bapusaheb Rajbhoj*, pp. 108–9.
151 Ibid., pp. 130–31.
152 Ibid., pp. 137–42.

153 Ibid., p. 172.

154 Bhalchandra Phadke, *Phule-Ambedkar Shodh ani Bhodh*, Aurangabad, 1985, p. 68.

155 Letter from A.O. Hume to S.H. Chiplunkar, 27 Nov. 1884 (cited in S.R. Mehrotra, *The Emergence of the Indian National Congress*, Delhi, 1971, p. 400).

156 Presidential Address to Calcutta Congress, 27 Dec. 1886 [*Speeches and Writings of Dadabhai Naoroji*, Madras, 1917 (2nd edn.), pp. 7–8].

157 The All-India Harijan Sewak Sangh, Report for the Year 1933–34 (H. N. Mitra, ed., *Indian Annual Register*, 1935, vol. I, Calcutta, 1935, p. 347).

158 M.K. Gandhi, 'Statement on Untouchability V', 14 Nov. 1932 (*The Collected Works of Mahatma Gandhi*, vol. LI, Ahmedabad, 1971, p. 427).

159 M.K. Gandhi's Interview with P.N. Rajbhoj, 11 Nov. 11932 (Ibid., p. 405).

160 R. Sardesai, 'Atrocities on Dalit: Who will break the status quo?', *The Times of India*, 9 Sep. 1991.

161 Letter from Gandhi to Samuel Hoare, 11 March 1932 (H.N. Mitra, ed., *Indian Annual Register*, 1932, vol. II, p. 237).

162 Ambedkar was also keenly conscious of the ethical and moral aspects of the problem of the untouchability and anti-untouchability movement but his standpoint on this matter was quite different from that of Gandhi. We can find at least some part of his thinking in a six-page-long editorial titled 'Asprushyata va Satyagrahachi Siddhi' (Untouchables and determination of Satyagraha) which appeared in the 24 November 1927 issue of *Bahishkrut Bharat.* In this editorial Ambedkar scrutinises the Gandhian ideas of satyagraha and ahimsa (non-violence) from the viewpoint of the anti-untouchability movement. It is interesting to know that at the stage of the mid-1920s Ambedkar understood that untouchables and caste Hindus belonged to one and the same religion and based his argument on the Bhagavad Gita, deemed as one of the sacred books in Hinduism. He argues that an agitation aiming at eliminating discrimination of Hindus by same Hindus is nothing less than satyagraha judged by any criterion given in the Gita and that though there is no denying that Gandhi is the first creator of the satyagraha movement, satyagraha does not always mean ahimsa and that the right attitude of satyagrahis is to choose their means, ahimsa if possible and himsa (violence) if necessary, as it is in the end the moral nature of their conduct that determines whether or not it is satyagraha. (*Bahishkrut Bharat*, 25 Nov. 1927 in *AACAS*, pp. 127–32.)

163 For example, 'Khoti urf shetkariwargachi gulamgiri', *Bahishkrut Bharat*, 3 May 1929 (*AACAS*, pp. 270–71).

164 G.B. Nirantar et al., eds., *Shri Bapusaheb Rajbhoj*, p. 163. Though this proposal is what was known as 'Dalitstan' (Land of Untouchables) in later years, the idea of a colony only for Mahars was discussed by him during the Mahar watan abolition movement in the late 1920s. ('Asprushyonnaticha arthik paya', *Bahishkrut Bharat*, 23 Dec. 1927 in

AACAS, p. 150) Shortly before his death in 1956, Ambedkar expressed his decision to 'start an agitation to enable untouchables to get uncultivated land' if he recovered his health. (*Prabuddha Bharat*, 24 March 1956 in S.R. Kharat, ed., *Dr. Babasaheb Ambedkaranchi Patren*, Pune, 1961, pp. 329–30.

165 According to Shankar Rao Kharat, a Mahar activist and writer, Jagjivan Ram and other Congress leaders declared after India's independence that the real problem of untouchables (Scheduled Castes) was an economic one. (S.R. Kharat, *Asprushyancha Muktisangram*, p. 219.) But it is doubtful whether or not the post-independence Congress has ever implemented policies which would solve their real economic problem.

166 E. Zelliot, *From Untouchable to Dalit*, pp. 173–74.

11

Pushed towards the Partition: Jogendranath Mandal and the Constrained Namasudra Movement

MASAYUKI USUDA

INTRODUCTION

Jogendranath Mandal (1904–68) is a forgotten politician. Born as an 'untouchable' Namasudra in the Barisal District (now in Bangladesh), he was appointed the Law Minister in the Interim Government in October 1946 and sworn in as the first Law and Labour Minister of Pakistan in August 1947. His career may be outwardly compared to that of Ambedkar. Despite that, he is not mentioned even in the national biography of India[1] published in Calcutta, the centre of Bengali culture to which he belonged. *Sansad Caritabhidhan*, a representative biographical dictionary in Bengali, treats him unjustly in the shortest six lines without ever making the effort to note the year of his birth or referring to the fact that he was the first Law and Labour Minister of Pakistan.[2] He seems to have fallen in the chasm created at the time of partition of India and Pakistan, having been regarded as an ambiguous and thus suspicious figure worth being neglected by both sides.

This paper aims to clarify the process of his alienation from the mainstream of politics in the subcontinent. However, the emergence of Jogen Mandal as an all-India figure must be connected fundamentally with the political rise of the depressed communities. Therefore, I propose to analyse his political career against the background of the depressed class movements, especially that of the Namasudra community in the *bil* (marsh) area of the Bakharganj and Faridpur districts.

The first section discusses the formation of the Namasudra movement in the middle of the nineteenth century and its subsequent developments. In the second section I shall depict Jogendranath Mandal's life by placing considerable emphasis on his political career between 1936 and 1947. In the third section, I shall throw light upon the image of Jogendranath Mandal as seen by his fellow villagers. The required information was collected by me between 1985 and 1986 when I conducted a village survey in the district of Barisal (a part of the former Bakharganj District).

THE MODE OF EXISTENCE OF 'UNTOUCHABLES' AND THEIR MOVEMENTS

It is not possible to state the mode of existence of the Scheduled Castes (SC, not exactly the same as the 'untouchable' castes) of Bengal as a whole, because their statistics have not been taken following the independence of Bangladesh. As a result we must be satisfied with their present statistics in West Bengal given by the 1981 census. Thus, the total population of the Scheduled Castes in West Bengal amounted to 12 million which occupied 22 per cent of the whole population of the state. This percentage is exceeded only by that of Punjab (26.9 per cent) and Himachal Pradesh (24.6 per cent), much surpassing the figure of the all-India average (15.8 per cent).[3]

The earlier-mentioned fact, however, does not mean that the 'untouchhable' problem has assumed an important position in the socio-political life of Bengal. The major fissure of Bengali society runs between the Hindu and Muslim communities. The contradiction within the Hindu community tends to be only secondary. This is quite different from the conditions of central and south India in and beyond the Deccan, where the Muslim population is relatively small and as a result anti-Brahman movements came to the fore. Here lies the primary and structural reason why anti-untouchability movements experienced oscillation between the two poles of the Hindu-Muslim antagonism.

According to a passage from Bipin Chandra Pal's autobiography, forms of discrimination against untouchables in Bengal do not seem to have been so severe as in Maharashtra or south India. A senior in age was addressed as *dada* (elder brother) even if he was an untouchable.[4] The actual condition of the forms of discrimination and the degree of discriminating consciousness are difficult to gauge, and Pal's description is open to challenge. Yet, in our context, it is true that the types of discrimination experienced by Jogen Mandal are not mentioned so bitterly as are those by Ambedkar.[5] The Namasudra community to which Mandal belonged was a principal agricultural caste in southeast Bengal. Their population amounted to 45 per cent (in 1911) of the total Hindus in the district of Bakharganj[6] in which he was born and concentrated in its north-western portion where the Hindus were equal to or even outnumbered the Muslims.

So far as Bengal was concerned, landowning peasants dominant in a certain area tended to raise themselves in the caste ladder as was evident from the Sanskritization of the Kaivartas (now designated as Mahisyas) in south-western Bengal. The Chasha-Kaivartas broke away from the Kaivartas betweeen the middle of the sixteenth and the middle of the eighteenth century through their professional conversion from fishing to agriculture. Thus they elevated themselves from the *ajalchal* to the intermediary rank as a full-fledged caste.[7] Comparing them to the Mahisyas of Midnapur who were 'a locally dominant caste which includẹd petty landlords and substantial peasants'[8] the 'untouchable' Namasudras were poor peasants with very little social power. For all that, they had enough power to mitigate Mandal's feelings of suffering. At least they were not so lowly placed as to be denied the status of landed peasantry as was the case with the Paraiyars who constituted a quarter portion of the whole population in south India.[9]

Heretofore we have used the Scheduled Castes as a synonym of the 'untouchables'. As is evident from Table 1, however, the Scheduled Castes include not only the 'untouchables' but also several *ajachal* castes ritually ranked a step above them. The Scheduled Castes are attributed as such not according to the ritual status but chiefly by their economic condition (social backwardness in judicial terms). In Bengal the intensity of untouchability was relatively weak so that the temple entry movement, for example, could not emerge as a major task for the removal of untouchability. There the movements themselves did not demand the complete removal of untouchability. They were proposed as movements to step up and out from the social backwardness. Therefore they took the form of joint efforts in which socially backward castes engaged. Since the *ajalchal* castes as shown by their designation were *a-jal-chal* (not capable of giving drinking water to the superior castes), the problem of untouchability occurred decidedly not between the 'untouchables' and the caste Hindus but among different castes with different degrees of variation. Hence it tended to be reduced to the antagonism between the poor *chotolok*s and the affluent *bhadralok*s or *baralok*s which was a vertical division of society observed in Bengal. Movements among the Bengali 'untouchables' were, so to say, promoted as an indispensable link of the Scheduled Caste movements directed against the haves by the not-haves.

As a result of the above-mentioned process, the ritual criteria of untouchability within the Scheduled Castes should have been vaguer than before. In Bengal self-emancipating endeavours among the 'untouchables' as a part of the Scheduled Caste movements were ardent enough to expect satisfactory results. The status of their movements within the all-India framework, however, remained marginal on account of their strategy which would not set the removal of untouchability as their central task. Ironically enough, one of the reasons that Mandal could not be Ambedkar is attributable to this fact.

Now it would be desirable to examine more concretely the development of the Namasudra movements in the southern part of Bengal. Traditionally they were called Chandals. As is widely known, the term Chandal is derived from Sanskrit Caṇḍāla, a representative term for the 'untouchables' [10] which has been used even in old Japanese in the form of *Sendara.* The Namasudras, densely distributed in the southern part of East Bengal, numbered 2,087,162 according to the 1911 census, constituting the biggest community among the 'untouchables'. The Rajbansis in north Bengal (2,049,454) and the Bagdis in west Bengal (1,041,892) came next to them.[11] All three castes were of tribal origin.[12] The Namasudras and the Rajbansis are considered to have been transformed 'at a comparatively recent date'.[13] The Namasudras are assumed to be Hinduised tribes 'who were driven into the marshes of the interior by successive waves of invasion'.[14] They have been despised by the caste Hindus and forced to live in separate quarters on the outskirts of villages.[15]

So far as I know, the oldest colonial document recording the movement of the Namasudras is dated at 1873. In this incident, an affluent Namasudra peasant named Dwarkanath Mandal, who lived at Mushlundpore in the *bil* area spanning in the southwestern part of Faridpur planned to invite 10,000 people[16] of every caste to his father's *sraddha* ceremony in 1872. The Kayasthas responded to this invitation with insulting answers and instigated other castes not to accept it. The offended Namasudra headmen including Dwarkanath Mandal agreed in protest neither to give any service to other castes and the Muslims nor to allow their women to visit *hats* and *bazars*. This agreement was forced upon their fellow caste men with the threat of excommunication should violation occur. This movement had spread to the adjoining Bakharganj District by the next spring. The protestors told the

Table 1 Traditional ritual position of the Scheduled Castes in West Bengal

Name of Castes	*Percentage to total SC population in WB* (%)	*Classification in Brihad-dharma Purana*	*Classification in Brahma-vaivarta Purana*
1 Rajbansi	15.38		
2 Bagdi/Duley	14.65	3	(c)
3 Namasudra	11.12	3	c
4 Pod/Poundra	11.06		b
5 Barui	7.09	3	
6 Chamar/Muchi	5.77	3	b
7 Hari/Methor/Bhangi	2.56		c
8 Jalia Kaibarta	2.32	(2)	b
9 Dhoba/Dhobi	2.17	2	b
10 Dom/Dhangad	1.99		c
11 Sunri (excluding Saha)	1.89	2	b
12 Kaora	1.64		
13 Lohar	1.18		
14 Paliya	1.14		
15 Jhalo Malor/Malo	1.02	3	

Note: The classification of Sudra castes according to *Brihad-dharma Purana*: (1)Uttama Sankara (2)Madyama Sankara (3)Adhama Sankara or Antyaja. The same classification according to *Brahma-vaivarta Purana*: (a)Sat Sudra (b)Asat Sudra (c)Antyaja.

Number/alphabet in parentheses indicates inference.

Source: Jyotirmoyee Sarma, *Caste Dynamics among the Bengali Hindus*, Calcutta, 1980, pp. 11–13, 14–15.

Magistrate of Faridpur who came to inspect the movement (a kind of 'strike' in Pradip Sinha's wording[17]) on the spot that their object was 'to obtain a better position in place of being the despised and degraded class' they were 'in the eyes of their neighbours'.[18]

In his report on this Chandal movement, the British Magistrate referred to them as 'Nomoshudros' in the bracket after mentioning their common name Chandals. Though it is not clear only from this remark that since when they had called themselves Namasudras, their socially elevating movements apparently began to quicken before the 1870s. At this point of time, however, Namasudras[19] remained as their self-designation and they were commonly called Chandals. Since that time onwards they continued to try to get an official sanction for assuming the name of their choice. They were thus 'entered in the census table of castes as Namasudra or Chandal in 1891, as Namasudra (Chandal) in 1901 and as Namasudra only in 1911 and 1921'.[20]

The census had definitely great relevance to the self-elevating movements of the Namasudras. It is not a matter of coincidence that the first (preliminary) census was taken in 1872 when the Chandal movement gained ground. The Kayasthas who stood against the Namasudras in this movement were the latter's natural enemies as either land owners or intermediate tenure-holders. In this regard, Jack, the settlement officer of Bakharganj and an author of *Bakarganj District Gazetteer* stated that the Kayasthas showed 'an apparent increase of over 20 per cent in the last decade (1901 to 1911), but most of these were men of lower caste who took advantage of the opportunity offered by the census to claim an improvement in their status'.[21] The Kayasthas ranked topmost among the Sudras demanded to be registered as the Kshatriyas. Most of the castes regarded therefore the census as an opportunity offered them officially to improve their social status.[22]

The objection raised by the Namasudra prisoners in the Faridpur Jail against their selected employment as scavengers[23] was nothing more than the extension of the above-stated Chandal movement into the jail wall. Undoubtedly jails were pioneer institutions in shaping the modern character that would render caste seclusion difficult. This incident probably first cracked the official practice of employing Namasudra prisoners as *mehtrs* according to the custom presumed to be 'of ancient date'[24] and thus of maintaining caste order within modern jails.

In consequence, the colonial authorities were also pressed to reach a decision. Two choices were available at the time. W.S. Wells, Magistrate of Faridpur, considered that 'Government should in justice and fairness require all men to take their share in this unpleasant and degrading duty.'[25] On the other hand, W.L. Heely, Inspector General of Jails, Lower Provinces, took the position that the government would be justified in non-interference with the long standing practice though he suggested future reform.[26] Ultimately the colonial government decided to choose the latter.[27] However, Namasudras' assertion of 'self-respect' was an epoch-making event and also an indication of the permeability of the Namasudra combinations arising in the early 1870s.

The Namasudra (Chandal) movement between 1872 and 1873 was led by the rich headmen among them on the basis of caste solidarity. The general conditions of the caste show that relatively poor tenants and agricultural labourers constituted the majority and that they were forced to resort to agriculture from different occupations as was the case of other labour castes in nineteenth century Bengal. It is also noteworthy that there were a few industrious Namasudra peasants who had succeeded in gaining the status of zamindar or talukdar. The Nandis of Jamgram in the Hooghly District were one of such families. Shankar, the fourth of the lineage, purchased zamindari in 1862[28] the date itself of much interest in my study.

Suspension of any service to other castes, the core of the movement in the early 1870s was of a character not to be maintained for a long period by the majority of poor tenants and agricultural labourers among the Namasudra peasants exclusive of their affluent segment of leaders. The end of the movement remains unknown because of the dearth of relevant materials, yet the available official documents suggest its decline.[29] To disallow their women to attend market may have been regarded as a form of protest easily imposed upon poor peasants due to its small economical demerit.[30]

The affluent segment of the Namasudras started to impart higher education to their sons in the last quarter of the nineteenth century, as a consequence of which a band of educated youths was formed among them. Naturally they decided which course the whole community should take from this time onward. Yet it would be open to question to take their roles as being too significant. Wells, Magistrate of Faridpur, found in 1873 that the Namasudras were 'eager to learn, but hardly able anywhere to support a school' and hoped to encourage their educational zeal by investing official funds.[31] It is probable that public opinion was formed by their educated youths against the background of this prevailing zeal for primary education. The District Magistrate's sympathy for the Namasudras was also noteworthy.[32] It would ultimately open a circuit to induce them to rely on official support. According to Sekhar Bandyopadhyay's judgement, the movement 'began to break down as the poorer sections found it difficult to sustain without work'.[33] The demand for the removal of untouchability was also not accomplished because of the opposition posed by the upper castes. This breakdown seems to have acted in two forms on the subsequent Namasudra movements for the period from the end of the nineteenth century to the early decades of the twentieth century.

First, they assumed a religious form. From the early times the Vaisnava Kartabhaja sect spread over the entire region.[34] 'The lowest among the lowly is really the best, for he is God'[35] was the creed of the sect. Their unorthodox doctrine admitting neither idolatry nor caste distinction must have been attractive to the 'untouchable' Namasudras. As the most upper castes followed Saivism in Faridpur and Bakharganj, the spread of Vaisnavism among the 'untouchable' Namasudras was charged with social significance. On this foundation the Vaisnava Matua sect expanded its influence at the end of the nineteenth century. The essence of its teachings lay in the assertion of complete social equality and possibility for spiritual relief by means of the performance of secular duties, embodied by their motto 'hate kam mukhe nam' (Work with the hands, chant by mouth). Such teachings must have definitely charmed the Namasudras. The Matua sect expanded mostly among the Namasudras between the end of the nineteenth century and the early twentieth century in defiance of the contemptuous treatment inflicted by the upper castes.[36]

Prabhu Jagatbandhu (1871–1921) is also notable for his zeal in his missionary work among the untouchables. He was a 'Brahman who (had) read up to the Matriculation standard, renounced the world early in his youth, and worked among the Doms of North Calcutta and the Namasudras of Faridpur and Jessore'. His teachings were moderate and mystical in character. His Namasudra followers in Faridpur and Jessore founded 'a caste-sect of their own which was known as the Mahanta sect'.[37]

The conversion of the Namasudra to Christianity was another phenomenon worthy of notice. It was in the *bil* area along the border of Faridpur and Bakharganj that the Christian missionaries made an exceptional success in rural Bengal. According to the 1911 census, the number of Christians was 6,541 in the Bakharganj District, most of whom were Baptists. The remainder comprised about 1,000 members of the Church of England and 1,000 Roman Catholics. The majority of the Catholics lived in Sibpur, a village with a heavy Portuguese concentration.[38] In Faridpur Christians numbered 6,299 according to the 1921 census.[39] Apart from the Goa Church at Sibpur, the propagation of Christianity started in Bakharganj in around 1830.[40]

The result of conversion, however, seems to have had a social impact on the local society after 1850. There occurred a case in 1855 in which several families of converts were kidnapped and confined by the landlords against whom they had formed a combination in the spirit of revolt. This was the famous 'Baropakhya case' which was appealed to the Calcutta High Court.[41] In the old District Gazetteers of both Bakharganj and Faridpur, however the number of Christians is recorded to have increased since 1872. The conversion is related to the rebellious spirit 'against caste bondage and zamindari oppression'.[42] Therefore, the conversion to Christianity shared the same reason for the spread of Vaisnava faith throughout the region.

It was of no little significance that these groups of Christian converts were formed in the *bil* area along the Faridpur and Bakharganj border. The missionaries attempted to spread education, in consequence of which modern European thought was gradually instilled into the minds of the local people in general, not to mention the Christian converts.

The second form in which the breakdown seem to have acted was that despite its breakdown, the Chandal movement in 1872–73 contributed much to their recognition of the vital importance of caste organizations and their search for new socio-political movements. N.K. Bose states that there was a caste organization existing under the name of Namasudra Hitaishini Samiti.[43] *Khulna District Gazetteer* records that 'a conference was held in March 1908, which was attended by Namasudras from Khulna, the adjoining districts, and some districts of Eastern Bengal'. Thus, in the author's judgement, the Namasudras showed considerable aptitude for having their own organizations. Judging from the published report on the conference, its objects were the spread of education, the establishment of a permanent fund, and the removal of social evils.

In pursuance of these objects, the following four resolutions were passed: First, that the Namasudra conference be made permanent through annual meetings to be held in different districts for the discussion of relevant social matters and the spread of education; Second, that a village committee was to be formed in every Namasudra village, and unions of 15 such villages, and a district committee in every district; Third, that for acquiring funds for the Namasudra contribution fund, village committees, unions and district committees were to be authorized to collect subscriptions. Here, a handful of rice was to have been set apart before meals in every family, and collected weekly by the village committee. Every member of the village committee was to pay a monthly subscription of one anna, of the unions two annas, and of the district committee four annas. Three per cent of the expenses incurred in *sraddha*, marriages and other occasions must be reserved for this fund. Finally, as some active measures should be adopted towards initiating social reform, it was resolved that any Namasudra marrying his son under 20 or daughter under 10 will be excommunicated. The committee and unions was to have been especially careful about strict compliance with this resolution.[44]

It is not certain to what extent these three-tier committees actually functioned, yet it is clear in what direction the Namasudra community was motivated.

In order to form public opinion within the caste, the publication of caste journals was essential. The following four caste journals were thus published during the first two decades of the twentieth century. (Given in turn are the name of each journal, period of publication, place of publication, name of editor, amount of annual subscription, and number of publications.): (1) *Namasudra Hitaishi*, monthly, Dacca, Bharatchandra Sarkar, Rs. 2, 2,000 (in 1921); (2) *Namasudra Sakha*, monthly, Dacca, Rajanikanta Das, Re. 1, 1,000 (in 1921); (3) *Namasudra Suhrid*, monthly, Orakandi in the Faridpur District, Rev. Gopalchandra Datta and Aditkumar Chaudhuri, Re.1, 600 (in 1911); and (4) *Pataka*, monthly, Calcutta, Mukundabihari Mallik, Re.1, 500 (in 1921).[45]

The tone of these journals was both anti-Hindu (upper castes) and pro-British. N.K. Bose states that the two reasons why the Namasudras were alienated from the Hindus and sided with the British were the numerical strength of their community and the insults inflicted upon them by the caste Hindus after they had been educated.[46]

Since the breakdown of the 'strike' between 1872 and 1873, the Namasudras had tried to remove caste discrimination and elevate their social status by means of the aquisition of education. However, as it was not possible within the caste to raise the huge amount of funds for the enhancement of education, they had no alternative but to receive support from the government. The colonial government was also responsive to this request as illustrated with the sympathetic statement made by Wells, Magistrate of Faridpur.

Needless to say, the political stance of the Namasudras shared the same structure with that of the Muslims. Both of them showed the same response to this official bait. The sympathy extended to poor and hard working peasants by conscientious bureaucrats like Wells and Jack appears to have been genuine, but within the framework of colonial rule, their initiative turned into none other than a kind of divide and rule ideology. It was during the Swadeshi Movement that the political position of the Muslims and the lower castes was made clear.

The Swadeshi Movement was the first large-scale nationalist movement initiated by the middle class against the administrative division of Bengal in 1905. The greatest problem with the Swadeshi Movement was that its actual core, almost exclusively composed of the educated upper-caste Hindus, could not effectively win over to their side the Muslim community and the lower-caste Hindus. All the worse, they alienated the latter from the main current of the nationalist movement. The entrance of the terrorist movement in the last scene of the Swadeshi stage bespeaks a great deal about the isolation of the middle class and their organizational failure in the expansion of the movement to the lower strata of the society.[47]

The Namasudras sent a deputation in 1905 to meet Bampfylde Fuller, Lieutenant-Governor of Eastern Bengal and Assam. Another was sent in 1907 to meet Lancelot Hare, Lieutenant-Governor in succession to Fuller. The October 1907 issue of *Namasudra Suhrid* reports that the deputation told Hare that the Namasudra caste was praying for the permanency of British rule. According to N.K. Bose, two Namasudra '*bhadraloks*' (gentlemen) named Nabagopal Majumdar and Raghunath Sarkar called on Fuller. This was most probably the deputation to the Lieutenant-Governor in 1905. They prayed for state patronage to educational facilities and government employment for the members of their community, promoting in return they promised to support the government.[48]

It is noteworthy that the anti-Swadeshi and pro-British stance of the Namasudras was not created with the development of the Swadeshi Movement itself (as an instance, it was one result of a grievance against the enforced boycott of cheaper British goods), but had been there since the very beginning of the movement as a settled line of work. This is well understandable from our study of the social trend among the Namasudras. The friction between the upper-caste Hindus and the others, i.e. the lower-caste Hindus and the Muslims, had already come into being in 1905 as a fixed social element. Therefore, the task of the Swadeshi Movement was not one of simply expanding its social base by winning support from the lower castes and the Muslims, but as much more difficult attempts to involve the opposing social groups in the movement.

A Namasudra meeting was held with Brajendranath Mandal, a zamindar, in the chair at Orakandi (Gopalganj Subdivision, Faridpur District) on 2 October 1906. The resolutions passed in the meeting are interesting enough to be quoted here: (1) that 'This meeting is greatly indebted to the Secretary of State for India for his declaring the partition of Bengal as a settled fact and admissible of no amendment'; (2) that 'This meeting prays most earnestly that the Hon'ble Mr. Hare will bestow the same rights and privileges upon the Namasudras as have been done upon the Mahomedans, in as much as the Namasudras and the Mahomedans are predominating communities of Eastern Bengal, and the latter unlike the Hindus possess a good deal of sympathy for the Namasudras'; and (3) that 'It is simply owing to the dislike and hatred of the Brahmins, the Vaidyas, and the Kayasthas that this vast Namasudra community has remained backward; this community has therefore not the least sympathy with them and their agitation, and will henceforth work hand in hand with their Mahomedan brethren'.[49]

Orakandi where the above-mentioned meeting was held is situated at the western edge of the *bil* land spreading across the border of Faridpur and Bakharganj on which sat a mansion of a Namasudra zamindar, the Australian Baptist Mission and a high school. The Baptist Mission opened a vocational school and a widows' home in the 1910s.[50]

Namasudra Suhrid was also published in this village. Almost every feature typical of the Namasudra movement was seen there. The intermediary role of the Christian missions which connected the Namasudras with the government is clearly shown by the fact that their petition in 1911 was recommended by Rev. C.S. Mead of the Australian Baptist Mission.[51] In addition, Orakandi was the headquarters of the Matua sect since it was the ancestral village of Sri Guruchand Thakur who was the founder of the sect.[52]

The Namasudras' position was the same as that of the Rajbansis in north Bengal and was also shared by the Jogis and Bhuimalis who exhibited a strong upward social orientation.[53]

At the already stated Namasudras' meeting held at Khulna in March 1908 the right was demanded to buy British goods freely.[54] Tagore in his article 'Sadupay' (Proper Means) contributed to the *Prabashi* of Sraban, 1315 B.S. (July–August 1908) analysed the boycott movement in Bakharganj. 'According to the information received from a reliable source in Barisal, despite the fact that *karkachlaban* (sea-salt produced internally) has become cheaper than imported rock salt, the Muslims who are known to our informant use the imported one at a price. He says that the local Muslims use imported cloth and salt not in consideration of loss and gain but solely out of their sense of honour. The information has come to us that the same tendency is also observed among the Namasudras.'[55]

Tagore pointed out that the enforcement of the boycott was a fatal folly, for it alienated the tenants of the lower classes of the country, let alone resolved to combine them. The situation in which the Muslims and the lower-caste Hindus were opposed to the Swadeshi Movement pressed other intellectuals to review it. Binod Lal Ghose, a pleader of Madaripur, made more concrete proposals in his article 'What can be done for the Namasudras' contributed to the *Modern Review* of June 1909. Madaripur is a subdivision located east of the Gopalganj Subdivision and north of the Gaurnadi Thana of the Bakharganj District. Madaripur and Gaurnadi were notorious for their dense distribution of minor talukdars and as one of the centres of the Swadeshi Movement. There were as many as 80 pleaders only in Madaripur.[56] Ghose wrote the article in response to a sense of growing crisis that the Namasudra neighbours were fast alienating themselves from the Hindu society.

Ghose concluded that the Namasudras, who were an inseparable part of the Hindu society, tried to sever their relationship with the upper castes, rely on the Muslims, and lean upon the Christian missions constituted the wrong course of action. Yet he frankly admitted that it was the upper-caste Hindus who had driven them into this sad plight. His question, therefore, was meant to ask what could be done for the Namas in order to win back their reliance. He proposed to take such concrete steps as the removal of untouchability and the establishment of schools and dispensaries.

Ghose stated in his article that the Namasudra sharecroppers stopped cultivating lands belonging to upper-caste landlords and did not offer service to them by forming a combination in some places.[57] The prototype of 1872–73 was again followed.

Some Swadeshi leaders tried to win over the Namasudras. Aswinikumar Datta (1856–1923) and Ambikacharan Majumdar (1851–1922) were two of them. Not a few Namasudras like Bhegai Haldar were drawn to Datta's lofty personality. At the Calcutta session of the Congress in 1917, Haldar was introduced by Surendranath Banerjee as a philanthropist who opened a charitable dispensary. He made a speech in Bengali 'to repudiate the attitude of a dozen Namasudras who are assisting the Anglo-Indian community in their fight against home rule'.[58]

Majumdar was more political in his efforts to tackle the Namasudra problem. He presided over the Calcutta session of the Bengal Provincial Conference in 1910 and played a vital part in passing a resolution to elevate the depressed classes. This resolution was criticized by the Bengali paper *Nayak* on the ground that it would ultimately destroy the caste system. It appears that the *Nayak* spoke frankly for the majority of the middle-class Hindus in Calcutta.[59] In the following year 1911, an annual session of the Bengal Provincial Conference was held at Faridpur which was Majumdar's headquarters. This session has been called Ambikacharan's Nama conference.[60] Most papers, however, took no notice of Majumdar's efforts. Among the accounts collected in *Report on Native Papers* of Bengal, only *Hitavadi* made the following sarcastic comments: 'the body of ultra-radical social reformers made themselves ridiculous at the Social Conference. These men, who delight in transgressing social regulations and who have been expelled from the pale of society, pretend to an equal position with the Hindu Social Legislators of old'.[61]

A band of ultra-extremist social reformers of Faridpur led by Ambikacharan Majumdar might be understood in relation to the Depressed Classes Mission established by Sibnath Sastri (1847–1919) who was a mentor of the Sadharan Brahmo Samaj.[62] This mission was established with the object of fighting against untouchability in Bengal. The mission changed its name to the Society for the Improvement of the Backward Classes in 1913. The society concentrated its work on the spread of education as illustrated by the fact that it established 104 schools in Bengal and Assam between 1916 and 1921 and imparted literacy to about 45,000 people between 1909 and 1921.[63]

The main trend of the Namasudra community which was against the nationalist movement and for the patronage of the government created two different reactions. On the one hand, a minor part of the upper-caste Hindus experienced a sense of crisis and they searched for effective measures for the uplifting of the depressed classes. On the other hand, however, a majority continued to neglect them under suspicion and disgust. The introduction of an election system gave political importance to the depressed classes and nationalist ideology itself demanded their support. As an inevitable result of this process, their political participation was promoted. On a deeper level, however, the middle-class public entertained a tacit distrust of them. The discrepancy of the reaction between political and psychological spheres appears to be a key to understanding Indian political history in the twentieth century.

What the Namasudras demanded during the Swadeshi Movement did not produce such dramatic changes as in the case of the Muslims after the annulment of the partition and the outbreak of World War I. Therefore, the same demands were repeated in the 1910s.[64] The government also responded favourably to their request and increased expenditure on 'education of the backward classes' from Rs. 19,732 in 1914–15 to Rs. 36,929 in 1915–16. This amount was largely allotted to the cost of reserved scholarships.[65] As a result the number of the depressed classes' students increased. A problem came into being in connection with their accommodation. As the problem of untouchability and segregation had not been solved, separate hostels were required for their accommodation. Government hostels for the Namasudra students were opened in Jhalakati, Perojpur, Barisal (these three in Bakharganj), Orakandi (in Faridpur), Dacca and Rajshahi.[66] In July 1918 the government started two special messes, one for the Jogis and the other for the Namasudras.[67]

The investment of money for education had the expected effect. The educated middle class among the Namasudras steadly increased in size. In 1911 there were 522 medical practitioners and 192 persons in educational posts among the Namasudras. In 1931 these numbers leapt to 784 persons in government services including gazetted and non-gazetted and 4, 263 persons in law, medicine and teaching.[68] The ratio of the middle class in the whole population of the Namasudra caste rose from 1.1 per cent in 1911 to 6.0 per cent in 1931.[69] This ratio in 1931 was much less than the Brahmans' 30.8 per cent, the Baidyas' 49.4 per cent and the Kayasthas' 22.4 per cent, but almost the same as the ratio of the Nabashak category (Napits' 7.4 per cent and Baruis' 8.7 per cent). The upward curve of the Namasudras was far sharper than that of the Nabashaks (the ratio of the same kind was 3.3 per cent with the Napits and 2.1 per cent with the Baruis in 1911). There were castes which did not come up to the Namasudras' standard even in the Nabashak category (Gops' 5.4 per cent and Kumars' 4.3 per cent). The 'Ajalchal' and 'Antaja' (untouchable) category like the Bagdis (1.2 per cent), Dopas (3.1 per cent) and Bauris (0.8 per cent) showed a much lower ratio than the Namasudras in 1931. Moreover, the ratio of the Brahmans, Baidyas and Kayasthas was 43.7 per cent, 54.7 per cent and

21.4 per cent respectively.[70] That is to say, the ratio of the three upper castes was either decreasing or following a crab-like course.

The middle class had changed its composition from the collective dominated by the three upper castes to that consisting of various castes. The depressed castes large in population like the Namasudras began to enter the middle class, which became a menace to the upper castes. In actuality, however, there existed the difference in quality within the middle class and the expansion in quantity did not produce any shift in hegemony whatsoever. The Bengali society until and even long after the independence was a top-heavy society dominated as ever by the three upper castes. It was only after the death of Jogen Mandal that the protective discrimination evolved into a social problem. At the end of this section, I shall briefly survey the problem of the entrance of the depressed classes into politics in relation to the introduction of an election system.

The Indian Council Act of 1909 introduced the separate Muslim electorate. This acted in a large way on the state of affairs around the lower-caste Hindus who had been moving on the same principles as the Muslims. It was during the 1910s that the Government of India started to tackle the problem of the depressed classes. The separate enumeration of the 'depressed classes' was planned but could not be undertaken owing to public protest.[71] Since the preparation of lists of such castes constituted the basic work essential to incorporating them into the Raj, it was attempted 'on no less than eight occasions between 1917 and 1936'.[72] Lists always remained arbitrary and could not be endowed with objective criteria. In principle it was not possible to fix in lists communities that went on moving according to various motives. It is obvious that the specification of Scheduled Castes following the independence involves the problem of the same kind.

Most of the depressed classes responded favourably to the government policy. Their efforts were concentrated on the acquisition of more opportunities for education and government services.[73] As a result, they refused to join the nationalist movement and occasionally opposed it in the first Non-Cooperation Movement between 1919 and 1922[74] in just the same way as during the days of the Swadeshi Movement. The pattern of their actions did not change even in the Civil Disobedience Movement.[75]

In 1917 the All-India Depressed Classes Association was formed. In Bengal, the Bangiya Janasangha (Bengal People's Association) was established in 1922 but did not last long owing to 'the lack of committed volunteers, general apathy and mutual jealousies'. In 1926 the Bengal Depressed Classes Association came into being with the Namasudra leader Mukunda Behari Mullick sitting in presidency. Through the activities of this association, the depressed classes' movement in Bengal came into contact with their all-India organization. From its very inception, this asociation was so closely related to the Bengal Namasudra Association which was also headed by M.B. Mullick that the dissatisfied other castes formed the All-Bengal Depressed Classes Federation in 1932. In the late 1930s the depressed classes began to be called under the legal term of the Scheduled Castes. Yet the new term hardly had any relevance to their movement which was disrupted because of violent internal oppositions created by the difference of personality rather than by that of principle.[76]

The reservation of the official services for the depressed classes did not work well owing to the dearth of qualified candidates, as in the case of the Muslims during the Swadeshi days. According to a government nortification of 1922, not less than one sixth of the candidates for the examination for the governmental services was reserved for either Anglo-Indians or members of the depressed classes. The result of the examination was imaginable. The candidates of the depressed classes could not compete with Anglo-Indians who had been well educated in English. Thus, they claimed that their appointment to official posting should be changed from that based on examination to that on nomination. Even in this case the minimum qualification was to be set aside to ensure the required number.[77]

According to the Government of India Act of 1919, a representative from the depressed classes was included among the 14 nominated non-official members in the Central Legislative Assembly. In the provincial legislatures, the number of their nomination was four in the Central Provinces, two each in Bombay and Bihar and one each in Bengal and the United Provinces.[78] Among the depressed castes of Bengal it was only the Namasudras that articulately demanded such special representation.[79] In the early 1930s, out of the 46 Hindu members in the Bengal Legislative Council, eight were members of the depressed classes who were either the Namasudras or the Rajbansis.

The Communal Award in August 1932 alloted 10 reserved seats in the Bengal Legislative Council to the depressed classes. This Award, as everybody knows, was repealed by Gandhi's fast observed at the risk of his life. Under this circumstance, the Poona Pact was concluded. All through Gandhi's fast, an all-out campaign against untouchability was organized across Bengal, and Kalighat Temple in Calcutta opened its door to the untouchables under the pressure of Congress volunteers.[80] Thanks to the Poona Pact, the number of the reserved seats for the depressed classes rose to 30. Even the 10 seats allotted by the Communal Award received repulsion from the caste Hindus who felt that this infringed upon their vested interests. In this context, the number of 30 was beyond any expectation. Responsible Hindu leaders were not in the position to protest because of Gandhi's life being at stake.[81]

In rural Bengal where the process of privation had already set in owing to the loss of frontier for agricultural expansion since the early 1920s,[82] rivalries between the landlords and tenants came to be strained. In East Bengal there were some reports in which the Namasudra and Muslim sharecroppers went on strike against high-caste Hindu landlords.[83] In the 1930s, however, the attempts to mobilize the masses are said to have shown a remarkable decline. The leaders of the depressed classes had accomplished their three tasks of spreading education, providing government jobs and being represented in legislature to a certain extent, and began to alienate themselves from their rural supporters. They were from either landlords or rich peasants and no way in a position to be interested in the privation of share-croppers and agricultural labourers from the 1930s onward.[84]

Jogendranath Mandal entered the Bengal political stage as a highly educated man when the Namasudra movement lost its dynamics.

POLITICAL LIFE OF JOGENDRANATH MANDAL

Jogendranath Mandal was born on 29 January 1904 in the village Maistarkandi of the Gaurnadi Thana in the district of Bakharganj. His father Ramdayal and his mother Sandhya had as many as six sons and four daughters. He was the youngest. His grandfather Nabinchandra was an affluent peasant and hired a private teacher for his children's education. Nabinchandra had made a pilgrimage as far as to Gaya, Benares and Vrindaban on foot.[85]

The Mandals were a joint family. Little Jogen was brought up by his childless uncle and his wife like their own son. His first learning was also imparted by this uncle and it was at the age of eight when he first went to school. This lower primary school was soon abolished and he was obliged to take a two-year vacancy in his educational career.

After he finished class IV in the reopened school, he entered Barthi Tara Institution located 2.5 miles north of his house. After finishing class V, he had again to leave school for a year for family reasons. Since his readmission to the school on his own expense, he stood first in every examination up to his graduation. Barthi was a rich village of Brahman concentration. He was five years senior to his classmates but he had to study in spare moments from his odd job in a home where there was neither table nor chair. Besides he was the only untouchable in the school. His biography written by his own son praises his brilliancy with a usual set phrase of 'making nothing of neglect inflicted upon him by fellow students of upper castes'. Yet in more concrete descriptions, Mandal, who was a sincere student, distinguished in study and physical power, was sufficiently loved by his teachers including the headmaster. On the other hand, there is an episode which shows that discrimination was not nonetheless absent. One day when he sat by a Brahman classmate, the boy exclaimed, 'Look! How cheeky this Namasudra is! He has come to me and wants to sit keeping very close to my body.' Other caste Hindu boys blindly followed him, saying, 'Well said! Let's throw him out.' Mandal protested on the instant. 'I won't move an inch. This school is not only for you, but for me too. I believe everybody equally has his right to sit here.' Teachers supported Mandal and praised his firm resolution.[86]

It goes without saying that Mandal suffered a certain degree of harassment. Yet what is much more noteworthy are the facts that Mandal had the courage to overcome this abuse and that the school had the logic to denounce it. In consequence, Mandal did not have such humiliating experiences as had Ambedkar. Unlike the latter's case, no teacher refused to touch his notebook nor did he have any need to have some one pour his drinking water from above so that no pollution might be produced on the pitcher through his touch. Besides, Barthi Tara Institution was not an urban school but a rural school located in the village with a large Brahman concentration. Logic to rise above caste ideology had already penetrated deep into such remote rural schools. Nevertheless there was an undercurrent of discrimination flowing side by side with the opening of modern consciousness.

In 1924 Mandal passed the Matriculation Examination in the first division with distinction in mathematics and Sanskrit.[87] He entered B.M. College located at Barisal, the headquarters of the Bakharganj District. B.M. College was founded by celebrated Aswinikumar Datta who upheld the district in the vanguard of the whole Swadeshi

Movement. B.M. Institution (consisting of a college and a high school) was famous for its lofty moral education and as the core of the nationalist movement in the district.[88] Owing to the government interference, although it had lost its former vitality and loftiness to a great extent, nonetheless its stoic tradition was kept alive thanks to the personality of Jagadishchandra Mukherji, headmaster of B.M. School. Mandal joined the Little Brothers of the Poor, an organization of teachers and students for social services which had been prominent in developing the moral education of B.M. Institution. Mandal inherited the idealistic essence of the nationalist movement created by Aswinikumar Datta by actively placing himself in its key organization.

Discrimination against the untouchables was rooted even in B.M. College. At the time of the Saraswati Puja, there was a custom that the lower-caste students offered flowers standing outside the temporarily built shrine. In spite of Mandal's protest upper-caste students turned a deaf ear to it. Mandal consulted with other lower-caste students and built a separate site for the puja. He could not bear to see an educational institution that pretended to be egalitarian infested with a discriminatory conscience.[89]

There took place an incident in Barisal town that a Namasudra student was found setting foot in the *natyamandir* (dance hall) attached to Kali Temple to offer worship, and beaten up. Mandal held a large protest meeting in which he made a fiery speech in support of human dignity. This lower-caste agitation rocked the town and the influential men stepped in with a mediation plan. The situation was saved for the time being.[90]

Mandal won fame as an orator outside college too. At a *praja mahasammelan* (large tenant meeting) held at Agailjhara village of Gaurnadi Thana in 1926, he made a speech which clearly demonstrated the basic line for his future political activities. He stressed the need of uniting the lower castes together if they wanted to win human dignity and social respect. For that purpose they were required to give up their minor, selfish interests. He professed that it was the way of the world that the strong oppressed the weak and the superior insulted the inferior, but realistic measures should be taken for emancipation from such a situation. The first means to attaining this purpose should be extrication from the state of illiteracy. An honorable status could be obtained not by means of mere prayer but by dint of self-help.[91]

In 1926 Mandal received his I.A. degree and married Kamala who was the second daughter of Praphullachandra Barui in Khagbari village of Gaurnadi Thana. Thereafter, the school fees were to be defrayed by his father-in-law until his graduation. He passed his B.A. examination in 1929.[92]

For a year after getting his B.A., Mandal lived at Jamalpur in Mymensingh to help his elder sister who had lost her husband. There he suffered from malaria for a long period. After that he ultimately managed to come to Calcutta to enter Law College. As his father-in-law had no intention of defraying further educational expenses for him, he had to work to continue his own studies. He was thus provided with accommodation and meals under a contract with a doctor from the same district that he taught his children at home. Yet he had to work his way through college as a proof-reader in a press. He tried to educate himself well to realize his conviction that the spread of education was the most urgent task for the backward communities to promote their social welfare. He passed the law examination in July 1934.[93]

Mandal received practical training in law at the Calcutta Small Causes Court under Advocate Chandmohan Chakrabarti. In January 1936 he was registered in the list of *ukils*. He entered the Small Causes Court but he had still to work in a press to earn money for his daily meals.[94] In July 1934 Mandal started to practice at the Bar in Barisal and began to win fame as an able pleader and would take a case in hand without fees from a poor peasant or artisan. He was censured for this way of doing business by his colleagues but did not depart from his principle. Thus he came to be regarded as an influential and popular pleader within a short time. Even before coming back to Barisal, he had been elected from Gaurnadi Thana to the Local Board by a substantial majority. Vast Namasudra support must have been behind his election. His return to Barisal might have been encouraged by this victory. On the occasion of appointment of chairman in the Local Board, he was asked to take up the post, but he adamantly declined to receive the offer. He let a former vice chairman have the credit for this. Naturally, he could raise himself in public esteem in the society in which elders won respect. This is reminiscent of young Aswinikumar's decision in connection with the management of the Barisal People's Association.[95] In 1937 Mandal was appointed to the District Board.[96]

In the 1937 election, Mandal stood for the Bengal Legislative Assembly (hereafter BLA) on the recommendation of a band of fellow pleaders and young government servants. He ran as a candidate in the Bakerganj North East General Rural Constituency which was a general constituency not reserved for the Scheduled Castes. It consisted of three subdivisions (Barisal Central, North and South) and 16 thanas under the Bhola Subdivision in the Dakshin Sahabajpur Island with an area of 1,657 square miles and a population of 427,728 out of which 183,390 were people of the Scheduled Castes.[97]

His opponent was Saralkumar Datta who was Aswinikumar's nephew and the president of the district committee of the Congress at that time. Both of them were based in the Gaurnadi Thana. While Datta came of a distinguished family and was the apparent heir of Aswinikumar Datta who had founded the nationalist movement in the district, Mandal was only a 33-year-old novice in the legal business who came of an untouchable peasant family.

In the Bakharganj District, the constituency which most attracted public attention was the Patuakhali Constituency located in the south where the Muslim population predominated. There a single contest was waged between Fazlul Huq, president of the Krishak Praja Party challenging the zamindari system and Nazimuddin, a member of the Dacca Nawab family who was running on the Muslim League ticket.[98]

The relative importance of the Patuakhali Constituency in comparison with the Bakerganj North East General Rural Constituency reflected changes in Bengal politics in a clear-cut form. The expansion of the franchise brought the populous Muslim community to the forefront of politics. The problem of whether or not the zamindari system should continue was also mainly contested not between the Hindu landlords and their untouchable tenants but between the Muslim landlords and their Muslim tenants. In this sense the contrast of the two constituencies was symbolic. So far as the Bakharganj District was concerned, the focus of politics had been shifted from the northern part where there was a slight possibility of the Hindus pitting themselves against the Muslims to the southern part where the Muslims overwhelmingly predominated. In the 1920s the rivalry between the Hindus and the Muslims came to take place in the south as in the case of the Patuakhali Satyagraha in 1926,[99] in which the Hindus claimed their age-old right to play music in front of mosques. It was quite obvious that the main rivalry had been shifted to that among supporters of the Muslim political parties, while the traditional rivalry between the Hindu landlords and their Namasudra tenants had already receded from the main stage.

Not expecting to gain a victory over Saralkumar Datta, Mandal hesitated to be a candidate. At the end of the vote counting, however, it was Mandal who came out victorious. The total votes in 62 polling places altogether amounted to 22,723 in which only 307 votes were cast by women. The turnout was 32.3 per cent. Mandal gained 12,069 votes (53.2 per cent), while Datta accrued 10,653 votes (46.8 per cent).[100]

There were several causes for Mandal's election. First of all, the Namasudra votes were firmly behind him. The biography of Mandal alloted a half page to listing his influential supporters.[101] Not only the Namasudras, however, voted for him, but the other Scheduled Caste voters enthusiastically supported him.[102] Even a part of the caste Hindus voted for him. This was largely brought forth by the support given by the 30 pleaders of the Barisal Bar.[103] The fact that Mandal received favours from Khan Bahadur Hashem Ali Khan, chairman of the District Board, and Khan Bahadur Muhammad Ismail Chaudhuri, a member of the Central Legislative Assembly,[104] may have considerably affected the result of the Muslim votes.

Another cause could most probably be attributed to the articles written by Durgamohan Sen. Sen was a Congress activist and the editor of *Barisal Hitaishi*, one of the papers punished with the suspension of publication in the Swadeshi days.[105] He was known to be very critical of social reformers. Unexpectedly, however, he made a favourable comment on Mandal's political speech delivered at Barisal Town Hall (now Aswinikumar Town Hall). Sen who had been dissatisfied with the state of affairs in Barisal after Aswinikumar's death, might have found in him a leader who could revitalize the social service ideal in the changed circumstances.

In the 1937 election, the Scheduled Castes won 32 out of 250 seats in the Legislative Assembly. Of the seats won by them 30 were from the reserved seats allotted for them and two were from the general seats. Apart from Mandal, a candidate who had run on the Congress ticket was returned to the general seat. The composition of the 32 successful candidates based upon the division of political parties was 7 Congress and 2 Hindu Sabha nominees in addition to 23 'independent' members.[106] Mandal took the office of the secretary of the Independent Scheduled Caste Assembly Party.[107]

The first work that Mandal set about after his election was to raise the status of the Bhegai Haldar Public Academy at Agailjhara to a high-level English school. Having stayed at Calcutta to act for the Assembly from April to July, he returned home and held a large meeting on the campus of the school at Agailjhara chaired by Khan Bahadur Hashem Ali. Mandal preached the importance of education and made an appeal for subscription to improve school facilities and increase the number of students. A total subscription of Rs. 2,700 was promised on the spot and was later paid in full. The number of students also rose from 93 to nearly 300 in the following year. Mandal managed to persuade ministers of the provincial government and Syamaprasad Mookerjee, Vice Chancellor of the Calcutta University to promote the school to a high-level English school for the coming three years. He served as secretary to the school until he was appointed provincial minister. At the time of the renewal of the school site which was owned by the District Board, he exercised his political influence to keep it intact.[108]

Mandal's activities in the legislature were directed to the uplifting of the status of the Scheduled Castes (the establishment of boarding facilities for Scheduled Caste policemen, the expansion of scholarships, boarding subsidies for students, reservation for the government services[109]) and the introduction of funds to the Bakharganj District. (Building an embankment along the *bil* land in the Wazirpur Thana or attempts to construct a railway between Barisal and Khulna, though it did not come about as a result of its being opposed by the steamer company.[110]) Thus, he presented himself as a typical member of the legislature who did his best to act for his supporting body and constituency. Yet he had the remarkable character of a politician as well. He won the confidence of Naliniranjan Sarkar who was the Finance Minister and through him achieved his political purposes. Sarkar had high regard for Mandal's claims, as they were free from selfish motives.[111]

Mandal's selfless behaviour was esteemed highly by the Bose brothers of the Congress.[112] Up to 1940 Mandal kept in touch with their Congress and was in the camp of the opposition parties. At the time of tabling non-confidence motions against the Huq Ministry in August 1938, he moved against Prasanna Deb Raikat (Rajbansi), the Minister for Forest and Excise.[113] When the Calcutta Municipal Amendment Bill was brought under deliberation, Mandal spoke against it on the ground that the introduction of the separate election, according to which seven seats would be reserved for the Scheduled Castes, was contrary to the principle of democracy. The bill was finally legalized along the lines of a joint election with reserved seats, for which Mandal argued. Subhas Chandra Bose's influence on him was obvious when he stated that he would make every effort to build an undivided Hindu society.[114]

In the Calcutta Corporation election in April 1940, Mandal, who was not a member of the Congress, ran as a candidate for the reserved seat in Ward 3 on the recommendation of the Congress and was returned on account of the effective backing given him by the Bose brothers.[115]

In the early part of 1940,[116] Subhas Bose set the Forward Bloc to work. And when he visited Barisal to expand its organization, Mandal presided over a large meeting at the request of Bose. A happy mutual reliance arose there between them. Bose had sufficient insight to find in a young untouchable member of the Legislative Assembly a man selflessly dedicated to the social services and to win him to his side by giving him his patronage. On the other hand, Mandal could increase his popularity from a political scenario in which he looked well trusted by Bose.[117] Mandal was fully impressed by Bose's posture in that the latter was ignoring all the distinctions of castes and sects for the sake of the great cause of independence.

Mandal's leaning toward the Congress was solely owing to the inspiration and patronage given by the Bose brothers. Therefore, Subhas Bose's de facto expulsion from the Congress, which was brought forth in rapid succession within a few months after he had been forced to resign his Presidency in April 1939, was a great shock to Mandal. He lost his faith in the Congress under the leadership of Mahatma as did many Bengali contemporaries.[118] In view of this situation, he found that any policy worth mentioning had not been put into effect in the provinces under the Congress governments. He realized keenly that the social promotion of the Scheduled Castes would not be materialized through reliance on the Congress and that their self-support and unity were highly needed.[119]

A political situation had already come into being, in which any Scheduled Caste politician would be forced to take the position of the pro-Muslim League once he took a stance aginst the Congress. And the necessity for the self-support and unity among the Scheduled Castes induced Mandal to come under Ambedkar's influence. The way for their self-help and unity should have been theoretically cleared by strengthening their organizational movements from below. As already stated at the end of the previous section, however, their movement had stepped into the phase of decline, and Mandal himself had to shift the place of his activities to Calcutta. It was difficult for him to lead any substantial movement in his base in Barisal. At this point of time he was alienated upwardly; thereby he was no more a grass-roots worker. His position was a Scheduled Caste notable who represented their interests at the centre of the province as a spokesman. The age had been completely changed from the time when Aswinikumar Datta could dedicate himself to building the nationalist movement in Barisal without regard for gaining fame in Calcutta. The introduction of a regular election system sent men like Mandal to Calcutta. If it was difficult to organize the movement from below, there was no alternative to improve the collective interests of the Scheduled Castes but from the centre of politics. Mandal met Ambedkar in such a situation as the urgently called for all-India unity of the Scheduled Castes.

Before that, however, we shall examine the circumstances under which Mandal joined the Nazimuddin Ministry. The second Huq Ministry which was in power between December 1941 and March 1943 was a coalition with the Forward Bloc (27 MLAs led by Saratchandra Bose) and the Mahasabha (11 MLAs led by Shyamaprasad Mookerjee). As Bose was removed from the scene after his arrest early in the morning on the day of the formation of the new cabinet, it is customary to call it the 'Shyama-Huq' Ministry.[120] Twelve members of independent Scheduled Castes members were in the coalition but the number of their ministers was reduced from two in the first Huq Cabinet to one in this cabinet. This incurred the wrath of the Scheduled Castes, who held their district meetings demanding that another minister be appointed from among them.[121] In addition, the Scheduled Castes were not appointed to official posts according to the quota set by the Communal Ratio Rule which had been legalized under this government. They claimed the allotment of Rs. 500,000 for their education but in fact only Rs. 200,000 was allotted. All these factors made Mandal, the Secretary of the Scheduled Caste Assembly Party, stand against the Shyama-Huq Ministry.[122] The main opposition party at that time was the Muslim League led by Nazimuddin. Mukund Behari Mullick, a veteran Namasudra politician who was a minister of the first Huq Ministry, had joined it with his brother as its only non Muslim members.[123] This then was the background of Mandal's entry to the Nazimuddin Ministry.

When the second Huq Cabinet failed, the Scheduled Caste MLAs got together at the Savoy Hotel in Calcutta under the leadership of Mandal. They agreed to join the camp which would accept their following demands: (1) Three ministers should be appointed from the Scheduled Castes; (2) Rs. 500,000 should be allotted to the Scheduled Castes for educational expenditures; and (3) Candidates from the

Scheduled Castes should be appointed to all governmental services, including senior posts, according to the quota set by the Communal Ratio Rule.[124]

It was Nazimuddin who accepted all of these demands. In return he demanded the support of 20 Scheduled Caste members for his Ministry. The Scheduled Caste side agreed this. Thus, the Muslim League succeeded in incorporating the Scheduled Caste members into their camp. Out of the 13 ministers of the Nazimuddin cabinet, there were 6 Hindu ministers out of whom 3 were Scheduled Castes. Mandal was appointed to the Minister for Co-operative Credit and Rural Indebtedness, Premhari Barman to the Minister for Forest and Excise, and Pulinbehari Mullick to the Minister for Publicity.[125]

Mandal set about work to form a Bengal branch for purposes of the integration of the Scheduled Castes on the all-India level, as a part of forming organizations for the Forward Bloc. It is said that this movement, spreading over the Namasudra-dominated areas like Dacca, Mymensingh, Barisal, Faridpur, Noakhali, Jessore and Khulna, worried Gandhi.[126] After the 'exodus' of Subhas Bose in January 1941, however, the attitudes of the Forward Bloc became ambiguous. Thus the cooperation with the nationalist movement receded from the front. Instead, the integration of the Scheduled Castes on the all-India level was to be chosen as its main object.[127]

Ultimately in July 1942, this movement under Mandal's leadership was connected with the All-India Scheduled Castes Federation (AISCF) founded at the instance of Ambedkar. In May 1943 its Bengal branch was formed and Mandal made strenuous efforts to solidify it further.[128] The executive office of the branch was set up at the office of the weekly *Jagaran* (Awakening), the organ of the Scheduled Caste movement, which Mandal founded at his own expense.[129] Mandal took office as the President of the Bengal Provincial Scheduled Castes Federation (BPSCF). The appeal, which he distributed after his assumption of office, is an interesting document acclaiming the AISCF 'as the only patriotic organization of the Scheduled Castes committed to deliver the down-trodden communities to the final goal of emancipation' and also observing that 'The tremendous gust of people's liberation throughout the world has inspired us greatly and we are determined to create a new future for us in a free and prosperous world.'[130] The establishment of branches in districts and subdivisions started in Faridpur, especially in the Gopalganj Subdivision where people's activities were very active.[131] Gopalganj was a subdivision where the Namasudras were predominant, occupying 41 per cent of the total population and as many as 73 per cent of the Hindu population.[132] While the formation of the branches of the AISCF was progressing, Mandal met Ambedkar for the first time in Bombay where the meeting of the provincial ministers for cooperation was held in October 1943.

Mandal's movements, however, did not have the universal support of the Namasudra community. When Ambedkar visited Calcutta in 1944, leading politicians except one, of the Namasudra community that appeared to receive him at his saloon brought the following criticism of Mandal to his notice. As Mandal was a committed follower of Subhas Bose and returned to the Calcutta Corporation on the Congress ticket, he lost the confidence of the Scheduled Castes. Ambedkar told them that the question was not how he was elected but whether his actions were really against the interests of the Scheduled Castes in its aftermath. Mandal's biography claims that nobody could give such an example. Moreover, Premhari Barman (Rajbansi, Minister for Forest and Excise), Kshetramohan Sinha (Rajbansi) and Anukulchandra Das (Paundra Kshatrya) came forward to support him and hereupon Ambedkar decided not to attend any meeting except the one held by the Scheduled Castes Federation.[133]

The above-mentioned episode may endorse in our biographer's view that Mandal and Ambedkar attracted each other. At the same time, it also shows that the Namasudra community did not give solid support to the BPSCF and yet Mandal found some support in other influential Scheduled Castes.

Ambedkar made an assertion in a pamphlet on the Pakistan problem published at the end of 1940 that the Muslim League's demand for 'partition' was supportable. In a sense, a foundation of the collaboration with the Muslim League was created at the time when Mandal accepted Ambedkar as the leader of the all-India Scheduled Caste movement. Yet this was nothing but a political collaboration meant for the expansion of the rights of the Scheduled Castes. Later Mandal's actions in connection to the partition of Bengal would confirm this.

The Nazimuddin Cabinet carried out almost all of the plans for the Scheduled Castes which the Huq Ministry had shelved. There were three main items here: (1) The expenses of Rs. 500,000 per year for educational grants; (2) 20 per cent reservation of government services for the Scheduled Castes, irrespective of category, gazetted or non-gazetted; and (3) The introduction of the reservation system for the

Scheduled Caste students to medical schools and colleges.[134] To put these items in operation, Mandal, on the authority of his ministership, took actions so coercively that he incurred criticism. At the time of the new recruitment in large numbers in the Food Rationing Department, Mandal noticed the Scheduled Castes had not been brought in according to the stipulated quota. Mandal took action without delay. He made a bomb shell demand that so long as the anomaly was going on, the Ministry under his charge would adopt only Scheduled Caste candidates without taking Muslims or caste Hindus. The meeting became embroiled in dealing with this problem. The Chief Minister Nazimuddin and the Minister for Civil Supply Suhrawardy decided to accept his demand. In the course of discussion Mandal threatened them with unseating the Cabinet. The 20 Scheduled Caste members held the casting vote in the legislature consisting of the 140 membered Government party and the 108 opposition. This definitely explains Mandal's firm attitude and the realization of the policies favourable for the Scheduled Castes.[135]

Certainly, some progress had been made in the recruitment of the Scheduled Castes for government services. Yet there remained major problems. For instance, Mandal pointed out in a letter addressed to the Secretary to the Public Service Commission that the candidates of Scheduled Castes were placed in circumstances disadvantageous to them on the occasion of their interview. Often they were not even given an opportunity to having an interview, though they possessed the requisite qualifications. Unusual and pinpricking questions were put to them and generally, in the exact expression given by Mandal, 'They do not possess so healthy and beautiful a physique as is possessed by the candidates of the other two communities.'[136] As a countermeasure, Mandal suggested the necessity of incorporating a Scheduled Caste member in the Commission.[137]

From this time onward, Mandal assisted many youths of Scheduled Castes with regard to their service, promotion, studying abroad and so on, sometimes paying out of his own pocket. Yet not a few of these Scheduled Caste elites forgot their debts to Mandal or committed a breach of trust. His son's reproaches on them are a pitiful undercurrent of Mandal's biography.[138] Clearly, this is a piteous plight to be experienced by a fallen leader. Viewed as a social problem, however, it is not surprising that men who have risen in the world by means of their private merit of education would exhibit every possibility of being the selfish elite if they have been alienated from their own community.

They are inclined to go adrift if the movement of their own community does not pull them toward it. In those days, however, such a condition no longer existed since higher education and employment in the reserved posts were sought after as a means of caste emancipiation in place of the caste movements.[139]

On 28 March 1945 the Nazimuddin Ministry failed. Between 1944 and 1945 Mandal conducted a campaign for disseminating the policies of the Scheduled Castes Federation over the area centring on the north-eastern part of the Bakharganj District.[140] The campaign culminated in the Gopalganj session of the Bengal Provincial Scheduled Castes Federation which was held on 24–25 April 1945 soon after the collapse of the Nazimuddin Ministry. Ambedkar had given word that he would attend it but a sect opposing Mandal within the Scheduled Castes managed to persuade Ambedkar to cancel it. Mandal's biography states fully how Mandal worked hard to cope with the situation.[141]

This meeting achieved a phenomenal success as a session of the Scheduled Castes Federation. About a thousand volunteers busied themselves in setting up the meeting grounds to accommodate 100,000 people and for handling other tasks. At least 50,000 people attended it, coming from Namasudra dominated districts like Bakharganj, Khulna, and Jessore, not to mention the home district Faridpur and farther from Dacca, Mymensingh, Comilla, Pabna, Rangpur, Bogra, and Jalpaiguri.[142] The handbill, 'What is the direction of emancipation? The requirements for organizing the Federation', published on this occasion by the office of this session, is of interest but is too long to be cited here. Instead I shall hereafter sum up the resolutions of the session as follows.

1. Support of the demands resolved at the Nagpur Session of the AISCF (July 1942) and its executive committees held at Madras and Kanpur and declaring Ambedkar as the only leader of 80 million people of the Scheduled Castes.
2. A declaration of resolve to agitate for the realization of the following basic demands of the peasants and labourers who constitute the majority of the Scheduled Castes.
   (1) The distribution of land under the landlord's own holding to the landless peasants of the Scheduled Castes and the establishment of their rural colonies.
   (2) The abolition of the zamindari and intermediate tenure system and the introduction of the appropriate agricultural system by the government.

(3) The decision to set fair minimum prices of agricultural products and the establishment of cooperative sales centres for purposes of joint cultivation and agriculture.
(4) The granting of fishing rights in the low swampy lands to those who were engaged in fishery.
(5) The introducton of the legal minimum wage system to meet the needs of municipality and factory labourers.
(6) Employers should bear expenses for unemployment insurance, endowment insurance, sickness insurance and delivery by female workers.

3. The expression of a deep concern for the situation that the great famine and rampant epidemics experienced during the last three years had wielded a disastrous influence upon the Scheduled Castes; immediate relief measures were demanded.
4. The expression of concern for disadvantages incurred by Scheduled Caste candidates at the time of recruitment for government services and a consequent demand to the government of the appointment of a Scheduled Caste member to the Public Service Commission.[143]

After the fall of the Nazimuddin Ministry, Bengal was placed under the Governor's rule. In the circumstances, the elections were held during the winter of 1945–46. In the *Jagaran* (24 October 1945), Mandal stated that the coming provincial elections would produce the constitution making body, so that they should do their best to increase the power of Ambedkar who would speak for them in it. He analysed the situation that there were three all-India parties, i.e. the Congress, the League and the Federation (AISCF), all of which were led by strong leaders.[144] The weakness of the Federation, however, was quite obvious. It could offer its own candidates only for 24 seats out of 151 seats reserved for the Scheduled Castes throughout India. Its position was quite the same in Bengal. The candidates of the Federation could run only for 5 out of 30 reserved seats.[145]

Mandal stood as a candidate in the Bakerganj South (Reserved) Constituency in addition to the Bakharganj North-East General Rural Constituency from which he was elected in 1937. The result of the election was that he was defeated in the general seat and returned in the reserved seat.

The defeat in the general seat may be ascribed to three causes. Firstly, in this constituency where the voters of the caste Hindus surpassed by far those of the Scheduled Castes, the Congess offered a candidate whom the caste Hindus could unanimously support. The man of their choice for the Congress was Manoranjan Gupta, who had acted as a 'revolutionary terrorist' since the early 1910s, passed 24 years in jail and was still in Meerut Jail at that time.[146] There was strong support of a patriot who had dedicating his entire life to the nationalist cause without marrying. Secondly, Mandal was so very busy with his campaign in the reserved constituency that he had neither time nor funds to spare for the general seat. He lacked such necessary support, both organizational and financial, as to conduct campaigns in the two constituencies at the same time.[147] Finally, according to Mandal's protest telegraph sent to the Governor after the election, there seems to have been a considerable degree of obstruction arising during the campaign.[148] An incident connected with this obstruction experienced by Mandal's camp will be discussed later in the third section.

The Bakerganj South (Reserved) Constituency consisted of 18 thanas under the Perojpur and Patuakhali Subdivisions in the south of the district. Mandal had no local connections there. This constituency, however, had a previous record of electing a candidate brought in from outside.[149] In this election, too, some local leaders among the Namasudras there offered a safer constituency to Mandal whose election was precarious at best in his own constituency. Finally, however, five candidates ran in this constituency and a preliminary election was held on 24 January 1946 to decrease their number to four.

Mandal stood first by winning double as many votes as the second candidate, who thought of stepping down. Persuaded by the Congress, however, he gave up the idea. It was necessary for the Congress to nail Mandal down to this constituency, and thereby to prevent him from being returned to the general constituency. A candidate who had run on the Congress ticket narrowly passed the preliminary election in the last place, whose number of votes was a quarter less than Mandal. The Congress sent volunteers from Barisal and Calcutta with a sash on which was written the slogan of 'Jay Hind' (Victory to India) and attacked Mandal as a supporter of Ambedkar who denied the Hinduness of the Scheduled Castes. A dead heat was fought to and the election was held on 22 March. Mandal was returned with 28,560 votes. Upendranath Edbar, who was second in the preliminary election, followed him with 15,445. Congress nominee Agnikumar Mandal got only 1,140 votes.[150]

The 30 reserved seats in the 1946 election were divided into 26 for the Congress, 3 for independents and 1 for the Scheduled Castes Federation.[151] There was considerable possibility that the Federation would get a seat in Faridpur but it was lost owing to the lack of coordination among the Namasudras. Mukund Behari Mullick, a Namasudra leader opposing Mandal put up his own candidate, so that both sides shared the same fate.[152] Mullick himself was returned as an independent candidate in Khulna. In the result of the 1946 election, it was brought to light that the Scheduled Caste movement exhibited weakness in its organization and was defective in its leadership. Their leaders were engrossed in strife, seeking interests to be accrued from their institutional status.

In April Suhrawardy formed the cabinet of 12 ministers. For the first time the numerical balance among the communities was not considered in the formation of this cabinet. There were only 2 Hindu ministers in it and both of them were of the Scheduled Castes.[153] Mandal took office as the Law Minister and the Minister for the Public Work and the Construction of Houses.[154]

On 16 May 1946 the Cabinet Mission proposed a plan with a loose confederal structure. Both the Congress and the League accepted it. The interests of the Scheduled Castes, however, did not come into view in this plan owing to a crushing defeat sustained by the Scheduled Castes Federation in the last election. Thus, the Scheduled Castes were alert to the coming danger that their existence would be lost forever once this plan was implemented.[155] In Bengal the joint leaders' meeting of the BPSCF led by Mandal and the Scheduled Castes Association led by Mullick was held on 8 June through the good office of the Bengal Namasudra Samiti. It was decided in the meeting that they would take joint actions under Ambedkar's leadership.[156] On 28 June Ambedkar visited Calcutta and a great rally of the BPSCF was held on 30 June. On the one hand, the Constituent Assembly election was near at hand. The members of the Constituent Assembly were to be indirectly elected by the provincial legislatures. Ambedkar who was defeated in the Bombay Legislative Assembly election expected to be elected to the Constituent Assembly through having the support of European members in the Bengal legislature. Yet they gave up participating in the election and it was a great disappointment to Ambedkar. In view of such a situation, Mandal undertook the responsibility for sending Ambedkar to the Constituent Assembly.

The situation was hopeless, however, because two candidates, Pramatharanjan Thakur (Congress) and Mukund Behari Mullick, had already announced that they would stand from among the Namasudras. The educated youths of the Scheduled Castes came out with Mandal in support of Ambedkar. Mandal set about vote-securing with their support at his back. First he went to Rangpur and got support from Nagendranath Ray of the Rajbansi community. Gayanath Biswas, Congress MLA from Tangail, was a supporter of Ambedkar so that the Congress, not eager to have Ambedkar in the Constituent Assembly, held him in seclusion. He managed to send an emissary to Mandal and informed him that he would definitely vote for Ambedkar if he was sent to the Assembly Hall. On the night before the election, Mullick expressed his intension to vote for Ambedkar to Nazimuddin who passed the news to Mandal. Dwarkanatha Baruri, MLA from Faridpur, promised to give his second vote to Ambedkar. Two MLAs of the Matsyajibi (fisher caste), Bholanath Biswas (Jessore) and Haranchandra Barman (Pabna) assented to give their first vote to Ambedkar. Polling was taken on 18 July and the votes were counted on the following day. Ambedkar was found to be elected by the greatest majority.[157] This is dealt with as a mere episode as well as a matter of course in Ambedkar's biographies. Yet it had not come to pass without the dedicated canvassing of the educated youths of the Bengali Scheduled Castes.

Although crashed by the Direct Action Day on 16 August 1946, the All-India Satyagraha Day was implemented by the Scheduled Castes Federation in opposition to the Cabinet Mission Plan. There was a rally in Calcutta and meetings were held in various parts of East Bengal.[158] On 21 November some Scheduled Caste MLAs, mainly consisting of those who had voted for Ambedkar, left the Congress and joined the Federation. The primary cause for this transfer of allegiance was their grievance against the decision of the Interim Government inaugurated with Nehru as its head. Only one minister was appointed from among eight crore people of the Scheduled Castes and even that one was not Ambedkar.[159] And when the Muslim League joined the Interim Government on 26 October, the League sent Mandal to it as a Law Member.

This is a well-known fact mentioned in every historical text dealing with this period and is generally explained as follows. In order to maintain a balance with the assignment of a ministerial post to a Muslim (Asaf Ali) by the Congress, the League appointed one of Scheduled Caste members for the purpose of making it prominent that all of the Scheduled Castes were not represented by the Congress in just the same way as the efforts of the Congress to show that all of the Muslims were not necessarily represented by the League.[160]

On 14 October Mandal was informed of Jinnah's intention by Suhrawardy. The following day the news was flashed by all papers. In this situation what Mandal cared most about was meeting with Ambedkar's approval. At that time Ambedkar was on his way to London and Mandal had no means to contact him. On arriving in London, Ambedkar gave a statement of welcome.[161]

Jinnah seems to have cooly understood the merits and demerits of Ambedkar and Mandal. The fact that Mandal sent out Ambedkar to the Constituent Assembly from the Bengal Legislature means nothing more than the former's acknowledgement of the latter's superiority as a political leader. Undoubtedly Mandal was regarded by Jinnah as a politician easier to be handled. Moreover, while Ambedkar had his political base in Section A which had no relation with Pakistan, Mandal belonged to Muslim-dominated Section C so that he was to be useful even in connection with the founding of Pakistan. Ambedkar on his part considered Jinnah's decision to take Mandal into the cabinet as one of his extraordinary strategic manoeuvres. In his view the entry of two Scheduled Caste men (Jagjiwan Ram from the Congress and Mandal from the League) to the Interim Government was a double-edged event. He wrote to D.G. Jadhav on 29 October that 'Although we have got two seats, we have become the tools of the two major parties.'[162]

Just at that moment a violent storm of communal riots was blowing in Noakhali. Against a background of the attack of the Muslim majority on the Hindu minority, Gandhi's criticism that 'The League's whole mode of entrance into Government had not been straight'[163] was not easy to be brushed aside. At any rate, Mandal's entrance to the cabinet was of its nature vulnerable to criticism. It is also open to question whether or not Mandal who, unlike Ambedkar, was only a regional politician, had any executive ability.

Regarding this point, Mandal seems not to have overestimated his ability. First he postponed going to Delhi and rushed to Noakhali. Accompanied by the MLAs of the Scheduled Castes and the cadres of the Muslim League, he energetically traveled around to see the riot stricken areas for himself, tried to pacify the situation by preaching the identity of economic interests between the Scheduled Castes and the Muslims, and organized for relief works.[164] Starting with this, Mandal appears to have made speech tours outside Delhi too often than to act as a central minister. This was to have been endorsed by the following cutting remark made by Governor-General Wavell: 'Mandal, the League's Scheduled Caste nominee, is a Law Member. . . . He is usually travelling the country to attend Scheduled Caste political meetings; when he does come to the Cabinet he is silent or silly.'[165]

The cause for his 'silence' and 'silliness' in the cabinet seems to be attributable to his incompetency of speaking good English. An English high official made the following comment on Mandal in his confidential letter. 'I was least impressed with the Law Member, but he is somewhat handicapped by defective knowledge of English.'[166] Coming across such objective, cold remarks, we understand why he looked up to Ambedkar as their leader and satisfied himself as being his lieutenant. Once Viceroy Mountbatten asked Mandal why he only spoke about the Scheduled Castes whenever he came. He answered that other ministers spoke nothing about them; since they spoke about the general condition of the country, he had to speak about the neglected and down-trodden people.[167] Thus he knew his given position and expected role exactly.

Only one point remains to be made about Mandal at the time of his membership in the Interim Government: he started a movement against the partition of Bengal.

Since Mountbatten took office in March 1947, the process towards partition had gained momentum. In the third week of April the BPCC (Bengal Provincial Congress Committee) Executive Council put forth a plan for partition. Starting with Calcutta on Direct Action Day (16 August 1946), spreading to Noakhali and Tripura and coming back to Calcutta again between 26 March and 1 April 1947, the communal riots panicked the Bengali Hindus and drove them to accept the partition. On 21 April Mandal made a statement against partition in Delhi. He pointed out that communal riots would not last forever and a remedy in the form of panic-driven partition would be worse than riots, specifically, the source of panic. By partition, he argued, Bengal was to be reduced and to present a dangerous border line in-between.[168]

The greatest ground for his opposition to the partition was that it would crush the Scheduled Castes of East Bengal. The Namasudras, the largest among them, was to be divided into East and West Bengal and thereby would be under the threat of Muslim violence just at the time of the riot in Noakhali in East Bengal and prey to the caste Hindu domination in West Bengal. The proposed exchange of population would not work well for the Scheduled Castes. Being people of poor means they would not leave their homes as the upper-caste Hindus would do. Therefore, Mandal was convinced that it was essential for the Scheduled Castes in East Bengal to keep the united Bengal intact.[169]

From early May Mandal went round making speeches at various parts of the *mofussil* districts in support of anti-partition agitation.[170] This time, too, his position was not generally supported by the Scheduled Castes. On the contrary, as Sekhar Bandyopadhyay has demonstrated, the general trend among the Scheduled Castes had been moving towards the utterly opposite direction. The 'majority of the Scheduled Castes particularly in eastern and northern Bengal had identified themselves with the sentiments whipped up by the Mahasabha and had rejected the leadership of Jogendranath Mandal'.[171] His image as a man of the Muslim League connection was detrimental to his agitation. After all, his anti-partition agitation was too closely combined with the interests of the Namasudra community in East Bengal to attract wider public support beyond them at this critical moment in the history of Bengal.

The scheme for an independent Bengal argued by Suhrawardy and Abul Hashim, and Sarat Bose's attempt in response to it, were killed by Mountbatten's announcement of the partition plan on 3 June 1947, which compelled provincial legislatures to choose only beween India and Pakistan. Mandal's attempt was so deeply buried that history has left it unrecorded.

The only choice for Mandal, a Namasudra politician, was to remain in East Bengal where the majority of his fellow caste would be left behind and to work for safeguarding their political rights. He had no choice but to join Pakistan. On 5 August 1947 he was found on the train bound for Karachi.[172]

Mandal acted as temporary chairman at the Constituent Assembly of Pakistan which started on 10 August. He made an inaugural address, brief and to the point, to celebrate the founding of Pakistan. On that night Liaquat Ali Khan blessed him saying, 'Heartiest congratulations, Mr. Mandal, you have made a brilliant speech today. We did not expect it.'[173] In a sense it was a contemptuous comment. Liaqut Khan and other cadres of the League judged him in just the way as Wavell and Mountbatten did. In order to appeal to the world of the legitimacy of Pakistan, Mandal was still regarded as a useful puppet. From the comment made by Liaquat Khan, however, we can read their fear lest Mandal should spoil the foundation ceremony of Pakistan by his 'silly' speech.

With the independence of Pakistan on 14 August 1947, Mandal took up the post of Minister in Charge for Law and Labour. For three and half years from this time to October 1950 when he tendered his resignation from Calcutta, he did his best to safeguard the rights of the minorities, protect the living of labourers, and expand their rights.

In spite of his efforts, however, the conditions of the minorities in Pakistan deteriorated so that communal riots took place often during these three years. Mandal though, as a member of the cabinet, was not in a position to blame them openly but rather was to conceal them. His resignation and taking refuge in Calcutta in October 1950 meant that he would no longer put up with this kind of deception.

Until his death on October 1968, Mandal lived a life of another 18 years in Calcutta. Those years seem not entirely to be a retired life. The publication of the third volume of his biography by his own son is expected to provide further information about the last phase of his life.

JOGEN MANDAL AS SEEN FROM THE VILLAGE

I spent about a hundred days between November 1985 and February 1986 at Harhar village (popularly called Batajor together with two adjacent villages, Batajor and Deopara) where Aswinikumar Datta's ancestral home is located. During my stay there, I collected a certain amount of information about Mandal. Comparing what I found with the relevant parts of the published 'biography', I shall discuss Mandal as seen through the eyes of the villagers.

Originally Harhar was a Hindu village dominated by the Kayasthas. At present almost all of them had moved over to India. Consequently it has assumed the character of a Hindu village with very few upper-caste inhabitants, mostly consisting of the middle and lower castes. The Namasudras, along with the *pan* (betel leaf)-cultivating Baruis, form the influential castes in the village.[174] I can thus safely say that there is no real discrimination based on the untouchability system.

In the memory of the villagers, Mandal first appeared in connection with the 1937 election. It was the event which had taken place nearly 50 years before my survey in the mid-1980s. The election campaign between Mandal and Saral Datta of the landlord family took a wild turn and was sometimes marked by violent clashes. Those who led the campaign among the Namasudra community in the Gaurnadi Thana were men like Jitendranath Talukdar, Bipinbihari Sinha, Ramkrishna Mandal and Haralal Mistri.[175] Among them the 'biography' refers to Ramkrishna Mandal and Jitendranath Talukdar of the village Chandrahar and Bipinbihari Sinha of Batajor (more correctly Deopara).[176] The last mentioned person was incidentally the father of my assistant. He had served for many years as a headmaster of a primary school and was shot dead by the Pakistan army at the time of the Bangladesh Independence War. All his children, except the youngest son who remained in the village with his mother, had been properly educated, left for Calcutta, and engaged in white collar jobs. The network of local leaders who had received secondary education like Bipin Sinha functioned as the base in support of Mandal.

According to the village oral tradition, when Mandal took up the office of provincial minister, the Namasudra community was exposed to stronger opposition of the caste Hindus. To contend with such a situation the Namasudras of Batajor held a large meeting on Bipin Sinha's land in Deopara with Jogen Mandal as its main guest.[177]

In the 'biography', this meeting is described as that of the BPSCF which was held at Batajor through the good offices of the villagers of Batajor and Chandrahar in 1944.[178]

The subject of the speech made by Mandal from the chair of this meeting was a severe crticism of the *Manu-Smṛti*, particularly its provisions on the untouchables as to how they should behave.[179] Mandal's position is understandable because at that time he was much influenced by Ambedkar who was an unflinching critic of *dharmashastra* literature like *Manu*. According to the village tradition, however, Mandal is said to have made a speech on *Gita* to the effect:

> The only innate distinction between the castes (jatis) was that between the Aryas and the non-Aryas. Those who were envious and oppressive to others were non-Aryan Asuras (demons). There were no other criteria for applying the social distinctions to the contemporary world.[180]

Mandal therefore advised the Namasudra community to side with the Aryas.

The version from the 'biography' seems to be nearer to the truth than does the village oral tradition. In the latter, *Manu-Smṛti* was changed to *Gita*, which was also affirmatively mentioned. As is well known, Ambedkar regarded *Gita* as a book significantly exerting an evil influence on society. Among the Namasudra community in East Bengal, however, *Gita* was the main source of inspiration in their Vaisnava faith. Therefore it would not have been wise for Mandal to have spoken ill of it. The change in religious situation following the partition would also contribute much to this replacement of the sacred books. The villagers of the middle and lower castes, who are now free from the upper-caste domination, are losing their original faith on the village level and are accepting a higher Hindu faith to enable them to pit themselves against the constant Muslim pressures.[181]

According to the village oral tradition, Mandal went abroad after this meeting. The political situation of the Namasudras grew worse in his absence. In fact Mandal did not venture abroad at that time, but to his supporters in the village, going abroad was thought to be one of the achievements to be attained by their hero. In this regard, it would be interesting if the analysis of the formation of the 'Mandal legend' were to be made in comparison with the pattern of narration prominent in the folk tales or *mangal kabyas*.

The deterioration of the political situation of the Namasudras was nothing more than an intensification of the caste strife. The composition of the rivalry in Batajor took the form of the lower castes like the Namasudras and Dhopas being opposed to the Kayastha landlord families and the middle caste (the Nabashak) Baruis taking sides with the landlords. As is revealed from the description of the event, however, the opposition of such kind, on many occasions, depended on the individual 'who likes whom' relationship, rather than on the caste rivalry of the commonly understood character. We can mention, for example, Benu Mukherji (Brahman) and Hiren Datta (Kayastha) as the sympathizers of the Namasudra-Dhopa combination. The basic social opposition existed between the landlords and the tenants. Caste alliances, more or less, overlapped economic relations. The actual shape it would take seems to have depended upon more amorphous elements like the temper and thoughts of those concerned.

There took place two remarkable events during the time prior to the partition: (1) presentation of a drama and establishment of a cinema hall; and (2) a series of strifes between the upper and lower castes. The first set of events appears only in the village tradition. A villager said that it had taken place in the year 1347 B.S. (A.D. 1940–41). The second one definitely occurred in relation to the 1946 election. Let me discuss these in turn to demonstrate their relevance. Regarding the presentation of a drama and establishment of a cinema hall, some time during the autumn holidays, a young lady named Doli Datta returned from abroad to participate in the Durga Puja. She was a daughter of Ray Bahadur Surendranath Datta, the then head of the senior branch of the family, popularly called *Paschimer Bari* (west house).[182] Her real name was Phularenu Datta (becoming Guha after marriage). She was educated up to her M.A. in Calcutta, then went to France to obtain her D.Lit. at Sorbonne. After the partition she engaged herself in political activities as a Congress worker. She was once a member of Indira Gandhi's cabinet.

Being fond of dramas, she proposed to stage 'Ravanabadha' (The Killing of Ravana) after the Puja. An audition was held to assign the roles to the actors and actresses. It was decided that Doli herself would play the part of Mandodari and Manoranjan that of Ravana. Educated Baruis, considering themselves to be culturally advanced, felt themselves discontented with the decision but could not air it in the face of the highly educated daughter of their landlord. Three masters were called from Barisal to direct the group in its rehearsals. To deprive Manoranjan of the part of Ravana, dissenters demanded that only those who could afford to buy their costumes by themselves should be allowed to appear on the stage. Manoranjan at once proceeded to Dhaka and purchased a set of gorgeous costumes. His quick responses to the challenge put his opponents to silence. The play was staged after four days of reheasal and Manoranjan won plaudits for his excellent acting.[183]

Manoranjan Dhupi and his friends planned to purchase a house at Batajor Bandal (market) to hold cinema shows. The Namasudras agreed to bear the share of its capital. Earnest money to buy a cineprojector was paid to a dealer. Ignoring the original proponents, however, a rival group set up a 'cinema hall' at an *atchala* (a thatched house with eight roofs) in Dwijendranath Datta's *Paschimer Bari.* This situation served to disgrace Manoranjan and his chief associate Bipinbihari Sinha. A meeting was held at the *tapasil* office to consider how to handle this issue. At one point, Dwijendranath Datta deplored that the cinema hall could not be set up because of the *chotolok* (lower-caste men). A confrontation between both parties became naturally aggravated.

Around this time, a bull belonging to Dwijendranath found its way one day into the garden adjoining Manoranjan's house. People there attacked it with a spear. It fled back to the landlord's compound and died there. The landlord was inflamed with rage and declared that he would not let Manoranjan set foot on his land. Manoranjan, however, was not in a position to reach his own house from the main road without taking a road across the landlord's. Hearing his trouble, Bipinbihari Sinha called his caste folks together and constructed a road overnight on his own land to join the main road to Manoranjan's house.

The road still exists and villagers conveniently use it.[184]

With regard to the second incident, the series of events climaxed in January 1947 when the Provincial Assembly election was held, though it is not mentioned in the village legend as an event taking place at the time of the election. Before seeking to explain its reason, I shall briefly bring the two versions from the 'biography' and the village of the episode into view.

According to the biography, on the occsaion of the 1946 Provincial Assembly election, the caste Hindus energetically canvassed for Manoranjan Gupta under the leadership of Dwijendranath Datta in order to defeat Mandal. For the purpose of curtailing voting for Mandal, they penetrated into villages like Batajor, Harhar, Deopara, Bachar, Bankura, Paschim Chandrahar, Dakshin Chandrahar and Shinga where many Scheduled Caste people lived. There they engaged in committing barbarous atrocities against the supporters of Mandal under police assistance. The police went to houses specified by the caste Hindus, shattered household goods and utensils, arrested people and beat them up. The armed police contingent was sent from Barisal. The caste Hindu men bribed the police into employing violence upon the Scheduled Caste people, so that their men retired to other villages. Then the police turned their attack on the village women. Many of women were kicked with the police's high boots, bayonetted, and suffered injuries brought about by lathi charges. Pregnant women were not the exception either. Thereafter the police arrested 28 Scheduled Caste activists with Bipinbihari Sinha and Manoranjan Dhupi at the head of the list. All of them were prosecuted for false crimes like burglary or murder and sent to Barisal. Mandal rushed to the spot on the following day and helped them in a lawsuit both in terms of costs and proceedings. The local people well remembered this violent event still in the mid-1970s, and Batajor Day in its commemoration was still observed by the Scheduled Caste people.[185]

Now I shall see the village story of the same event. Kartik Sarkar who is the narrator of it was himself involved in this event. The event occurred in the year 1352 B.S. (A.D. 1945–46). The Baruis had set up *paner baraj* (betel garden) on 1.20 acres of *bita* land in Chandrahar village 15 years before under the agreement that they would pay Tk. 15 for it.

Unfortunately, *pan* plants decayed that year because of an unusual rise in the water level in the month of Sraban (July–August) and a flood in the month of Bhadra (August–September) completely damaged the *baraj*. According to the agreement, the Baruis were obliged to pay rent as long as the *baraj* remained on the ground. Some poor Males (a Dravidian-cultivating caste) served as their day labourers. Deprived of their means of earning, they entreated lower-caste villagers to help them. Thereupon, Bipinbihari Sinha and Manoranjan Dhupi, taking the *matbars* of four villages along with them, went to Dwijendranath Datta, Union Chairman, to discuss the matter.

In the month of Aswin (September–October), the Males planted the land with radish. One night in the month of Agrahayan (November–December), the Baruis set up a *baraj* on a quarter of the area. In protest, the Males again took the matter up with Bipin and Manoranjan, who took some of their men to the spot and crushed the *baraj*. On a night a few days later, the Baruis reconstructed it. Bipin and Manoranjan's group informed Dwijendranath Datta of the matter. The Union Chairman told them, however, that he had no control over the situation. Bipin's party decided to break up the construction again that night.Their decision was transmitted through a trimmer to the Baruis, who consulted among themselves to call the police to meet the threat. The news could not be kept secret either. Muhammad Aham Haoladar, *peyada* of the Dattas, confided this plan to Bipin's party.

The violent clash that occurred that night resulted in the murder of a policeman. Bipin's party with about a thousand men marched to the spot. The Baruis also came with a police force. Frightened to face the sight of lower-caste villagers who had already gathered there, the Baruis retreated with the police. But, from a vantage point some distance back, the police opened fire. To this the lower-caste party responded with a concerted cry of *ullah*, which frightened the Baruis away from the spot. At about three o'clock, three Baruis were caught by the lower-caste party but subsequently sent home unhurt. The victorious villagers also dispersed and went home.

As for the policeman who lost his life in the confusion, the Namasudra villagers believed that he was killed by one of the group of five influential Barui brothers who, of course, intended to implicate the Namasudras in the crime. Nevertheless, a thorough investigation was instituted to find the actual criminal. At eight o'clock the next morning, a police contingent under a commander arrived from Barisal in four separate cars, surrounded the Batajor Bandar, and arrested Bipinbihari Sinha and Kartik Sarkar who happened to be on the spot. The event stirred a panic in the market.

Muhammad Aham Haoladar sent a secret agent to inform the

leaders of lower castes of the news. On the other hand, the *lal-pagris* (red turbans) or policemen of Batajor and Gaurnadi came in and joined the contingent from Barisal.

The police, with the upper-caste youths joining hands with them, set about staging a *gherao* (besiegement) around Batajor and Chandrahar, plundering villagers and employing violence. The victims of these outrages included everybody irrespective of gender and age. Six or seven men were arrested. About three o'clock, the police started applying physical torture on those who had been arrested. In around two hours this progressed to such a point that some of them stood on the brink of death. Meanwhile, sympathizers like Sonamuddin Mincha, Siraj Mincha, Menajuddin Mincha, Biren Datta, Benu Mukherji and Mahendra Thakur went to the thana to inquire about the men and there they were shocked to observe the outrage. They went straight to Mafijuddin Saheb, a respected gentleman in the area and informed him of the details of the police oppression. Mafijuddin Saheb immediately went to see Dwijendranath Datta and told him that if an accused was killed, it was Datta who would get the blame. Next he went to the police camp to see the physical conditions of those who had been arrested, and found them lying unconscious. It was not until two o'clock in the morning that the men regained consciousness and came round through proper treatment. Again, Hiren Datta and Benu Mukherji, accompanied by several men, went to see Sayyad Mincha Saheb of Nalchila village and inform him of the situation. Sayyad Saheb sympathized with them and hid Kartik Sarkar to save him from trouble. Kartik threw himself at the Saheb's feet and begged of him to save his brother, Bipinbihari Sinha's life. Sayyad Saheb sent him to Barisal with a message to Jagatbandhu Pande, *mukhtar* of the local court, to wire the news to Jagendranath Mandal.

Sayyad Saheb made for Batajor for first-hand information on how matters stood there. He stayed at Mafijuddin's house and visited each and every house at night of those who had been tortured with food, clothes and medicine. The police outrages, however, continued even on the following day. As for Jagatbandhu Pande in Barisal, he sent a telegram every two hours to Mandal. Kartik Sarkar went to Bhurghata, a village bordering Barisal and Faridpur surrounded by a predominantly Namasudra area, and collected relief funds.

Six days later Jogendranath Mandal reached Barisal and proceeded straight to Batajor with Pande. He was moved to tears seeing Bipin and Manoranjan lying half-dead. Calling the police chief, he said, 'I demand you return to your own duties. I will take the accused to Barisal on my own. Stop the violence unless you want to invite trouble.' Hearing of Mandal's arrival, leaders and sympathizers of the lower caste rallied to Batajor. The appearance of Jogen Mandal so overwhelmed Bipin that he clung to his feet, burst into tears and ultimately lost his senses.

Jogen Mandal called for a doctor from Barisal to treat the malhandled. He himself went round locality with his supporters to soothe and assure the villagers who had suffered from police outrages and distributed medicines among them. He stayed that night at Bipin's and at nine o'clock the following day, 40 out of 56 arrested were transferred to Barisal by police van and placed in custody for trial. The accused who had been injured were sent to a hospital where they were treated by Jogen Mandal's doctor. Sayyad Saheb who stood all along beside Jogen Mandal, instructed a jailor he knew to treat the unconvicted prisoners with care. That evening Jogen Mandal returned to Calcutta by steamer. Later, Jogen Mandal sent a competent barrister of the Calcutta High Court to Batajor to conduct an on-the-spot investigation. The Namasudra community still remembers his brilliant defense of the accused at the Barisal Court. Finally, all the accused were found not guilty and acquitted and freed from prison. Thousands of people proceeded to Barisal to receive them. Their triumphant march to Barisal resonant with rousing cheers is a memorable event in the long history of their movement against the upper castes.[186]

Comparing the two versions mentioned earlier, I am certain that a series of similar events that took place during the autumn of 1945 and in January 1946 are dealt with accordingly. In the version of the 'biography', all the events are told related to Mandal's election campaign in 1945–46. On the other hand, in the village version, the aspects of Mandal's election are concealed and entirely spoken of as a local caste strife between the upper and lower castes. In this election Mandal was defeated in this constituency. However, the story of his defeat does not match the cheerful tune of victory which colours the village legend. As a result, it has been ignored in the course of time. Moreover, the villagers have added a story that Mandal exercised his power of Law Minister to change judges to ensure the manipulation of the suit. Thus, the image of a powerful Mandal crowned with glory has been shaped.

The features of the village legend might have something to do with the fact that at present the Namasudra peasants enjoy relatively free status in the society, though they are economically not free from poverty. On the other hand, however, they do not think they are completely safe in Bangladeshi society which has become more and more Islam oriented. This might be one of the causes for them wanting to create this image of a powerful Mandal. Yet, in return, it sometimes provokes their criticism of Mandal. In their view they had to remain on the eastern side of the border owing to their leader's choice. The present position of the Namasudra owner-cultivators entertaining a deep-rooted hope to settle on the other side of the border at the first opportunity[187] might be projected on their criticism of Mandal.

The violent clash between the upper and lower castes related here appears similar to the atrocities committed against the 'untouchables' and ensuing reactions, violent or suppressed, which often take place in today's rural India. This event may summarily be called their prototype. The atrocities against the 'untouchables' do not necessarily reveal their weakness, but rather often occur on the heels of their legitimate claims. The Namasudra villagers who are no longer shadowed by untouchability now may be said to have realized the possibility of emancipation that is ardently longed for by their brethren in India. Thus, Jogen Mandal is not a forgotten politician among them but is ever memorable as their leader who worked sincerely and tirelessly to secure their emancipation.

NOTES

1 S.P. Sen, ed., *Dictionary of National Biography*, 4 vols, Calcutta, 1972–74. Supplementary volumes have been published under the editorship of N.R. Ray since 1988. As I have seen only the first volume, I am not in a position to say whether Mandal is mentioned somewhere in any of the following volumes.

2 Anjali Basu, ed., *Sansad Bangali Caritabhidhan*, Kalikata, 1976, p. 435.

3 Government of India, *India 1992: A Reference Annual*, New Delhi, 1993, p. 17.

4 Bipin Chandra Pal, *Memories of My life and Times*, Calcutta, 1973, pp. 87–88. Generally it is admitted that 'the problem of untouchability and social discrimination or disability was relatively less severe in Bengal than in other parts of India'. Sekhar Bandyopadhyay, *Caste, Politics and the Raj*, Calcutta, 1990 [hereafter Sekhar Bandyopadhyay(1)], pp. 81–82.

5 A good work on Ambedkar is available in Japanese. Gen'ichi Yamazaki, *Indo Shakai to Shin-Bukkyo* (Indian Society and Neo-

Buddhism—Ambedkar's Personality and Thought), Tokyo, 1979.

6 *Bengal District Gazetteers, B Volume, Backergunge: Statistics 1900–1901 to 1910–1911*, Calcutta, 1914, pp. 5, 7.

7 Castes in Bengal are categorized into the following six groups: (1) Brahman, (2) Baidya and Kayastha, (3) Nabasakh (artisan castes), (4) Intermediary castes, (5) Ajalchal castes (members of which are not entitled to offer water to the Brahmans and Sat Sudras), and (6) Antyaja castes (the untouchables). See, Hitesranjan Sanyal, *Social Mobility in Bengal*, Calcutta, 1981, p. 41.

8 Sumit Sarkar, *Modern India 1885–1947*, Delhi, 1983 [hereafter Sumit Sarkar (1)] p. 58.

9 Abbé J.A. Dubois, *Hindu Manners, Customs and Ceremonies*, English tr. by H.K. Beauchamp, Oxford, 1968 (1st edn. in 1906), p. 49.

10 Gen'ichi Yamazaki, *Indo Shakai to Shin-Bukkyo*, p. 216.

11 H.H. Risley, *People of India*, Delhi, 1969 (1st edn. in 1915).

12 Sukumar Sen states that the Chandals, along with the Doms, have been speaking an Aryan language throughout history. As for the tribal origin of the Bagdi, see Masayuki Usuda, 'The transformation of the Malla dynasty of Bengal' (in Japanese), *Toyo Gakuho* 71, nos. 3, 4, 1990, p. 171–73.

13 H.H. Risley, *People of India*, p. 126.

14 J.C. Jack, *Bengal District Gazetteers*, *Bakarganj*, Calcutta, 1918, p. 35.

15 Nirmalkumar Bose, *Hindu Samajer Garan*, Kalikata, 1365 B.S., pp. 140–41. This description seems contradictory to the commonly accepted view that the untouchability of the Namasudras was less severe in Bengal. Probably their untouchability decreased in great measure during the twentieth century owing to either the results of the Namasudra movement and to the changes in public consciousness brought about by the social reform movement. As for the influence of the social reform movement in rural areas, Amales Tripathi argues in favour of Aswinikumar Datta's movement (Amales Tripathi et al., *Freedom Struggle*, New Delhi, 1972, p. 91).

16 The number of 10,000 people is not an exaggeration. A veteran Muslim *matbar*, who worked for me as an assistant during my survey at Batajor, told me while he was preparing dinner for 1, 500 guests on a *sraddha* ceremony, that he had once prepared dinner for 10,000 people.

17 Pradip Sinha, *Nineteenth Century Bengal: Aspects of Social History*, Calcutta, 1965, pp. 8–10.

18 W.S. Wells, Magistrate of Furreedpore to the Commissioner of the Dacca Division, dated 8 April 1873, *Judicial Proceedings*, 56–60, 17 May 1873. Referring to a letter of a District Superintendent of Police, Pradip Sinha gives a clear picture of the situation. Some Kayasthas taunted the Namasudras, saying, 'Eat with men who send their women to market and who are employed as "mehters" in jail for removing filth and everything unclean? What next?' (Pradip Sinha, *Nineteenth Century Bengal*, p. 8).

19 'Namasudra' means 'respected sudra'. In an article contributed to the January 1908 issue of the *Namasudra Suhrid*, Raycharan Biswas

asserted that 'The Namasudras are the Brahmans. But, out of either anger or envy, many people do not like us. We make our living by agriculture, the glorious Aryan way of living in the ancient as well as the present' (Nirmalkumar Basu, *Hindu Samajer Garan*, p. 141).

20 L.S.S. O'Malley, *Bengal District Gazetteers*, *Faridpur*, Calcutta, 1925, p. 47 [hereafter O'Malley (1)].

21 J.C. Jack, *Bengal District Gazetteers*, *Bakarganj*, p. 35.

22 Sekhar Bandyopadhyay (1), p. 100

23 W.L. Heeley, General of Jails, Lower Provinces to the Secretary to the Government of Bengal, Judicial Department, dated 22 May 1873, *Judicial Proceedings*, Nos. 84–87.

24 M.D. Bose, Superintendent of the Furreedpore Jail to W.S. Wells, Magistrate of Furreedpore, dated 19 April 1873, *Judicial Proceedings* Nos. 84–87, 7 June 1873.

25 W.S. Wells, Magistrate of Furreedpore to the Inspector-General of Jails, Lower Provinces, dated 7 June 1873, *Judicial Proceedings*, Nos. 84–87, 7 June 1873.

26 Same as note 23.

27 A. Mackenzie, Junior Secretary to the Government of Bengal to the Inspector-General of Jails, Lower Provinces, dated 7 June 1873, *Judicial Proceedings*, Nos. 84–87, June 1873.

28 Chie Nakane, *Kazoku no Kozo* (The Structure of Family: A Socio-Anthropological Analysis), Tokyo, 1970, p. 255.

29 Same as note 18, especially para. 23.

30 Nirmalkumar Basu stated that the Namasudras, who had had the custom of widow remarriage, set themselves to suppressing it when they asserted their status as Brahmans (Nirmalkumar Basu, *Hindu Samajer Garan*, p. 141). According to Risley's *The Tribes ans Castes of Bengal*, vol. I, p. 187, published in 1891, 'Widow-marriage, once universally practised, has within the last generation been prohibited'. H. Beveridge stated about the Namasudras in 1876 that 'They practise widow marriage, or at least often live in adulterous intercourse with widows' (H. Beveridge, *The District of Bakarganj: Its History and Statistics*, Barisal, 1970, rept. edn., p. 230).

31 Same as note 18, especially para. 30.

32 Sympathy of Wells, Magistrate of Faridpur, for the Namasudras is evident from the official files. It seems to have been noticed among the officials. H. Beveridge, once Magistrate of Bakharganj, cited Well's letter on the Namasudras which were included in the Census Report (H. Beveridge, *The District of Bakarganj*, pp. 242–44).

33 Sekhar Bandyopadhyay (1), p. 98.

34 H. Beveridge, *The District of Bakarganj*, p. 232.

35 Ramkanta Chakrabarty, *Vaiṣṇavism in Bengal 1486–1900*, Calcutta, 1985, p. 377.

36 Sekhar Bandyopadhyay (1), p. 99.

37 Ramkanta Chakrabarty, *Vaiṣṇavism in Bengal*, p. 398.

38 J.C. Jack, *Bengal District Gazetteer*, *Bakarganj*, pp. 31–2, H. Beveridge, *The District of Bakarganj*, p. 232.

39 O'Malley (1), p. 36.
40 H.Beveridge, *The Distri ·f Bakarganj*, p. 233.
41 J.C. Jack, *Bengal Distri. ;azetteers*, *Bakarganj*, p. 32.
42 Ibid., p. 31.
43 Nirmalkumar Basu, *Hindu Samajer Garan*, p. 141.
44 L.S.S. O'Malley, *Bengal Disrict Gazetteeers*, *Khulna*, Calcutta, 1908, pp. 66–67.
45 Sekhar Bandyopadhyay (1), p. 208–9.
46 Nirmalkumar Basu, *Hindu Samajer Garan*, p. 141.
47 This is the point of issue which Sumit Sarkar has maintained. (Sumit Sarkar, *The Swadeshi Movement in Bengal 1903–1908*, New Delhi, 1973 [hereafter Sumit Sarkar (2)], pp. 490–92.
48 Nirmalkumar Basu, *Hindu Samajer Garan*, p. 142.
49 Sufia Ahmad, *Muslim Community in Bengal 1884–1912*, Dacca, 1974, p. 257.
50 O'Malley (1), pp. 113–14.
51 Sekhar Bandyopadhyay (1), p. 102.
52 Sekhar Bandyopadhyay, 'Development, differentiation and caste: the Namasudra movement in Bengal', in Sekhar Bandyopadhyay, Abhijit Dasgupta and Willem van Scendel, eds., *Bengal: Community, Development and State*, New Delhi, 1994, p. 97.
53 Sekhar Bandyopadhyay (1), pp. 154–55.
54 Sumit Sarkar (2), p. 330.
55 Rabindranath Thakur, 'Sadupay', *Purabasi*, Sraban 1315 B.S., p. 221.
56 Sumit Sarkar (1), p. 109.
57 Binod Lal Ghose, 'What can be done for the Namasudras', *Modern Review*, June 1909, pp. 553–55.
58 B.B. Majumdar, *Congress and Congressmen in the pre-Gandhian Era, 1885–1917*, Calcutta, 1967, p. 305. Masayuki Usuda, *Aswiṇikumar Datta's Role in the Political, Social and Cultural Life of Bengal* (Unpublished Ph.D. thesis, Calcutta University), 1977, p. 352.
59 *Nayak*, 22 September in *Report on Native Papers in Bengal* (hereafter RNPB) for the week ending 1 October 1910.
60 Masayuki Usuda, 'Local leaders during the period of the formation of the nationalist movement in East Bengal' (in Japanese), *Ajia Kenkyu* 26, no. 3, 1979, p. 12.
61 *Hitavadi*, September 22, 1911, RNPB for the week ending 23 September 1911.
62 Sekhar Bandyaopadhyay (1), pp. 156–57.
63 Ibid., p. 157.
64 Nirmalkumar Basu, *Hindu Samajer Garan*, p. 142.
65 Sekhar Bandyopadhyay (1), p. 56.
66 Ibid.
67 Ibid., p. 57.
68 Ibid., pp. 110–11.
69 Nirmalkumar Basu, *Hindu Samajer Garan*, p. 130.
70 Ibid., pp, 126–32.
71 Sekhar Bandyopadhyay (1), p. 42.

72 Ibid., p. 82.
73 Ibid., pp. 60–66.
74 Ibid., p. 152.
75 Tanika Sarkar, *Bengal 1928–1934: The Politics of Protest*, Delhi, 1987, p. 147.
76 Sekhar Bandyopadhyay (1), pp. 164–67.
77 Ibid., p. 64.
78 Ibid., p. 61.
79 Ibid., p. 62.
80 Ibid., pp. 168–69.
81 Ibid., p. 167.
82 M.M. Islam, *Bengal Agriculture 1920–1946: A Quantitative Study*, Cambridge, 1978, p. 1.
83 Tanika Sarkar, *Bengal 1928–1934*, pp. 40–41. She does not ascribe the Muslim-Namasudra combinations solely to their pauperization. They were the substantial peasants who had raised their aspirations. See, Partha Chatterjee, *Bengal 1920–1947: The Land Question*, Calcutta, 1984, p. 183.
84 Sekhar Bandyopadhyay (1), pp. 177–78.
85 Jagadiscandra Mandal, *Mahapran Jogendranath Mandal*, vol. I, Kalikata, 1382 B.S. (1975) (hereafter MJ-I), p. 1. This biography has so far been published in two volumes, the second of which ends in 1950 when Mandal broke away from Pakistan. It is a fairly voluminous biography (271 pages for the first volume and 342 pages for the second volume). The author is Mandal's only son. Though he has made considerable effort to collect materials, it is rather more a dedicated son's homage to his late father than an objective estimation of a political worker. I am thus impressed with his dedication but urge caution when it is used as a historical document.
86 Ibid., pp. 2–8
87 Ibid., p. 10.
88 Masayuki Usuda, 'The Formation of public opinion in the Bakharganj District, East Bengal' (in Japanese) in *Studies on Agrarian Societies in South Asia* 1, Institute of the Study of Languages and Cultures of Asia and Africa, Tokyo, 1978, pp. 67–74.
89 MJ-I, p. 15.
90 Ibid., pp. 16–17.
91 Ibid., pp. 13, 17.
92 Ibid., pp. 18–19.
93 Ibid., p. 21.
94 Ibid., p. 22.
95 Same as note 88, p. 78.
96 MJ-I, pp. 24–27.
97 Ibid., pp. 22, 33.
98 Shila Sen, *Muslim Politics in Bengal 1937–1947*, New Delhi, 1976, pp. 87–88.
99 Buddhadeva Bhattacharrya, *Satyagrahas in Bengal 1921–39*, Calcutta, 1977, pp. 128–58.

100 MJ-I, p. 33.
101 Ibid., p. 31.
102 Ibid., pp. 30–31.
103 Ibid., p. 30.
104 Ibid., pp. 40–41.
105 Ibid., p. 41.
106 Sekhar Bandyopadhyay (1), p. 81., Sekhar Bandyopadhyay, 'From alieation to integration: Changes in the politics of caste in Bengal, 1937–47', *The Indian Economic and Social History Review* (*IESHR*), 31–3, 1994, [hereafter Sekhar Bandyopadhyay (2)] p. 349.
107 MJ-I, p. 36.
108 Ibid., pp. 35–37.
109 Ibid., pp. 37–38, 44–47.
110 Ibid., pp. 38–39.
111 Ibid., pp. 45–46.
112 Ibid., p. 63.
113 Ibid., pp. 60–61.
114 Ibid., pp. 53–58.
115 Ibid., pp. 61–63.
116 According to MJ-I, the time when Subhas Bose visited Barisal to expand the organization of the Forward Bloc was January 1939. However, this is an obvious mistake, since the Forward Bloc was not formed until May of the same year. It was in the early 1940s that Bose undertook a campaign at various parts of East Bengal.
117 MJ-I, pp. 47–49.
118 As Tagore wrote to Gandhi on 29 March 1939, 'At the last Congress session some rude hands have deeply hurt Bengal with an ungracious persistence' [Amales Tripathi, *Svadhinata Samgrame Bharatiya Jatiya Kamgres*, 1885–1947, Kalikata, 1397 B.S. (1990), p. 268]. Bose became all the more popular 'as the regional hero who had been given a raw deal' [Sumit Sarkar (1), p. 374]. Mandal responded to the expulsion of Bose in the typically Bengali manner. Here, however, we would be allowed to see Mandal's devotion to Bose who tried to involve everyone irrespective of community, caste or belief in the struggle for independence.
119 MJ-I, p. 50.
120 Shila Sen, *Muslim Politics in Bengal*, p. 132, Sugata Bose, *Agrarian Bengal: Economy, Social Structure and Politics, 1919–1947*, Cambridge, 1986, p. 218.
121 MJ-I, pp. 66–67.
122 Ibid., p. 77.
123 Kalipada Biswas, *Jukta Banglar Shesh Adhyay*, Kalikata, 1966, p. 357. Upendranath Barman, who entered the Huq Cabinet belonged to the Rajbansi community (MJ-I, p. 66). It is also noteworthy that Mandal commented as follows in a speech delivered at the session of BLA on 24 March 1943. 'Today it seems that Huq Saheb stands to weaken the Namasudra community in particular' (ibid., p. 70). The Huq Ministry not only 'failed to win the trust of a large majority of Muslims' (Sugata

Bose, *Agrarian Bengal*, p. 218) but also that of the Scheduled Castes, especially the Namasudras.

124 MJ-I, pp. 81–82.

125 Ibid., p. 83. Of 28 Scheduled Caste members, 20 were among government supporters and eight stood in the camp of the opposition under the Congress leadership (Shila Sen, *Muslim Politics in Bengal*, p. 173).

126 MJ-I, pp. 76–77.

127 MJ does not mention changes taken place during these times. To discuss Mandal's life, however, the fact that Mandal was a supporter of Subhas Bose cannot be overlooked. Without taking this into account, his ensuing checkered political life would come to nothing but a confusing state of affairs.

128 MJ-I, p. 98.

129 Ibid., p. 94. The circulation of the *Jagaran* stood at 1,000 at the time of its foundation, 2,000 in the second year, 3,000 in the third year and reached 4,000 within a short time. Many in the editing board became politicians or bureaucrats in their later life (ibid., pp. 94–96).

130 Ibid., pp. 99–100.

131 Ibid., p. 100.

132 According to the 1931 Census (*Bengal District Gazetteers*, *B Volume*, *Faridpur District: Statistics, 1921–22 to 1930–31*, Calcutta, 1933, pp. 5–6).

133 MJ–I, pp. 101–2.

134 Ibid., pp. 83–93.

135 Ibid., p. 85.

136 Ibid., pp. 88–89. The lack in physical attractiveness of the Scheduled Caste people (regarding the expression of this assumption, see, for example, an old Brahman's remark on Indira's beauty as that hardly seen among lower-caste households in Bankimchandra's novel *Indira; Bankim Racanabali*, vol. I, Sahitya Samsad, Kalikata, 1391 B.S., p. 295) seems to be working on the psychology of the middle-class Indians as a visible sign of the lack in their ability. Once an air company officer of my acquaintance told me about the abuses of the reservation system. He said, 'Passengers would not enjoy their trip even if they receive services from any air hostess as ugly as "ghost".' This anti-reservation feeling is so strong among the greater part of the middle class. Their seemingly physical unattractiveness is used as a convenient vent to their discontent.

137 Ibid., p. 89.

138 Ibid., pp. 94–95, 153–57.

139 The alienation of the Scheduled Caste elite became more obvious after Independence. 'Barring a few exceptions, in most of the cases, the majority of the elite are not in any way concerned with the problems of their community. Those who have climbed up, in most cases, do not take interest in the measures for uplifting their bretheren lying at the lowest rung of the society' (Sachchidananda, *The Harijan Elite*, Faridabad, 1977, pp. 132–33).

140 MJ-I, pp. 103–4.
141 Ibid., pp. 106–10. Reproduced on pages 113 to 114 of MJ is Ambedkar's letter addressed to Mandal dated 23 April 1945. Ambedkar attributes his absence from the Gopalganj session of BPSCF to the delay of Wavell's return to India.
142 Ibid., pp. 104–11.
143 Ibid., p. 114–15.
144 Ibid., pp. 121–31.
145 Ibid., pp, 122, 132.
146 S.P. Sen, ed., *Dictionary of National Biography*, vol. II, Calcutta, 1973, pp. 114–15. While I was staying in India in the mid-1970s, I had an opportunity to interview Manoranjan Gupta in his last days. The old, stout and reticent terrorist looked like a toad covered with aged moss whose interior was scarcely discernible. The intensity of his personality is unforgettable.
147 MJ-I, p. 132–33.
148 Ibid., pp. 151–52. Here, the whole telegraph excluding the date is reproduced.
149 In the 1922 BLC election, Nirodbihari Mallik, an inhabitant of Calcutta, was returned in this constituency.
150 Ibid., p. 146.
151 Ibid., p. 152.
152 Ibid., p. 132.
153 Shila Sen, *Muslim Politics in Bengal*, p. 203.
154 MJ-I, p. 153.
155 Ibid., p. 167.
156 Mullick himself was absent from the joint meeting held on 8 June. Yet amalgamation of the 'Association' to the 'Federation' was decided at this meeting.
157 Ibid., pp. 172–74. Those who actually voted for Ambedkar were the following six MLAs: (1) Jogen Mandal (Barisal), (2) Dwarikanath Baruri (Faridpur), (3) Gayanath Biswas (Tangail), (4) Nagendranarayan Ray (Rangpur), (5) Kshetranath Sinha (Rangpur), and (6) Mukunda Behari Mullick (Khulna).
158 Ibid., pp. 176–81.
159 Ibid., pp. 184–85.
160 Amales Tripathi, *Svadhinata Samgrame Bharatiya Jatiya Kamgres*, p. 448, Sumit Sarkar (2), p. 435, Kalipada Biswas, *Jukta Banglara Shesh Adhyay*, p. 194.
161 MJ-I, pp. 189–91, 216.
162 Ambedkar to D.J. Jadhav, 29 October 1946, cited in MJ-I, pp. 207–8.
163 *Statesman*, 18 October 1946, cited in MJ-I, p. 197.
164 MJ-I, pp. 224–29.
165 Field Marshall Viscount Wavell to H.M. King George VI, Wavell Papers, Private Correspondence: H.M. The King, pp. 139–48, New Delhi, 24 February 1947, in *Transfer of Power*, IX, London, 1980, p. 804.
166 As mentioned, for example, in Sir J. Colville to Lord Petrick-Lawrence,

New Delhi, 18 December 1946, in *Transfer of Power*, IX, p. 380.

167 Jagadiscandra Mandal, *Mahapran Jogendranath Mandal*, Vol. II, Kalikata, 1979 (hereafter MJ-II), p. 5. Just as Wavell did, however, Mountbatten lost interest in Mandal as a Cabinet Member. Thus Mandal for his part was deprived of opportunities to lay his opinion against partition.

168 'Partition will not solve problem, Majority of Non-Muslims against proposal, Mr. J.N. Mandal', *Statesman*, 23 April 1947 in MJ-II, pp. 11–16.

169 'Partition of Bengal move to crush Scheduled Castes', *Free Press* (Madras), 18 May, 1947 in MJ-II, pp. 27–28, 'Partition opposed by Scheduled Castes', *Statesman*, 17 May 1947 in MJ-II pp. 45–47.

170 MJ-II, pp. 22–25, 49–55.

171 Sekhar Bandyopadhyay (2), p. 383, Bidyut Chakrabarty, 'The 1947 united Bengal movement: A thesis without a synthesis', *IESHR*, 30–4, October-December 1993, p. 475. Chakrabarty does not mention Mandal's movement at all in his neatly-written article.

172 MJ-II, p. 87.

173 Ibid., p. 94.

174 Masayuki Usuda, 'Historical evolution of a Talukdari village in southern Bangladesh (1)' [hereafter Usuda (1)], *The Bulletin of the Faculty of Letters*, *Tokai University*, no. 51, 1989, p. 19.

175 Masayuki Usuda, 'Historical evolution of a Talukdari village in southern Bangladesh (3)' [hereafter Usuda (3)], *The Bulletin of the Faculty of Letters*, *Tokai University*, no. 55, 1991, p. 2. The original story given as a village version of the event was written in Bengali by Sri Kartik Sarkar, an inhabitant of Batajor, at my request. As is given in the text, he is one of those who were involved in this event.

176 MJ-I, p. 31.

177 Usuda (3), p. 2.

178 MJ-I. p. 103.

179 Ibid.

180 Usuda (3), p. 3.

181 Usuda (1), p. 21.

182 Aswinikumar Datta belonged to the junior branch called *nuton bari* (new house).

183 Usuda (3), p. 3.

184 Ibid., pp. 3–4.

185 MJ–I, p. 149–50.

186 Usuda (3), pp. 4–6.

187 Ibid., p. 9.

12

Untouchable or Scheduled Castes? A Gram Panchayat Election in West Bengal in 1993

MASAHIKO TOGAWA

INTRODUCTION

Untouchability has to date been considered to constitute a depressed status ranked at the very bottom of the India's caste system. The term 'untouchable' composing a dichotomy with 'Brahman' has been frequently adopted to explain the caste system in ethnographical studies on Hindu society.[1] However, the Constitution of India clearly proclaimed the abolition of untouchability after India's independence, and prescribes the compensatory discrimination to be awarded to the Scheduled Castes (SC) as well as to the Scheduled Tribes (ST).[2] In this respect, Harold Issacs (1965) once used the phrase 'ex-untouchables' for these people because untouchables no longer officially existed under the new Constitution. This, of course, does not imply in any way the immediate disappearance of their factors of discrimination, which have remained deeply rooted in the social structure and have hindered them from advancing in their social status, but neither does it seem to signify merely a nominal change. The reservation system prescribed by the Constitution covers the spheres of public employment, higher education, and election in the Parliament and the state assemblies. The various governmental programmes for rural development are also designed in to advance their social status. The largest portion of the rural poor still comprise the Scheduled Castes, and they mostly correspond to the target groups to which poverty alleviation programmes implemented by the local governments are aimed.

In this essay, I shall discuss the status of one Scheduled Caste group in a village society through the examination of their social, economic, and political activities, in which the administrative measures were given considerable weight. The people of the village have come to consider their social conditions, especially of which the reservation system brought them, not only as a status guaranteeing their welfare, but also as a strategic opportunity for them to participate in public affairs. Many social scientists have discussed the efficacy of the reservation in the state administration, especially after the dispute arose in 1990 on its further application to the Other Backward Classes (OBC).[3] To date, however, only few attempts have been made to assess these various measures within a village society in its aggregated form.

West Bengal exhibits an exceptional character in terms of Indian contemporary politics.[4] It has been relatively long ruled since 1977 by the Left Front Government (LFG). Any evaluations of the policy of rural development in West Bengal in most cases must therefore depend on the scholar's attitude toward the achievements made by the LFG since then.

Regarding the problem of untouchability, Ross Mallick (1992; 1993:80–84) criticizes severely the commonly held view on the relative weakness of caste consciousness in rural Bengal, and argues that untouchability continues to have a tenacious existence, because of the lack of policies formulated to contend with this lingering issue. On the other hand, G.K. Lieten (1992:237–50) presents plentiful data from a surveyed village in the Birbhum District, and discusses the progress of the social status of the Scheduled Castes there. He considered the villagers to be in a state of 'transitional ambivalence', though he endeavours to describe the village as a whole. In the course of my work, I applied here an anthropological method and concentrated on the social process operating within the relevant Scheduled Caste community so as to describe objectively their orientations toward political mobilization from their perspective. This brings to light the social circumstances surrounding the Scheduled Castes in rural society of today as well as their pressing problems.

In this essay, I will first examine the process involved in the formation of the rivalry dividing two Scheduled Caste localities during the gram panchayat election in 1993. Second, I will look at the differences in their social backgrounds and in their evaluations of the achievements of the panchayat, which have appeared to work to evolve their different attitudes toward the panchayat. I will then review the distribution patterns of the panchayat programmes, in particular the Integrated Rural Development Programme (IRDP) loans. Finally, I will discuss the influence of the reservation on their social life, which now leads the people consider the category of SC and ST as a significant social status as it is being permeated by the local administration in rural society. The sample community is located in the Surul Mauza, Ruppur Gram Panchayat Area, Bolpur Block, Birbhum District. This area is well known for its neighbouring Visva-Bharati University in West Bengal. The panchayat office was once reported by Westergaard (1986:45) with regard to its passive participation of the Scheduled Caste members in the panchayat office in 1978. The analysis on the fourth election in the panchayat will illustrate the extent of their change in the attitude toward the panchayat.

PROFILE OF THE VILLAGE

Surul Mauza (JL. No. 108) occupies 2,012 acres in area and the 1991 census gives its population as 8,190 people. Scheduled Castes in the Mauza number 2,213, and Scheduled Tribes 1,458, which constitute 27.0 per cent and 17.8 per cent respectively, both summed at 3,671 or 44.8 per cent. The total population of the panchayat area is 23,700 inhabitants, which includes the SC (5,458; 23 per cent) and ST (5,038; 21.3 per cent) populations.

The residential area of the village is divided into three constituencies (1, 2, and 3) for the gram panchayat election, and each constituency has two seats posted for its panchayat members. The gram panchayat has 25 seats in all, and of these, eight seats are allotted to the Surul Mauza and six to the village proper. The data for the case study presented in this essay were collected from a Bagdi caste community being mostly inhabitants of constituency 1. They are scattered in the four localities ('para' in Bengali) from the south end of the village to the northeast fringe, which I shall call A para, B para, C para, and D para in turn for the sake of clarification. In particular, the localities of A para and D para lie distant from each other. A para has easy access to the outside market and the university in contrast to D para, which fringes the surrounding cultivated fields. The village is composed entirely of about 30 caste groups from Brahman to Scheduled Castes, Scheduled Tribes, and Muslim. Constituency 1 includes most of the Bagdi people in the village as well as the residences of the Sadgop families. The Bagdi caste is one of the largest population groups of SC in West Bengal, and is concentrated in the historical region of Rarh, in particular, Bardhaman District. The Bagdi were previously considered to be untouchable commonly in rural Bengal (e.g. Risley 1898). On the other hand, the Sadgop used to be in an influential position in the area (e.g. Acarya 1982). The Brahman castes, and the other caste groups are scattered over constituency 1, but they are relatively small in number.

Table 1 details the composition of the population of adults (18 years of age or over) classified by caste group according to the voter's list prepared in 1993. As is evident from the table, the subtotal of the Bagdi caste occupies 42.2 per cent of the total in this constituency, and constitutes the principal majority among the other SC households. On the other hand, the Sadgop caste holds the second-ranked position, though they still maintain their dominance in the village with respect to such social status as landholding, education, and employment. Specifically, this constituency simultaneously represents the dominant force of the village and the largest groups of SC. Notably, this information enables us to comprehend the economic and political relationship operating between the village's dominant force and the community of poor tenants and agricultural labourers, and it was also explicitly reflected in the panchayat election. In this connection, it would behoove us to examine the voting tendency in this constituency.

GRAM PANCHAYAT ELECTION

The Reserved Seats

Before the enforcement of the regulation for the reserved seats by the state government, the vacancy seats for SC, ST, and women were filled by nomination in the name of the District Magistrate (DM) so as to secure at least two seats each for members of a gram panchayat. This new regulation in 1993 prescribes the introduction of reserved seats for SC, ST, and women as members of gram panchayat, as in the reserved seats posted for SC and ST in the Parliament and Legislative Assembly.[5] The seats for SC and ST are allotted in proportion to the population, and not less than one third of the seats for women are secured within the reserved seats for SC and ST, as well as amounting to one third to the total seats. A seat was allotted by 500 voters in a gram panchayat in 1993, though this constituency is fixed at 1,000 voters for every two seats. Thus, two seats for SC, two general seats, one seat for women, and one seat for women as well as for SC were allotted in the village.

Although the Indian National Congress (I) (INC) obtained one seat in the second election held in 1983 in the village, CPI(M), the

Table 1 Population composition of constituency 1

Caste	*Subdivision*	*HH*	*AP*	*Total HH*	*Total AP*
Bagdi	D para	69	264	147	526 (42.2%)
	A para	34	120		
	B para	26	87		
	C para	18	55		
Sadgop		-	-	77	322 (25.9%)
Brahman	Kulin brahman	33	136	51	193 (15.5%)
	Barna brahman	13	39		
	Other brahman	5	18		
Others (middle-ranked castes)		-	-	53	166 (13.3%)
Others (Scheduled Castes)	Suri	6	32	10	38 (3.1%)
	Bauri	1	2		
	Mete	1	2		
	Dom	1	1		
	Muci	1	1		
Total		-	-	338	1245 (100.0%)

Note: HH: Number of households
AP: Number of adults(18 years old and over)
Source: Extracted from Bidhansabha Nirbacan Kshetrer Nirbacik Talika, 1993 and the research data gathered by the author.

Communist Party of India (Marxist), won all six seats in the third election held in 1988. In 1993 the Bharatiya Janata Party (BJP) newly stood for the panchayat of the area. Table 2 presents the election results of the constituencies in 1993 from the election record preserved at the Block Development Office (BDO). It lists the names of the caste or religion of each candidate, the party affiliations, and those polled. In constituency 1, the Brahman candidate officially adopted by the CPI(M) was elected to his fourth term for the general seat. A Bagdi caste candidate adopted by the CPI(M) won the reserved seat for the SC for his first time. The former member elected to this seat obtained only 17 votes as an independent candidate this time. He was elected the past two elections as a CPI(M) member, but he lost his candidate seat this time. In his place, the leader of the youth club in D para won the seat with the approval of CPI(M). As this table denotes, the candidates of CPI(M) won over the BJP by a narrow margin of only 10 votes in the general seat, and 32 in the seat for SC. Similar performances of BJP were observed in the many gram panchayat elections held throughout West Bengal at this time. Table 3 summarizes the transitions in the number of the gram panchayat seats of West Bengal classified by the party affiliations over the past four elections.

Table 2 Results of the 1993 panchayat election

Constituency 1

General Seat		
Caste/Sect	*Party affil.*	*Votes*
1 Brahman	CPI(M)	427
2 Brahman	BJP	417
3 Brahman	INC	60
4 Sadgop	Independent	19
5 Napit	Independent	2
6 Kul	Independent	2
Reserved Seat for SC		
1 Badgi	CPI(M)	442
2 Badgi	BJP	410
3 Suri	INC	70
4 Badgi	Independent	17

Constituency 2

General Seat		
Caste/Sect	*Party affil.*	*Votes(721)*
1 Sadgop	CPI(M)	310
2 Brahman	BJP	289
3 Mayura	INC	84
4 Brahman	Independent	38
Reserved Seat for SC as well as Women		
1 Bauri	CPI(M)	305
2 Suri	BJP	286
3 Dom	INC	91
4 Suri	Independent	19

Constituency 3

Caste/Sect	Party affil.	Votes
Reserved Seat for Women		
1 Muslim	CPI(M)	394
2 Santal	BJP	318
3 Muslim	INC	145
4 Dom	Independent	110
Reserved Seat for SC		
1 Bauri	CPI(M)	414
2 Muci	BJP	320
3 Muci	INC	128
4 Mahal	Independent	102

Source: Extracted from the record in the panchayat section, Bolpur-Sriniketan Block Development Office.

Table 3 Number of seats in gram panchayat election in West Bengal

Year	*Total*	*CPI(M)*	*RSP*	*FB*	*CPI*	*INC*	*BJP*	*Others*
1978	46401	28105	1674	1539	825	4536	-	9722
		60.6%	3.6%	3.3%	1.8%	9.8%	-	21%
1983	45675	24410	1241	1084	716	14733	34	3457
		53.4%	2.7%	2.4%	1.6%	32.3%	0.1%	7.6%
1988	52473	33834	1581	1398	907	12239	32	2482
		64.5%	3.0%	2.7%	1.7%	23.3%	0.1%	4.7%
1993	60965	35342	1526	1238	799	16292	2367	3401
		58%	2.5%	2%	1.3%	26.7%	3.9%	5.6%

Note: RSP: Revolutionary Socialist Party
FB: Forward Bloc

Source: *Panchayati Raj; Bishes Nirbacan Sankha 1, May-June, 1993*, Department of Panchayat, Govt. of West Bengal, pp. 4–16.

Since the first election held in 1978 for the gram panchayat, where the two candidates of the CPI(M), belonging to the Brahman and Bagdi caste, were allotted to the two seats of this constituency, the CPI(M)

have never lost both seats. With regard to the allotment of candidates, the local branch of the party seems to have a reasonable selection in view of the caste composition of the voters in the constituency. According to the voter's list prepared in 1993, the distribution of the communities of the Bagdi (42.2 per cent), Sadgop (25.9 per cent), and Brahman (15.5 per cent) show roughly a three-two-one ratio as evidenced in Table 1. Although the most numerous population is that of the community of the Bagdi caste, they do not comprise any more than half. The second-ranked population is that of the Sadgop caste, who mostly draw their members from the households of landowners, and generally form a political counterpoise to the inhabiting tenant farmers and agricultural labourers. They belong to the households called 'bhadra-lok' in Bengali, which means upper- and upper-middle-ranked farmers in rural areas in comparison with the lower-ranked tenants and agricultural labourers called 'choto-lok'. The households of the Brahman are not coherent politically like these two groups, especially in the divergence between what is called the Brahmans belonging to the 'kaulinna-pratha' (highest-ranked Brahman) and 'barna-brahman' (lower-ranked Brahman) in Bengali.

Of the election campaign in 1993, the main difference from the last three is that new candidates of the BJP appeared in the village politics. This change was due to the following two reasons.[6] First, many of the households of the Sadgop began to support the BJP since the 1991 election for the Legislative Assembly. At the time of the panchayat election in 1988, they voted mostly INC. The basic point of contention, which has figured in village politics, is a counterbalance between the poor peasants as well as some intellectuals, and the upper- and middle-ranked farmers. The latter are cognizant of the state of things, knowing that under the present policies of the panchayat, which have for the most part been formulated for the benefit of the poor peasants, they are not able to receive any more benefits from them. They thus maintain their political consistency as a counterpoise to CPI(M) in spite of changing their stance toward the INC. This is therefore an important factor in explaining the narrow margin of 10 votes that, although the Bagdi community remained consistent in being the largest supporter of CPI(M), most of the households in A para split with the other Bagdi caste for the first time, and lent their support to their own candidate standing for the BJP. It is this second point that I shall discuss in greater detail in the section that follows.

The Election Campaign in A Para

The first visit of a BJP member to A para is said to have been at the time of the election campaign for the Assembly in 1991, even though the BJP was not active in organizing the residents. Apart from any influence directed by party members from outside, it was during Durga Puja in 1990 that the opposition of A para to D para was distinctly revealed.

It is customary for the youth of the Bagdi community to carry the image of the goddess Durga offered by the landlords on their shoulders during the procession of the goddess on the final day of Durga Puja. Notably, however, this procession has recently became apt to be ever more uproarious with the setting off of firecrackers. When the procession of the youth of D para passed by the locality of A para, a conflict occurred between them due to the firecracker bursting, resulting in several of the procession bearers being injured. After the incident, the police ordered them to report any kind of procession beforehand in which they intended to engage. The occasion of their next dispute arose during a marriage ceremony a few months before the election. As it is not unusual for a relationship through marriage among the Bagdi people in the village such as between the A and D paras, hence each locality has its own relatives by marriage (*kutum*), and they often visit mutually on several ritual occasions. Since they harboured ill feelings between them after Durga Puja, however, another incident occurred where the members of D para excluded the youth of A para from the marriage ceremony site, even though this ceremony was for their own relatives.

In such a circumstance, the BJP members and their candidate launched their hard-hitting campaign in A para. They held meetings almost daily at various places, such as at the market place for a mass meeting and at the locality for small gatherings, and thereby the residents of A para expressed the support for their candidate with one accord and strengthened their solidarity all the more. The other parties such as CPI(M) and INC had held their meetings in the same manner, but these were limited only to a few times within the locality. It was obvious that the candidate of A para had a greater advantage in the locality than did any other candidates from outside. At the time of the gatherings and the door-to-door soliciting by the candidate, the people discussed their dissatisfaction with the gram panchayat, such as the insufficient facilities of hand tube wells, sewage drains, the anganawadi centre (to be mentioned later), and the meeting place in their locality.

In particular, they complained about the IRDP loans, which had been given considerable weight by the administration through the gram panchayat, as noted below:

> The distribution of the loans of IRDP by the panchayat has been less to the households of A para than to D para. This will become clearer when comparing both localities by statistical percentages. The inclination is apparent not only in the numbers of loans received but also in the number of people who were not sanctioned despite their applications for various kinds of livestock and shops in A para.

This kind of opinion was persuasive to the many people residing in the locality, all the more so as these facilities are part of their daily life. At the same time, however, it can be readily pointed out that this opinion does not take into consideration the limits of the budgetary and authorized rights of the panchayat. Not all claims can possibly be solved by the panchayat alone. For example, the foundation of the anganawadi centre is under the jurisdiction of the Department of Social Welfare. They expressed their long-held dissatisfactions with D para, however, which seemed for them to have been given more facilities by the panchayat than they were, in the form of criticisms of the present panchayat administration during the election campaign. The candidate of A para pledged to the canvassed voters that he would resolve these issues if they would elect him to the panchayat, and consequently the people of A para did indeed give him their solid support.

The people of A para thought that the panchayat programmes such as the IRDP were only partially distributed in D para among the Bagdi community. But they also belonged to the Scheduled Castes with many of them living below the poverty line making them eligible to benefits from the panchayat programmes. Thus, if a member of the panchayat were to be elected from their own locality, he could hence bring them greater benefits from the panchayat programmes. In this regard, it did not matter to the voters for which party he stood. Most important for them was to have a panchayat member seated from their own locality to represent their interests.

The second fact we should consider is the emotional discord existing between the localities which sparked the conflicts ensuing during certain ritual occasions such as the Durga Puja and marriage ceremonies. And during the time of the election campaign, they aired their discontent with the panchayat administration as if it were the result of the unequal treatment given to D para, which then could readily evolve into criticism of the panchayat. The complaints against the panchayat in recent years such as the decrease in the number of IRDP loans sanctioned and the increased cases rejected by regional banks seem to have become widespread over the area. Generally speaking, however, there has been a tendency to turn their ill-feelings not toward the limitations in the system itself, but toward the relative disparity between the localities. The competition for the limited resources of the panchayat hence gave rise to discontent all the more, thereby leading to the separation of A para from the unity of CPI(M) and resulting in its win by only a narrow margin. This then leads us to the next topic, namely, the difference in the socio-economic backgrounds of each locality, which ultimately gave rise to the varied attitudes expressed toward the panchayat.

ECONOMIC BACKGROUND

General View of the Income Levels

Survey data on income levels in rural areas give rise to the question of how precisely they reflect the actual state of rural life. Granting the methodological limitation, we shall first adopt to our purpose data from the book usually referred to as the 'survey report' conducted at each anganawadi centre. Under the Integrated Children Development Scheme, an anganawadi centre is founded for every one-thousand-population unit in rural areas and provides welfare mainly to infants and mothers. The survey records the composition of each family, its state of health, income and other factors of this whole unit. Obtaining the data on the family incomes is especially important for restricting the beneficiaries to the centre. In 1993, the households receiving under Rs. 500 of family income per month corresponded to the target group of the anganawadi centre.

The area of the centre sited at D para covers 129 households in the southern part of the village consisting of the Bagdi caste (79), Sadgop (36), and others (14) in 1993, though it did not include the A and B para localities.

According to the report, the average family income of the total households is Rs. 1,175, though the average of the Bagdi caste alone is Rs. 469 in contrast to the Sadgop which amounts to Rs. 2,636. The other caste groups average Rs. 1,350. This result exemplifies the economic state contrasting the Sadgop and Bagdi castes. 64 households surveyed correspond to the target group, 81 per cent of which are of the Bagdi caste as compared with only one Sadgop household. Regarding the income distribution, 51 households (65 per cent) of the Bagdi range from Rs. 301 to Rs. 500 per month, while only four households, who are all employees in Visva-Bharati University, fall within from Rs. 901 to Rs. 1,600.

Another target group meeting the conditions as a beneficiary of IRDP, which shall be discussed later, averages less than around Rs. 917 per month (Rs. 11,000 per year in 1993). Except for the four higher-income families, all of the Bagdi families (i.e. 73 households, 92.4 per cent) correspond to the target group for IRDP as compared to only two Sadgop families.

The survey report is, however, not necessarily a totally reliable source for this purpose because it was prepared mainly by non-professional researchers, the research was not conducted regularly, and members of the Bagdi caste were apt to under-report their incomes. Nevertheless, the survey has proved illustratively the contrasting economic state existing between the Sadgop and Bagdi castes. We shall subsequently examine the administrative records of landholding, Operation Barga, vested lands, and occupational composition of the households sufficiently accurate to evaluate the economic state regarding the Bagdi residents.

Landholding

The total of 126 Bagdi caste are registered as land owners on the pages of the land records at the Block Land Reform Office (BLRO), but the total amount of the land area is only 4.53 acres because most of these tracts are residential land. Only three names are registered as holders of cultivated lands, one in D para (0.62 acre) and two in A para (0.71 and 0.4). These data show that even many families of landless labourers are at least assured of their residential rights, though some families have built their houses on the banks of the canal, which is actually government land (*khas-jami*). Additionally, the data concerning recent transfers indicate that another two persons in D para and A para bought plots, and one in A para sold a plot of 0.4 acre in 1993. As a result, the two households hold one plot for cultivation in D para and one in A para.

Operation Barga

In the entire village, the number of registered tenants under Operation Barga includes 124 names, with 16 of them belonging to the Bagdi caste. Of these 11 are in D para, 2 are in A para, and 3 are in other localities. The total size of the registered plots for Barga cultivation by the Bagdi caste is 39.01 acres, with 11.7 acres in D para, 7.45 acres in A para, and 9.86 acres in other localities. One of the plots registered in D para is only 0.03 acre, which is only just large enough on which to build a house. This infers that a main aim of Operation Barga was to improve the relationship with these tenants and their landlords rather than to secure tenancy land itself. In fact, when Operation Barga was introduced, many conflicts were observed between tenants and landowners all over West Bengal, though such cases are very rare now in this area. Recently, there have been a few newly registered Barga lands. In this regard, some tenants even said that there is no need to register their Barga lands because they currently enjoy a good relationship with their landowners. There are still 8 households in D para and one in A para who continue their tenant cultivation with their landowners without registration. This is known as 'krishan-casi' and 'hal-casi' according to the customary apportionment.[7]

Vested Lands

Due to the provision of the land ceiling, 75.63 acres have been registered as surplus land within the Mauza by the BLRO prior to 1993, but some plots are still pending in the High Court. This total comprises 3.8 per cent of the total Mauza. The beneficiaries of the vested lands are selected by a committee present in every block. They decide the deserving cases for the vested lands according to a prearranged priority list, which records the caste or religion and other data of the applicants.

In this endeavour, we can use the records housed in the BLRO until 1988, and supplement this with the data subsequently garnered through interviews with the villagers. As might be imagined, this is a very difficult task even for the staffs because there are so many plots registered in the case records as pending long term in the court. Moreover, some plots of the vested lands are still awaiting a certificate of registration (*patta*).

There were 18 total beneficiaries in D para in 1988. The sum of the vested lands was 5.23 acres. Additionally, five names were granted after 1989. On the other hand, the beneficiaries in A para have not been recorded as yet, but three names are known as beneficiaries after 1989. However, one of the plots was leased to another person. Therefore, there were 23 cultivators on vested lands in D para and two in A para.

Occupational Composition of the Households

Table 4 briefly compares the occupational compositions of both localities in units of households. The occupation denoted as 'cultivator' means a household which includes at least one owner of field land except for the beneficiaries of vested land. The Barga household means that they registered during the time of Operation Barga, and 'other barga' refers to those households engaging in the traditional forms of tenancy without such registration. The remaining occupation denotes households of agricultural labourers who mainly depend on daily work in the fields without holding any kind of cultivated land or tenancy right. In the non-agricultural sector, the 'employee' households are those that have at least one person employed in the university or other institutions. In the same way, the shopkeeper, woodworker, and fish broker households includes a shopkeeper, a woodworker, and a fish broker respectively. The remaining households are those of daily labourers who mainly depend on construction work for their income.

Table 4 clearly denotes the distinctive difference in the labour environment in the ratio of the employees working at the university. While the 12 households in A para have members employed in the university, only 4 households in D para hold such work. This means that although more than 35 per cent of 34 households of A para are thus employed, less than 6 per cent of the 69 households are so engaged in D para. Furthermore, regarding the state of daily labour in both localities, though the labourers in D para are mainly engaged in agricultural work, the people of A para find their work mostly away from the fields such as in doing construction labour in neighbouring towns. In the town of Bolpur, for example, demand for construction labourers has been increasing with the recent growth in the number of concrete buildings. It is important here to underscore the greater progress in the labour environment of A para because more than one third of the households maintain stable employment at the university and none of them depend on agricultural labour. Such a development could not be possible, of course, without the large-scale institution sited next to the village.

Only a few families of both localities hold cultivated lands

Table 4 Comparison of households per locality by type of work

	Locality	*A para*		*D para*	
Non-agricultural Sector					
	Occupation	*HH*	*Total*	*HH*	*Total*
1	Employee	12	25	4	8
2	Shopkeeper	1		0	
3	Woodworker	2		0	
4	Fish broker	0		3	
5	Daily labourer	10		1	
Agricultural Sector					
1	Cultivator	1	6	2	60
2	Operation Barga	2		11	
3	Other barga	1		8	
4	Vested land	2		23	
5	Agricultural labourer	0		16	
	Other	3	3	1	1
	Total		34		69

Source: Author's research data gathered in 1993

sufficient to meet their living needs. In this respect, both A and D paras seem to be operating under similar conditions. But this would not signify the same concerns to them. Although most of the D para households do not have enough cultivated land, they depend on agricultural labour to make their living. Accordingly, they meet the conditions necessary to receive the benefits of the panchayat programmes, and, in practice, most households owed much as shown in the table such as the vested land and the Operation Barga. On the other hand, the people in A para have less chance to receive such benefits, though one third of the locality are still engaged as daily labourers. They pursue more jobs outside the fields, and consequently receive less opportunities of the panchayat, which are mainly designed for rural development. This would be clarified more so with the analysis of the IRDP distribution in both localities, which will be discussed later.

Many villagers have the impression that A para is a developed (*unnayan*) and rich locality in contrast to D para. Even the people of D para agree with this opinion taking into consideration the state of higher employment in A para. Although within the locality of A para, there is a gap between the rich and the poor, it is noteworthy that they are apt to hold the impression that the locality of A para has developed as a whole, while, on the other hand, the locality of D para has received more benefits from the panchayat generally, irrespective of the differentials within the locality itself.

The same observation applies to the educational disparity between both localities. The numbers of students registered in middle high schools (from the fifth to tenth grades) in 1993 were 18 in A para and 13 in D para. There were 1 student entered in higher secondary school, 3 undergraduate students, and 1 postgraduate student, all from A para and enjoying the reservation of higher education for SC.

Notably, each department of the university provides the reservation for SC and ST student. Also, the state government offers various benefits such as compensation for SC and ST students in public high school. However, the ratio of the students at the secondary and higher education levels clearly denotes a disparity between the student in both localities. The difference in incentives to go on to a higher education clearly depends on the social background of the prospective students' parents in each locality.

RURAL DEVELOPMENT PROGRAMMES ACHIEVED THROUGH PANCHAYAT

Hand Tube Wells

First, we shall examine the achievement of the development programmes through Jawahar Rozgar Yojana (JRY), National Rural Employment Programme (NREP, to 1989), and Food for Works (FFW, to 1980). These programmes were designed to increase employment opportunities in rural areas through the provision of construction work which serves to improve rural infrastructure. In 1992–93, the panchayat has allotted Rs. 101,163.38 to the village under study for the various programmes of JRY which includes the installation of 3 hand tube wells and sewage drains, maintenance work for 15 hand tube wells, a motor pump, and three roads. With regard to the hand tube wells, the panchayat has altogether installed 61 tube wells since 1978 in the panchayat area and 21 in the Surul Mauza. The sites for the tube wells are generally scattered among the densely built localities of the lower class.

In the Bagdi community, there are six tube wells installed adjoining their localities. Two tube wells are in A para, one in B para, one in C para, and two in D para. These sites seem to be reasonably selected according to the population ratio of each locality. However, the residents in A para claimed that one tube well in A para has been in disrepair for many years, but the panchayat office has yet to send an engineer to fix it. This seems to be a result of a lack of their influence to the panchayat members who send their claims to the office. In the case of IRDP loans for individuals, as will follow, this problem is more clearly demonstrated.

IRDP

IRDP has been offered in the area since 1981–82, and since 1984–85 the distribution of loans was introduced to the households of the Bagdi community. The SC and ST recipients are subsidized by the government for 50 per cent of their loans. The total number of loans given out by the panchayat office to the village thus far are 259, though another 14 applications were rejected by the regional bank. The total monetary amount of the 259 loans is Rs. 983,591. The average amount per case is Rs. 3,798, demonstrating that is more often made available in the form of IRDP small loans distributed among the many poor households. The greatest number of the loans was awarded in 1985–86, and after that the number decreased gradually. According to the manager of the regional bank, the rate of loan repayments by the villagers is worse than that of other villages. This has resulted in very strict examination for the loan applicants of the village these days.

Table 5 shows the number and total amount of the distributed loans to the Bagdi localities every year since 1981. Each column compares the subtotals of the loans in D para, A para, the entire Bagdi community, and the whole village total. As is readily evident from the table, D para has generally been allotted more loans than has A para. Specifically, the total amount of the loans in D para is about 4 times that of A para with the number being 4.8 times more, even though the ratio of the adult population is about nine to five. This means that D para locality received more than twice the number of loans than did A para. Moreover, when IRDP began in the Bagdi localities in 1984, 26 loans were distributed in D para, none to A para, and only 4 in the next year. These facts seem to support the opinion of the people of A para that they have been treated unfairly compared with those in D para with regard to the distribution of the IRDP loans. They have recognized this seeming disparity through witnessing many experiences such as more

Table 5 Distribution of IRDP loans per year

	D para		*A para*		*Bagdi total*		*Village total*	
	No.	*Sum(Rs.)*	*No.*	*Sum(Rs.)*	*No.*	*Sum(Rs.)*	*No.*	*Sum(Rs.)*
1981-82	0	0	0	0	0	0	9	15692
1984-85	26	50520	0	0	32	58420	59	139325
1985-86	14	32060	4	7300	23	57320	78	189450
1986-87	1	4750	2	8450	3	13200	16	68840
1987-88	3	12890	1	4680	4	17570	18	87621
1988-89	8	37420	4	12834	20	82474	50	262158
1989-90	1	7480	0	0	1	7480	5	28280
1990-91	3	22500	0	0	5	36900	14	117800
1991-92	2	15000	1	9000	7	50400	10	74425
Total	58	182620	12	42264	95	323764	259	983591

Source: Extracted from the record in the Ruppur Gram Panchayat Office

livestock been distributed to D para than to themselves and the increasing number of rejections of their applications.

The average amount of the loans per household, however, is Rs. 3,049 in D para, whereas that of A para is Rs. 3,522. This fact might show up in the difference of items distributed to both localities despite their impression based on the number of loans granted. Table 6 compares the total number of the loans classified by the items distributed between both localities. Clearly, agricultural sector loans were significantly more allotted to D para, while A para received its loans principally for petty trade and industries except for livestock which has a comparatively lesser relation to their occupations. This seems quite natural because the people of D para depend on their agricultural labour in the fields for their living, whereas those residing in A para depend almost exclusively on employment and labour in occupations outside of the fields. This distribution pattern corresponds well to the existing situation and intention of the beneficiaries and it is not necessarily the result of any partiality. Furthermore, of the 12 cases of the Bagdi applicants cited on the records of the rejected applications, there were 5 cases in D para and the other 7 were in other localities, with no case being recorded for A para. The rejection of loan applications can indeed happen in every step of the examination processes from a joint selection with panchayat members to a committee in the regional banks. Apart from those, the rejection case

Table 6 Distribution of IRDP items in two localities

Sector	*Loan Items*	*Number*	
		D para	*A para*
Agriculture	Bull and cart	6	0
	Bull for plough	9	0
Subtotal		15	0
Livestock	Sheep	24	0
	Bull	4	0
	Pregnant cow	9(3)	1
	Calf	12	3
	Goat	5	3
	Pig	0	1
	Goose	0	1
Subtotal		54	9
Handicraft	Threshing machine	9	0
	Woodworking tools	0	2
Subtotal		9	2
Small business	Rickishaw	0	1
	Shop	1	2
	Tailor	1	0
Subtotal		2	3
Total		80	14

Source: Extracted from the record in the Ruppur Gram Panchayat Office

on this record do not support the opinion held by A para.

IRDP is intended to provide loans individually to poor families being below the poverty line and these are assessed by the annual income of each household. As we have seen, more than one third of households in A para are employed. This may rather signify the improvement of the community of A para. This then requires a more thorough discussion of the target groups of IRDP in both localities.

The IRDP Target Group

The candidates for becoming recipients of IRDP loans are selected according to a qualification list of poor families, which is generally called the 'survey list'. This list records the yearly income, caste or religion, family composition, and landholding of each household, and arranges them in order of decreasing income. The reservation quota of IRDP is that 50 per cent of the recipients are allotted to SC or ST households, 40 per cent to women, and 3 per cent to physically disadvantaged persons.[8] An officer of the BDO conducts out the survey in each gram panchayat area, and the list is kept in every panchayat office. An essential condition for applying to the IRDP by villagers is first whether their names are found on the list. The currently used list surveyed in 1989–90 indicates 688 households as the total number of families in the village being below the poverty line including 150 Bagdi caste households. Notably, the number of Bagdi households is weighted with 81.9 per cent of all of the names entered on the list of those residing within constituency 1.[9]

Table 7 notes the distribution of household income by each consecutive Rs. 1,000 on the list. Each column is classified by locality, namely D para, A para, the entire Bagdi community, and constituency 1. Three points are apparent from the table. First, in D para there are seven names classified as 'the poorest of the poor families', which means under Rs. 4,000 of annual income, while there are none in A para. Second, the number of names in D para is proportionately 2.7 times that of A para. Third, the ratio of the recipients in each locality is

Table 7 Income levels of the Bagdi localities in the IRDP survey report

Rs.	*D para*	*A para*	*Bagdi Total*	*Total*
0-1000	0	0	0	0
1001-2000	4	0	4	6
2001-3000	1	0	1	1
3001-4000	2	0	5	7
4001-5000	23	12	48	53
5001-6000	16	8	44	44
6001-7000	7	4	15	13
7001-8000	5	1	10	11
8001-9000	9	2	16	18
9001-10000	3	0	5	5
10001-11000	2	0	2	8
Total	72	27	150	166

Source: Extracted from the record, *Daridryasimar Nice Basabaskari Paribargurir Elaka Bhittik Talika, Part No.115/114, 1992* in the Ruppur Gram Panchayat Office.

80.6 per cent in D para, 44.4 per cent in A para, and 63.3 per cent in the Bagdi community as a whole. These facts indicate at the very least that the gap between D para and A para is estimated to be less than that of the seeming number on the voters' list. In other words, this list shows a higher ratio of families qualifying in D para than in A para as the recipient of IRDP. In the dispute over the equal distribution of the IRDP, we cannot deny the tendency of D para receiving 6 times more livestock than A para. We can be fairly certain that this resulted from the different level of political influence which A para and D para extend on their panchayat members. However, it is difficult to say that there was some form of political unfairness at work here if we consider the difference in the backgrounds of each locality shown on the survey list. It is, therefore, possible to assume that there is an effort under way to seek favour for their own localities. The more important thing to consider is that their discontentment with the seeming number of the distributed loans has given substance to the image of political unfairness, if they compare their circumstances with those of D para; nevertheless such an opinion is not necessarily based on detailed administrative data.

CONCLUDING REMARKS

The facts just mentioned signify that the distribution of loans to individuals tends to intensify the sentiment of rivalry between the successful and the rejected applicant, or the qualified and the unqualified marked by the poverty line over the limited resources. This easily creates an image of unfairness among the discontented, as far as the distribution is implemented only for public favour without being properly integrated with the other development plans, or providing enough information on the total plans.[10]

The sample area neighbours a national university. We cannot therefore generalize about the advanced state of employment and education in the area as being broadly applicable to the overall situation in West Bengal. However, this case does clearly portray an aspect of the structural characteristics of the rural society.

G.K. Lieten (1992:216) argues that the combined operation of land reforms, devolution of power to the panchayat, and a strong peasant movement are the conditions for the successful implementation of poverty alleviation programmes. The present case seems to support his view generally. The land reforms such as vested lands and Operation

Barga for the poor peasants in the area have led to their increased political awareness and the rise in economic and social position in close connection with the local branch of Krishak Samiti. This has enabled them to place their reliance on the Left Front Government to a certain extent which was evidenced in the results of the panchayat elections in the area. Such stability in local administration based on the panchayat is an essential condition for enhancing the practical efficacy of the development programmes, especially for poverty alleviation such as the IRDP.

At the same time, however, it would be unable to deal sufficiently with the needs of the people who have less opportunities for the panchayat benefits as in A para unless the distributions were to be implemented with adequate integration with the other programmes and sufficient information. On this point, there appears to be an essential difference between the target group formula distributed to individuals since the 1980s and the land reforms begun since 1953 which led to a structural reform in agrarian society under the strong peasant movement. In this sense, in spite of Harriss' opinion (1993), it seems not merely a matter of the policy formulated concerning the spread of boro-casi based on minor irrigation, although it certainly increased agricultural productivity. The New Industrial Policy of the LFG will become more important even for rural society in view of the emerging needs of the people which seem to include unsolvable problems within the agrarian framework.

In the case of a Tamil village, Deliege (1996) pointed out the Pallar have received no real support from the reservation system. But my study has shown that the administrative category of the SC as well as the ST have fulfilled a significant function even in local administration in present West Bengal. This therefore implies a double-edged sword, in the sense that the enlargement of the reservation in public employment of the state government for the SC and ST from 20 per cent to 28 per cent, and the newly made appointments of the OBC since 1994 would rather intensify the tensions all the more among the people over the reservation system.[11]

In any case, in place of the traditional concept of untouchability, people have become aware of the category of SC as a notable social status due to the penetration of the administrative measures carried out in rural society. This is, however, not necessarily in the direction of eliminating untouchability in people's mind, but rather, it seems to have become a keen issue raising the people's social consciousness about the reservation.[12] Thus, the foregoing observations of West Bengal villages fairly well elucidate the prospective situation of the SC in rural society living and working under the present Indian Constitution.

NOTES

1 It is well known that L. Dumont (1980) developed this view in an influential study on Hindu society. However, a great deal of criticism has been levelled at the book already. C.J. Fuller (1996) edited the latest renewal of interst in the subject among anthoropologists .

2 The Constitution of India, Clause 17. The selection of Scheduled Castes has proceeded primarily on the basis of 'untouchability', but criterion has left scope for various estimations. In this respect, see, in particular, Galanter (1984:131–47).

3 On the reservation for the OBC, anthoropolgists in India are under the apprehension lest it may strengthen the caste consciousness further; see Béteille (1990). M.N. Srinivas (1996) edited the recent studies by Indian scholars on the changing role of caste in contemporary India.

4 See Echeverri-Gent (1992), Kolhi (1990;1991), Lieten (1990;1992), Mallick (1992;1993), Nossiter (1988), Sato (1980), Webster (1992), and Westergaard (1986).

5 On the new regulation in West Bengal, see *Compendium of the West Bengal Panchayat Act, 1973 and The West Bengal Panchayat (Election) Rules, 1974*, The Department of Panchayat, Calcutta, 1993. For the analysis of the fourth election in general, see Lieten (1994), Bandyapaday (1993).

6 The following descriptions mainly depend on the interviews from the villagers. The interviews were conducted after the election.

7 In Krishan-casi, tenants cultivate without the provision of plough and bull, and usually recieve 40 per cent of the crop. In Hal-casi, tenants reccive 75 per cent of the crop if they offer a plough and bulls. But it is also called Hal-casi when the agricultural labourers provide their own plough and bulls hired by the hour.

8 *Sarbik Gramin Unnayan Karmmasuci (IRDP)*, Birbhum Jela Unnayn Sangastha (Birubum, DRDA), Siuri, 1992, p. iv.

9 The 14 names being registered separately in another book corresponding to constituency 3, 136 of the Bagdi caste are actually within constituency 1. Table 7 shows the total number of names in both constituencies.

10 In this respect, G.K. Lieten (1994) points out the importance of the IRDP of integrating with the other development plans. J. Echeverri-Gent (1992) also refers to the same problem regarding the NREP.

11 Of a controversy on the reservation, see, for example, *Anandbajar-patrika*, 23 May, 4 June, 21 July, 25 July, and 20 August 1994.

12 Cultural patterns regarding untouchability rooted in the structure of the people's mind appear to be not easily solved merely by improving the

economic conditions of the discriminated. As a good example of this, in Japan, although the government has been implementing compensation policies expressly formulated for improving the economic conditions of a historically discriminated segment of Japanese, the prejudice against them still lingers in the disparate social lives and the discriminating expression often unconsciously being refered to them in everyday life.

REFERENCE

Acarya, Buddhadeb
1982 *Surul Sarkarbari o Maharsh Shantiniketan*, Bolpur, Sri Durga Press.

Bandyopadhyay, D
1993 'Fourth general elections of panchayats in West Bengal (May 1993)', *Mainstream*, 26 June 1993, 15–21.

Béteille, A.
1990 'Caste and politics', *Times of India*, 11 September.

Deliege, Robert
1996 'At the threshold of untouchability: Pallars and Valaiyars in a Tamil village', in C.J. Fuller, ed., *Caste Today*.

Dumont, L.
1980 (1966) *Homo Hierarchicus: The Caste System and Its Implications*, Complete revised English edition, Chicago, University of Chicago Press.

Echeverri-Gent, J.
1992 'Public participation and poverty alleviation: the experience of reform communists in India's West Bengal', *World Development*, vol. 20 (10).

Fuller, C.J. (ed.)
1996 *Caste Today*, Delhi, Oxford University Press.

Galanter, M.
1984 *Competing Equalities: Law and the Backward Classes in India*, Berkeley, University of California Press.

Harriss, John
1993 'What is happening in rural West Bengal?: agrarian reform, growth and distribution', *EPW* 28, no. 24, 1237–47.

Isaacs, Harold R.
1965 *India's ex-Untouchables*, Massachusetts Institute of Technology.

Kholi, Atul
1990 'From elite activism to democratic consolidation: political change in West Bengal', *Dominance and State Power in Modern India: Decline of a Social Order*, 2 vols., F. Frankel and M.S.A. Rao, eds., Delhi, Oxford University Press.
1991 *Democracy and Discontent: India's Growing Crisis of Governability*, Cambridge, Cambridge University Press.

Lieten, G.K.
1990 'Depeasantisation discontinued: land reforms in West Bengal', *EPW* 25, no. 40, 2265–71.

1992 *Continuity and Change in Rural West Bengal*, Delhi, Sage Publications.
1994 'For a new debate on West Bengal', *EPW* 29, no. 29, 1835–38.

Mallick, Ross
1992 'Agrarian reform in West Bengal: the end of an illusion', *World Development*, vol. 20, no. 5, May.
1993 *Development Policy of a Communist Government: West Bengal since 1977*, Cambridge South Asian Studies, Cambridge, Cambridge University Press.

Nossiter, T. J.
1988 *Marxist State Governments in India*, London, Printer Publishers.

Nicholas, Ralph W.
1963 'Village factions and political parties in rural West Bengal', *Journal of Commonwealth Political Studies* 2, no. 1, November, 17–32.

Risley, H.H.
1891 (1981) *The Tribes and Castes of Bengal*, Calcutta, Firma KL Mukhopadhyay.

Sato, Hiroshi
1980 'The rural and agricultural policy of the Left Front Government of West Bengal, India' (in Japanese), *Ajiakeizai* (Asian Economics), January, 2–19.

Srinivas, M.N. (ed.)
1996 *Caste: Its Twentieth Century Avatar*, New Delhi, Viking, Penguin India.

Webster, Neil
1992 *Panchayati Raj and the Decentralization of Development Planning in West Bengal*, Calcutta, K.P. Bagchi.

Westergaard, Kirsten
1986 *People's Participation, Local Government and Rural Development: The Case of West Bengal*, Copenhagen, Centre for Development Research.

(P.S. I wish to thank the District Magistrate of Birbhum and other authorities concerned for permission to use the official records in this paper. Special thanks are also due to Dr. André Béteille for his reading of the draft and making helpful suggestion, although, of course, I am solely responsible for any errors. This paper especially owes much to the persevering cooperation given by the villagers.)